THE BIRDWATCHER'S
A-Z

Dedicated to my friends and colleagues
in The West Midland Bird Club

Alan J Richards
THE BIRDWATCHER'S
A-Z

with drawings by Rob Hume

DAVID & CHARLES
Newton Abbot   London   North Pomfret (VT)

ISBN 0 7153 8016 8

Typeset by ABM Typographics Ltd., Hull
and printed in The Netherlands
by Smeets Offset B V, Weert
for David & Charles (Publishers) Limited
Brunel House   Newton Abbot   Devon

Published in the United States of America
by David & Charles Inc.
North Pomfret   Vermont 05053   USA

In compiling this book I have attempted to bring together between the covers of a single volume as comprehensive a selection as possible of birdwatching knowledge and jargon, and ornithological terminology; for these one has otherwise to consult a whole library of bird books. Hopefully, therefore, this publication will provide not only the beginner, but also the more advanced birdwatcher, with a quick source of information on all aspects of birdwatching and the wonderful world of birds; information that will not only add to enjoyment but also lead to a fuller understanding of the subject as a whole.

Included in the book are references to the Orders of the world's birds as well as most of the major bird families. The amount of information given on these depends on their importance to the British birdwatcher. Individual birds and groups of birds are also dealt with; again, particularly those birds that might be seen in Britain, or certainly in the Western Palearctic, are included as well as some of the more interesting species from other faunal regions. I have dealt with the names of birds and the way they are named, aspects of bird study, birdwatching organisations, bird observatories, equipment, some of the major birdwatching areas and, particularly, I have included birdwatchers' 'slang', so that you will be able to hold your own in conversation with the local experts when terms like 'jizz', 'rush' or 'lifer' are bandied about!

The study of wild birds, or birdwatching—with or without any scientific motives—can be an exciting and satisfying business. I hope with the aid of this book it will prove to be even more so.

It is inevitable in a work of this nature that something gets left out that should be included, or something is included that might well have been left out. I would, therefore, be grateful to any reader who cares to give me his opinion on such matters in order that possible future editions might be improved.

Alan J. Richards
1980

Abberton Reservoir, Essex

Regarded as one of the finest reservoirs for wildfowl in the country, it benefits greatly from its near-coastal location. Midway between Colchester and the Blackwater estuary, about 4 miles (7km) from each, its total water surface is over 1,200 acres (486h). The numbers of wildfowl which gather there can be quite staggering with Wigeon, Teal, Pochard and Tufted in their thousands during early autumn. Waders and Terns are regular and almost anything is possible. Access is restricted to a limited number of members of the Essex Birdwatching Preservation Society, though much can be seen from two causeways crossing the reservoir and from a public hide on the B1026 Colchester to Maldon Road where it crosses the reservoir between the main and middle sections.

Abbotsbury, Dorset

Situated at the western end of Chesil fleet, the area near to Abbotsbury has long been the site of a swannery since it was established by monks as a source of food over 900 years ago. This largest (about 50-60 pairs) of only two breeding colonies of Mute Swan in Britain (the other colony is at nearby Radipole Lake, Weymouth) has been a protected site for many years. A tourist attraction more than a birdwatching locale, the swannery is closed to the public in mid-September. However, the fleet itself can be quite interesting in the winter with various wildfowl, Divers and Grebes.
See Swan; Radipole Lake

Aberrant

Diverging from the normal type in the biological sense, eg coloration of the plumage not appropriate to the described species, possibly due to a genetic malfunction.

Abmigration

Abnormal migration, a term introduced by Sir Landsborough Thomson in 1923 to denote spring migration on the part of a bird that had remained in its native area during winter. This abnormality occurs with some frequency among Ducks, due to pairing by resident birds with winter visitors, the hitherto resident bird leaving with the winter visitors in the spring.

Bird-watching country: RSPB warden looks across the flat, flooded pastureland of the Ouse Washes, Cambridgeshire

Abrasion

The effect of wear on feathers. Towards the end of the breeding season plumage abrasion is evident in some species, and the reduction of the barbs or their barbules can substantially change the pattern or hue of the plumage. Abrasion of the feathers, particularly of the retrices (tail), is often indicative of the bird having been kept in captivity and vagrant species showing this sort of abrasion would be suspect for this reason. Apparent plumage changes due to abrasion, eg the spring plumage of Finches etc, gradually develop due to wear and not moult.
See Moult

Accentor

Former generic name used as a substantive name for most species of the Prunellidae of which there are 12 species, found mainly in the Western Palearctic. All unobtrusive, rather solitary and largely ground-feeding birds; only two species occur in Europe, the more widespread Dunnock (*Prunella modularis*) or Hedge Sparrow and the localised Alpine Accentor (*Prunella collaris*) whose habitat preference confines it to mountainous regions from 5,000 ft (1,500m) to the snowline. There are only 33 records of Alpine Accentor in Britain, 5 of these occurring in the last 20 years.
See Dunnock

Accidental (species)

A term applied to a bird that turns up in an area where it does not normally occur, usually a migrant species that has wandered outside its normal range. (In a British context usually restricted to species recorded less than twenty times in total.)

Accipiter

A member of the sub-family Accipitridae which includes such 'Hawks' as Sparrowhawk (*Accipiter nisus*) and Goshawk (*Accipiter gentilis*). The term is perhaps more frequently used in North America as a vernacular for Accipiter spp, 'Hawk' having a wider connotation than in Britain.
See Falconiformes; Hawk

Accipitridae

A family of Falconiformes, sub-order Falcones, comprising the Old World Vultures, Hawks and Harriers.

Acrocephalus

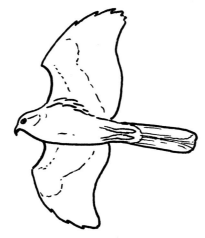

General form of birds of the Accipiter group

Sedge Warbler (above) and Reed Warbler (below, left), Britain's commonest Acrocephalus Warblers

Acrocephalus Warblers

A group of Old World Warblers of the sub-family Sylviinae (Passeriformes sub-order Oscines), the genus Acrocephalus. Mainly haunting swampy, marshy habitats. In Britain the commonest of these are the Sedge Warbler (*Acrocephalus schoenobaenus*) and Reed Warbler (*Acrocephalus scirpaceus*). Some rarer members of this group include Mous-tached Warbler (*Acrocephalus melanopogon*) and Aquatic Warbler (*Acrocephalus paludi-cola*).

The general term Acrocephalus Warbler is applied to any of these birds, and often the group is further divided into unstreaked and streaked—those with uniform-coloured plu-mage (Reed Warbler), those with dark marks in the plumage (Sedge Warbler). A slang term much used by 'twitchers' and perhaps more frequently by ringers, is 'Acrocephs'.
See Warbler

Adaptive Radiation

Denotes the divergence in the characters of related forms that enables them to exploit different kinds of opportunity.
See Convergence

Adult

A bird which has reached sexual maturity and displays all the characteristics of this state: ie, its plumage no longer changes with age.

Gannet (adult)

Blackcock (Black Grouse) at lek

Aftershaft

A small feather growing from the stem (rachis) of a proper feather and underlying it. Found on all body feathers of many kinds of birds and on certain of the body feathers of other kinds. In some orders of birds the aftershaft is comparable in size with the main feather, particularly many game birds, herons, storks, birds of prey and parrots. In some groups it is quite small, often vestigial. In a few it is entirely absent, eg the Pigeons (Columbidae).

See Feather; Plumage

Aggression

Serves an important function in the lives of most birds, significantly in the establishment and in the defence of territory, also when competing for food, mates, nesting and roosting sites. Threatening behaviour in birds rarely results in physical assault, though some species frequently make contact when displaying to each other at leks, eg Black Grouse (*Lyrurus tetrix*) and Ruff (*Philomachus pugnax*). The Robin (*Erithacus rubecula*) is also a bird which is well known for its aggression to other birds, physically driving away intruders. The physiological state of a

bird has great bearing on the degree of aggression it shows and most important in determining this is the level of gonadal hormones in circulation. This is invariably greatest in the breeding period. The term 'aggression' is not usually used when describing aspects of predation, eg Falcons killing other birds, Skuas chasing Terns.

Aigrette

A soft plume grown by Egrets and used in their nuptial display. Due to their softness and beauty these feathers were widely used in the millinery industry in the late 19th century. In North America many thousands of Egrets were slaughtered for their plumes. Prominent in the movement against such exploitation was the Audubon Society. In Britain similar protests against the use of bird plumes resulted in the formation of the movement which was to become the Royal Society for the Protection of Birds.
See Audubon; RSPB

Sooty Albatross, most graceful of all Albatrosses

Albatross

Name for some members of the Diomedeidae family, pelagic species notable for their spectacular powers of flight. Mainly birds of the southern hemisphere, there are 13 species in 2 genera, Diomedea and Phoebetria. They are rare birds to British waters: the Black-browed Albatross (*Diomedea melanophris*) is the most frequently recorded species, having occurred 31 times (including 3 inland records).

Albinism

A total or partial absence of pigment in feathers and soft parts normally coloured. In a true albino, pigment is completely lacking even from the irides and bill, legs and feet. Birds showing partial albinism or a pied state frequently occur; the condition may be patchy, forming a mosaic, or it may be symmetrical. Albinism has been recorded in practically every species of bird, but it is frequently noticed in normally dark-coloured species such as Blackbird (*Turdus merula*), Crow (*Corvus corone*), Starling (*Sturnus vulgaris*), Swallow (*Hirundo rustica*) and House Sparrow (*Passer domesticus*).
See Leucism; Melanism
Read Sage, B. L., 'Albinism and Melanism in Birds', *British Birds*, June 1962, pp. 201-225.

Robin showing albinism

Albumen

The egg white which surrounds the yolk, being enclosed within the membranes and shell of the egg. It exists as a viscous liquid, and also in gelatinous and semi-solid form. The albumen is arranged in four concentric layers. It has been extensively studied and has provided much taxonomically valuable information.

Razorbill, a diving sea bird

Alcidae
A family of diving sea birds generally referred to as the 'Auks'. It includes such well-known species as Razorbill (*Alca torda*) and Guillemot (*Uria aalge*).
See Auk; Guillemot; Razorbill

Alimentary Canal
Also called the digestive tract. In all vertebrates it consists essentially of a coiled tube or gut leading from the mouth to the anus, through which food passes during the process of digestion. As food passes through the alimentary canal it is broken down into nutrients and water which are absorbed, and the waste material expelled as droppings.

Allen's Rule
In warm-blooded animals the relative size of exposed parts (limbs, tails, ears, etc) decreases with the decrease of the mean temperature of the habitat.

Allopatric
A term used to designate closely allied species or families of birds living in different geographical areas, eg Sugarbirds (*Meliphagidae*), (Passeriformes, sub-order Oscines) found in South Africa, belong to the same family as the Australian Honeyeaters.
See Sympatric; Sugarbird; Honeyeater

Allopreening
Birds preening each other at the same time or taking it in turns, the procedure often being a highly ritualised affair, formerly termed mutual preening.

Altitudinal Migration
The movement of mountain-nesting species to and from their breeding areas, to lower altitudes in winter, and back to the higher altitudes where they breed in spring. Alpine species, such as Wallcreeper (*Tichodroma muraria*) and Snow Finch (*Montifringilla nivalis*) undertake altitudinal migration.

Altricial
A term denoting a young bird incapable of locomotion when hatched. All passerines particularly and some other species whose life begins in highly developed nest situations or in holes in trees, underground, etc, are altricial.
See Nidicolous; Nidifugous; Young

Alula
See Bastard Wing

Ambivalence
A behavioural term applied to a movement that is the outcome of two incompatible behaviour tendencies, such as approach and

11

Anatidae

avoidance or flying and walking, one movement suggesting one act and a second the other.

Anatidae
Family of birds comprising those species variously designated Ducks, Geese and Swans.
See Anseriformes; Duck; Goose; Swan

Anglesey
The island of Anglesey is linked to the mainland of North Wales by the Menai Bridge which crosses the narrow straits at that point. The island has long been an attraction to birdwatchers and though industrial development and increased tourism have taken away much of its wildness (still apparent even in the early sixties), the area retains great appeal, with the precipitous cliffs of South Stack, with its sea birds and Chough, the Maltraeth sands and Red Wharf Bay for its waders being of particular note. Cemlyn Bay, Penmon Point and some of the inland lakes have their bird specialities.

Anhinga
Used (in America) as vernacular name for Darter (*Anhinga anhinga*).
See Darter

Anis
Belong to the sub-family Crotophaginae of the Cuculidae (Cuculiformes). They are medium-sized non-parasitic Cuckoos with almost black plumage. Gregarious birds, they build communal nests in which several females lay their eggs. There are three species occurring in North, Central and South America.

Anseriformes
Order comprising the Ducks, Geese, Swans and Screamers, over 140 species in all. The order is divided into three families, Anhimidae (Screamers) 3 species, Paranyrocidae (extinct) and Anatidae (Ducks, Geese and Swans) 146 species. The Anatidae are further divided into three sub-families. Members of the Anseriformes are easily recognised; the bill alone is sufficient to distinguish them. On the edge of each mandible are rows of lamellae regularly arranged and more or less developed, these acting as filters in water. In the dabbling ducks they are truly remarkable instruments, comparable to the baleen of whales, with innumerable nerve ends which makes their sense of touch very delicate. In geese the lamellae are external, hard and horny, enabling the birds to graze and pull up grass. In the 'sawbills' the lamellae are in the form of teeth which facilitate the capture of fish.
See Duck; Goose; Sawbill; Screamer; Swan

Antagonistic behaviour
This term was coined to replace in part the motivational term 'agonistic behaviour' of both comparative psychology and ethology. In general the term is applied to behaviour in disputes over food or mates, during the establishment or maintenance of territories. Forms of antagonistic behaviour include:
1 Threat displays, to force withdrawal of rival
2 Advertising displays, song, song flight
3 Appeasing displays to forestall attack well in advance
4 Submissive displays to inhibit or stop an attack that is imminent or in progress
5 Attack and fighting, hostile approach, to full combat
6 Escape behaviour, fleeing
See Aggression; Threat

Antbird
Substantive name for some species of Formicariidae (Passeriformes, sub-order Tyranni). A neotropical group of 230 species. Small dull-coloured birds, they are confined to Central and South America.

Anting
A still largely unexplained behaviour by some species of birds (mainly the Starlings and Jays) which apply ants to their feathers (active anting) or allow them to run over the body (passive anting). The formic acid exuded by the ants possibly provides some cleansing action.
See Bathing; Dusting

Antiphonal Song
A type of singing performed by certain species of bird (mainly tropical) when sexes respond to one another often with different phrases, the timing making it almost impossible to tell that the song comes from two birds rather than one. Normally restricted to the formation and maintenance of the pair bond.
See Countersinging; Pair Formation

Antpipit

Substantive name, alternatively Gnateater, of species of Conopophagidae (Passeriformes, sub-order Tyranni). A neotropical group of 11 species of insect-eating ground birds of the tropical forests of South America.

Apodiformes

An order comprising the sub-order Apodi with the families Apodidae (Swifts) and Hemiprocnidae (Crested Swifts), and sub-order Trochuli with the sole family Trochilidae (Hummingbirds).
See Hummingbird; Swift

Apterygiformes

An order comprising the one family Apterygidae (Kiwis), of which there are 3 species.
See Kiwi

Arboreal

Living in or connected with trees, eg Woodpeckers (Picidae).

Archaeopteryx

A species of fossil bird (*Archaeopteryx lithographica*) discovered in limestone of the Upper Jurassic, Middle Kimmeridgian zone of Bavaria. It is known from three specimens of skeletal remains and the impression of feathers. The first find was made in 1861 in a quarry near Solnhofen Pappenheim, Bavaria, the others discovered nearby in 1877 and in 1956. Differing from modern birds in having teeth, its feathers classified it as a bird. It was probably not capable of prolonged active flight but it could certainly glide. These specimens have been extensively studied and scientific opinion supports the belief that they form a link with the reptilian ancestors of birds and the correctness of the so-called 'pro-avis' theory of the origin of flight.
Read Swinton, W. E. *Fossil Birds*, British Museum (Nat Hist), London, 1968; de Beer, G. B., *Archaeopteryx lithographica*, British Museum (Nat Hist), London, 1954

Arne, Dorset

A 740 acre (299Ha) RSPB reserve situated on a peninsula on the western side of Poole harbour. The main habitat is heathland and the most important species the Dartford Warbler. Since 1965 the population has been built up from 2 pairs (to 21 in 1973) with others breeding outside the reserve area. Visitors are always welcome to the Shipstal

Archaeopteryx

Point area of the reserve which is approached along a public footpath from Arne village. Access to the rest of the reserve is by permit only obtainable at the reserve (in advance for parties).
See Reserve; Royal Society for the Protection of Birds

Arundel, Sussex

A Wildfowl Trust centre situated less than one mile from the town of Arundel between Swanbourne Lake and the River Arun. The wooded hillside of Offham Hanger and the imposing structure of Arundel Castle provide an attractive setting for the 55 acrea (22Ha) of landscaped pens, lakes and paddocks which will ultimately contain 1500 wildfowl from many parts of the world. The central attraction is the Swan Lake with its colony of Australian Black Swans and other wildfowl.
See Wildfowl Trust

Assembly

Collective noun used when referring to a number of birds (or other animals) of one kind occurring together. However, the most frequently used expression for an assemblage of birds is 'flock', or sometimes 'flight' if on the wing, though this latter term is more associated with wildfowling, eg morning and evening flights of Duck, etc. The term 'party' is often used when the number of birds is quite small. There are many collective nouns especially applied to certain species which are supposedly correct but are now more or less obsolete and rarely used. They are of interest, however, if only in the historical sense, and some of them are listed below.

Bitterns (or Herons): a seige or sedge
Bustards: a flock
Choughs: a clattering
Crane (or curlew): a herd
Crows: a murder
Ducks (in flight): a team

Asity

Eagles: a convocation
Geese: a gaggle
Geese (in flight): a skein
Lapwings: a deceit
Larks: an exaltation
Mallards: a flush
Nightingales: a watch
Partridges: a covey
Quails: a bevy
Starlings: a murmuration

Asity

Substantive name of the two species of Philepitta in the Philepittidae (Passeriformes sub-order Tyranni) namely Velvet Asity (*Philepitta castanea*) and Schlegel's Asity (*Philepitta schlegeli*). The group also includes two species of *Neodrepanis* False Sunbirds. All restricted to the forests of Madagascar.

Asynchronous Hatching

Staggered hatching of a single clutch of eggs. Most birds do not begin to incubate their eggs until the complete clutch has been laid and then all the young hatch at about the same time. The Owls, Hawks, Eagles and some other species, however, begin incubating when just the first egg has been laid. Consequently, the eggs hatch at intervals and the chicks show great disparity of growth. When food is short, the youngest and weakest frequently fail to survive, often being eaten by their older brothers and sisters in the case of raptorial birds.

Atlas (The)

More fully *The Atlas of Breeding Birds in Britain and Ireland*. The published result of a five-year enquiry into the distribution of breeding birds of the British Isles organised by the British Trust for Ornithology and the Irish Wildbird Conservancy during the years 1968-72. Based on the 10km sq national grid (Ordnance Survey), probably as many as 10,000 birdwatchers and helpers mapped the presence or absence of breeding birds throughout Britain. Every part of Britain and Ireland was visited and each of the 3,862 squares was covered during the period of the survey.

Over 285,000 records were summarised and the distribution of all but 11 of the 229 bird species which breed in the British Isles plotted on maps, providing a unique visual record, each a measure for future changes of breeding-bird distribution. The success and

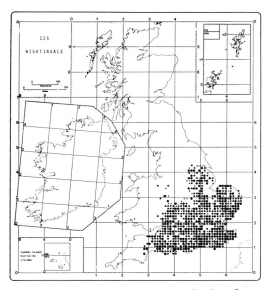

A map from the *Atlas*: Breeding distribution of the Nightingale. (Large dots show confirmed breeding, medium dots probable breeding and small dots possible breeding)

value of the survey and the results offered have led to many other European countries mapping their own breeding birds in a similar way.

Published for the BTO by T. & A. D. Poyser Ltd. Twelve transparent overlays can also be obtained; these show such things as altitude, annual rainfall, lowland heath, moorland, etc, providing opportunity to discover various correlations of birds, habitat, climate etc.

See British Trust for Ornithology

Audubon, John James (1785-1851)

America's greatest naturalist and probably the world's best-known bird artist. His name not only lives on through his magnificent works of art but also in the names of three birds: Audubon's Caracara (*Polyborus plancus auduboni*), Audubon's Shearwater (*Puffinus therminieri*) and Audubon's Warbler (*Dendroica auduboni*). His most important memorial, however, is undoubtedly the powerful American conservation organisation, the Audubon Society, which came into being through his inspiration. Born in Hispaniola he lived for a short time in France before moving to the United States at the age of 18. There he studied painting, making a living

as a portrait painter. However, he soon
became interested in ornithology and later
devised plans to combine his talents and
interest, in a great publishing venture, a
mammoth, superbly illustrated *Birds of
America*. Attempts to find a publisher brought
him to England for a time, and it was here he
obtained backing for his great enterprise.
This he followed up with *Quadrupeds of
North America* and today the original double-
elephant-sized folios and subsequent smaller
sized editions of these works command great
prices whenever they come up for auction.
His contribution to the study and appreciation
of wildlife is beyond price.

Read Chacellor, John, *Audubon a biography*,
Viking Press, New York. There are also others
by Frances Herrick (1917), Alice Ford (1964)
and Alexander Adams (1966).

Auk

A member of the family Alcidae. Auks are
small to medium-sized sea birds, generally
black and white in colour, with short and more
or less pointed wings, short legs and fully
webbed feet. The bill can be almost cylin-
drical and pointed, rather broad or laterally
compressed, some having coloured plates

Two of the four Auks that breed in Britain:
Guillemot (right) and Razorbill (below)

which are shed after the breeding season. Auks are colonial in their breeding behaviour, either nesting on inaccessible cliff ledges, in holes among rocks or in burrows underground. Food is mainly fish caught under water, the birds propelling themselves with their wings. There are four British breeding species, Razorbill (*Alca torda*), Guillemot (*Uria aalge*), Black Guillemot (*Cepphus grylle*) and Puffin (*Fratercula arctica*). The Little Auk (*Plautus alle*) is a winter visitor and on some occasions quite a number are storm-blown inland, during 'wrecks'. The Great Auk (*Pinguinus impennis*) formerly bred but is now extinct. Brunnich's Guillemot (*Uria lamvia*) is a rare visitor to British waters from the Arctic. Other names used for this group, or for species in the group, are 'Auklet', 'Dovekie', 'Murre' and 'Tystie' (old Norse name for Black Guillemot). The term Murre, an old local name in Britain, is now exclusive to the USA. Birdwatchers use the term 'Auk' when they cannot be specific, eg 'there were a number of Auks on the sea'.

See Guillemot; Great Auk; Puffin; Razorbill

The other two 'British' Auks: Puffin (left) and Black Guillemot (below)

Auklet
Substantive name of a number of small sea birds that are related to the Puffins. Term generally applied to the genera Aethia and Ptychoramphus. All found in the North Pacific.

Australasian Region
One of the faunal zones. It comprises the Australian and New Zealand regions of some zoogeographers, but in respect of its avifauna is more appropriately treated as a unit with sub-divisions. The major part of the region is the island continent of Australia. New Zealand, its dependencies and New Guinea and Papua are also included.
See Zoogeography

Autolycism
Term applied by R. Meinertzhagen to the utilisation by birds of other species of animal (including man) when this is not done in a true parasitic manner.

Aves
Plural of the Latin *avis* and used as the scientific name of the class of animals known as birds.

Aviculture
The practice of keeping wild birds in aviaries or enclosures with the object of studying their habits and when possible inducing them to breed.
See Cage and Aviary Birds, a weekly newspaper for aviculturists

Avifauna
All the bird species of a region (or period).

Avocet (*Recurvirostra avosetta*)
A black-and-white wading bird with distinctive upturned bill. It belongs to the family Recurvirostridae (Charadriiformes, sub-order Charadrii). There are other species of Avocet which, along with the Stilts, also belong to that family, all generally black-and-white long-legged wading birds; they are found in all continents except Antarctica. The Avocet has special significance to British bird-watchers, being the symbol of the Royal Society for the Protection of Birds, epitomising the protection movement and the successful recolonisation by this bird since it nested again in Britain in 1947 after a hundred years' absence. Its main breeding

Avocet, our most beautiful wader

places in Britain are Minsmere and Havergate, both RSPB reserves on the Suffolk coast.

Axillaries
The feathers at the base of the underside of the wing—in the armpit of a bird. The black axillaries of the Grey Plover (*Pluvialis squatarola*) are a distinctive feature of the species.

The position of the axillaries

17

Babbler

Substantive name of many species of the sub-family Timaliinae of the Muscicapidae (Passeriformes, sub-order Oscines). Possessing a loud and varied voice which is constantly used (to which they owe their name). Abundant birds of the oriental region; there are 252 species.

Baldpate

North American name for the American Wigeon (*Anas americana*). Slightly larger than the Wigeon (*Anas penelope*) it is a mostly pinkish-brown bird with a broader creamy-white crown patch. A vagrant from North America; there have been 70 records of this species in Britain in the last 20 years.

Barb

A branch of the feather stem; alternatively, a ramus—a constituent unit of the vane of the feather.
See Feather

Barbet

Name of the species Capitonidae (Piciformes, sub-order Galbulae). The name comes from the tufts of feathers around the nostrils and the rictal and chin bristles that are well developed in most species of this family. The Barbets are strictly arboreal and primarily forest birds. Of the world's 78 species, most are found in Africa, some also in South America and SE Asia.

Barbicel

A small branch off the barbule, which on the distal barbule is hooked, on the proximal barbule is spoon-shaped. Thus the distal barbicel off one barbule hooks into the proximal barbicel of the next barbule. This maintains the smoothness and continuity of surface of the vane of the feather.
See Feather

Barbule

A branch off a barb of a feather.
See Feather

Bardsey

Lying some 2 miles (3km) off the tip of the Lleyn peninsula, Gwynedd, it is a most scenically varied and beautiful island in the Irish sea. Its 444 acres (180Ha) are dominated by a 500ft (152m) moutain in the east, and at the southern end there is a lighthouse. The island's farmhouses, now largely disused, are scattered along the only road which runs north to south, linking the lighthouse and the abbey ruins.

A bird and field observatory were established on the island in 1953 and this is open from March to October. The autumn particularly provides exciting times, with spectacular overnight arrivals of Redwings, Blackbirds and Goldcrests, matched by a massive diurnal passage of Finches, Skylarks and Starlings. Bardsey also gets its share of rarities and Summer Tanager, Short-toed Lark and Pallas's Warbler are recent additions to the list. Resident birds of note are Chough, Manx Shearwater and Storm Petrel.
See Observatory

Barn Owl (*Tyto alba*)

A member of the Tytonidae family of Owls (Strigiformes), with 10 species throughout the world. In Britain a species well known in myth and legend, haunting churchyards and ruins. Its shrieking call and its habit of quartering low over the ground at dusk, with slow, buoyant, wavering flight alternating with short glides, have enhanced its reputation for having supernatural associations. Sometimes it hunts in daylight, when its beautiful orange-buff and vermiculated upper parts can be seen. When perched, its typical round flat owl-face, large dark eyes and long legs are very apparent. Considered to be a beneficial species, feeding mainly on rodents, it also takes some small birds, occasionally insects, frogs and fish. Generally distributed throughout Britain, though scarce in some areas, it has an estimated population around 10,000 pairs.
See Owls; Strigiformes

Barred Woodpecker

A name sometimes used for the Lesser Spotted Woodpecker (*Dendrocopos minor*), the black-and-white plumage of the upper parts having a barred appearance.
See Woodpecker

Bass Rock

In the Firth of Forth, $1\frac{1}{2}$ miles offshore and 3 miles NE of North Berwick. This small island, only a $\frac{1}{4}$ mile by 300 yd, is one of Britain's major gannetries. There are regular boat trips round the island during summer, starting from North Berwick.

Bastard Wing
The alula, 'ala spuria' or bastard wing consists of a number of small quill feathers
attached to the first digit situated at the bend
of the wing. It is used in swimming by
certain ducks, and also in flight, particularly
by birds of prey—it is important in the
prevention of stalling.

Bastard wing or alula

Barn Owl (left)
Gannets on Bass Rock (below)

Bathing

Highly co-ordinated innate behaviour essential to the care and maintenance of feathers. Most birds will bathe in water, though certain groups such as Pheasants and Grouse only 'dust' bathe. They bathe in various ways, according to the type of bird. The general pattern consists of movements of the head, the wings and to a lesser extent the tail, together with ruffling of the body feathers, while the bird is standing in shallow water. Most water birds bathe while floating in the water, normally ducking the head and shoulders under water, raising them quickly in a scooping motion which sends water on to the back, then rubbing the head sideways along the flanks or folded wings. The loosely held wings are vigorously beaten against the water, splashing it over the plumage. Some species, Geese and Swans particularly, will turn completely over in the water. Semi-aquatic birds such as waders bathe while standing in shallow water, but otherwise use the method of true water birds. Most birds stay in water for the duration of their bath, but some land birds move in and out, never staying in for more than a few seconds. Aerial birds such as Swallows, Swifts etc, bathe from the air, dropping repeatedly into the water for a brief moment. Kingfishers, Pigeons and Owls also plunge-bathe.

The main purpose of bathing seems to be to facilitate subsequent oiling and preening rather than actually to cleanse the feathers.
See Dusting

Beak

Synonomous with bill, perhaps. Beak is more frequently used when describing the bill of birds of prey—ie hooked beak rather than hooked bill—while the term 'bill' is ascribed to Herons, Storks, waders, etc.
See Bill

Bearded Reedling (*Panurus biarmicus*)

The correct name for the Bearded Tit, which is not a member of the Tit family (Paridae) but related to the Babblers (Timaliinae).

Bee-eater

Name applied to all members of the family Meropidae (Coraciiformes, sub-order Meropes). There are 23 species of Bee-eater confined entirely to the Old World and predominantly Afro-Asian and tropical. Highly colourful birds, their prey consists

Sparrowhawk about to bathe

mostly of bees and wasps caught in the air, either in continuous hawking flight or during short-duration sallies from a perch. In Britain the species most frequently noted is the Common Bee-eater (*Merops apiaster*), on average 5 records a year. It has bred on two occasions (Midlothian 1920 and Sussex 1955). The much rarer Blue-cheeked Bee-eater (*Merops superciliosus*) has been recorded once.

Sparrowhawk bathing

White-throated Bee-eater

Behaviour
As in other animals, behaviour in birds includes a great variety of reactions to stimuli, internal as well as external. The results of their behaviour make it possible for each species to survive and procreate. Behaviour patterns can be triggered by instinct or through learning or imprinting. In connection with a bird's survival, behavioural patterns are concerned with feeding (aggression and dominance), feather maintenance (bathing) and avoidance of predators (flocking, freezing). Related to reproduction, distinct behavioural patterns concern territory (singing, display), courtship and rituals of nest building and raising young, etc.
Read Sparks, John, *Bird Behaviour*, Hamlyn, 1969

Bergmann's Rule
In a polytypic species, body size tends to be larger in cooler parts of the total range and smaller in the warmer parts.
See Allen's Rule

Bewick, Thomas (1753-1828)

Bewick, Thomas (1753-1828)

A Northumberland farmer's son, Bewick was a self-taught artist, achieving in his lifetime recognition as one of the world's finest wood engravers.

Bewick's three works are *A General History of Quadrupeds*, first published in 1770 when he was 37, which made his name, *History of British Birds*, Volume I, *Land Birds*, first published in 1797, Volume II, *Water Birds*, first published in 1804 and *The Aesop's Fables*, first published in 1818. The *History of British Birds* is his best-loved and greatest work, going through six editions in his lifetime. He spent seven years cutting the blocks. A limited facsimile of the 6th edition was published by Frank Graham of Newcastle-upon-Tyne in 1971. The Bewick's Swan (*Cygnus bewickii*) was named after him. *Read* Bewick, Thomas, *A History of British Birds*, Vols I and II (1797) (facsimile edition, Graham, Newcastle-upon-Tyne, 1971).

Bill

Alternatively 'beak', the projecting jaws of a bird with their horny coverings, comprising two major parts, the upper mandible and the lower mandible. For descriptive purposes the upper mandible may be divided into the culmen (or dorsal ridge from the top of the bill to the forehead) and the upper mandibular tomia (or lateral cutting edges). In the lower mandible, chief characteristics are the lower mandibular tomia or cutting edges, the mandible ramus extending posteriorly on either side of the jaw and the gonys or ventral ridge formed by the distal fusing of the two halves of the jaw. The horny coverings of both mandibles can regenerate as the bill becomes

Two engravings from Bewick's *History of British Birds*: left, Starling; right, Jay

worn, while in some species of Alcidae this horny coverage can be extensive and colourful in the breeding season, but shed in the winter.

The shape and size of a bird's bill vary enormously and are clearly adapted to the procurement of its food. For example, the long dagger-shaped bills of most Herons and Bitterns are well adapted for seizing quick-moving prey in shallow water, whilst other fish-eating birds (eg the Merganser) have evolved a serrated bill. Many wading birds' (Charadriiformes) bills are long and straight, enabling food to be obtained from soft mud or sand; often these have very sensitive pliable tips, as in the case of the Woodcock (*Scooplax rusticola*) and Snipe (*Gallinago gallinago*). Highly specialised and different modes of feeding are well demonstrated by such species as the Spoonbill (*Platalea leucorodia*) with its spatulate bill for sifting muddy ooze, and the Crossbill (*Loxia curvirostra*) with its crossed mandibles used in the extraction of seeds from fir cones. The hooked beak of a bird of prey is of course another well-known example of bill development, in this case allowing for the tearing and ripping of flesh.

As well as for feeding, the bill also serves many other purposes and is used notably in nest building and in preening. The bill often figures in display rituals and can, though not primarily, be used as a weapon.

Billing

Caressing with the beak, as billing and cooing of the doves; also called nebbing.

Forms of bill: 1 Gull; 2 dabbling Duck; 3 Phalarope; 4 Diver; 5 Dove; 6 Crossbill; 7 Warbler; 8 Finch

Binoculars

The indispensable aid to birdwatching, binoculars owe their origins to a 17th-century Dutch spectacle-grinder, John Lippershey, whose design was simply two telescopes placed side by side. Some 250 years were to pass before the prism combination that we know today was to become an integral part of binocular construction. The interim period, however, saw the development of the straight-through or Galilean-type glasses (named after Galileo) or what are termed 'opera glasses', providing only low magnification and a small field of view. None the less, with only four air-to-glass surfaces, light transmission is relatively high and good-quality 'field glasses' as they are also called (military term) can provide a reasonably bright image under quite dull conditions.

The modern prismatic binocular employing all the latest constructional techniques and high-quality lenses (invariably coated or 'bloomed' with a thin layer of some suitable transparent substance, usually magnesium fluoride, which cuts out unwanted reflections, thus increasing light transmission) is a scientific instrument which at the top end of the market can be expensive. The latest prism arrangement (roof prism binoculars) provides for an even more compact stream-lined 'glass' also giving improved performance in most cases. German and Japanese manufacturers reign supreme, offering an almost bewildering choice of makes and sizes.

Binocular Vision

Specification of all binoculars is given thus: 8 x 30, 10 x 40 or 12 x 60, etc, the first figure denoting the magnification, the second the diameter of the object lens in millimetres. Most birdwatchers choose something between 7x and 10x. This magnification, coupled with a suitable field of view, bulk and weight, provides a useful performance under most conditions.

Brightness factors (and price) also need to be considered, and no binocular should be bought without trying them out. Most reputable dealers allow you this privilege—after all you could be spending up to £250 or more. There are, of course, much lower-priced models. The thing to do is shop around; but always *caveat emptor*!

A survey of binoculars and telescopes was published in *British Birds* in October 1978, providing a then up-to-date assessment of models available. All leading dealers will provide literature on the various makes they have on offer and one of these, Charles Frank of Glasgow, publishes a booklet on the subject of choosing binoculars.
See Brightness Factor; Field of View

Binocular Vision

The area of vision where the fields of view of the two eyes overlap. This is greatest in birds of prey with forward-facing eyes, particularly Owls. This area of binocular, or three-dimensional, vision allows distances to be judged more accurately, essential in the pursuit of moving prey. However, the field of view is limited, compared with that of a Pigeon, for example, which virtually has all-round vision, but only a 24° arc of binocular vision.

Binominal (or Binomial) System

The system universally adopted for scientifically naming natural forms. Introduced by the Swedish naturalist Linné or Linnaeus, and first consistently applied in the 10th edition of his *Systema Naturae*, published in 1758. In essence the system identifies each species of animal or plant by using two Latin names. The first one refers to the genus, the second to the species within the genus.
See Genus; Nomenclature; Species; Trinominal System

Bird

Belonging to the Class 'Aves'. A warm-blooded air-breathing bipedal vertebrate covered with feathers (the feature which distinguishes it from all other animals) and having the forelimbs modified into wings, giving it the power of flight (though in a few 'orders' of birds these are rudimentary,

OWL

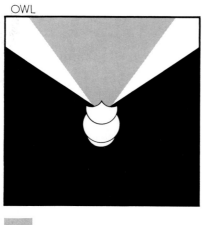

PIGEON

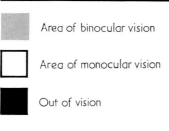

Area of binocular vision

Area of monocular vision

Out of vision

Binocular vision

'Straight-through' or Galilean-type binocular (above) and prismatic type (below)

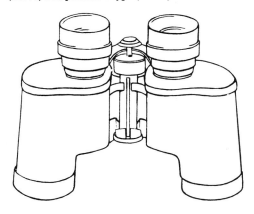

rendering them flightless, eg Ostriches, Kiwis, Cassowaries. The brain is well developed, the jaws covered with a horny sheath forming a beak, and the young are produced from eggs. Other features include a four-chambered heart and an essentially high constant body temperature because of the tremendous energy output required to sustain flight over a long period.

The largest living bird is the Ostrich (*Struthio camelus*) up to 8ft (2.4m) tall. The heaviest flying bird is the Kori Bustard *Ardeotis kori*), up to 30lb (14.5g).

The smallest bird is the Bee Hummingbird (*Mellisuga helenae*), measuring 2.28in (58mm) from bill tip to tail tip.

Bird Artists

Birds have served as an inspiration since man first scratched likenesses on cave walls, though until relatively recent times birds and animals have usually only formed part of a picture or have been incidental to the main study. Certainly an artist whose work is mainly concerned with the portrayal of birds is a fairly new phenomenon.

The beginnings of animal or wildlife painting really date from the 18th century with the commissioning of pictures depicting dogs, horses and hunting scenes, the indulgences of the British landed gentry. Later that century saw a more definite move to bird and animal portraiture in its own right and possibly the greatest of all 'true' bird artists of that period was John James Audubon (1785-1851), whose magnificent *Birds of America* captured the imagination of the public of the time and whose work is still a stimulating inspiration today.

John Gould (1804-1881) was in a sense Britain's answer to Audubon and his output was possibly even greater, including nearly 3000 lithographs of birds in 18 folio works, totalling 41 volumes. The first of his famous series of illustrated folios, *A Century of Birds of the Himalayas*, was published in 1832. His tremendous output was aided by artists equally important in their own right, such as Edward Lear, H. C. Richter, Joseph Wolf and others who helped him with the preparation of the many lithograph plates.

The beginning of the 20th century found Archibald Thorburn (1863-1935) pre-eminent in the field of bird painting and his illustrations for Lord Lilford's *Coloured Figures of the Birds of the British Isles* may well be the most widely reproduced bird pictures of all time, and still appear today in modern editions of T. A. Coward's *Birds of the British Isles*. The original of his great four-volume work *British Birds* would now fetch a fortune, but a single-volume version (much reduced in size), edited by the late James Fisher, can delight the beholder at a much more modest price.

Another outstanding bird artist of the same era was George Lodge (1863-1953). A keen falconer, much of his best work consisted of portraits of birds of prey. Lodge worked right up to his death, and saw the first volume of the mammoth 12-volume *Birds of the British Isles* written by David Bannerman, for which he painted all the illustrations. Other notable bird artists of the early 20th century include J. G. Keulemans, H. Gronvöld, Axel Amuchastegui, D. M. Reid Henry, Winifred Austen, Roland Green, J. C. Harrison, Paul Barruel, Robert Hainard; and some recent names must include Peter

Bird Bath

Scott, Roger Tory Peterson, Fenwick Lansdowne, Charles Tunnicliffe, Robert Gillmor, Eric Ennion, Arthur Singer, Michael Warren.

Bird Bath

An artificially constructed bathing place for birds, usually of stone or fibreglass, but improvisation can provide a bird bath from any number of materials. As virtually all birds bathe, the provision of a bird bath is a useful means of encouraging birds to a garden.
See 'Do-it-yourself Bird Baths', RSPB *Birds* Magazine, Autumn 1979, p. 73
Read Soper, Tony, *The Bird Table Book in Colour*, David & Charles, Newton Abbot, 1977

Bird Clubs

All sports and pastimes have their clubs, and birdwatching is no exception—it is probably true to say the network of bird clubs and ornithological societies is more extensive in Britain than in any other country in the world. Most bird clubs are of relatively recent origin though many natural history societies that have bird sections began during the Victorian era when the collecting mania was the driving force behind most aspects of natural history.

The year 1858 was important in the development of such interests for it saw the formation of one of the first regional natural-history societies, the London Natural History Society, and also saw the founding of the British Ornithologists' Union, the first society whose preoccupation was birds. Certainly no provincial bird club dates that far back and most began life this century. One of the larger established clubs is the West Midland Bird Club, formed in 1929; it

West Midland Bird Club symbol, the Ruddy Duck, a breeding bird in the Midlands area

covers four counties and has almost 2,000 members. Nearly every county in Britain has its own bird club and sometimes one or more localised area bird clubs exist within a county as well.

Within the last decade the RSPB has encouraged the setting up of local RSPB groups and quite a number of these in many areas of the country, operate harmoniously side by side with longer-established county bird clubs, having a rather different role. The local library will usually yield an address to contact.

Birder

An American vernacular term for someone who watches birds or whose aim is to see as many birds as possible. This is gradually coming into more frequent use in Britain.

Bird Fancier

Term for someone who keeps cage birds, an aviculturist, and *never* applied to someone interested in watching wild birds.

Bird Life (Magazine)

A colourful and informative bi-monthly magazine published by the RSPB for its Young Ornithologists' Club members.
See Young Ornithologists' Club

Bird of Paradise

Member of the family Paradisaeidae (Passeriformes, sub-order Oscines). In the plural, a general name for the family, which comprises 40 species, all found in New Guinea and neighbouring areas. Small to medium-sized forest-dwelling birds, the males have extremely colourful plumage, often with long tails and other spectacular plumes. These feature in elaborate displays that can involve a great variety of positions, even to hanging upside-down. A few species, however, are wholly black, with only coloured wattles. Paradise feathers are used for decorative head-dresses by local natives, and some species are endangered by this practice.

Bird of Prey

In the widest sense any bird which preys on another bird or animal, but the term is normally applied to members of the order Falconiformes: the Accipiters, Buzzards, Eagles, Falcons, Harriers, Hawks, Osprey,

Secretary Bird and Vultures. Sometimes used to include Owls (Strigiformes), the terms *diurnal* and *nocturnal* then being used to distinguish the two groups.
See Diurnal; Nocturnal
Read Brown, Leslie, *Birds of Prey*, Hamlyn, 1976, *British Birds of Prey*, Collins, 1976; Newton, I., *Population Ecology of Raptors*, Poyser, Berkhamstead, 1971; Parry, G. and Putnam, R., *The Country Life Book of Birds of Prey*, Country Life Books, 1979

Bird Protection Acts
The basic principle of the Protection of Birds Acts 1954-1967 is that all birds, their nests and eggs, are protected by law. There are certain specified exceptions, notably 'pest' species and sporting birds of various kinds. Any species not mentioned in the First, Second or Third Schedules or in the Statutory Instruments is fully protected throughout the year. These schedules provide exceptions, listing species which can be killed or taken and those which are afforded special extra protection. The laws also control ringing and trapping, disturbance of certain birds at or near the nest, possessing recently taken wild birds, the sale of birds, skins and eggs, the standard of caging for captive birds and the methods allowable for killing and taking those birds which can legally be killed or taken. Scientific, agricultural and other activities (eg falconry) are covered by special licence schemes. Penalties are regularly reviewed. Schedule I birds, though referred to as being specially protected, are in effect given the same protection but special penalties apply. The schedules consist of the following:

First Schedule—Part 1 Wild birds and their eggs protected by special penalties at all times.

Part 2 Wild birds and their eggs protected by special penalties during the close season.

Second Schedule—Wild birds which may be killed or taken by authorised persons.

Third Schedule—Wild birds which may be killed or taken outside the close season.

Fourth Schedule—Wild birds which may not be sold alive unless close-ringed and bred in captivity.

During 1980 legislation was passing through parliament which would alter and in some parts revolutionise the Bird Protection Acts in detail—the Wildlife and Countryside Bill. This would especially affect the methods of investigation of alleged offences.
See Schedule I
Read Wild Birds and the Law (RSPB)

Bird Recorder
The title usually applies to the member of a local bird club who maintains data on birds observed in the club's area, and is also often applied to the editor of a club's bird report. The magazine *British Birds* periodically publishes the names and addresses of bird-club recorders, which enables observers on holiday, away from their home areas, to send records of interesting or unusual birds to the right people.
NB: A person who records bird sounds on tape is usually known as a sound *recordist*.
See British Birds: Bird Clubs; Bird Reports

The Derbyshire
BIRD REPORT 1978

THE DERBYSHIRE ORNITHOLOGICAL SOCIETY

Typical county bird report

Bird Report (County)
Most, if not all, county bird clubs produce a report of some sort on the birds observed in their area. This may be only a duplicated list, but many publish quite comprehensive and expensively printed, frequently well-illustrated, booklets. Generally these deal with the birds observed over a year, though some cover a longer period. A bird report is one of the best means of finding out about the birds of an area unfamiliar to you, as well as being a permanent record which becomes of value to the analyst over a period of time.

RSPB reserve, Bempton Cliffs, Yorkshire—it has
the only mainland colony of breeding Gannets

Bird Reserve

A nature reserve principally managed to maintain or increase its natural wild bird population, normally with equal concern for the complete bird community but often with a particular species, or group of species, having special importance. Reserves are not in any sense zoos—none of the birds are captive or introduced. Visitors, if access is allowed, must look for the birds which occur naturally, though this is often facilitated by the provision of hides and nature trails. Most reserves require carefully researched and planned management to realise their full potential. The RSPB reserve at Minsmere, Suffolk, is a good example of this; new habitats have been created (the Scrape), existing ones encouraged by scrub clearance, reed control, etc, and certain birds and mammalian predators or pests are controlled, in order to improve conditions for those species most desirable from a conservation viewpoint (in this case Bittern, Marsh Harrier, Avocet, Bearded Tit, etc.) Most bird reserves, nevertheless, have a variety of other interesting wildlife which benefit from the protection afforded to the area. Many reserves owned or managed by local organisations such as county trusts are primarily for the protection of the flora or insect life, but birds benefit as well.

Several National Nature Reserves, managed by the Nature Conservancy Council, are important for birds but usually they are primarily designated for their overall ecological significance. The largest group of bird reserves managed by a single body are those of the RSPB, which number over 70 and cover more than 85,000 acres. The aim of the society is to have as good a representation as possible of the major habitat types and to concentrate on areas nationally and internationally significant for their 'bird populations'. Certain sites, however, are acquired for their value as educational centres. Most reserves are open to visitors, usually by permit only and parties only by prior arrangement, others are wholly or partly open to the public.

Sanctuary areas are specially designated sites with different legal implications; all species of birds are protected within the limits of the sanctuary, even those which do not have protection elsewhere.

See Minsmere; Nature Conservancy Council; Royal Society for the Protection of Birds.

Bird Sanctuary

An area set aside specifically for the protection of the birds that occur there. The term 'bird reserve' is now more generally used; sanctuary has slightly different legal connotations, denoting an area in which even birds not usually protected may not be touched or disturbed in any way.

Bird Strike

A collision between birds and aircraft. A number of serious incidents have arisen from such collisions and some planes have even crashed as a result of the impact, either because birds shattered the cockpit or because they were sucked into the jet air intake causing engine failure. All bird strikes are officially logged, and many airfields, particularly military ones, employ some means to clear runways of birds in an attempt to reduce the hazard.

Bird Table

In its simplest form a flat surface, supported by a single post or pole, or suspended from above, on which food can be set out for wild birds. More elaborate constructions can be made or bought, with roofs, perches and roosting quarters. In principle a bird table should provide a safe feeding area for garden birds and stand where it can easily be watched from the house. A leaflet detailing the construction of a simple bird table can be obtained from the Royal Society for the

A simple bird table—its construction is described in the YOC magazine *Bird Life's* leaflet 'D.I.Y. Bird Table' by John Taunton, illustrated by Robert Gillmor

Protection of Birds. Directions are also given in Soper, T., *The Bird Table Book in Colour*, David & Charles, Newton Abbot, 1977.

Tony Soper also discusses the types of food that should be offered.

Birds (Magazine)

A quarterly sent to all RSPB members. It contains news and comment about bird protection, details and reports of the Society's many bird reserves, and articles and features about birds. Extensively illustrated with colour photographs, and with a lot of advertising useful to birdwatchers—suitable holiday accommodation, makes of binoculars, etc. Details of membership of the RSPB can be obtained from its headquarters, The Lodge, Sandy, Bedfordshire SG19 2DL.

Birdwatching

The observation of birds for enjoyment, rather than the scientific study undertaken by the biologist or behavioural scientist whose motives are usually more academic. Some birdwatchers do, however, undertake census work and other forms of study on behalf of scientifically orientated organisations, notably the British Trust for Ornithology. In the early 1950s ornithologists tended to believe that all birdwatching should yield some scientific return; in more recent years this attitude has disappeared, and birdwatching is usually done for sheer pleasure and interest. This is now generally related to a protection and conservation theme, as propagated by the Royal Society for the Protection of Birds and by county naturalists' trusts, and many birdwatchers are members of these organisations or a local bird club or society.

Read Alexander, H. G., *Seventy Years of Birdwatching*, Poyser, Berkhamsted, 1974; Conder, P., *RSPB Guide to Birdwatching*, Hamlyn, 1979; Fisher, James and Flegg, Jim, *Watching Birds*, Poyser, Berkhamsted, 1974; Lack, D., *Enjoying Ornithology*, Methuen, 1965; Wallace, I., *Discover Birds*, Whizzard Press/Deutsch, 1979

Bittern (*Botaurus stellaris*)

A shy secretive bird, whose mottled and barred brown-and-black plumage provides ideal protective colouration for the reedy

Birdwatchers—and telescopes

world in which it lives. In flight its kinship to the Herons is more apparent, though the darker plumage and shorter neck is not at all like the Grey Heron (*Ardea cinerea*). The Bittern is very local as a breeding bird, the total UK breeding population being probably under 80 pairs, most of which are found in Norfolk and Suffolk. The Bittern is noted for its resonant booming call, mainly uttered at dusk and audible half a mile away. The American Bittern (*Botaurus lentiginosus*) is a vagrant from North America. The Little Bittern (*Ixobrychus minutus*) is a rare visitor from Southern and Eastern Europe.

Blackbird (*Turdus merula*)
In Britain the all-black male with his orange-yellow bill and yellow eye-ring is one of our most familiar birds. The brown female, with her pale streaked throat, is not so striking and might be mis-identified by the beginner. Not only is it a common garden bird, but it has penetrated into the heart of cities and towns, and in wilder areas can overlap with the mountain-loving Ring Ousel (*Turdus torquatus*). The total British and Irish population is put at 7 million pairs. In North America the name Blackbird is applied to certain of the Orioles (Icteridae).

Bittern

Read Snow, D. W., *A Study of Blackbirds*, Collins, 1958; Sims, E., *British Thrushes*, Collins, 1978

Blackcap (*Sylvia atricapilla*)
A member of the sub-family Sylviinae of the Muscicapidae (Passeriformes, sub-order Oscines). The Blackcap is regarded by many as rivalling the Nightingale (*Luscinia megarhynchos*) with its song; it is in fact sometimes called the Northern Nightingale. The male Blackcap does have a black cap which makes him easy to distinguish from the female even when not singing, for she has a chestnut-brown cap. Mainly a summer visitor to Britain, but some Blackcaps do overwinter and visit garden bird tables, when confusion can occur with Marsh Tits or Willow Tits, which also have black caps.

Blackcock (*Lyrurus tetrix*)
Name generally applied to the male Black Grouse, a game bird with a distinctive lyre-shaped tail. The less conspicuous female is known as the Greyhen. Present throughout the year, it was formerly more widespread in Britain; now mainly found in suitable areas of

Blackcap

Scotland, with a few in Northern England, the Peak District, and the North Staffordshire moors. Also present in parts of Wales, with a few on Exmoor and Dartmoor. Total population around 25,000 pairs.
See Grouse

Black Geese

Those species of wild Geese that are predominantly black (with varying amounts of white) on head and neck, are collectively referred to by this term.
See Geese

Blakeney Point, Norfolk

A National Trust Reserve since 1912, it comprises a spit of some 1,300 acres (526Ha) of sand dunes, shingle and saltings, which can be reached by boat from Morston or Blakeney opposite or by walking up the beach from Cley-next-the-Sea some 4 miles to the west. Notable as a ternery, with over 1,000 Common Terns nesting most years, and at times other species of Tern, as well as Redshank, Oystercatcher, Ringed Plover and Shelduck. It can also provide exciting watching in spring and autumn with many rare migrants to its credit.

Blakeney harbour is also the haunt of waders, particularly in autumn, and in the winter there are always plenty of Brent Geese and other interesting wildfowl, Grebes and Divers to be seen.

Read Blakeney Point and Scolt Head Island, National Trust, 1971

Bluethroat (*Luscinia svecica*)

Belonging to the genus Luscinia, which includes Nightingale (*Luscinia megarhynchos*) and Rubythroat (*Luscinia calliope*), the Bluethroat occurs in two forms. The Scandinavian form, Red-spotted Bluethroat (*L.s. svecica*) has a chestnut spot in the centre of its blue throat, while the Central and Southern European form (*L.s. cyaneucla*) has a white spot there. As scarce passage migrants to Britain both forms have occurred. In autumn when adults have lost breast colouration, it becomes impossible to separate the two forms.

Bobwhite (Quail) (*Colinus virginianus*)

One of the American Quails, a native of the Eastern USA, north of the Great Lakes and the Dakotas and west to Eastern Texas, Colorado and SE Wyoming. A game bird with a considerable sporting reputation, and attempts to introduce it in Britain have met some limited success. The areas where birds have been bred and released include Suffolk, and Tresco in the Isles of Scilly.
Read Lever, C., *The Naturalised Animals of the British Isles*, Paladin/Granada, 1977; Rosene, W., Jr, *The Bob-white Quail*, Rutgers University Press, USA, 1969

Bonxie (*Stercorarius skua*)
Local Shetland name for the Great Skua.

Booby
The name used for certain species of the Sulidae family (Gannets and Boobies). There are six species of Boobies which replace the Northern Gannet (*Sula bassana*) in tropical waters: the Blue-footed Booby (*Sula nebouxii*), Peruvian Booby (*Sula variegata*), Abbott's Booby (*Sula abbotti*), Masked Booby (*Sula dactylatra*), Red-footed Booby (*Sula sula*) and Brown Booby (*Sula leucogaster*). The name 'Booby' was first applied by seamen because of the apparent stupidity of the birds when approached on the nest.

Booming
The act of calling by the Bittern (*Botaurus stellaris*), which emits a deep resonant note that can be heard half a mile away and may be likened to a foghorn.

Booted
Equipped with a horny covering to the tarsus (leg), most of it in an undivided state, a condition found in most Passerines. The Booted Warbler (*Hippolais caligata*), smallest of the *Hippolais* warblers, only $4\frac{1}{2}$in (114mm) long, is a vagrant to Britain from Asia. The Booted Eagle (*Hieraaetus pennatus*) is so called because of its feathered tarsus, though the expression is normally used when referring to poultry with feathered legs.
See Scutelate; Tarsus

Bo'sun Bird
An old nautical name for Tropicbirds (Phaethon spp). Also spelt Boatswain Bird.

Botulism
Poisoning caused by an exceptionally powerful toxin that attacks the nervous system. Produced by the bacillus *Clostridium botulinus* which exists in decaying organic matter, it is most frequent in alkaline marshes, especially in periods of drought when water level is low

Blue-footed Booby

Bowerbird

and decaying material abundant. In such conditions many birds die from this cause, particularly wildfowl. One of the most serious outbreaks known occurred in 1929, when an estimated 3 million birds died on the Great Salt Lake in the United States of America.
See Disease

Bowerbird

Species belonging to the Ptilonorhynchidae (Passeriformes, sub-order Oscines). There are 17 species, restricted to the forests of Australia and New Guinea. Their most interesting characteristic is the one that gives them their common name: the construction of bowers, used in their display, having no direct connection with the nest. Bowers are generally strewn with bright objects or light-reflecting materials and can include bottle-tops, bits of plastic and other man-made debris. Each item is selected with great discrimination. Some species paint their bowers with fruit pulp or charcoal, or dry grass mixed with saliva.
Read Gilliard, E. T., *Birds of Paradise and Bower Birds*, Weidenfeld & Nicholson, 1969

Great Bowerbird

Brailing

Rendering a bird flightless by binding the wing so that it cannot be extended.
See Clipping: Pinioning

Brambling (*Fringilla montifringilla*)

Or Bramble Finch. Mainly a winter visitor to Britain, its numbers varying considerably from year to year. A frequent companion of the Chaffinch (*Fringilla coelebs*) in stackyards and open fields, it also favours beech woods feeding on the fallen seeds.
See Finch

Breckland (Norfolk/Suffolk)

Formerly an area of sandy wastes, much of the original 'brecks' has been turned over to agriculture and forestry. Most is now coniferous forest which has brought in Crossbills as a breeding species, and though the Stone-curlew is adapting to the changed habitat it is much scarcer than it used to be. The main area of the brecks lies within the rectangle between Mildenhall, Bury St Edmunds, Watton and Methwold. Some of the best remaining heaths are Norfolk Naturalists' Trust Reserves such as Thetford and Weeting

Heaths, and Cavenham Heath is a National Nature Reserve.

Brambling (male)

Breeding

This term refers to all activities associated with reproduction:

1 Holding territory
2 Nest building (including excavating)
3 Courtship and display
4 Egg laying
5 Incubation
6 Feeding young
7 Nest sanitation
8 Protection of nest and young

See Breeding Season

Breeding Season

The period of time during which breeding takes place. This does vary from species to species and sometimes even within the same species. Most birds, however, have a well-defined season which is determined by their physiological state and the availability of food. In the northern temperate and Arctic zones, breeding is confined to the spring and early summer; the physiological readiness for breeding is influenced by lengthening days

House Martins may raise three broods in a season

and by the availability of food for the young.

In such species as the Crossbill (*Loxia curvirostra*), which can be seen sitting on eggs in February, however, the availability of food plays a more significant part.

Most species breed once a year, though some of the smaller passerines raise more than one brood, and in some species, eg House Martin (*Delichon urbica*), as many as three. In the tropics the breeding season can be correlated to the periods of rainfall, and in Australia where rainfall is unpredictable and irregular many species appear to commence breeding activities at the onset of rain. Some of the larger birds, eg Condors, Albatrosses, only breed every other year as the young take so long to reach the free-flying stage—in the case of the Wandering Albatross (*Diomedea exulans*) eleven months.

Breeding Territory

An area defended by a bird (or pair) against others, for the purposes of nesting. Its size varies greatly between species. In some, only the site of the nest itself is defended. Others defend a large territory, sufficient to meet all the needs of both adults and the family of young. Others compromise, defending a sizeable area around the nest but overlapping with other pairs in their feeding range. These breeding strategies are generally dependent on the type, distribution and availability of food.

Bridling

Facial plumage markings that resemble a bridle or spectacles on certain species. For example, some Guillemots (*Uria aalge*) have a white ring round the eye and a white line running back from it. In Britain this variety comprises about 1 per cent of the population

Bridling

in S and SW England, increasing northwards to about 25 per cent in the Shetlands. The Bridled Tern (*Sterna anaethetus*) is named after the white mark over its forehead extending backwards past its eye. A bird of the tropics, it is a rare vagrant to Britain.

Brightness Factor

An important performance aspect of any binocular is the clarity of image and this is measured by its brightness factor. The diameter of the object lens governs the amount of light entering the instrument and the brightness of the image depends on its relationship to the magnification, eg an 8 x 30 binoculars has a brightness factor of 3.75:

$$30 \div 8 = 3.75$$

A 10 x 50 binocular has a brightness factor of 5.0.

$$50 \div 10 = 5.0$$

Binoculars with a brightness factor of less than 3.75 will give poor illumination except under really good light conditions and as birdwatching is often undertaken in dull weather the greater the brightness factor the better.

See Binoculars; Field of View

British Birds (Magazine)

Known simply and affectionately as 'BB' to many of its subscribers *British Birds* is regarded as the premier journal for British birdwatchers. Though prefixed 'British', articles on birds of the whole western Palearctic are included. Founded in 1907 by H. F. Witherby, co-author and publisher of the unrivalled and as yet unsurpassed *The Handbook of British Birds* (Witherby, Jourdain, Ticehurst, Tucker), BB flourished for over 30 years under his enthusiastic editorial direction. Since then, the journal's senior editors have been other notable British ornithologists: B. W. Tucker (1943-50), E. M. Nicholson (1951-59), P. A. D. Hollom (1960-62) and now Stanley Cramp. Since mid-1976, the managing editor has been Dr J. T. R. Sharrock, formerly the national organiser of the Atlas project (qv).

In 1973, ownership of 'BB' was transferred from the firm of H. F. & G. Witherby, its founders, to Macmillan Journals Ltd. In recent years, the magazine's appeal has been greatly widened, yet it still maintains its scientific accuracy and undisputed role as guardian of the British rarities lists. The introduction of photographic and bird-illustration competitions, news and recent report features and a monthly mystery bird photograph have done a great deal to make this monthly magazine even more appealing to the ordinary birdwatcher.

Obtainable on subscription from Macmillan Journals Ltd, Brunel Road, Basingstoke, Hampshire RG21 2XS, from whom a free sample copy may be obtained.

British Library of Wildlife Sound,
The British Institute of Recorded Sound was established some years ago and is recognised as the national collection of sound recordings. In 1969 a new department of the Institute was set up specifically to handle bio-acoustic recordings and is known as the British Library of Wildlife Sounds. It has been presented with quantities of commercial, BBC and privately made recordings. The aim of the library is to provide a national repository for natural history recordings which can be made available for scientific and cultural purposes. Recordings of all types of natural history sounds are accepted from amateurs and professional recordists alike. Full details of BLOWS can be obtained from the Librarian, The British Institute of Recorded Sound, 29 Exhibition Road, London SW7.

British List
The official list of British and Irish birds, maintained jointly by the British Ornithologists' Union and the Irish Wildbird Conservancy. There are four categories under which birds are listed:

A Species which have been recorded in an apparently wild state in Britain and Ireland at least once within the last 50 years.

B Species which have been recorded in an apparently wild state in Britain or Ireland at least once, but not within the last 50 years.

C Species which although originally introduced by man have now established a regular feral breeding stock which apparently maintains itself without necessarily having recourse to further introductions.

D Species which have been recorded within the last 50 years and would otherwise appear in category 1 except that either (a) there is a reasonable doubt that they have ever occurred in a wild state or (b) that they have certainly arrived with ship assistance or (c) they have only

been found dead on the tideline; also that their feral populations may or may not be self-supporting.

Individually, many birdwatchers keep their own 'British list', a record of species they have seen in the wild in Britain.

British Ornithologists' Club
Founded in 1892 as a dining club for members of the British Ornithologists' Union.

British Ornithologists' Union (BOU)
The BOU was founded in Cambridge in 1858 by Professor Alfred Newton, FRS, and brought together a very small body of 'gentlemen attached to the study of Ornithology'. From this beginning the society has expanded to an international membership of around 2,000, and has among its ranks some of the most eminent ornithologists in the world. Through its membership and quarterly journal *Ibis* it has a respected world-wide influence. The Union organizes an annual conference and scientific meetings and provides grants for ornithological research. Members of the Union have the exclusive privilege of joining the British Ornithologists' Club. The club itself publishes a regular quarterly bulletin, its usually short papers dealing with taxonomy. It also holds a dinner in London every other month. The BOU is not for the average 'birder' but experienced birdwatchers interested in more scientific matters can obtain application forms from: The Assistant Secretary, British Ornithologists' Union, c/o Zoological Society of London, Regents Park, London NW1 4RY.

British Trust for Ornithology (BTO)
Founded in 1932 to promote the scientific study of birds, especially among amateur birdwatchers, the BTO is the premier scientific authoritative body in Britain today. The first research activities of the Trust set the pattern for future years with studies of the distribution and status of the Woodcock; size of Swallow broods and the relation of the species to climate; and the connection between vole plagues and the breeding of Short-eared Owls. Censuses were also carried out of some common species of bird and one of the earliest undertaken by the Trust (and still continued today) was a census of heronries. Other annual censuses started in its early days and still carried on, concern the Great Crested Grebe and Mute Swan. Major projects such as the Common Bird Census,

Great Crested Grebe—subject of an annual BTO census

BTO NEWS

**A BULLETIN
FOR BIRD WATCHERS**

Edited by David Glue and Robert Morgan for
THE BRITISH TRUST FOR ORNITHOLOGY

DECEMBER 1979   NUMBER 104

DEATH ON THE MERSEY

For several weeks, dead and crippled birds have been picked up in large numbers on the Mersey Estuary, mainly on the north shore, west of Hale. A wide range of species have been involved, the largest number being Dunlins, the commonest wader on the estuary. This is not an isolated incident since birds have been reported as found dying there in smaller numbers for some years — mortality this year has been very much worse than usual. Many organizations are involved in trying to determine the cause of these deaths and, so far, it is obvious from the analysis of corpses that birds are suffering from lead poisoning. Furthermore this is acute poisoning, the birds having ingested a lethal dose over a short period of time, rather than chronic long-term poisoning.

The Mersey is heavily industrialised and there are many potential sources of pollution. It is possible that the deaths are a result of lead deposited in the estuarine silt many years ago and only recently stirred up by dredging operations. Some mud samples have contained very high levels of lead indeed. The inorganic lead in the mud is not, in itself, an immediate danger to the birds. However, many species of mud-living invertebrates, which are horrifyingly efficient concentrators of lead, form the main food of many of the estuary's birds: this is probably how birds are being poisoned.

A minimum count of the birds so far affected and found on the north shore of the Mersey up to early November comprises:

Part of the Mersey Estuary's death toll of waders and ducks.
Photo: Malcolm Lord.

DUNLIN	1,020
BLACK-HEADED GULL	306
REDSHANK	156
CURLEW	62
TEAL	49
PINTAIL	19
MALLARD	15
COMMON GULL	15
GREY PLOVER	5
KNOT	5
LITTLE STINT	5
GREEN SANDPIPER	4
ELEVEN OTHER SPECIES	34
Total of Birds	**1,695**

In addition eleven rats and a hedgehog have been found dead, probably poisoned from eating contaminated corpses. As we write in early November fresh casualties are being washed ashore with the high tides, a single day producing 170 Dunlin, plus some Redshank, Grey Plover, Pintail, Teal and Black-headed Gulls.

Over the last ten or fifteen years the Mersey has 'come alive' in an ornithological sense. It has progressed from being a minor estuary for birds to one of international importance for several species of ducks and waders. This improvement has coincided with a general cleaning-up of the effluents draining into the waterway. It is now particularly noted for its Pintail, Teal, Shelduck, Redshank and Dunlin populations. During the winter more than 5% of the British population of wintering Dunlin are to be found on the Mersey and this is the species worst affected throughout this incident. Indeed a newly arrived flock of 7,000 birds seem currently to be at risk in the Dungeon Bank area and methods of scaring them away from this part of the estuary are being discussed.

Such incidents, affecting waders, have not previously been reported from Britain. However the number of birds involved puts the disaster on a par with the ten worst oiling incidents affecting seabirds to have happened round our coasts over the last decade. The particularly worrying aspect is that, unlike ordinary oiling, the underlying cause of the pollution has yet to be identified and we have no idea how long the mortality may continue.

CHRIS MEAD and ROB COCKBAIN

which has been under way since 1961, and the nest record scheme, which first began as the Hatching and Fledging enquiry back in 1939, along with migration and ringing studies, form a large part of the Trust's work. The co-ordination and administration of ringing activities are particularly important.

The BTO operates from its headquarters at Tring in Hertfordshire with a full-time professional staff. With the aid of a network of regional representatives, a regular bulletin (*BTO News*) and its magazine *Bird Study*, it maintains close contact with its many members, who participate in the various studies and enquiries that the BTO organises. Undoubtedly the largest survey ever undertaken by the BTO, involving probably 10,000 birdwatchers over a five-year period (1968-72), was the 10km sq breeding-bird survey which culminated in the *Atlas of Breeding Birds in Britain and Ireland* published in 1976.

A more recent major survey has been made of the sites of major ornithological importance in Britain and this 'register' of such places is to be published shortly.

For details about the British Trust for Ornithology write to the BTO, Beech Grove, Tring, Herts.
See Atlas; Common Bird Census; Ringing

Broadbill

Substantive name of species of Eurylaimidae (Passeriformes, sub-order Eurylaimi). A group of brightly coloured birds inhabiting the Old World tropics from Africa to the Philippines. There are 14 species recorded. The name Broadbill is also used in North America for the Scaup (*Aythya marila*).

Broads, Norfolk

A series of freshwater lakes lying in the valleys of the Norfolk rivers, which eventually drain into Breydon water and into the sea at Yarmouth. The area is synonymous with boating holidays, a use not always in harmony with the wildlife of the area. However, it is still a wonderland of aquatic and reed-haunting species of birds and other creatures. Bure Marshes and Hickling Broad, both National Nature Reserves, and Horsey Mere which is the property of the National Trust, are of particularly great interest to the birdwatcher. Bearded Tit, Bittern and Harriers can still be seen in some areas, as well as the more usual wildfowl.

Broken-wing Trick

A bird may feign injury to lure a predator, animal or human, away from the nest or young.
See Distraction Display

Brood

Collectively, the young hatched from a single clutch of eggs.

Brooding

The act of sitting on the young by the parent bird, mainly to keep them warm. Most birds brood their young for lengthy periods immediately after hatching, the amount of time spent brooding decreasing as the young grow. Adult birds will also brood their young to protect them from rain and also from hot sun. Brooding might also be employed on occasions as protection against predators.

Brood Patch

An area on the underside of the adult bird where the feathers are shed. Usually more than one is present. Brood patches are richly supplied with blood and the skin becomes swollen at incubation times, an adaptation facilitating the transfer of heat from parents to eggs.

Blackcap male brooding the young

Brown Owl
Alternative name for the Tawny Owl (*Strix aluco*), also sometimes called the Wood Owl.

BTO News
A bulletin published by the BTO and circulated to members about every two months. It contains mainly details of current BTO surveys and studies, but also has other news and information of interest to birdwatchers.
See British Trust for Ornithology

Bufflehead (*Bucephala albeola*)
A small duck allied to the Goldeneye (*Bucephala clangula*), it has a similar flight pattern to this species but shows a white head patch on the drake. A North American species, it has been recorded half a dozen times in Britain.

Buffon, George Louis Leclerc, Comte de (1707-1788)
French naturalist and author of the famous *Histoire Naturelle*, the first book to present natural history in an intelligible form. The Long-tailed Skua (or Jaeger) (*Stercorarius longicaudus*) was formerly called Buffon's Skua in his honour.

Bulbul
Substantive name of most species of Pycnonotidae (Passeriformes, sub-order Oscines). An Old World, largely tropical, group of birds varying in size from that of a Sparrow (*Passer domesticus*) to that of a Blackbird (*Turdus merula*). There are 118 species of these noisy gregarious forest birds. Most feed on fruit and berries, some feed on buds and the nectar of flowers, and several are insectivorous.

Bullfinch (*Pyrrhula pyrrhula*)
The male bird is exceedingly handsome with deep pink breast, blue-grey back and glossy black cap, the female has the same basic plumage pattern but the breast is brownish. A resident and widely distributed species, the total population of Britain and Ireland is probably around 600,000 pairs. In fruit-growing areas it can be a nuisance as it is extremely fond of fruit buds.
See Finch

Bullfinches with young

Reed Bunting—Sparrow-like back but distinguished by white outer tail feathers

Bunting

The substantive name of the Old World species of Emberizinae, a sub-family included either in the Emberizidae, if that be kept as a separate family, or in the Fringillidae (Passeriformes, sub-order Oscines). In the plural, a general term for the sub-family. In North America most birds of this sub-family have the substantive name Finch or Sparrow, the name Bunting being applied to brightly coloured species of the Pyrrhuloxiinae. Buntings are small sparrow-like birds, averaging 6in (152mm) in length. Predominantly ground-feeding, they eat mainly seeds. The usually short conical bill is in some species provided with a hump on the roof of the mouth for crushing seeds. In the Old World there are 40 species of bunting, 29 of which are found in the palearctic region. In Britain the best-known is the Yellow Bunting (*Emberiza citrinella*), more often called the Yellowhammer. This is a bird of heaths,

Corn Bunting

Snow Bunting

commons, agricultural land and open country-side. The male bird's monotonous song, 'a-little-bit-of-bread-and-no-cheese' is a familiar summer sound as the song period goes on long after most other species have finished. Additionally the bright yellow head and underparts make him easy to identify. The female is less striking, but the rufous rump common to both, and the longish tail which is continuously flicked, should help identify her.

The male Reed Bunting, with his black head and throat and white collar, is a mainly waterside-haunting member of the family; even the smallest reedy, marshy area will support one or two pairs of this widely distributed bird. In recent years it has been resorting to drier situations and even visiting suburban gardens in winter.

Less well known is the Corn Bunting (*Emberiza calandra*), a bird of arable grass-land and cultivated areas. A drab-looking bird, its distinctive song is likened to the jangling of a bunch of keys. Even less well known is the Cirl Bunting (*Emberiza cirlus*), whose breeding range in Britain is restricted to SW England where there are probably less than 1,000 pairs all told.

The Snow Bunting (*Plectrophenax nivalis*) nests in Britain in even smaller numbers, probably no more than half a dozen pairs in any year and these confined to the area of the Cairngorms. However, it is commoner in winter, when flocks of visiting birds (some-times 100 or more together) can be seen, particularly along parts of the East Coast.

The Ortolan Bunting (*Emberiza hortulana*) and Lapland Bunting (*Calcarius lapponicus*) are regular but scarce visitors, and the Little Bunting (*Emberiza pusilla*) and Rustic Bunt-ing (*Emberiza rustica*) are only rarely noted.

Busking
Territorial display by the male Mute Swan (*Cygnus olor*). When swimming, the wing feathers are raised, neck ruffled and head laid back, the bird making itself as conspicuous as possible.

Bustard
The most usual substantive name of species Otididae (Gruiformes, sub-order Otides); in the plural the general term for the family. Medium-sized to large (the heaviest known flying bird is the Kori Bustard (*Ardeotis kori*), some specimens weighing 30lb (14.54kg). Long-legged, long-necked, mainly ground-dwelling birds, there are 21 species, most of which are found in Africa. In Britain the Great Bustard (*Otis tarda*) once nested. Attempts have been made recently to reintro-duce the species on Salisbury Plain. The Little Bustard (*Otis tetrax*) and Houbara Bustard (*Chlamydotis undulata*) are vagrants to Britain.

Butcherbird
A name often used for members of the Shrike family (Laniidae) after their unsavoury habit of impaling their prey (small rodents, birds, insects) on thorns or spikes, forming so-called 'larders'. In Britain applied to the Red-backed Shrike (*Lanius collurio*) and Great Grey Shrike (*Lanius excubitor*) parti-cularly. Name also used for this last mentioned species in North America where it is called the Northern Shrike. In Australia the term is also used for some species of Cracticidae, again related to the forming of a 'larder of prey'.
See Shrike

Buteo
A North American term used by birdwatchers as vernacular for *Buteo* spp where these are

Butcherbird with 'larder'

included under the general term Hawk; in Britain they are called Buzzards, eg Common Buzzard (*Buteo buteo*).

Butterfly Flight
A form of flight used by some birds during courtship displays. The slow flickering wing-beats are reminiscent of a butterfly's wing

action. Species frequently using this form of display include Little Ringed Plover (*Charadrius dubius*), Ringed Plover (*Charadrius hiaticula*) and Lesser Spotted Woodpecker (*Dendrocopos minor*).

Buzzard (*Buteo buteo*)
A broad-winged, round-tailed bird of prey, well known for its soaring flight. Frequenting mainly hilly country with wooded valleys, open moorland and secluded open regions, it is commonest in parts of West Scotland, the Lake District, Wales and South West England. A small number breed in Northern Ireland. Total population probably around 10,000 pairs.

Other species which occur in Britain include the Rough-legged Buzzard (*Buteo lagopus*), a winter visitor in small numbers, and the Honey Buzzard (*Pernis apivorus*), a summer visitor with a few pairs breeding.

Buzzard

Barnacle Geese at the Caerlaverock Wildfowl Trust Refuge

Caerlaverock

Situated on the northern shore of the Solway Firth, this area is one of the outstanding bird haunts in Britain, famed for its wintering geese and wildfowl. A principal haunt of the Barnacle Goose, with upwards of 5,000 recorded. The flocks of 10,000 or more Pinkfeet and smaller numbers of Greylags are no less impressive. There are two controlled areas: the Caerlaverock National Nature Reserve, which can be visited, but usually only on Sundays and then by prior arrangement with the warden, Mr E. L. Roberts, Tadorna, Hollands Farm Road, Caerlaverock; and the Caerlaverock Wildfowl Refuge which can be visited throughout the winter, 11.00-14.00 hrs, except Tuesdays and Wednesdays. Applications to Warden, Eastpark Farm, Caerlaverock, East Dumfriesshire. However, good views of geese can be obtained from various points along the B725.

Cahow (*Pterodroma cahow*)

Another name for the Black-capped Petrel, which breeds in small numbers on Bermuda where it was rediscovered in recent years, after being thought to have become extinct. It has been recorded in Britain, once— a single bird of this species obtained at Swaffham, Norfolk, in 1850.

The rare Cahow or Black-capped Petrel

Cain-Abel Conflict

In some large birds of prey, the oldest nest-ling repeatedly and mercilessly attacks its smaller nest mate, the younger bird often dying from starvation or injury. Such aggression occurs chiefly in the first half of the nesting period at times when the young are not being brooded. Such behaviour has become known as the Cain-Abel conflict.
See Asynchronous hatching

Calamus

The quill or main supporting shaft of a feather below the vane, the base of which is embedded in the skin.
See Feather

Calf of Man

An island of 350h, it lies off the south-west tip of the Isle of Man separated from the main island by a sound some 600m wide. In 1959 an observatory was established on the island which has had an important and continuing influence on Manx ornithology. The Calf of Man has long been famous for breeding sea birds, though the once large Manx Shearwater population is now only represented by a few pairs. An important part of the observatory's work has been an annual census of the breeding-bird population, along with its study of migratory bird movements and ringing activities. Among the many usual observatory species the Calf of Man has had its rarities, which have included Black-eared Wheatear, Subalpine Warbler, Dusky Thrush and Scops Owl, to name but a few.

Call Note

Song is primarily controlled by the sex hor-mones, and is generally concerned with such basic functions as the defence of territory or its establishment. Call notes, on the other hand, are concerned with the co-ordination of behaviour of other members of the species in situations that are not primarily sexual but connected with such activities as feeding, flocking, migration and response to predators. Virtually all birds have call notes which communicate such information to other members of their kind or in some instances to other species, particularly in the case of alarm calls. The call note seems to be inborn, as is the response. Thus for example a newly hatched chick of a Ringed Plover (*Charadrius hiaticula*) or Lapwing (*Vanellus vanellus*) will 'freeze' immediately its parent's alarm is uttered. The parent bird's call is also of great

Peregrine calling in flight

importance in making contact with its off-spring when the young become scattered for some reason.

Call notes are useful to the birdwatcher as an aid to identification and can often be the clinching factor in distinguishing between similar species. Also as often as not they serve as the only means of establishing a bird's presence, eg with the Water Rail (*Rallus aquaticus*) and other Rallidae spp. Perhaps one of the best-known examples of a bird's presence being detected by its call is provided by the Redwing (*Turdus iliacus*), whose plaintive 'seep' note can be heard as it migrates overhead unseen at night, arriving in Britain usually from early October on-wards. But this is not so well known to non-birdwatchers as the call of the Cuckoo (*Cuculus canorus*) which is so eagerly awaited each spring.

Camargue

One of the best places for birdwatching in Europe, it comprises a vast expanse of saline lagoons and freshwater marshes lying between the two branches of the Rhone in SE France. Penetrated from the south by the sea, the fresh waters of the Rhone flow in from the north. In recent years much of its wildness and remoteness have been eroded by tourist development and rice production. Despite these incursions it remains a great attraction

Canary

to birdwatchers, and at least part of it will be preserved, thanks to the creation of a 52 square mile reserve, almost a third of the delta proper. The sanctuary, created in 1928 by the Société Nationale d'Acclimation, can only be visited by permit which must be obtained in advance. However, it is not necessary to go to the reserve to see birds. A good centre for working the Camargue is Arles and from there forays can be made to the Etang de Vaccerès where it is still possible to see the Greater Flamingo (*Phoenicopterus ruber*) and other such species as Purple Heron (*Ardea purpurea*), Marsh Harrier (*Circus aeruginosus*) and Little Egret (*Egretta garzetta*). Other parts of the region such as Les Alpilles still hold Bonelli's Eagle (*Hieraaetus fasciatus*), Blue Rock Thrush (*Monticola solitarius*) and Crag Martin (*Hirundo rupestris*); Le Crau (stone desert) has Calandra Lark (*Melanocorypha calandra*) and Pin-tailed Sandgrouse (*Pterocles alchata*).

Read Ferguson-Lees, Hockliffe and Zweeres, *A Guide to Birdwatching in Europe*, Bodley Head, 1975

Canary

The Canary (*Serinus canaria*) of the Canary Islands, Madeira and the Azores was first brought into Europe during the sixteenth century, and as a cagebird now exists in a diversity of form, colour and plumage patterns. The so-called Roller Canary is famed for the beauty and variety of its song. Hybrids between the Canary and other Finches are known as 'mules'.

The wild Canary is about the size of a Linnet and is a greyish-green colour with darker streaks and greenish-yellow breast and rump. It is very similar to its European relative the Serin (*Serinus serinus*).
See Serin

Cannon Netting

A means of capturing birds for ringing purposes. Projectiles attached to one edge of a net are fired from cannons, thus drawing the net over the catching area where birds are feeding or roosting. Normally used in connection with waders, Gulls and Wildfowl.
See Rocket Netting

Cap

An area of distinctive colour in some plumage patterns, covering part of the top of the head, as on Blackcap (*Sylvia atricapilla*); sometimes it extends down to the nape, as on Willow Tit (*Parus montanus*) (see drawing opposite).

Cape Clear

Lying off the coast of Co. Cork, it is the most southerly piece of Ireland (apart from Fastnet Rock). This small island (5 x 2km) has been the site of a bird observatory since 1959. Tim

Greater Flamingos in the Camargue

Cap on Willow Tit

Sharrock, current managing editor of the magazine *British Birds* and organiser of the BTO/IWC *Atlas* project, was a founder-member and later its committee chairman. Though there is no permanent warden, the observatory is manned each spring and autumn (often summer and winter as well) by amateurs on holiday. The observatory is famous for two things; the large number of rarities seen on the island (Little Crake, Little Swift, Rufous Bush Robin, White-throated Sparrow), and as one of Europe's foremost sites for observing seabird movements (30,000 Manx Shearwaters an hour, 2,000 Great Shearwaters an hour, 900 Storm

North Harbour, Cape Clear, Co Cork: bird observatory house is left centre, at end of harbour

Caprimulgiformes

Petrels an hour, 2,000 Gannets an hour and nearly 100 Great Skuas in one day is the sort of excitement that Cape Clear is renowned for).

Read Sharrock, J. T. R., *The Natural History of Cape Clear Island*, Poyser, Berkhamsted, 1973

Capercaillie (*Tetrao urogallus*)
A very large Turkey-like game bird. The males can be between 33in (838mm) and 35in (889mm) in length, with females somewhat smaller at 23in (584mm) to 25in (635mm). The name has Gaelic origins and is sometimes spelt Capercailzie. The species became extinct in Britain in the middle of the eighteenth century but was reintroduced in the first half of the nineteenth century, and is now established in NW Scotland, where over 10,000 birds are probably present. A bird of coniferous woodland with plenty of undergrowth, it feeds mainly on conifer shoots.

Caprimulgiformes
An order of birds comprising the following sub-orders and families:
Sub-order Steatornithes
    Family—Oilbirds (Steatornithidae)

Sub-order Caprimulgi
   Family—Frogmouths (Podargidae)
         Potoos (Nyctibiidae)
         Owlet-Nightjars (Aegothelidae)
         Nightjars, Goatsuckers (Capri-
         mulgidae)
In Britain the order is represented only by
the Nightjar (*Caprimulgus europaeus*).

Caracara

Substantive name of some species of Dap-
triinae of the Falconidae (Falconiformes, sub-
order Falcones). A group of large (Buzzard-
sized) long-legged birds with hooked beaks,
they are quite unlike Falcons. Insect-eating or
omnivorous, also having a strong taste for
carrion, they are common in parts of Central
and South America, where they often
associate with Vultures. The Common
Caracara (*Polyborus plancus*) which occurs in
California, Florida, New Mexico and Central
America, is also known as the Mexican Eagle.

Cardinal Grosbeaks

Members of the sub-family Cardinalinae of
the Emberizidae (Passeriformes, sub-order
Oscines). There are 37 recorded species in
this sub-family, the commonest substantive
name being Grosbeak, with others called
Bunting, Cardinal, Dickcissel, Pyrrhuloxia
and Saltator. Confined to the New World,
they are predominantly tropical in distribution. Some of the North American species

Hen Capercaillie at nest

are highly migratory. The best known species
is the Cardinal (*Cardinalis cardinalis*). The
male is a vivid red bird with a black throat. In
parts of North America it is common in
suburban gardens.

Carinatae

The class Aves was originally divided into
two sub-classes, the Ratites (running birds,
the Ostriches and Rheas) and the Carinatae
(flying birds), but is now combined as one
class, split into 28 orders.
See Carinate; Order

Carinate

Having a keel (carina) on the sternum.

Carpal

The small bones of the 'wrist' in a bird's wing,
the carpal joint being the bend of the wing.
This is equivalent to the wrist but is sometimes misleadingly referred to as the 'elbow'.
In describing a bird, the proper term, carpal
joint, is preferable as it allows no ambiguity.
See diagram for Ulna

Carpometacarpus

The main bony structure of the 'hand' in
birds, formed by the fusion of carpal and
metacarpal elements.
See Wing

48

Casque on the Black-casqued Hornbill

Casque
An enlargement of the upper surface of the bill in front of the head, typically in most species of Hornbill (Bucerotidae), or on top of the head as in Cassowaries (Casuariidae).

Cassowary
See Casuariiformes

Cast
In falconry, a cast of Hawks means two flown together, not necessarily a pair.
See Pellet

Casuariiformes
An order of ratite birds comprising families

The Cassowary has a big bony 'crest'—it may be for protection as the bird pushes through undergrowth, or a sexual adornment

Casuariidae and Dromaiidae (Cassowary and Emu). Very large running birds, the Cassowaries are found in Australia and New Guinea, and the sole surviving species of Emu only in Australia.

Catbird
A name applied to a number of unrelated species in various parts of the world. In North America the name is used for a species of Mocking Bird, in Australia for a type of Bowerbird.

Caudal
Pertaining to the tail or region of the tail.

Census
The term usually applied to estimates of breeding populations of birds. In Britain the first census on any scale was the 1928 Census of the Heron (*Ardea cinerea*), organised by E. M. Nicholson. Other larger-scale breeding-season surveys carried out under the auspices of the British Trust for Ornithology have related to such species as Great Crested Grebe (*Podiceps cristatus*), Gannet (*Sula bassana*) and Mute Swan (*Cygnus olor*). Perhaps the best-known and longest-running census is the Common Bird Census, which differs from those previously mentioned in that it provides an index, by means of sample counts, instead of attempting to give a complete total.
See Common Bird Census

Cere
The soft fleshy covering at the base of a bird's bill. Most obvious in birds of prey (Falconiformes), Pigeons (Columbiformes) and Parrots (Psittaciformes).

The cere at the base of a bird of prey's bill

Cereopsis (Goose)

Name sometimes used for the Cape Barren Goose (*Cereopsis novaehollandiae*). A large grey-coloured Goose, confined as a breeding species to the islands off the coast of Australia. Formerly persecuted due to damage it did to crops, its numbers were considerably reduced. Thanks to protection they are slowly recovering. A current estimate of birds in the wild would be around 6,000.

Certhiidae

A family of the Passeriformes, sub-order Oscines, which includes the Treecreeper (*Certhia familiaris*), a well-known British bird whose behaviour gives it its name. The Short-toed Treecreeper (*Certhia brachydactyla*) in the main replaces our own bird in SE Europe. A small number, however, have been recorded in Britain.
See Treecreeper

Chachalaca

Name given to some species of Cracidae (Curassow).

Chaffinch (*Fringilla coelebs*)

A colourful member of the Finch family, breeding widely throughout Britain, in fact one of our commonest birds, with an estimated population of around 700,000 pairs. The male particularly is a distinctive bird, with slate-blue crown, chestnut-brown back and pinkish under parts. When at rest, however, the most notable feature is a broad white shoulder patch with a less prominent wing bar behind it. In flight these show as a distinct double white wing bar. The female lacks the male's bright colours, though she has similar markings, and looks very greenish on the back in flight. In winter Chaffinches associate with other Finches, roaming the countryside in large flocks. The call is a metallic 'chwink-chwink' which has given rise to a local name of 'Spink'. The song is a cheery, short, vigorous, rattling succession of rather unmusical notes which have been parodied as 'You naughty little boy I'm going to beat you'.

Charadriidae

Family within the order Charadriiformes. Generally the 'waders' or in American usage shorebirds, includes such species as Dunlin, Knot, Turnstone, the Godwits, Sandpipers, Stints etc.

Charadriiformes

An order of mainly shore birds (waders, such as Dunlin, the Godwits, Knot, Sandpipers, Stints, Turnstone, etc) but also includes the Auks and the Gulls.

Charm

An assembly, flock or group of Goldfinches (*Carduelis carduelis*).

Chaffinch, our commonest Finch

Chat

Name applied particularly to Whinchat (*Saxicola rubetra*), Stonechat (*Saxicola torquata*), Wheatear (*Oenanthe oenanthe*), and Redstart (*Phoenicurus phoenicurus*) which are generally referred to as 'Chats', the name referring to the harsh chacking notes of many of these birds. The name is also used in various parts of the world for unrelated species, and in North America it is applied to some of the New World Warblers (Parulidae spp).

Whinchat (above) and Stonechat (below) are easily mistaken for each other

Check List

A list of the birds of a given area. Printed lists are produced by many bird clubs and organisations and these are used by bird-watchers to check the total number of different species they may record in the area to which the list relates, usually in a given time. Some bird reserves and nature trails have check lists which visitors use during the course of the visit. For an area with a limited avifauna, the list will of course be short, but some are extensive: for example, a check list published by the Zambian Ornithological Society (for the whole of Zambia) lists 699 species. The most complete check list in book form, however, is *A Check List of the Birds of the World*, by Edward S. Gruson, a complete record of the world's bird species (Collins, 1976). The magazine *British Birds* publishes a printed list of *Birds of the Western Palearctic*, and this is available to subscribers. (For details write to *British Birds*, Macmillan Journals Ltd, Fountains, Park Lane, Blunhan, Bedford.)

![ZAMBIAN ORNITHOLOGICAL SOCIETY]	SPECIES RECORD CARD BIRDS OF ZAMBIA	REF

LOCALITY:

CO-ORDINATES: ALTITUDE:

DATE: TIME:

WEATHER:

OBSERVERS:

NOTES

NAMES AND NUMBERS
ARE FROM 'THE BIRDS OF ZAMBIA' — 1971.
SPECIES RECORD CARD — MAY 1974

Chicks of Kestrel, Blue Tit and Redshank

Chick

In general speech, the term usually applied to a young bird still in the nest in the case of nidicolous types, or in the case of nidifugous types, to a young bird still unable to fly.
See Juvenile; Nestling; Pullus; Nidicolous; Nidifugous

Chickadee

Name for some North American 'titmice', *Parus* spp. Derived from the call, particularly that of the Black-capped Chickadee (*Parus atricapillus*) which utters a clearly enunciated 'chick-a-dee-dee-dee, a-dee-dee-dee'.

Three more 'Chats' are shown on the left: Wheatear (top left), Redstart (top right) and Black Redstart (below)

West Midland Bird Club

A Field List of British Birds

Two check or field lists

Chromatic Aberration
The rainbow effect round the edge of the image of a binocular or telescope that has inferior lenses.

Chukar (*Alectoris chukar*)
A Partridge similar in appearance to the Red-legged Partridge (*Alectoris rufa*) but with a distinctive clucking or cackling voice like a barnyard fowl's. Not found in Britain, it occurs in stony and rocky areas of Italy, Greece, Bulgaria and the Aegean.

Chukar

Churring
Term applied particularly to the song of the Nightjar (*Caprimulgus europaeus*). A sustained vibrant sound continued on occasions for up to 5 minutes without a break. During this time a rhythmic rise and fall is heard as the bird turns its head from side to side. Only uttered at night, usually beginning at dusk.
See Nightjar

Ciconiiformes
An order of mainly large birds, characteristically with long legs and bills adapted for wading in shallow water or marshes, and living mostly on fish or other animal prey. The order comprises the following families:
   Herons and Bitterns (Ardeidae)
   Shoebill (Balaenicipitidae)
   Hammerhead (Scopidae)
   Storks (Ciconiidae)
   Ibises and Spoonbills (Threskiornithidae)
   Flamingos (Phoenicopteridae)

Circadian
A term applied to a biological rhythm of about a day, ie 24 hours.

Class
A primary category in the classification of living organisms, comprising one or more orders. Classes are grouped into a Phylum (plural phyla) in the animal kingdom or a division in the vegetable kingdom. All birds, including those known from fossils, constitute a single class of animals—the class Aves.
See Classification

Classification
All living things—plants, animals, etc.—are classified (grouped) into categories which can then be further sub-divided into other groupings, and so on, according to taxonomic differences as described by the scientist studying the subject in question. Classification is a continuous process and is constantly being adapted to fit new knowledge.
See Class; Family; Genus; Linnaeus; Nomanclature; Order; Taxonomy

Claw
A specialised horny appendage on a bird's toe. The shape is variable and adapted for different uses: eg strongly curved claws are used for gripping firmly, as in such birds as Tree Creepers (*Certhidae*), Woodpeckers (*Picidae*) and some birds of prey. They can be blunt, as in the case of most species which scratch on the ground in search of food (*Phasianidae*), or be extremely long, as in the Jacanas (*Jancanidae*). The Herons (*Ardeidae*), Nightjars (*Caprimulgidae*) and Pratincoles (*Glareola* spp) have a serrated edge or comb on the inner border of the third claw, the function of which is unknown.
See Foot

Cleidoic
Term describing the totally enclosed condition of a bird's egg.

Cley Marshes (Norfolk)
The North Norfolk coast has long been a magnet for birdwatchers and nowhere is the concentration greater than the area between the villages of Cley-next-the-Sea and Salthouse, where on a weekend at peak migration times the assemblage of binoculars and telescopes has to be seen to be believed. Seawards a large shingle beach running east-west protects a series of marshes, of which the best-known is 'Arnolds' (owned by the National Trust), lying immediately east of the famed East Bank. An earth bank with a

Cley-next-the-Sea (above) and Salthouse Broad,
Norfolk—places to see birds and birdwatchers

footpath from the A149 coast road to the sea,
it provides elevated viewing of both Arnolds
Marsh and Bishops Marsh (administered by
the Norfolk Naturalists Trust) to the west.
Over 275 species have been recorded within
the parish boundaries of Cley and annually
this is added to. It is certainly one of the best
places in England to see not only rare birds
but also well-known birdwatchers!
Read Clarke, P. R., *Birdwatching in Norfolk*,
Norfolk Ornithologists Association in co-
operation with the Holme Bird Observatory.
Seago, M. J., *Birds of Norfolk*, Jarrolds,
Norwich, 1967.

Cline

A term introduced by J. S. Huxley (1939).
A gradient of types. Certain characters in an
animal or plant population tend to change
gradually and continuously over large areas,
so that the populations at each end of the
cline may be substantially different from each
other, but within which no abrupt divisions
are apparent. Exemplified particularly by
some species of birds which inhabit the
Pacific islands.

Clipping
Cutting the primary feathers of one wing, thus rendering a captive bird temporarily incapable of flight.
See Brailing; Pinioning

Cloaca
The combined terminal opening of alimentary tract, excretory system and reproductive system of a bird.
See Alimentary Canal

Clutch
A complete set of eggs laid in one breeding attempt by one female.

This can vary tremendously in different species of birds ranging from one (written c/1) in the case of the Gannet (*Sula bassana*) to 15 (written c/15) or more in the case of the Partridge (*Perdix perdix*) and other game birds.

Many species may lay more than one clutch in a season. Some, eg Red-legged Partridge (*Alectoris rufa*) and Sanderling (*Calidris alba*), may lay two clutches at the same time, one being incubated by the male and one by the female.

Cob
Special term for the male Swan.
See Swan

Clutch of Grey Partridge eggs

Cock
A male bird. Special terms apply to the males of some species, eg drake (Duck spp), gander (Goose spp), cob (Swan spp), tiercel (Falcon spp), Blackcock (Black Grouse).

Cockatoo
Substantive name of members of the sub-family Kakatoeinae of Psittacidae (Psittaciformes). Large parrots with long erectile crests. Several species are mainly white.
See Parrot

Cock nest
Name given to extra nests, not finally used for laying eggs in. In particular the male Wren (*Troglodytes troglodytes*) is well known for building such nests, often several being constructed. The hen is supposed to choose the most suitable one, which is then lined, an exclusively female activity.

Cock-of-the-Rock
Substantive name of the *Rupicola* spp of the Cotingidae (Passeriformes, sub-order Tyranni). The males of the two species, Guyanan Cock-of-the-Rock (*Rupicola rupicola*) and Andean Cock-of-the-Rock (*R. peruviana*), are brilliantly coloured birds with a helmet-like crest which conceals the bill.

Cold Searching
Looking for nests or birds without pre-knowledge of their exact whereabouts (ie a methodical, systematic search).

Colony
A number of birds nesting in close proximity to one another. Colonial-nesting species include many sea birds, Gulls, Terns etc, also such Passeriformes as House Martins, Sand Martins and Rooks.

Colour
Birds are among the most colourful of animals. The colours of the feather are produced in two ways:

1 By pigmentation. The commonest of the coloured elements is melanin, which gives black or brown. Carotenoids show red or orange, porphyrins and some other pigments provide other colours.

2 By feather structure. Interference or scattering of light waves gives both iridescent and non-iridescent colours; many

colours are caused by a combination of pigment and feather structure.

Colours serve two major and contradictory functions—namely concealment and recognition/advertisement.

Colour Ringing

In some bird studies birds are ringed with coloured plastic rings, which aid the immediate identification of individuals. This is only useful in controlled situations, eg among colonial-nesting birds and with sedentary species which keep to a particular area that is under regular observation. The BTO registers colour ringing schemes to avoid duplication of colour combinations. Details are given in the BTO *Bulletin* from time to time.

Columbiformes

An order comprising the sub-orders Ptercodetes (family Pteroclidae—Sandgrouse) and Columbae (families Columbidae—Pigeons and the extinct Raphidae—Dodo).

Sandwich Tern colony

In full breeding dress and in sunlight, the Starling's plumage is splendidly iridescent

Coly
Alternative name for Mousebird.
See Mousebird

Colymbidae
With Colymbiformes, discarded name originally applied to the Divers, now Gaviiformes, Gaviidae.

Comb
Unfeathered flap or appendage, usually fleshy and brightly coloured. A familiar example of a comb is that on the crown of the domestic fowl, being much larger and brighter in the cock bird. The name is derived from the serrated edge. Its function is probably related to display and recognition.
See Lappet; Wattle

Comfort Movements
The various movements made by many birds especially to put their feathers in order, eg ruffling, shaking, stretching, etc.

Commic Tern
The combined names of the Common Tern (*Sterna hirundo*) and Arctic Tern (*Sterna paradisaea*). A vernacular term applied to either of these two species when the observer is unable to be specific! It is sometimes impossible to distinguish between the two, particularly when adults in autumn and winter are involved.

Commissural Line
Line of contact between upper and lower mandibles when closed.

Common Bird Census
More accurately, a Breeding Season Census of birds: it is a census on a number of fixed areas, of either farmland or woodland, organised by the British Trust for Ornithology. It was started at the request of the then Nature Conservancy as a pilot scheme in 1961, as a year-by-year comparison of breeding numbers. It has been going on ever since. An observer or team of observers plot sightings of any of 70 common breeding birds included in the census on a 1:2500 map. At least 10 visits in a season are needed to make the census meaningful and at the present almost 200 teams provide details of the breeding birds in their census areas each year. The results are analysed by the full-time experts at BTO headquarters and from these returns a population index is obtained. This shows how the population level in these sample areas changes from year to year and thus indicates any general trends nationally.
See British Trust for Ornithology, count

Opposite: Examples of bird population trends obtained through CBC

Common (on left) and Arctic Terns—'Commic Terns'

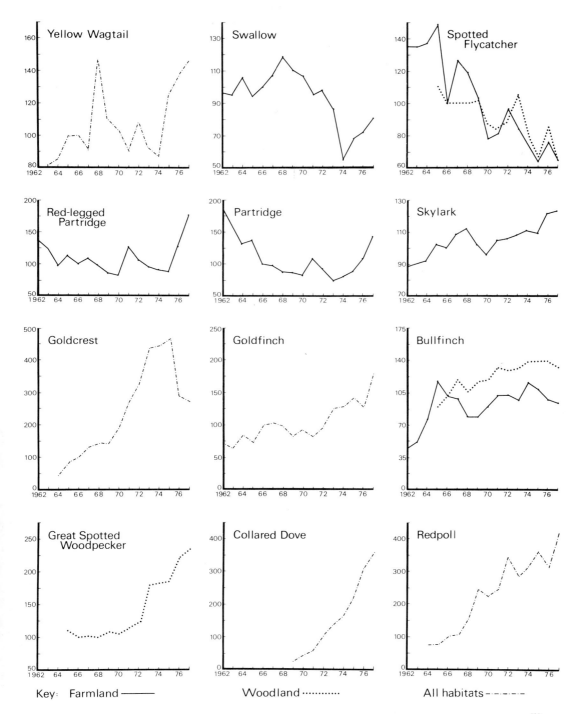

Key: Farmland ——— Woodland ·········· All habitats –·–·–·–

59

Condor

Name of two species of the family Cathartidae: the Californian Condor (*Vultur californianus*) and Andean Condor (*Vultur gryphus*). This latter bird is the largest bird of prey in the world, living in the Andes mountains of Venezuela and Columbia south to the Straits of Magellan. The Californian Condor is the third rarest bird in America and features in the *Red Data Book*. It is in grave danger of extinction, with only around 50 individuals existing in the wild.

Condor

Congeneric

Of two or more species, meaning they are, or should be, placed in the same genus.
See Genus

Conspecific

Denoting that two or more sub-species or other forms belong to the same species. For example, the White Wagtail and the Pied Wagtail look noticeably different but the differences are superficial and both belong to the same species *Motacilla alba*.
See Taxonomy

Contour Feather

Any feather visible on the outer surface of a bird.
See Feather; Plumage

Control

Deliberate action to limit or reduce numbers of wild birds where potential increase or existing numbers are thought to be detrimental to human interests. In very few instances is there complete agreement that measures to control should be undertaken, or are even effective. In Britain, species which are normally thought to need control are the House Sparrow (*Passer domesticus*), Starling (*Sternus vulgaris*) and Feral Pigeon, certainly in city and urban areas where they can be quite a nuisance. On the basis of health risk alone, local authorities or councils take measures to reduce numbers of these birds, sometimes using controversial means (eg narcoticising). The Wood Pigeon (*Columba palumbus*) is perhaps the only species of wild bird in Britain that can be described as an agricultural pest to the extent that officially organised countermeasures have been undertaken. A degree of control is often needed at airports where birds have to be cleared from runways, eg by the use of trained falcons, which is not always effective. (It is probably better to let the grass grow!).

Control measures are even carried out on bird reserves where some species increase under the protection afforded to another particular species and thus endanger the protected one, eg Black-headed Gull (*Larus ridibundus*), predating Avocets (*Avosetta recurvirostra*). In some instances egg-pricking is considered to be an acceptable means of control. Fortunately this country does not have to contend with the problem of the Quelea-finch or Red-billed, Black-faced or Sudan Dioch (*Quelea quelea*). A small bird less than 5in (127mm) long, and weighing just over 1 oz, it has been known from its earliest recorded history as a menace to crops of small grain. Despite the use of explosives and flame-throwers it still continues to be the problem bird of Africa. The Bird Protection Acts (1945 and 1952) have four Schedules which allow only a few species on the British list to be controlled.

Control is also a term for a normal or unaffected bird used to measure the effects of experimentation on others. Also used when a habitat is altered—the control being a measured area of unaltered habitat, so that the bird community in the changed area can be compared with that in the unaffected, 'control' area.
See Bird Protection Acts; Schedule I

Conure

A name for several species of neotropical Parrots.

Convergence

Similar evolutionary adaptations by unrelated

species in unconnected areas. The Yellow-throated Longclaw (*Macronyx croceus*) of Africa and the Meadowlark (*Sterna magba*) of America provide an example of convergence of appearance.

Coot (*Fulica atra*)

A common water bird. Its black plumage and white frontal shield quickly identify it. Widely distributed throughout Britain it is, however, scarce in NW Scotland and absent from parts of W Wales and SW England. Also scarce in parts of Ireland. Total population around 10,000 pairs. Formerly considered as secondary game, notably the sporting calendar included an annual Coot Drive on Hickling Broad. On 25 February 1927, twenty guns killed 1,175 Coots there. Fortunately such carnage in the name of sport has been abandoned. In North America the name Coot is misapplied to relatives of the Rails and Gallinules.

Copeland

The Copeland islands are situated outside the entrance to Belfast Lough on the south side of the shipping lanes. There are three islands in the group, and St John's Island, one of the two small outer islands, almost 3 miles (5km) off Orlock Point, Co Down, is the site of an observatory. Housed in the old lighthouse, this has been in operation since 1954. The Copeland observatory has as its main aim the study of the bird life of St John's Island, one of the major attractions being the colony of Manx Shearwaters, a great proportion of which have been ringed, with a considerable amount of re-trap data having been collected. The trapping and ringing of migrants is also a primary pursuit, and along with the more usual observatory species, Melodious Warbler, Icterine Warbler, Sub-alpine Warbler, Yellow-browed Warbler, Woodchat Shrike and Fox Sparrow have been recorded.

Copulation

The sexual act leading to the fertilisation of the ova of the female by the male. Also termed coition. This usually takes place with maximum frequency a day or two before the first egg is laid. Generally preceded by special displays which are normally necessary to break down the normal resistance towards physical contact between individuals, especially where aggressive or predatory species are involved.

Coot—more gregarious than the Moorhen, forming large flocks in winter

Coraciiformes

An order of mainly brightly coloured birds, many of which have other striking features such as long tails, crests and large bills. Most are partly arboreal, but many feed on the ground (Hoopoes), some in the air (Bee-eaters) or in water (some Kingfishers). They all usually nest in holes, some excavating burrows (Kingfishers, Todies, Motmots, Bee-eaters). The nesting habits of the Hornbill are particularly remarkable. The order

Coraciiformes

as a whole is cosmopolitan. It comprises the following sub-orders and families:

Sub-order Alcedines
   Super-family Alcedinoidea
      Family
      Kingfishers (Alcedinidae)
   Super-family Todoidea
      Family
      Todies (Todidae)
   Super-family Momotoidea
      Family
      Motmots (Momotidae)
Sub-order Meropes
   Family
   Bee-eaters (Meropidae)
Sub-order Coracii
   Family
   Cuckoo Rollers (Leptosomatidae)
   Rollers, Ground Rollers (Coraciidae)
   Hoopoes (Upupidae)
   Wood Hoopoes (Phoeniculidae)
Sub-order Bucerotes
   Family
   Hornbills (Bucerotidae)

Cordon-Bleu
Name of some Waxbills, *Estrilda* spp, popular cage birds which originate in Africa.

Cormorant
Name applied to nearly all species of the Phalacrocoracidae (Pelecaniformes, sub-order Pelecanidae). In Britain the family is represented by *Phalacrocorax carbo*, a large dark bird of sea coasts, but also occurring inland. The Shag (*Phalacrocorax aristotelis*) sometimes called the Green Cormorant, is a similar slightly smaller bird. Both feed entirely on fish.

Corncrake (*Crex crex*)
A species of Rail, sometimes—though now rarely—called the Land Rail. A shy, secretive bird, often only its rasping call or crekking indicating its presence. It has declined markedly in Britain during the last 50 years. The increasing mechanisation of farming contributed to this, as it nests in grass meadows. Once a widespread breeding bird in

Cormorants tree-nesting

England, there is now only an irregular scattering of nesting occurrences. The species was the subject of enquiries in 1933 and 1939, and more recently in 1978, when it was found that the total British population of around 600 pairs was almost entirely confined to the Inner and Outer Hebrides (80 per cent). It is still relatively common in Ireland, but less so than formerly.
See Crake; Rails

Corncrake

Corncrake, largest of the Rails

Corvid
General term for any of the Crow (Corvidae) family.

Corvidae
The Crows, a family of the order Passeriformes, sub-order Oscines.
See Crow

Cosmopolitan
Term applied to species distributed generally through the major zoogeographical regions of the world, or at least most of them and certainly in both Old and New Worlds and in both southern and northern hemispheres. The Barn Owl (*Tyto alba*) and the Roseate Tern (*Sterna dougallii*) are examples of cosmopolitan species.

Cotinga
Substantive name of some species of Cotingidae (Passeriformes, sub-order Tyranni). A neotropical group of about 90 species of forest birds, ranging in size from that of a Finch (Fringillidae spp) to that of a Crow (Corvidae spp), they are nearly all confined to the tropical areas of Central and South America. Strange-looking colourful birds with an assortment of equally weird calls, the family is exemplified by such species as the Cock-of-the-Rocks (*Rupicola* spp.)
See Cock-of-the-Rock

Rooks—'One Rook is a Crow and a flock of Crows are Rooks'

Coto Doñana
Wild marshy area in SE Spain, notable for its variety of birdlife which can only be visited by prior arrangement with the Spanish authorities. A new visiting centre is, however, being prepared with the advice of the RSPB.
See Marismas

Council for Nature
Founded in 1958 with its headquarters at the Zoological Gardens in Regents Park, London, it represented the voluntary natural-history movement in Britain until its dissolution in 1979.

Most of its major functions have since been taken up by the Council for Environmental Conservation (CoEnCo), including the publication of a regular bulletin (*Habitat*) and the continuation of the youth programme and the provision of an information service. CoEnCo will also work closely with the Society for the Promotion of Nature Conservation and will operate from 29 Greville Street, London EC1N 8AX.

Count
Counting birds is a method of studying their population trends and when counts are made on a regular basis over a considerable period they can yield valuable information. Whereas the term 'census' is usually applied to breeding populations, a 'count' is always applied to non-breeding birds, notably winter flocks of wildfowl etc.
See Wildfowl Counts
Read Dobinson, H. M., *Bird Count: a Practical Guide to Bird Surveys*, Penguin, 1976

Countershading
A common feature of the coloration of mammals and birds which helps to make them less conspicuous in their natural environment. Colour, shape and movement all contribute to the detection of an animal by sight; a bird or mammal which keeps still reduces its chances of being seen by a predator, and cryptic coloration will then help to make it blend into its background. Even without the complex camouflage of, for example, Nightjars and Woodcock, many birds achieve this by being darker on the upperside than on the underside. This effectively counteracts the effects of light (from above) and shade (below), so that the three-dimensional mass of the bird is less noticeable; it tends to look more evenly toned and flatter. Countershading is perhaps best appreciated on mammals (such as Rabbit and Wood Mouse) in which the area of the body normally in shadow is white in colour and thus prevents an obvious, eye-catching dark patch beneath the animal.

Countersinging
Singing in rivalry with another male bird within hearing; or duetting between male and female of a pair.
See Antiphonal Song

Country Code
Guard against all risk of fire
Fasten all gates
Keep dogs under proper control
Keep to paths across farmland
Avoid damage to fences, hedges and walls
Leave no litter
Safeguard water supplies
Protect wildlife, plants and trees
Go carefully on country roads
Respect the life of the countryside

This simple set of rules is still very pertinent and there can be few, if any, who disagree with its principles. However something more precise is needed for the guidance of the growing army of birdwatchers who may have greater repercussions on the countryside than the everyday visitor.

Courser
Name of most species of Cursoriinae, a sub-family of the Old World family Glareolidae (Charadriiformes, sub-order Charadrii), but which also includes the Pratincoles. Medium-sized Plover-like birds, there are 17 species occurring in Eurasia, Africa and Australia. The Cream-coloured Courser (*Cursorius cursor*), a slim, pale sandy-coloured bird with long pale creamy legs, is a rare vagrant to the British Isles.
See Pratincole

Courtship
Term applied to a wide range of behavioural activity in birds with the apparent aim of attracting a mate, maintaining the pair bond and facilitating copulation and parental activities. Singing plays an important part in the

courtship of many birds, and in some species feeding of one mate is significant. The display of particular parts of the plumage or anatomy and other rituals, eg the weed-exchange ceremony by Grebes, often have an important role.

See Copulation

Read Armstrong, E. A., *Discovering Bird Courtship*, Shire Publications, Aylesbury, 1978, Sparks, J., *Bird Behaviour*, Hamlyn, 1969, Welty, J. C., *The Life of Birds*, Saunders, 1975

Covert
Term for any of the contour feathers that overlie the base of the wings or the tail, eg wing coverts, tail coverts. Also applied to the ear coverts (auriculars).
See Wing

Crab Plover (*Dromas ardeola*)
Sole member of the Dromadidae (Charadriiformes, sub-order Charadrii). A very distinctive black-and-white bird with a large stout bill, it frequents open shores and reefs feeding on crustaceans, notably crabs. Found along the coasts of East Africa, the Persian Gulf and northwards to Egypt.

Crake
An alternative name of many species of Rail (Rallidae spp). In Britain the Corncrake (*Crex crex*) is perhaps the best-known of the Crakes, by reputation if not observation. However, all other Crakes are equally secretive, haunting marshy areas and rarely showing themselves. The Water Rail (*Rallus aquaticus*) is perhaps the most widespread and commonest species in Britain, breeding in suitable areas. The Spotted Crake (*Porzana porzana*) breeds sparingly in eastern Britain, while Little Crake (*Porzana parva*) and Baillon's Crake (*Porzana pusilla*) are vagrants to Britain. The Moorhen and Coot belong to the same family.
See Corncrake; Rail

Crane
Name of the species Gruidae (Gruiformes, sub-order Grues). Cranes are long-necked, long-legged birds, the largest species standing over 5ft (1½m) high and having a 7ft (2m) wing-span. They are powerful fliers and have loud trumpet-like calls. There are 14 species of Crane in the world, several of which are in

Crab Plover

Crane

danger of extinction, notably the American Whooping Crane (*Grus americana*) and the Japanese Crane (*Grus japonensis*). Europe has 2 species, the Crane (*Grus grus*) and the Demoiselle Crane (*Anthropoides virgo*). The Crane is a fairly frequent vagrant to Britain, breeding birds from Sweden occasionally wandering off course on their migration.

Crèche
A collection of still-dependent young of several pairs of a species with only one, or a few, adults present, seemingly as guardians, though this may not specifically be their role. Such birds as Eider (*Somateria mollisima*) and Shelduck (*Tadorna tadorna*) are typical species which form these collections of young birds.

Creeper
Name generally applied to members of the family Certhiidae. So called for their habit of

African Crowned Crane

creeping over the bark of trees, or over rocks, in search of their food, which is extracted from crevices with a fine curved bill. Although the name Creeper is used by American ornithologists for *Certhia*, it is more often written as part of a compound word for Certhiidae, ie Treecreeper, Wallcreeper.
See Treecreeper; Wallcreeper

Crepuscular
Active at dusk or in the dim light of evening or morning, rather than in full darkness. The Nightjars (Caprimulgidae spp) are crepuscular in their habits.
See Nightjar; Nocturnal

Crest
Usually a distinctive tuft of feathers on top of the bird's head, eg on Tufted Duck (*Aythya fuligula*), Lapwing (*Vanellus vanellus*), but can be apparent only when the bird raises the feathers of the head, usually an instinctive response to alarm or threat.

Crop
An enlargement of the gullet where food is

Crest on a Lapwing

prepared for digestion or feeding to the species' young, particularly by Pigeons, and some Finches. Also called the ingluvies.

66

Crossbill

Name of some members of the Fringillidae family which have crossed mandibles facilitating the extraction of seeds from tree-cones. In Britain the Crossbill (*Loxia curvirostra*) is present throughout the year, being resident and indigenous in Scotland. Scattered breeding also occurs in other parts of the British Isles, particularly in the Norfolk Brecklands and the New Forest with a total population of probably 5,000 pairs. It does not breed regularly in Ireland. However, from time to time large influxes from the continent take place and parties of Crossbills appear all over the place. The Two-barred Crossbill (*Loxia leucoptera*) is an occasional visitor.
Read Thompson, D. N., *Pine Crossbills*, Poyser, Berkhamsted, 1975

Crow

The name of many species of the Corvidae (Passeriformes, sub-order Oscines). The family also includes the Jays, Ravens, Magpies, Nutcrackers and Choughs. The Crow family is considered to represent the furthest stage so far attained in avian evolution. Their behaviour indicates a highly developed mentality and some species have a complex social organisation. They are certainly success-

Crossbill

Crows are a highly successful species

Cryptic

ful species, as their almost world-wide distribution would indicate. The name Crow is misapplied to a variety of birds throughout the world that are not members of the Corvidae—Bald Crow (North American Vulture) and Rain Crow (West Indian Great Lizard Cuckoo) are two examples.

See Under individual birds

Read Coombs, C. J. F., *The Crows: a Study of Corvids in Europe*, Batsford, Poole, 1978; Wilmore, S. B., *Crows, Jays, Ravens and their Relatives*, David & Charles, Newton Abbot, 1977

Cryptic

Term applied to birds' coloration or other characters that provide concealment or facilitate the capture of prey. Cryptic coloration is exemplified by the Nightjar (*Caprimulgus europaeus*) and Woodcock (*Scolopax rusticola*), but less obviously the colour of predators such as the Osprey (*Pandion haliaetus*) and Sandwich Tern (*Sterna sandvicensis*) may lessen the chance of their being detected by their prey species.

Cuckoo

Name for many members of the Cuculidae (Cuculiformes) but particularly in Britain denotes *Cuculus canorus*. Most Cuckoos are medium-sized, long-tailed birds, though they range from Sparrow-size to that of a Raven. As a rule the call is a monotonous repetition of loud notes which in the case of *Cuculus*

Great Spotted Cuckoo, a vagrant to Britain

canorus is the 'cuk-koo' which gives the bird its name. Parasitic behaviour, laying the eggs in other birds' nests, is also typical of the Cuckoo family, though this practice is not peculiar to the Cuculidae. The Cuckoo is a summer visitor to Britain arriving in April and departing around July to August. Some young birds are still around in September. The Great Spotted Cuckoo (*Clamator glandarius*), a bird of SE Europe, is a vagrant to Britain. The North American Yellow-billed Cuckoo (*Coccyzus americanus*) and Black-billed Cuckoo (*Coccyzus ery.. ~ophthalmus*) very occasionally reach Europe and have been recorded in Britain on a number of occasions.

When sitting on its eggs, the Woodcock's cryptic colouring renders it almost invisible against a background of woodland litter

Curlew, largest of our wading birds

Cuckoo's Mate
A common name for the Wryneck (*Jynx torquilla*). It refers to the approximately simultaneous appearance in spring of this species and the Cuckoo (*Cuculus canorus*). The appellation reflects the formerly more widespread distribution of the Wryneck, which is now restricted to a few breeding pairs in Southern England and a small recently established colony in Scotland.
See Wryneck

Cuculiformes
An order, alternatively Cuculi, comprising the sub-order Musophagi (family Musophagidae—Plantain-eaters, Turacos, Go-away Birds—22 species recorded) and the Cuculi (family Cuculidae, the Cuckoos, Roadrunners and Anis—127 species recorded).
See Cuckoo

Culmen
The dorsal ridge of the upper mandible from forehead to tip.
See Bill

Curlew (*Numenius arquata*)
Largest of our wading birds and unmistakable with its long downcurved bill and distinctive call; a familiar sight around our coasts, haunting especially mudflats and estuaries, with probably 250,000 present during the winter. In the breeding season it nests on moorland and is found extensively in the Orkneys, Shetlands and Scotland. It is also found commonly in Wales and N England. Some also breed in the low-lying river valleys of the Midlands and SE England.

Cygnet
A special term for a young Swan.

Dabchick
Alternative name for certain smaller members of the family Podicepitidae. In Britain commonly applied to the Little Grebe (*Tachybaptus ruficollis*) which as a breeding bird is generally distributed throughout England but scarce or absent from parts of Wales and the SW. It is less plentiful in parts of Scotland and is only a winter visitor to some places; widespread in Ireland. Total breeding population is around 20,000 pairs. As other Grebes it builds a nest of floating aquatic vegetation and also like other Grebes when disturbed covers the eggs on leaving the nest. Most Grebes have the unique habit of eating their own feathers and also feeding them to their young. The young birds are often carried on the back of the adults.
See Grebe

Dancing Ground
Special term in North America for the social display of the Sharp-tailed Grouse (*Tympanuchas phasianellus*).

Darter
Alternative name for the Anhinga or Snakebird. Looking like a long-necked Cormorant (*Phalacrocorax* spp) its habits are similar though it is purely a bird of inland waters. The family is represented in all the main continents except Europe.

Darter (or Anhinga or Snakebird)

Darwin, Charles Robert (1809-1882)
Undoubtedly the most important figure in the history of biology, his *Origin of Species*, first published in 1859, began a revolution not only in the biological sciences, but in western man's philosophical and moral conception of himself. There were six editions of the book in his lifetime, it has been constantly in print ever since and has been translated into over 30 languages.

The turning point of his career came when he was invited to sail on board HMS *Beagle* as the ship's naturalist, and it was during his five years on the *Beagle* that he made the many observations of living beings that formed the basis of his ideas of evolution.
Read Moorehead, A., *Darwin and the Beagle*, Hamish Hamilton, 1969; *Charles Darwin and the Illustrated Origin of Species* (abridged and introduced by R. E. Leakey), Faber, 1979

Darwin's Finches
General term for the group of Finches confined to the Galapagos Islands, except for one on Cocos Island, 600 miles to the north-east. Their nearest relatives on the American mainland are not known, but are presumed to have been Finches (Fringillidae). These birds are of historical interest because it is known they were discovered by Darwin and provided one of the chief stimuli for his theory of evolution.

There are about 13 species of Darwin's Finches (Galapagos Finches in American usage), the main morphological variation being found in the bill. This ranges from the usual seed-eating Finch type, to being almost Warbler-type. One of these Finches also has the unique habit of using a cactus spine for levering out insects from crevices.
Read Lack, D., *Darwin's Finches*, Cambridge University Press, 1947

Daw
Popular abbreviation for Jackdaw.

Dawn Chorus
The great volume of birdsong which heralds the beginning of the day, especially in May and June. It far surpasses the total song output during the rest of the day. Certain species tend to commence singing before others, some starting before dawn has broken. It usually reaches its peak just before the sun actually rises.

The order in which different species start to

Darwin's Finches

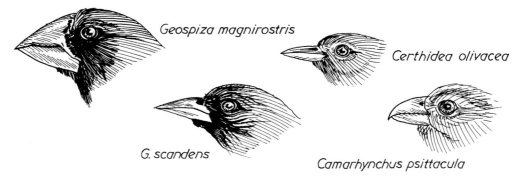

Geospiza magnirostris

Certhidea olivacea

G. scandens

Camarhynchus psittacula

sing is pretty constant and among woodland birds the Blackbird (*Turdus merula*), Song Thrush (*Turdus philomelos*) and Wood Pigeon (*Columba palumbus*) are usually in the first three, quickly followed by Robin (*Erithacus rubecula*), Redstart (*Phoenicurus phoenicurus*), Garden Warbler (*Sylvia borin*), Blackcap (*Sylvia atricapilla*) and others.

It can be a pleasant and exhilarating exercise to get up before light, go to a nearby piece of woodland and list the order in which birds begin to sing. It will certainly prove the saying 'up with the lark' is not accurate, as this species is not among the first to sing. There is a similar but less striking increase in birdsong at dusk (evening chorus), when it can be equally interesting to note the order of cessation of song, the Song Thrush and the Robin usually providing the final notes of the day.

Decoy

An artificial bird, used to attract other birds, mainly used for wildfowling, for which reason most decoys produced resemble Ducks and these days are invariably plastic.
See Duck Decoy

Dee Estuary, Cheshire/Clwyd

The Dee Estuary is approximately 12 miles by 5 miles, providing one of the finest haunts for wading birds and wildfowl in Britain. Originally the estuary was 20 miles long, extending as far as Chester, which was a major port from the 11th to the 14th centuries. Though siltation has greatly reduced the area, it still remains a vast wilderness of mud and sand at low tide. The Cheshire—Clwyd border runs down the middle of the estuary. Access to much of the western, Welsh side is difficult, due to industrial development, but Shotton Pools Nature Reserve lying within the British Steel Corporation complex can be visited by permit. By far the best spots, however, to see birds are the Hilbre islands which can be reached by walking across the sands from West Kirby at low tide. There are three islands, Little Eye, Middle Eye and Hilbre (the largest). Their position in the

Wader flock on the Dee estuary

mouth of the estuary makes the islands a natural vantage-point for birdwatching, the incoming tide driving birds to seek refuge on the surrounding rocks. The crossing can be dangerous and the times of tides should be ascertained. It is also necessary to obtain a permit to visit Hilbre itself.

Part of the upper estuary has recently been established as a reserve by the RSPB (Gayton Sands).
Read The Dee Estuary: A Surviving Wilderness, Dee Estuary Conservation Group, 1976

Density Dependence

In general terms many things may be explained in relation to density. For example, a territory-holding male bird in an area with a high density of its species may sing very much more (stimulated by the number and proximity of neighbouring males) than one in an isolated situation which has less 'need' to sing. However, the concept is usually referred to in studies of colonial birds, especially seabirds, and may be illustrated by reference to the Gannet (*Sula bassana*). Gannetries are variable in size but small ones become more successful above a certain minimum threshold, above which colony growth and breeding numbers can increase considerably. Young Gannets probably settle to breed at a colony with a high level of social activity which is related in turn to the density of the colony. The high density of all Gannet breeding colonies is practically uniform and is related to the social stimulation brought about by the close proximity of nesting pairs. Breeding success is influenced by the size of the groups and thus the amount of social stimulation, which helps to produce consistency in timing of breeding throughout the colony. The Gannetry at Bempton Cliffs (N Yorkshire) grew slowly over a lengthy period until the size was sufficient to generate the necessary social activity to attract new immigrants and to increase breeding success; since that point, growth has been much more rapid with an earlier return of birds in spring, an earlier laying date, a greater proportion of immature birds present, and greater breeding success. It is, therefore, advantageous for the birds to gain a nest site in an area of high density of breeders.
See Nelson, B., *The Gannet*, Poyser, 1978

Dikkop

African name for a member of the Burhinidae, the Thick-knees, ie Cape Dikkop (*Burhinus capensis*) and Water Dikkop (*Burhinus vermiculatus*), African equivalents of the Stone Curlew (*Burhinus oedicnemus*).
See Burhinidae

Dimorphic

Having two or more sharply contrasting forms (often known as 'phases').
See 'Sexual Dimorphism', Polymorphism

Arctic Skua in light and dark phases—an example of dimorphism

Dipper

Name for all members of the family Cinclidae (Passeriformes, sub-order Oscines). Birds of hilly country with rapidly flowing streams, they are remarkable for their aquatic habits, particularly for walking under water. There are four species in a single genus found in the New World and western palearctic. In Britain the Dipper (*Cinclus cinclus*) was formerly quite widely known as the Water Ousel, while in other European countries translation of its name means 'Water Blackbird' and 'Water Starling'. Its specific habitat requirement confines it mainly to the upland regions of Britain, with a total population of around 30,000 pairs. The nest is a large dome-shaped affair, always located near water and often under waterfalls.

Disease

Disease is quite common among birds though the condition or effect is rarely obvious in the wild. Some bird diseases are transmissible to man and can be serious, such as psittacosis or Parrot disease. Other viral infections are known, but are less serious. It has been suggested that birds are also the carriers of foot-and-mouth disease, though there is no

The Dipper—easily identified if seen bobbing and curtseying on a boulder in midstream

evidence of any substance to support this. Many bird deaths are caused by poisoning rather than disease; lead poisoning amongst water birds is responsible for a large number of deaths. Most birds are infected with fleas or mites (ectoparasites) and also worms (endoparasites), but only an overwhelming infestation seriously affects the health of the bird.

Listed below are some of the more commonly encountered diseases of wild birds, some of the conditions also occuring in domestic and caged birds.

Aspergillosis
Infection from a mould commonly present in decaying vegetable matter.

Botulism
An anaerobic bacterial organism produces this very powerful toxin.

Candida albicans infection
Also known as 'thrush' or 'canker' by bird keepers, it is a disease of the mouth or crop.

Coryza
An infection of the upper respiratory tract; a mild condition resembling the 'common cold' in man. Common in domestic poultry and in game birds where intensive rearing is carried out.

Encephalitis
Inflammation of the brain by a virus; in poultry known as an endemic tremor, due to muscular spasms.

Erysipelas infection
A micro organism, *Erysipelothrix rhusiopathiae*, it usually produces fatal results.

Fowl leucosis
The term 'leucosis complex' refers to a group of diseases characterised by abnormal production of white blood cells. Little known in wild birds, it is important in domestic poultry.

Fowl plague
Commonly known as fowl pest, this and Newcastle disease are serious viral diseases in domestic fowls.

Pasteurellosis
A common pathogen of wild life producing white necrotic lesions.

Protozoal infections
Various infections are caused by protozoa, the resultant conditions depending upon the type of parasite involved; often fatal.

Psittacosis (Ornithosis)
Has a worldwide distribution and over 20 species, including many non-'Parrots', have been proved to be infected by the virus. There are no characteristic clinical signs and at a postmortem examination an enlarged spleen may be the only lesion.

Quail disease
An ulcerative enteritis with heavy mortality, particularly in Bobwhite Quail and some other types of game birds.

Salmonellosis
A frequent problem with poultry but also found in wild birds. The organism is excreted in their droppings.

Dispersion

Tuberculosis (avian type)
A commonly occurring condition among birds.
Read Cooper, J. E., and Eley, J. T., *First Aid and Care of Wild Birds*, David & Charles, 1979

Dispersion
Defined by V. C. Wynne Edwards as the placement of individuals or groups of individuals within the habitats they occupy and the processes by which this is brought about.
Read Wynne Edwards, V. C., *Animal Dispersion in Relation to Social Behaviour*, Edinburgh and London, 1962

Displacement Activity
A common behavioural action amongst birds, synonymous with 'substitute activity', 'displacement reaction', 'false activity', 'false feeding', 'false preening' etc. Such behaviour frequently seems to occur out of context when a bird or birds are engaged in a particular action which is displaced by another; eg a bird may suddenly interrupt sexual behaviour and attack the mate. Displacement activity also frequently occurs when a bird is suddenly faced with some unknown situation—a bird will then seemingly commence to preen or feed, ie false activity, false feeding at the approach of danger.
See Ambivalence

Display
A means of communication by animals especially birds. Primarily restricted to visual signals but often associated with characteristic calls. The major forms of display are related to:
1 Threat when encountering rivals
2 Submission used between rivals or mates
3 Acceptance of dominance
4 Greeting—usually at change-over time at the nest
5 Social—pertaining mainly to flock migration
6 Anti-predator (distraction), mobbing, injury feigning
See Ambivalence; Displacement Activity; Distraction Display

Distal
Furthest from the centre of the body or from the point of attachment—opposite of proximal.

Distraction Display
Display by parent bird to distract predator away from eggs or young. Widespread amongst birds, it is particularly common in ground-nesting species. The most frequently observed form of distraction display is injury-feigning, the adult bird simulating some incapacity, usually a broken wing, fluttering in front of the predator dragging its wing, but always just out of reach. When the threat is removed far enough away from the young or the nest, the bird takes flight. Some waders also distract a predator by simu-

Threat display—between Yellow Wagtails

lating a mammal, crouching low and running rapidly over the ground like some rodent.

Ringed Plover feigning a broken wing—a distraction display

Distribution

In the geographical sense, the total range of a family or species of bird. Distribution can be limited by a multitude of factors, climate being a basic one, particularly through its effect on the terrain, in turn related to the conditions to which particular kinds of birds are adapted. The study of the distribution of animals is known as zoogeography. In some bird books the total distribution may not be given—only the area where each bird may be found within the scope of that book may be defined, eg a book on British birds may only give the British range of a bird also found elsewhere.

See Faunal Region; Zoogeography
Read Sharrock, J. T. R., *Atlas of Breeding Birds of Britain and Ireland*, Poyser, Berkhamsted, 1976; Voous, K. H., *Atlas of European Birds*, Nelson, 1960

Diurnal

Active during the daytime; characteristic of a great majority of bird species. Most often used in relation to birds of prey when owls are not included in those being discussed: eg a Buzzard is a diurnal bird of prey, a Barn Owl a nocturnal bird of prey.

See Crepuscular; Nocturnal

Diver

In Britain the term is generally applied to all 4 species of the Gaviidae (Gaviiformes), the Diver spp (in North America the Loons). All Divers have slender, cigar-shaped bodies with legs at the rear to aid propulson through the water, where they spend most of their lives, only coming to land for nesting.

The most familiar to birdwatchers is the Red-throated Diver (*Gavia stellata*), the smallest of the family, known as the Red-throated Loon in North America. It has a slender uptilted bill which identifies it immediately, even at a distance, though only at close quarters can the dark red colour of the throat patch be seen. It breeds in small numbers in North and West Scotland, the Hebrides, Shetlands and Orkneys. In winter this is the diver most frequently seen on the sea.

Red-throated Diver (above); if frightened it can sink like a submarine, only head and neck staying above the water.
The Black-throated Diver (below) has a distinctive summer appearance, but in winter can be confused with Red-throated or Great Northern Divers

The handsome Black-throated Diver (*Gavia arctica*), with grey head and black-and-white striping on the neck, is somewhat scarcer as a breeding bird in Britain, with probably only 100-150 pairs nesting in the Hebrides, some Scottish islands and parts of the NW Scottish mainland. Also to be found round our coasts in winter, and frequently recorded at some of our larger inland waters. In North America the Black-throated Diver is known as the Arctic Loon.

The Great Northern Diver (or Common Loon) (*Gavia immer*) is mainly a winter visitor, but is suspected of having bred on a couple of occasions. Mostly to be seen round British coasts from October to March, but a few visit inland waters.

The White-billed Diver (*Gavia adamsii*) breeds in the high Arctic and is a rare visitor to Britain. It has been recorded about 40 times over the last 20 years. In North America this is the Yellow-billed Loon.

Diving Petrel

Substantive name of the species Pelecanoididae (Procellariiformes). Small Auk-like sea birds, restricted to the southern hemisphere. Diving Petrels are mainly crustacean-eaters, diving to obtain their food, swimming under water using their wings. This group of birds is a good example of evolutionary convergence, Diving Petrels developing in much the same way as the Alcidae—particularly the Little Auk (*Plautus alle*) of the northern hemisphere.

See Auk; Evolutionary Convergence

Dodo

As an example of an extinct species there is none so well-known as the Dodo. The expression as 'dead as the Dodo' is part of everyday language. The Dodo (*Raphus cucullatus*) belonged to the Raphidae (Columbiformes, sub-order Columbae), the Pigeons, though this affinity has been questioned and it is suggested it should be linked with the Rails (Rallidae). The Dodo was peculiar to the Mascarene islands in the Indian Ocean east of Madagascar. Massive in size, it was as big as a turkey with strong feet and bill. The Dodo was a clumsy creature with a very large head, heavy hooked bill, short legs and a little tail of a few curly feathers. General colouration of the plumage was blue-grey. It moved slowly and was considered to be stupid, showing little or no fear of man. The arrival of Europeans, with their pigs and dogs and

The Dodo

accompanying rats, spelled the end of the Dodo and it had disappeared from Mauritius by 1680, from Réunion by 1750 and from Rodriguez perhaps as late as 1790 to 1800. There were two similar-looking members of the Raphidae, called Solitaires, and these suffered a similar fate, disappearing around the same period.

Read Greenway, J. C., *Extinct and Vanishing Birds of the World*, Dover Publications, New York, 1967

Domesticated Birds

Birds whose life cycle and maintenance are controlled by man, particularly for their economic value. In present times this mainly applies to domestic fowl, ducks, geese and turkeys for food, pigeons and game birds for sport and to a lesser extent such species as Ostrich (*Struthio camelus*) for their feathers and Cormorant (*Phalacrocorax* spp) for fishing in the Far East.

The domestication of animals and birds goes back to at least 3000 BC when domesticated pigeons were known. The domestic fowl, descended from the Red Jungle Fowl, became domesticated in Southern Asia about 2000 BC. The domestic goose is descended from the Greylag Goose (*Anser anser*) and the Chinese Goose (*Cygnopsis cygnoid*) and both were domesticated before 500 BC.

Dominance

The outcome of any confrontation between two birds, usually in defence of territory, is relatively predictable. The bird which achieves

victory, invariably the holder of the territory, is called the dominant bird and the vanquished the subordinate bird. Dominance is also established in groups of birds—the so-called 'pecking order' and once the dominant bird has emerged, the *status quo* is unlikely to be altered by birds within the group. This is particularly noticeable in barnyard domestic fowl and in caged birds.

Dotterel (*Eudromias morinellus*)

This member of the Plover family is one of Britain's scarcer breeding birds, mainly confined to the Grampians and Cairngorms with probably no more than 100 breeding pairs. Some birds, though not all, can be extraordinarily tame (the reason for the English name). It is the male Dotterel that does the incubating while the females gather together in small bands. A summer visitor, it can be seen on migration, particularly in the autumn when small parties called 'trips' are occasionally noted.

In Australia the name is used for several wading birds (*Charadrius* spp).
Read Thompson, D. N., *Dotterel*, Collins, 1972

Dove

Name of some species of Columbidae. The

Dotterel; broad white eyestripes joining in a V on the nape are a distinctive feature

names Dove and Pigeon are to some extent interchangeable. Generally the smaller species are called Doves.
See Pigeon

Dovekie

Alternative name of the Little Auk (*Plautus alle*). A small black-and-white sea bird breeding in the Arctic regions, it is a winter visitor to Britain's sea coasts. Occasionally storms 'wreck' numbers of this species, often far inland.
See Little Auk

Dowitcher

A wading bird formerly called the Red-breasted Snipe, this rarity to Britain often presents an identification problem for bird-watchers as there are two species, the Long-billed Dowitcher (*Limnodromus scolopaceus*) and the Short-billed Dowitcher (*Limnodromus griseus*) which are very hard to distinguish. In the last 20 years over 100 Dowitchers have been recorded in Britain with relatively few specifically identified, but

most of those have been ascribed to the long-billed species.

Read Sharrock, J. T. R. and E. M., *Rare Birds in Britain and Ireland*, Poyser, Berkhamsted, 1976

Down

Soft feathers usually underlying the contour feathers of the under parts. The use of down plucked by the female from her own body is characteristic of Ducks (*Anatidae*) and Lyrebirds (*Menura* spp) in the construction of their nests. Among the Ducks, the Eider Duck is probably most widely known for this behaviour.

See Eider

Drake

Name applied to the male Duck.

Drift

The displacement of a migrating bird by cross-wind. Often the cause of some species occurring far outside their normal range—'a wind-drifted migrant'.

Drinking

Water is as essential to birds as it is to any other living organism, but the method of drinking varies among different species, as

Mallard drake

The Wood Pigeon imbibes continuously without looking up; for a different drinking style see next page

does the amount directly absorbed in that manner. All food contains some water, but obviously the amount obtained from a diet of dry seeds must be much less than from succulent vegetable or animal food. Conditions of humidity and the bird's degree of activity also have some effect on requirements. Some species show an adaptation to conditions which allows them to go for long periods without water, while others deprived of water die within a few days. Basically there are two ways in which birds drink (as opposed to ingesting water from food). Most Passerines, for example, repeatedly fill the bill or mouth with water and raise the head each time to let the liquid run down the throat. Pigeons, Sandgrouse and Button Quails imbibe continuously without raising their heads. Some aerial species, notably the Swift, drink in flight, taking water from the surface of a pond or stream as they pass over it.

Drongo

Name of nearly all species of Dicruridae (Passeriformes, sub-order Oscines). The 20 species of Drongo are found in the Old World tropics. Though not related, their behaviour is 'Flycatcher-like'.

Droppings

Term applied to a bird's excreta, a mixture of urine and intestinal waste (faeces) expelled from the cloaca. Before the droppings are

The House Sparrow, like most Passerine birds, raises its head when drinking to let each billfull of water run down

Glossy-backed Drongo

expelled much of the liquidity is removed by the reabsorption of the water content through the cloacal walls. The white material often present in the droppings of many species consists of uric acid and salts. Droppings are also often tinged by the pigments contained in the food that has passed through the alimentary canal, eg the purple colour in the droppings of sea birds is due to their feeding on mussels.

In the case of many passerine nestlings, the faeces are enclosed in a gelatinous capsule which can be removed by the parent without soiling the nest. In some cases it is eaten by the parent bird.

Some bird droppings are characteristic and can be identified as emanating from particular birds, notably those of Grouse (Tetraonidae) and Geese (Anserini). Droppings can be valuable in the location of a bird such as a roosting Owl which would otherwise be difficult to spot.

Drumming
The term normally used for a non-vocal sound created by woodpeckers when the bill is used to rain a succession of rapid blows at a selected point of a tree or branch. A broken or dead branch is most frequently chosen, the bird usually operating towards its end; exceptionally, it may drum on other sounding-boards such as corrugated-iron roofs etc. The pitch of the sound is in proportion to the diameter of the branch and the normal frequency is around 8-10 blows per second. The sound may be audible at distances up to a quarter of a mile away. In Britain the main drumming period is from February to May. The sound serves to attract a mate.

The Great Spotted Woodpecker (*Dendrocopos major*) is responsible for most drumming heard. The Lesser Spotted Woodpecker (*Dendrocopos minor*) drums less frequently, and is less powerful, having a much higher pitch. It is of course a much smaller bird with a smaller bill. The Green Woodpecker (*Picus viridis*) makes loud tapping noises with its bill but does not drum in the manner of the Spotted Woodpeckers.

The term 'drumming' is also used to denote the sound or 'bleatings' of Snipe (*Gallinago gallinago*), which during their display flight in the breeding season produce a resonant tremulous sound with their tail feathers. In North America 'drumming' is the term used to describe the sound produced by the Ruffed Grouse (*Bonasa umbellus*) when it strikes its wings against its breast during display.

Great Spotted Woodpecker

Some familiar Ducks. Top left, Mallard duck and drake; top right, Teal drake; centre left, Pochard—duck at top, drake below; centre right, above, Scaup—female on left—and below, Tufted Duck, again with female on left; bottom left, Shelduck (female on left); bottom right, Wigeon (female on left)

Duck

Name of most of the smaller species of Anatidae (Anseriformes, sub-order Anseres). Ornithologically the term Duck is applied irrespective of sex, and it is often used (though incorrectly!) unchanged in the plural as a collective term, ie many Duck, large numbers of Duck. The Ducks are usually divided into three major groupings:

1 The surface feeders or dabblers—Mallard (*Anas platyrhynchos*), Teal (*Anas crecca*), Wigeon (*Anas penelope*) etc.
2 The diving Ducks—Pochard (*Aythya ferina*), Tufted (*Aythya fuligula*), Scaup (*Aythya marila*) etc
3 Sawbills-Goosander (*Mergus merganser*), Red-breasted Merganser (*Mergus serrator*) etc

See Anseriformes

Read Ogilvie, M. A., *Ducks of Britain and Europe*, Poyser, Berkhamsted, 1975; Owen, M., *Wildfowl of Europe*, Macmillan and the Wildfowl Trust, 1977; Soothill, E. and Whitehead, P., *Wildfowl of the World*, Blandford Press, Poole, 1978; Todd, F. S., *Waterfowl, Ducks, Geese and Swans of the World*, Sea World Press, California, 1979

Duck Decoy

The word decoy derives from the Dutch *eende*, Duck, and *kool*, cage or trap. A Duck 'decoy' is a device constructed on the edge of a lake, or round a pound specially dug for the purpose of catching wild Ducks. It typically comprises an area of water of one to three acres from which radiate 'pipes'—curved tapering ditches each covered by a tunnel of netting stretched over semi-circular hoops. The pipes narrow down to a small catching area. Ducks are lured into the pipes by a trained dog—the dog works along the pipe, appearing over the leaps and disappearing behind the screens, and the Ducks are drawn partly by bravado and partly by curiosity to follow it. When enough birds are well into the pipe, a decoyman shows himself at the end opening, and the birds' only means of escape leads them to the narrowing end of the tunnel and a catching net. The device was perfected in Holland in the late 16th century and introduced into Britain where there were more than 200 in operation. Today only a few remain and these are used for ringing; however they are still used in Holland to catch Ducks for food. The word decoy has now of course been extended in its use and is applied to include human deceptions.

Catching net of duck decoy at Borough Fen

Wildfowl Trust's duck decoy at Slimbridge, Glos (aerial view)

Duetting
Male and female of a pair singing or calling to each other as part of their courtship display. *See* Antiphonal Song

Dungeness, Kent
The site of a nuclear power station, a bird observatory and an RSPB reserve, Dungeness is a shingle promontory projecting seawards between Hastings and Folkestone. To its credit the power station has had breeding Black Redstarts (*Phoenicurus ochruros*). The observatory has recorded many vagrant species of migrants. The RSPB, in order to encourage many more nesting birds, has created suitable sites for Terns and Plovers, in conjunction with the planned excavation of gravel.

Dunlin (*Calidris alpina*)
A wader belonging to the Scolopacidae (Charadriiformes, sub-order Charadrii). In summer it has a chestnut and black back with a black patch on the lower breast. In winter the back is grey-brown and the under parts white. When feeding it has a distinctive round-shouldered look as it probes for crustaceans and molluscs with a series of rapid movements of its bill as if 'stitching'

Decoy dog leaping

the mud. The bill varies, being markedly larger and more curved towards the tip on some birds. There is even a considerable size difference between individuals, according to whether they belong to the Southern or Northern races, the Southern form being smaller though never as small as the Little Stint (*Calidris minuta*), which has a short

(left front) Dunlin in summer plumage; (above) Curlew Sandpiper, winter plumage; (right) Dunlin in winter plumage

Flock of Dunlin

straight bill; or in the case of the Northern form, never as big as the Curlew Sandpiper (*Calidris ferruginea*), which has a more curved bill and a white rump. The Dunlin is commonly found round Britain's coasts, particularly on muddy estuaries and sand-flats, with probably up to half a million birds present in winter. A number also breed— 5,000 to 10,000 pairs, mainly in the Shetlands, Orkneys, NE Scotland and the Hebrides; also in parts of N England, Wales and Dartmoor.

Dunnock

Alternative and often preferred name of the Hedge Sparrow (*Prunella modularis*). In any case the bird is not a Sparrow but belongs to the Accentor family. Other local names for the species include Shufflewing, Hedge Betty, Hedge Chat and Hedge Creeper, to list a few. Present all the year, breeding widely throughout Britain and Ireland, it is one of our commonest birds with an estimated British and Irish population of 5 million pairs. Not a showy species, it creeps about hedgerow bottoms, feeding on small insects. Its song is an unmusical hurried jangle of notes, shorter in duration and less powerful than that of the Wren (*Troglodytes troglodytes*). Its neat nest hidden in a hedge or bramble, with 4 or 5 turquoise-blue eggs, is often selected by the Cuckoo as home for its own offspring.

Dunnock or Hedge Sparrow, one of our commonest birds

Dusky Redshank

Name sometimes used for the Spotted Red-shank (*Tringa erythropus*), which in summer plumage is sooty-black speckled with white on the upper parts. In winter it looks more like the Redshank (*Tringa totanus*), with ash-grey upper parts copiously spotted with white, distinguished at all times from the commoner species by lack of wing bar, longer, thinner bill, longer legs projecting well beyond tail in flight, and distinctive call—a loud 'tchewit'.

Golden Eagle with chick

Dusting

Sometimes referred to as dust bathing. Dusting and bathing are not the same, though they may serve a similar purpose to some extent, both being concerned with the maintenance of feathers. Ectoparasites are probably dislodged or discouraged by both; preening and scratching often follow after dusting. Some species both bathe and dust. The House Sparrow (*Passer domesticus*) is a good example, and often small groups can be seen dusting together. Dusting is, however, more typical of birds of dry open country, particularly desert regions, where Larks, Sand-grouse and Bustards practise it.

Eagle

The name of large members of the Accipitrinae (*Aquila*, etc) particularly. In general Eagles are large broad-winged birds of prey feeding on mammals and on other birds. Though some have a wing-span which may exceed 7ft (over 2 metres) others are much smaller. In Britain the Golden Eagle (*Aquila chrysaetos*) is to be found in Scotland, where about 300 pairs breed. The White-tailed Eagle (*Haliaeetus albicilla*) formerly nested but is now only a rare visitor. There was a recent attempt to reintroduce this species to Shetland but it failed. However, a more promising attempt is continuing in the Hebrides. The Eagle has long been regarded as a symbol of power, boldness and daring and many countries use it as an heraldic device.
Read Brown, L., *Eagles of the World*, David & Charles, Newton Abbot, 1977

Ear

In birds the ear is not usually apparent, completely lacking the pinnae, the protruding part of the outer ear so characteristic of mammals. However, the avian ear resembles the human ear in its construction, the external ear consisting of a simple canal, the middle ear consisting of an air-filled space through which bony structures convey the vibrations of sound to the inner ear. The construction of the inner ear is identical with that of mammals, the cochlea containing the nerve endings and the auditory nerve. The range of frequency of sound audible to birds is similar to the human range of hearing. However, in some species of birds the ear shows special adaptations, as with the Owls (Strigiformes spp), where the structure of the outer and inner ear differs between the right and left sides which enables the bird to locate the source of sound with great accuracy.

Early (and Late) Dates

These are the dates when migrant birds are first noted on their arrival or last seen before their departure. Great interest has always been shown by birdwatchers in these first and last dates, and most bird clubs detail such sightings in their annual reports. *The Handbook of British Birds* (1938-1941) made a feature of listing small samples of early and late dates and this no doubt stimulated interest in this matter. Some early dates (and some late dates) are of course unrepresentative of the total movement of the species and the very earliest and latest dates are of little consequence when listed in isolation. The British Trust for Ornithology's Guide No 15, *Early and Late Dates for Summer Migrants*, gives the 15 earliest and 15 latest dates (up to 1973) for each of the species dealt with, plus any January records listed separately. This is a longer series than those given in the *Handbook*, and the *BTO Guide* enables extremes to be seen in some sort of perspective; each species is accompanied by a brief subjective statement giving some indication of the period when one might normally expect it to be present somewhere in Britain and Ireland.

Echo Location

The means of navigating during flight in the dark caves where certain species of birds breed. This has been developed by two widely separated types of birds, the Oilbirds (Steatornithidae) of neotropical regions and the Cave Swiftlets (Apodidae, *Collocalia* spp). The Oilbird utters a continuous stream of short pulses of sound, the Swiftlets a rapid succession of high clicking notes. These sounds echo back from the cave walls and other obstructing surfaces, and from the echoes the birds discern their whereabouts.

Eclipse

A plumage stage in certain species of birds, notably Ducks (Anatidae), when the drakes' bright breeding feathers are replaced by more cryptic-coloured ones, very like those of the female of the species. During the period of eclipse, which is mainly the latter part of summer until late autumn, birds may be rendered flightless as a simultaneous moult of the wing feathers takes place.

Ectoparasite

A parasite which lives on the outside of the host's body. Extremely common among birds, they include Hippoboscidae (louseflies), Siphonaptera (fleas), Ixodidae (ticks), Analgesidae (feather mites) and Mallophaga (lice). Apart from being vectors of certain diseases, ectoparasites are probably more of a nuisance than a danger to the bird; only in cases of extreme infestation do they have a deleterious effect on its health. Dust bathing, preening etc, no doubt play their part in keeping ectoparasites down to a tolerable level.
See Disease

Edible Nests

The nests of Cave Swiftlets (*Collocalia* spp). Some of these birds build pure white nests composed entirely of their own salivary secretion, while others make nests of secretion mixed with feathers or vegetable matter. They are esteemed by the Chinese and other Asians as a food, which is made into 'bird's-nest soup'.

Edward Grey Institute for Field Ornithology

Originally formed by the British Trust for Ornithology as a permanent institute for research into bird biology, it is now part of the University of Oxford's Department of Zoology. Links with the Trust are still maintained. It has given special study to the subject of bird population and migration, and it maintains one of the finest libraries of bird books in Britain.

Egg

The egg or ovum comprises:

1 The yolk, which is the female reproductive cell consisting of alternate layers of white and yellow yolk. On the surface of the yolk is the very small white germinal spot where the embryo develops.

2 The albumen ('white') which is covered by two membranes surrounding the yolk. These membranes are closely attached to the eggshell except at the broad pole. Here an air space is present between the two membranes, only the outer of which is attached to the shell.

3 The shell consists of a calcified layer of varying thickness which protects the egg from damage. Air, but not fluids, can penetrate the shell through its pores.

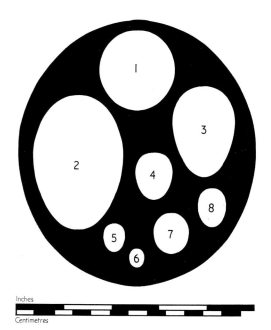

Mute Swan's nest and eggs

Inches

Centimetres

Against an Ostrich egg are the eggs of:
1 Tawny Owl, 2 Red-throated Diver, 3 Carrion
Crow, 4 Song Thrush, 5 Blue Tit, 6 Humming
Bird, 7 Kingfisher, 8 House Sparrow

Cryptically coloured eggs of the Oystercatcher

Eggs vary in size more or less according to the size of the bird. The largest egg is laid by the Ostrich (*Struthio camelus*) which is about 6in x 5in (150mm x 130mm), weighing about 3lb (1400g), while the smallest is laid by a Humming Bird (*Myrmia micrura*) $\frac{1}{2}$in x $\frac{1}{4}$in (11mm x 7mm), weighing only a few grammes. Shape varies from species to species but is consistent within each species. Some eggs are spherical, some oval and some conical. Colours are extremely varied and usually cryptic in ground-nesting species to white in most hole-nesting birds.

Egg Tooth
A calcareous scale-like development on the top of the upper mandible on a young bird still in the shell. This is used by the chick to cut its way out of the shell, and is shed within a few days of hatching.

Egret
The name of several species of the Ardeidae family (Herons). The Little Egret (*Egretta garzetta*), the Cattle Egret (*Bubulcus ibis*) and the Great White Egret (*Egretta alba*), formerly known as the Great White Heron, are rare visitors to Britain. The Little Egret is the most frequently recorded, with about 200 sightings over the last 20 years.

Little Egret

Eider
Sometimes called 'Eider Duck', of *Somateria* spp. In Britain the name refers to *Somateria mollissima*. A sea-haunting Duck, it breeds extensively in the Orkneys, Shetlands and the Hebrides, also on the east Scottish coast southwards to the Farne Islands. The drake is unmistakable with its black-and-white plumage and distinctive sloping forehead. The total British breeding population is about

The female Eider is distinctive only through size and shape. The male is the only duck with black belly and white back

20,000 pairs, with probably as many again present in winter. The King Eider (*Somateria spectabilis*) and Steller's Eider (*Polysticta stelleri*) are rare visitors to British waters from the Arctic. Eider-duck down is still commercially farmed in Iceland.

Eider's nest

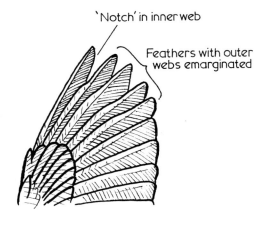

'Notch' in inner web

Feathers with outer webs emarginated

Elephant Bird
The extinct Aepyornithidae, large flightless birds whose remains have been found in Madagascar in deposits dating from the Pleistocene to geologically recent times. In general stature they resembled the Ostrich and some of the largest—about 8 species probably existed—may have weighed 1,000lb.

Emargination
A narrowing of the web on one side (usually the outer) towards the tip of certain primary feathers, producing a tapering effect. This produces 'notches' in the spread wing, of special importance to birds of prey. Also an additional aid in the identification of a number of closely allied species (when in the hand), particularly with some Old World Warblers. *See* Wing Formula

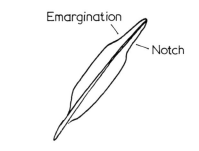

Emargination

Notch

Emberizidae
A family of the order Passeriformes, suborder Oscines, which includes the following sub-families:
    Buntings (Emberizinae)
    Cardinals, Grosbeaks (Pyrrhuloxidae)

Emargination on feathers

Emu

Embryo
The young bird from the earliest stage of its development within the egg until the time of hatching.
See Egg; Egg Tooth

Emu
Sole member of the Dromaiidae (Casuarii-formes), the Emu (*Dromaius novaehollandiae*) is the most widespread of the flightless ratite birds of Australia, being found all over that continent. Second largest of the world's birds (the Ostrich is the largest), it stands between 5 and 6ft high (1.5-2m) and attains a weight of 120lb (250kg).

Endocrine System
The glands which secrete hormones in the bloodstream. Endocrine glands in the bird include the pituitary, adrenals, gonads, parathyroid and thyroid, which affect such things as growth, heart-rate, respiration, behaviour, reproductive system and other physiological processes.

Endoparasite
A parasite inhabiting the interior of the host's body. Birds are hosts to an infinite variety of endoparasites, a number of which are quite common. Some of these, however, only affect certain species or groups of birds. The main groups of endoparasites are round-worms (Nematoda), thorny-headed worms (Acanthocephala), tapeworms (Cestoda), flukes (Trematoda) and unicellular animals (protozoa).
See Disease; Ectoparasite

Endysis
Renewal of plumage after moult.

Erne
Archaic and poetic name for the Eagle, especially the Sea or White-tailed Eagle (*Haliaeetus albicilla*).

Erythrism
The presence of an abnormal amount of red colouring in mammals or birds—black or brown is replaced by bright chestnut red in eggs or feathers.

Estuaries
Lying in the path of the major migratory routes of hundreds of thousands of birds, Britain plays a vital role as a staging post and wintering ground for many species of waders, wildfowl and Gulls which feed and roost in the numerous estuaries around the coasts. With reclamation and development schemes for industry and recreation, this valuable habitat is being severely reduced. Such is the importance ornithologists attach to estuaries that it was considered necessary to document as far as possible the comparative value of estuarine localities as passage areas and wintering grounds for waders, wildfowl and Gulls. To this end the BTO, with the active collaboration of the RSPB, undertook *A Birds of Estuaries Enquiry* in 1969.

Ethiopian Region
One of the classical zoogeographical regions,

it consists broadly of Africa south of the Sahara; at one time it included Madagascar, but this is now considered sufficiently different to be regarded as a separate region.
See Zoogeography

Ethology
The scientific study of behaviour.

Everglades
A wilderness of mangrove swamps, saw grass, plains, marshes and bald cypresses, the Everglades in Florida, USA, is one of the most important of the world's wetlands. Its tropical setting offers a paradise for bird-watchers, with almost every existing heron that may be found in North America as a whole. Limpkins, Snail Kites, Pelicans, Roseate Spoonbill, Frigate Birds, Boobies, Sooty and Noddy Terns and many others are also to be seen in this wonderland of birds.

Evolution
The theory which states that the different kinds of living things, animals, plants etc, have arrived at their present state by descent and modification from previously existing forms, and not by each one being created separately and having its present charac-teristics at the time of creation.
Read Darwin's *Origin of Species*;
    The Illustrated Origin of Species, abridged and introduced by R. E. Leakey, Faber, 1979

Excretory System
The organs involved in the elimination and excretion of waste materials, the most impor-tant being the kidneys and the urinary tract. As blood is filtered through the kidneys, waste materials in the form of excess salts and nitrogen and uric acid in particular are excreted as urine. The urine passes through the urinary tract to the cloaca, where it is expelled with the faeces in the form of droppings. Besides the kidneys, the bird's so-called salt glands help in the elimination of excess salt. These glands are highly developed in sea birds.

Exotic
Term applied to species of birds that are in the natural course alien to the area under consideration; eg, in Britain birds of tropical areas, such as Parrots, etc, are termed exotic. Many birds are kept in captivity, and a large number escape: observations of such birds

are usually referred to in bird reports under the heading 'Exotica'. The term is frequently misapplied (as for instance, in 'a bird of exotic appearance') when colourful, striking or distinctive is meant.

Extinct Birds

Species of birds that no longer exist. This term is usually applied to birds that have become extinct in historic times as opposed to species of birds known only as fossils. Of those birds which have become extinct within ornithologically recorded history, perhaps the best-known are the Dodo (*Raphus cucullatus*) which died out in the 17th century, the Great Auk (*Pinguinus impennis*), which survived until the 19th century, and the Passenger Pigeon (*Ectopistes migratorius*), the last-known living individual dying in 1913. Since the 17th century at least 78 full species of birds and 49 well-marked sub-species or races of birds have probably become extinct. At the present time there are numerous other species whose populations are dangerously low and which could well be extinct in a few years. Notable among these are the Whooping Crane, the Ivory-billed Woodpecker and the Californian Condor.

Read Greenway, J. C., Jr, *Extinct and Vanishing Birds of the World*, Dover Publications, 1967; Halliday, T., *Vanishing Birds*, Sidgwick & Jackson, 1978

Passenger Pigeon, now extinct

Eyas

The nestling of a falcon or hawk; the term is used especially in falconry. (Also spelled eyass, plural eyasses.)

Eye

In birds the eye is highly developed and often very large. The avian eye differs from the human eye in being much less spherical and by having an organ called the pecten situated in front of the retina. The function of this pecten, however, is unknown. The movement of a bird's eye is quite limited, though in many species the position of the eyes virtually provides all-round vision. In the case of Owls, however, their forward-looking eyes give poor peripheral vision. Compensation is provided by the birds' ability to swivel the head a full 270°. Birds have a third eyelid, or nictitating membrane, a transparent cover which can be pulled across the eye horizontally without shutting out the light. This protects the cornea without impairing the vision to any great extent.

See Binocular Vision

Eyelash

In birds this is a modified feather resembling a mammalian eyelash. Such eyelashes occur in a few groups of birds, notably the Ostrich, Eagles, Owls, Hornbills and some species of Cuckoo.

Eyrie

Term for the nest of a bird of prey, particularly applied to eagles (*Aquila* spp). Also eyry, aerie, aery.

Facies

Among other meanings in biology, it indicates the general appearance of a bird, without regard to details: its size, shape, posture or movement, perhaps with its general hue or any conspicuous feature. Not a term widely used by birdwatchers.

See Jizz

Fair Isle

A mere speck in the ocean, being 3 miles (5km) long by 1½ miles (2¼km) wide, Fair Isle lies north-east of the Scottish mainland, midway between Orkney and Shetland and separated to the north and south from both island groups by 25 miles (40km) of sea. The island is inhabited by a scattered community of some 70 souls, engaged in an enlightened policy of croft modernisation under the aegis of the National Trust for Scotland and with the support of the Shetland County Council on many projects. There has been an observatory on Fair Isle since 1948 when it was first established by George Waterson. In 1969 modern new buildings were opened providing sumptuous accommodation with a cafeteria food service for the many birdwatchers who make the pilgrimage.

The imposing cliff scenery provides breed-

Falcated

ing sites for Guillemot, Razorbill, Puffin, Kittiwake and Fulmar; Storm Petrel and Arctic Skua also nest, but it is the annual occurrence of numerous rarities that is such a 'draw'. Vagrant species rare elsewhere in Britain are almost regular; the Scarlet Grosbeak, Yellow-breasted and Little Buntings fall into this category, while the Barred Warbler, Bluethroat and Lapland Buntings are commonplace. A regular boat service runs between Grustness, Sumburgh and Shetland.

Falcated
Hooked or sickle-shaped.

Falcon
A name for many species of the Falconidae (Falconiformes, sub-order Falcones). General term for members of the whole family. Falcons are birds of prey, with long pointed wings and longish tails. Flight is generally fast, with rapid wingbeats followed by long glides. Some of the larger falcons kill their prey in the air by 'stooping' on it at great speed. The best known is the Peregrine (*Falco peregrinus*). Other falcons breeding in Britain include the Hobby (*Falco subbuteo*), Merlin (*Falco columbarius*) and Kestrel (*Falco tinnunculus*). Some rare visitors to Britain belonging to this family include the Gyr Falcon (*Falco rusticolus*) from the Arctic, which is the largest of the falcons, and the Red-footed Falcon (*Falco vespertinus*) from Eastern Europe.
See Hobby; Kestrel; Merlin; Peregrine; Stoop

Falconet
Name given to some small species of Falcon.

Falconiformes
An order of birds comprising the following sub-orders and families:
Sub-order Cathartae
Family—New World Vultures (Cathartidae); 7 species
Sub-order Falcones (or Accipitres)
Family—Hawks, Old World Vultures Harriers (Accipitridae); 211 species. Falcons, Caracas (Falconidae); 61 species
Sub-order Sagittarii
Family—Secretary Birds (Sagittariidae); 1 species

Falconry
The practice of taking wild quarry with birds of prey; also called 'hawking'. Of Eastern origins, it was practised as long ago as 1200 BC, notably in China, India, Pakistan, Persia and Arabia where it is still enthusiastically carried on. Introduced into Britain about AD 860, it was the chief sport of the nobility until the reign of James I, after which time it declined. In Britain today it has its band of devotees, whose interests are promoted by the British Falconers' Club. The trade in birds of prey by would-be falconers causes concern among bird protectionists, as not only are suitable birds imported from abroad but also

The Merlin, one of the Falcons breeding in Britain

94

our indigenous stock comes under threat: young falcons fetch high prices and too often are illegally taken from their nests. This is only allowed by special licence and severe penalties have been imposed on people taking birds unlawfully in recent years.

Fall

In birdwatchers' jargon, the sudden appearance of a considerable number of migrant birds, usually at a coastal observatory where this is more likely to be noticed. In autumn, particularly, sudden adverse changes in weather conditions which coincide with migratory bird movements can cause birds to be grounded, hence a 'fall' of birds. One day

Merlin (female) with prey (opposite)
(below) Trained Goshawk on the fist

there may be very few species to be seen, and the next day there could be many. The major species in a fall usually comprise Chats, Flycatchers, Warblers, etc, often with a sprinkling of rarer birds such as Wrynecks, Bluethroats etc.

Family
A primary taxonomic category of birds, being a sub-division of an order and a grouping of genera: ie, an order is made up of a number of related family groups. For example, the order Columbiformes comprises two families:

Pteroclidae—the Sandgrouse
Columbidae—the Pigeons

Each of these families contains a number of species. In the case of the Sandgrouse, there are 16 species in the world, and in the case of the Pigeons there are 280 species. Sometimes secondary categories are used, with sub-order and super-family used as higher divisions within the order, and sub-family and tribe used for subordinate groupings of genera. The names of sub-families end in 'inae' and names of tribes in 'ini'. In all cases the stem of the name is taken from the type genus.
See Classification; Genus; Nomenclature; Order; Species; Sub-species; Taxonomy

Farne Islands, Northumberland
The Farnes consists of some 30 islands lying 2-5 miles (3-8km) offshore from Bamburgh, most of which belong to the National Trust. The main attraction to birdwatchers is the easy viewing of breeding seabirds, particularly Eider, Cormorant, Shag and Kittiwake, plus the opportunity to see Sandwich, Common, Arctic and the rare Roseate Terns.

Faunal Region
In the study of the geographical distribution of animals, the world has been divided into several regions within which the animal life is relatively uniform, particularly where bird families are concerned. The major faunal regions are: Australasian; Ethiopian; Nearctic; Neotropical; Oriental; Palearctic. The Nearctic and Palearctic are sometimes referred to as the Holarctic Region. Some authorities consider the Pacific Islands a separate entity under the title Oceanic Region, and some also consider Madagascar as a separate region, the Malagasy Region. The Antarctic coasts and islands are also treated as a separate region.
See Zoogeography, for map

Feather
A component unit of the plumage and a structure unique to birds, probably a development from the scales of their reptilian ancestors. A typical feather consists of a shaft, made up of a hollow basal part, the calamus (quill) and a tapering part called the rachis. Along the rachis are rows of barbs that form the vane (webs) of the feather. Branching from each barb are two sets of barbules supporting barbicels; these are spoon-shaped on the proximal barbule and hooked on the distal barbule. These hooks fit into the grooves of the spoon-shaped barbules, and this arrangement gives the feather its strength and maintains its shape and contour. Contour feathers are those of head and body that form the outline of the bird. There are other kinds of feathers, such as semiplumes (usually the shorter body feathers which provide insulation) and down, the short feathers without a rachis which in the adult bird usually lie under the contour feathers. There are also filoplumes, hairlike feathers whose function is unknown. Some birds such as Nightjars (Caprimulgidae spp) have stiff hairlike feathers (bristles) around the gape which facilitate the capture of their prey (moths). The remiges are the main flight feathers (primaries and secondaries) and the retrices are the tail feathers.
See Topography; Wing

Feather Care
An extremely important aspect of routine behaviour which covers a range of highly stereotyped basic movements found in some form or other in all birds. The major pattern of feather care includes true bathing (in water), oiling and preening, with subsidiary acts such as anting, dusting and scratching. These various activities serve to keep the plumage in good order, so as to ensure effective insulation and/or powers of flight, both prerequisites for the bird's survival. Though much pioneer study of feather maintenance has been undertaken, it remains a somewhat neglected area of interest.
See Bathing; Dusting; Preening

Feigning Injury
See Distraction Display

Feral
Literally wild and untamed, but used of birds (or animals) that were once captive and have

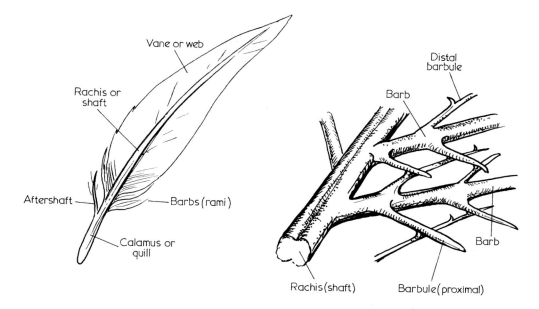

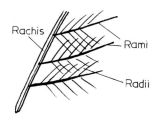

since been released or escaped and are now breeding freely in a natural manner (eg feral Pigeon). Also often used for populations of birds which have been artifically introduced into an area (eg feral Greylag Geese).

Field
An expression used by naturalists and bird-watchers for any outside environment. 'Out in the field', 'fieldwork', 'field guide' are terms for outdoor birdwatching or studying, or for a work of reference designed for outdoor use, as opposed to indoor or laboratory use.

Field Centre
A place where field studies can be undertaken, often sited at areas of major ornithological or general natural history interest. Some field centres have residential accommodation and fully equipped laboratories with a permanent staff as well as visiting tutors.
See Field Studies Council

Structure of the feather. The simplified view (top right) of the shaft, barbs and barbules shows how the minute hooks on the distal barbules fit into grooves beneath the proximal barbules, so holding the barbs together

Wood Duck, a feral species

Fieldcraft
The way in which a naturalist or birdwatcher achieves his aim of studying or watching wildlife in its natural environment. For example, obvious rules of fieldcraft if one is to approach wild birds and animals closely include keeping downwind and keeping below the skyline.

Fieldfare (*Turdus pilaris*)
Mainly a winter visitor to Britain from Scandinavia and Northern Europe, this handsome Thrush is a feature of the countryside from September to March. Noisy flocks foraging in the fields or feeding in the hedgerows call constantly with a harsh 'chack-chack-chack'. In really hard weather some resort to suburban gardens, where they will eat rotten fruit. Since 1967, when the first recorded instance of breeding in the Orkneys was noted, it has nested annually on Shetland and at several localities on the Scottish mainland. There are also a few scattered occurrences of birds nesting from Northern England south to Staffordshire.

Field Guide
A publication designed for use in the field, to help with the identification of birds (or other forms of wildlife), usually with the aid of comparative illustrations and brief descriptions of appearance, behaviour, call notes and song, etc. The first 'field guides' were about birds, and Roger Tory Peterson's *Field Guide* dealing with North American birds, published in 1934, was the first of many by the same author. This original concept has now been widely adopted, and the term 'field guide' is applied to any indentification book based on the Peterson style. One of the most successful and widely used today in Britain is *A Field Guide to the Birds of Britain and Europe* (1954), which Peterson illustrated and prepared with Guy Mountfort and P. A. D. Hollom. The first edition was reprinted eight times, the second edition (1965) was reprinted four times and a third edition was published in 1974. Additionally it has been translated into most European languages. Field guides on many aspects of natural history, on the birds of various different parts of the world, and on particular groups of birds, are obtainable; among British publishers, Collins have been pre-eminent in producing these.

Field Layer
One of several layers into which most plant communities can be divided. In an English broad-leaved wood, for example, four layers can be defined, each usually with one or more dominant species of plant. There is a high canopy formed by tall, mature trees, a low canopy of shrubs and saplings up to about 15ft

Fieldfare

(4.57m), the field layer of small flowering plants, ferns, brambles, grasses etc up to about 6ft (2m) and the ground layer of minute or prostrate plants, mosses, small herbs etc. The field layer may be sub-divided into upper 3-6ft (1-2m) and lower 6in-3ft (15cm-1m). Such broad divisions can be useful in describing the habitat of a bird and its utilisation of its environment.

Field Marks

Features of a bird's plumage which are discernible in the field, ie when it is observed in its natural habitat. Various species of birds have different field marks which aid identification and help to distinguish one species from another, eg spots or streaks, tail pattern, colour of rump, presence (or absence) of wing bars, eye stripes, coloured eye-rims, moustachial streaks, wing patterns, etc.
See Field Notes; Topography

Field Meeting

An organised visit to a specific area with the object of observing particular species of birds (or other wildlife). Most bird clubs arrange a programme of field meetings which, depending on the type and size of the club, range from visits to local areas with members using their own transport to long-distance trips by coach or train for a whole day or even a weekend. Even more ambitious field meetings are arranged by some clubs; for instance the West Midland Bird Club has included visits to Spain, Greece, Guyana and other countries.

Field Notes

In order to learn bird identification the taking of notes is essential. This helps to fix details in the mind and forces the observer to pay greater attention to the bird. To learn how to take effective field notes and how to go about describing a bird in a clear, unambiguous manner, it is important to learn some of the component parts of a bird (*see* Topography); 'a patch of yellow on the wing' might mean several different things but 'yellow on the outer primaries' gives a much clearer idea of the position of the distinctive field mark. With only a handful of terms to learn, this is far less difficult than some beginners imagine.

Birdwatcher making field notes

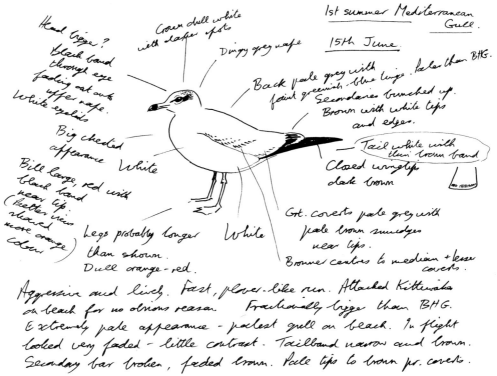

Example of an 'ideal' set of field notes made on the spot

Field notes may later be supplemented with details of such matters as optical aids, weather conditions, date and place etc, but it is of vital importance to write down descriptive details *at the time*. To do this well requires a good deal of practice and different people develop their own methods of 'field shorthand'. An annotated sketch such as that shown above—even if the sketch is nothing more than a few rough lines—helps to give guidelines for a basic description which can be written up into more permanent form later. Basically it is a method of labelling the various important features of the bird in question (eg such simple things as leg colour, bill colour, colour of back, tail pattern etc). Further notes on behaviour, call, comparison with other species, size and shape and so on should supplement the initial quick sketch. If the bird requires a full description, the rapid, labelled sketch should be made first—in case it flies away—but if the bird remains in view, a fuller, written version should also be made. As good a plan as any is to start with overall appearance, size and shape, then move on to individual features, starting at the head and working back over the upper parts and then doing the same for the underside, adding details of wings, tail, bill, eye and legs. Any method may be adopted, however, as long as the description is made in a regular, systematic way which helps to ensure that useful features are not accidentally missed out.

The use of a notebook in the field adds an extra dimension to simply watching birds—identification becomes a much more interesting and reliable process and notes on behaviour, habitat, voice and even such basic things as numbers are all likely to be far more detailed and more accurate—and therefore more useful—than the observer's later recollections.

Field Studies Council

A national body concerned with the organisation of field courses in biological, geographical and related subjects, including ornithology. It runs ten centres in England and Wales, with its headquarters at Preston Montford, Montford Bridge, Shrewsbury SY4 1HW. Its other centres are located at: Dale Fort, Haverfordwest, Dyfed; The Drapers Field Centre, Betws-y-coed, Gwynedd; Flatford Mill, Colchester, Essex; Juniper Hall, Dorking, Surrey; The Leonard Wills Field Centre, Taunton, Somerset; Malham Tarn, Settle, North Yorks; Orielton, Pembroke, Dyfed; and Slapton Ley, Kingsbridge, Devon.

Field of View
An important aspect of binocular performance is the field of view which is either given as an angle, usually 5° to 10° or in yards at 1,000 yards. As 1° is equal to approximately 17 yards at 1,000 yards, the greater the angle of view the better, as this is especially useful for following birds in flight. For general use at least 8° or 140 yards is preferable. Some manufacturers offer wide-angle versions of the various models available.
See Binocular; Brightness Factor

Filoplume
A hairlike feather.
See Feather

Finch
Name or part-name of many species of Fringillidae (Passeriformes, sub-order Oscines) in the plural general term for the family. Finches are primarily tree-haunting, seed-

The field of view decreases with magnification

Greenfinch, plump and short-bodied with cleft tail

eating birds with a bill specially adapted for extracting or shelling seeds. This is very hard and swollen at the base (being more or less conical in shape), but can vary enormously within the family, showing such extremes as in the Goldfinch (*Carduelis carduelis*), which has a slender needle-tipped bill, and the Hawfinch (*Coccothraustes coccothraustes*), which has a high pyramid-shaped bill that can exert a crushing power of 60lb or more, enabling it to extract the kernels from the stones of cherries and olives. One of the most curious adaptations of the bill form in this group is shown by the Crossbills (*Loxia* spp), in which the tips of the mandibles cross at an oblique angle, facilitating the extraction of seeds from the cones of pines and other conifers.

The Finches comprise the sub-families Fringillinae and Carduelinae. The former differ from the latter in having no crop, and due to other anatomical details are placed in a separate sub-family. There are only 3 species of the Fringillinae: the well-known Chaffinch (*Fringilla coelebs*), the Brambling (*Fringilla montifringilla*) and the Canary Islands Chaffinch (*Fringilla teydea*). The Carduelinae or Cardueline Finches are represented throughout the world by 122 species of which 18 occur in Britain. The best-known of these include the Greenfinch (*Carduelis chloris*),

Hawfinch, with enormous bill and bull-necked appearance

Goldfinch (*Carduelis carduelis*), Siskin (*Carduelis spinus*), Linnet (*Acanthis cannabina*), Redpoll (*Acanthis flammaea*), Crossbill (*Loxia curvirostra*), Bullfinch (*Pyrrhula pyrrhula*) and Hawfinch (*Coccothraustes coccothraustes*).
Read Newton, I., *Finches* (New Naturalist series), Collins, 1977

Finfoot
Name of all three species of Heliornithidae (Gruiformes, sub-order Heliornithes), also called Sungrebes. The family is confined to the tropical and sub-tropical zones. Mainly aquatic, they have the combined appearance and habits of Grebes (Podicipitidae), Cormorants (Phalacrocoracidae), Darters (Anhingidae), Ducks (Anatidae) and Coots (Fulicinae) though they are more closely allied to the Rails (Rallidae).

Firecrest (*Regulus ignicapillus*)
One of Europe's smallest birds, equivalent in size to the Goldcrest (*Regulus regulus*), which it resembles. However, it can be readily distinguished by a conspicuous white stripe above the eye and a black stripe through it. Much rarer in Britain than the Goldcrest, it is mainly a winter visitor and passage migrant,

Goldcrest (above) and Firecrest

though a few pairs have bred in parts of southern England in recent years, with some quite large but temporary concentrations being reported.

First Arrivals
Term applied to the first returning migrant birds noted in the spring or in the autumn—the summer or winter visitors respectively. *See* Early Dates

Fish Hawk
North American alternative name for the Osprey (*Pandion haliaetus*).

Fixed Action Pattern
Abbreviated to FAP, a behaviour pattern as defined by Konrad Lorenz. Characterised by its lack of variation, independence of environmental cues and spontaneous motivation, such behaviour is exemplified by the egg-rolling of the Greylag Goose (*Anser anser*). Here FAP consists of the Goose putting its bill over an egg and then drawing the egg towards its breast. The substitution of a model egg and its removal, and the consequent behaviour of the goose, demonstrate fixed action pattern.

Flamingo
Name of the species of Phoenicopteridae (Ciconiiformes, sub-order Phoenicopteri), large, long-legged, long-necked birds with a unique angled beak used to sieve food (minute organic matter) from muddy water. There are 4 species of Flamingo occurring

Greater Flamingo

in both the Old World and the New World. All Flamingos are highly gregarious and can be found in large numbers, especially in Africa where it is estimated there may be 6 million birds, of which the vast majority, perhaps 4½ million, are Lesser Flamingo (*Phoeniconaias minor*), the remainder being Greater Flamingo (*Phoenicopterus ruber*). The Andean Flamingo (*Phoenicoparrus andinus*) is found high up in the Bolivian Andes, as is the rarer James' Flamingo (*Phoenicoparrus jamesi*). The total world population of this last bird is only around 15,000. The Greater Flamingo is rarely if ever recorded in Britain in the wild, the few that may have wandered to these shores having come from either southern France or Spain, where small populations exist. Most Flamingos seen in Britain are escapees from captivity—they are widely kept in zoos, the most successful breeding results, and the most comprehensive collection, having been achieved at the Wildfowl Trust at Slimbridge.

Fledgling

A young bird which has acquired its first true feathers and is ready to leave the nest, or a bird which has just learned to fly.

Flicker

A North American species of Woodpecker (*Colaptes* spp). There is one record of a Common (Yellow-shafted) Flicker (*Colaptes auratus*) for the British Isles; it flew ashore at Cork on 13 October 1962. It had been aboard the RMS *Mauritania* since leaving New York on 7 October.

Flight

The outstanding characteristic of the class of Aves, though some birds have lost this ability in the evolutionary process. Different groups of birds have developed particular types of flight, and though in all species the principle is the same, the manner varies widely—from the hovering flight of the Humming Bird, with a maximum of 90 wing beats a second recorded, to the soaring flight of large birds of prey, which flap their wings only infrequently to maintain momentum. Aspects of flight can be a useful aid to identification, as some groups and some species have very distinctive flight; eg the twisting, turning flight of Snipe when flushed, the undulating flight of Woodpeckers and the hovering flight of the Kestrel when hunting. Some examples of rates of wing beat are given below:

Mute Swan	approx 3 beats per second
Heron	approx 2 beats per second
Pheasant	approx 9 beats per second
Peregrine	approx 4 beats per second
Guillemot	approx 8 beats per second
Blackbird	approx 6 beats per second

See Feather; Flightless Birds; Ratites; Wing

Flightless Birds

The earliest known birds could do no more than glide, but many distinctive characteristics of flying birds were present. It is believed that present-day birds that have lost their ability to fly have done so only in relatively recent times and that they had flying ancestors. The most notable examples of flightless birds are the so-called Ratites, the large running birds, which comprise the Ostrich (Struthioniformes), the two species of Rhea (Rheiformes), the three Cassowaries (Casuariiformes) and the Emu. The Kiwis (Apterygiformes) have also lost powers of flight, but this has come about through adaptation by leading a nocturnal existence, rather than relying on fleetness of foot like the running birds, for escape from predators. The Penguins (Sphenisciformes) form the other major order of birds that cannot fly: their marine existence has led to the development of flippers instead of wings, these being used to propel the birds through the water.

Ostrich dust bathing(opposite)

Undulating flight (below)

Flipper

Exceptionally there are several examples of flightless species within families of which the great majority of its members can fly, such as the now extinct Great Auk (*Pinguinus impennis*), the Flightless Grebe (*Centropelma micropterum*), of Lake Titicaca and the Flightless Cormorant (*Nannopterum harrisi*) of the Galapagos Islands.

There are also several flightless species, some recently extinct and some still surviving, amongst the Rails (Rallidae). Two of the three Steamer-Ducks (*Tachyeres* spp) are flightless, and the Owl Parrot or Kakapo (*Strigops habroptilus*) of New Zealand is flightless. A number of other species are virtually flightless, including the Ground Parrot (*Pezoporus wallicus*) and Night Parrot (*Geopsittacus occidentalis*) of Australia. Some of the New Zealand Wattlebirds (Callaeidae) are also nearly flightless.

Flipper
Term applied to the modified wing of Penguins (Sphenisciformes) with which they propel themselves under water. They are unable to fly.

Flock
See Assembly

Flocking
The positive social behaviour of individual birds resulting in the formation of a group or flock, often consisting solely of one species, though not always so. Many species are gregarious throughout the year, sea birds particularly. In the case of a large number of Passerines, especially Finches (Fringillidae) and Buntings (Emberizidae), groups are formed in the winter following the breeding season. Titmice (*Parus* spp) also form flocks and are often found in association with the Tree-creeper (*Certhia familiaris*) and Nuthatch (*Sitta europaea*) and in the autumn occasionally with some Warblers (*Phylloscopus* spp). Flocking has a survival value, in that concentrations of a food source can be exploited by the maximum number of birds, and additionally it gives increased awareness of the approach of predators.
See Assembly

Flowerpecker
Substantive name of some species of Dicaeidae (Passeriformes, sub-order Oscines). There are 58 species of these small nectar-feeding birds distributed throughout the oriental and Australasian regions.

Flycatcher (New World)
Substantive name of many species of Tyrannidae (Passeriformes, sub-order Tyranni). Also called Tyrant Flycatchers. Other substantive names in different genera include Tyrant, Kingbird, Phoebe and Pewee. The family of Tyrant Flycatchers includes over 300 species and is confined to the Americas, where it replaces, and in many respects resembles, the Old World Flycatchers (see below).

Gentoo Penguins, Falkland Islands

Flock of Knot about to land

The Spotted Flycatcher (above) is not spotted
at all; the male Pied Flycatcher (below) is a
more conspicuous bird

Flycatcher (Old World)

Name of many species of the sub-family Muscicapinae (Passeriformes, sub-order Oscines). In the plural, general term for the sub-family. There are 134 species of these insect-feeding birds throughout the world, but they are represented in Britain by only two breeding species, the Spotted Flycatcher (*Muscicapa striata*) and Pied Flycatcher (*Ficedula hypoleuca*). The Spotted Flycatcher is an inconspicuous mouse-brown bird (both sexes are similar) and is not spotted at all—it just has a few streaks on the upper breast. However, its pose and behaviour readily identify it. It sits in a very upright position on a branch or post, flicking its wings and tail, making frequent short aerial sallies after insects. A summer visitor, it is generally distributed throughout Britain with probably between 100,000 and 200,000 pairs. The Pied Flycatcher, on the other hand, is a handsome black-and-white bird (the female is less distinctly marked), though possibly not so adept at catching flies, feeding more on caterpillars taken from foliage. Also a summer visitor, it has a more westerly distribution, being common in most of Wales, the Lake District and parts of SW England. Total population around 20,000 pairs.

The similar-looking Collared Flycatcher (*Ficedula albicollis*) is a rare visitor from Eastern Europe, as is the Red-breasted Flycatcher (*Ficedula parva*).

Food Chain

Food chains always start with plants—the primary energy producers—and rarely exceed four or five links. The next link in the chain is the plant-eater and this is followed by the meat-eater which preys upon the plant-eater. The first meat-eaters are usually small and these are preyed upon by larger ones. The end of the food chain is the predator with no apparent enemies. This, however, is not the end of the energy cycle, which is what a food chain is—the eventual death of the large predator at the top of the food chain is followed by the decomposition of the body. Decaying bodies release nutrients which are available for plant growth, thus initiating the food chain once more. Food chains can involve widely differing groups of animals and though each link in the chain is dependent on the next link, some are able to make use of alternative food chains.

An example of a food chain:
Leaves fall from a growing plant in the autumn
Worm feeds on decaying leaves
Thrush feeds on worm
Sparrowhawk preys on Thrush

Food-chain effects have shown themselves in more sinister ways, when birds of prey at the end of the food chain have suffered from the accumulation of sub-lethal doses of agricultural chemical residues ingested by their prey (small birds) which have fed on treated seed or insects.

Food Pass

An aspect of the breeding behaviour of Harriers (*Circus* spp): the male passes food to the female with its feet, usually directly over the nest site. In the early stages of nesting activity this is invariably followed by copulation at the nest or nearby. Though the term is used especially with regard to the Harriers, similar behaviour can be observed amongst other birds of prey and can also take place between adults and their young.

A food pass

Foot

There are many different forms of feet amongst birds, all adapted to carry out one of three main functions: perching, walking or wading and swimming. Passerine birds perch and all the toes are free and mobile, the hind toe being highly developed and opposable, to give a firm grip. The zygodactyl foot (two toes pointing forward, two back) of Woodpeckers (Picidae) provides even greater grip. In raptors, the toes are widely spread and have sharp, highly curved claws. The undersurface of the toes has bulbous and roughened pads to improve holding power when the bird

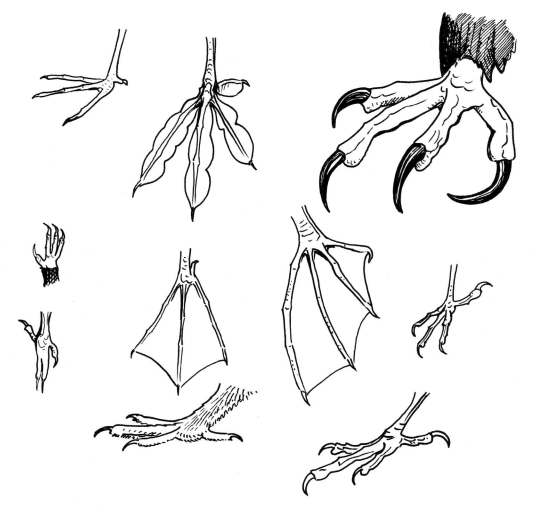

Forms of foot among birds: (left to right)
Lapwing, Coot, Eagle; Swift, Mallard,
Cormorant, Starling; Kingfisher, Grouse, Crow

is carrying prey. In the case of the Osprey (*Pandion haliaetus*), these pads have spines to grip slippery fish. Where walking or wading is the foot's major function, it tends to have less gripping power. The hind toe in many cases has become elevated and reduced in size, or even lost, as in the Kittiwake (*Rissa tridactyla*). In some wading birds the toes are partially or completely webbed, as for example in the Avocet (*Avosetta recurvirostra*). This aids walking over soft ground and also swimming when this becomes necessary. Rails (Rallidae spp) have developed long toes and claws to traverse the swampy and marshy areas in which they live. Another development is the feathered foot of the Ptarmigan (*Lagopus mutus*), which gives increased weight-bearing area for walking on snow, as well as extra insulation. For swimming birds, the foot has become a paddle, and many unrelated birds have developed in this way—notably Petrels (Procellariiformes), Gulls (Larinae), Auks (Alcidae), Ducks and Geese (Anatidae), with three toes connected by webs. The Pelecaniformes have all four toes webbed. In some birds the foot is only partially adapted in this way: the lobate variation, each toe carrying independent webs or lobes, is typical of the Coots (*Fulica* spp), Phalaropes (Phalaropodidae), and Grebes (Podicipitidae).

Coot, showing lobate foot

Fossil bird

The preserved remains of birds in a fossilised form are relatively rare due to their fragile skeletal structure. However around 1,500 species of fossilised birds have been found, half of which are of extinct species. The oldest known fossil is Archaeopteryx, which lived about 160 million years ago in the Upper Jurassic period.

No fossilised remains of any intermediate development from then until the Cretaceous period have been found, leaving a gap of 30 million years. By then birds were well established and represented by such species as Ichthyornis, a type of flying sea bird and Hesperornis, another sea bird perhaps similar to a Diver of today.

Fossils from the ensuing Tertiary period have included examples of the ancestors of present-day Herons, Flamingos, Vultures, Kingfishers and Rails.

See Archaeopteryx
Read: Swinton, W. G. *Fossil Birds*, British Museum (Natural History)

Fossorial

A term applied to the habit of digging or
  urrowing in the soil in order to prepare a

nesting hole, eg the Puffin (*Fratercula arctica*) and some Shearwaters.

Fowl

Term most often applied to the domestic fowl which originated from the Red Jungle Fowl of Asia, but also used for any members of the Galliformes, which include such game birds as Pheasants and Grouse, Guinea Fowls, Turkeys and some others. However the composite word 'wildfowl' refers to Ducks, Geese and Swans.

Francolin

A Partridge-like bird of Africa and Asia. The Black Francolin or Black Partridge (*Francolinus francolinus*), found from Turkey eastwards, and the Double-spurred Francolin (*Francolinus bicalcaratus*), found only in Morocco, are the two western palearctic representatives of this sub-family.

Frigatebird

Name of the species of Fregatidae (Pelecaniformes, sub-order Fregatae) in the plural general term for the family. Frigatebirds, or Man-of-War Birds, are inhabitants of tropical

111

and sub-tropical oceanic areas particularly where flying-fish are abundant. Frigatebirds tend to remain close to their breeding colonies and though they do wander some distance at sea the presence of several together has always been considered by sailors a sign that land is near. There are five species in this distinctive genus. The largest, the Magnificent Frigatebird (*Fregata magnificens*) has a wingspan of over 7ft. It has been recorded in British waters about half a dozen times.

Frigate Petrel (*Pelagodroma marina*)
A small Petrel with wholly white underparts. It has been likened to a huge long-legged fly.

Great Frigate Bird

It is an oceanic species breeding on the Salvage and Cape Verde Islands, other races occurring in the Tristan da Cunha group and in Australia and New Zealand islands. There are two records for Britain, one found dead, the other caught alive, both towards the end of the last century.

Fringillidae
A family of the Passeriformes, sub-order Oscines, consisting of three sub-families including the Fringillinae and Carduelinae (Finches), comprising such well-known birds

Frigatebird

as Chaffinch, Brambling, Bullfinch, etc.
See Finch

Frogmouth
Substantive name of the species Podargidae
(Caprimulgiformes, sub-order Caprimulgi).
A group of large Nightjars confined to the
oriental and Australasian regions (not New
Zealand). They have highly cryptic plumage
and some have a characteristic alarm posture,
'freezing' when perched and looking like a
broken branch of a tree. They have wide
gapes, with which they capture their prey—
beetles, scorpions, centipedes etc—mainly
taken from the ground or from branches,
and not in flight as Nightjars. They are active
after dusk and before dawn.
See Nightjar

Fulmar (*Fulmarus glacialis*)
A rather gull-like bird which, however,
belongs to the Petrel family, having the
external tube-like nostrils typical of this group.
It is a common bird round the coasts of
Britain, breeding wherever suitable cliff sites
are to be found. It has increased phenomenally
this century. At one time its stronghold was
the remote island of St Kilda, and before 1870

Fulmar: it will defend its young by spitting out
an oily evil-smelling liquid

Fulmar in flight

it bred nowhere else. Since then its expansion has continued with virtually every suitable site in Britain either colonised or prospected. In 1968-70 Operation Seafarer estimated that there were over 305,000 occupied sites in Britain and Ireland. One reason suggested for its increase is the availability of a greater food supply from fishing vessels gutting at sea.

Gadwall (*Anas strepera*)
Locally scarce, this Mallard-sized Duck with no startling plumage pattern (the female especially) is easily overlooked. It is not an abundant species anywhere in Britain, with no more than 250 pairs breeding in scattered localities, most of which are concentrated in East Anglia. In the winter immigration from the continent increases the population by 2,000 to 3,000 birds. A surface feeder like the Mallard, it prefers quiet lakes, marshy pools and other still waters, where it feeds on vegetable matter, chiefly seeds. The black-and-white speculum is a distinctive mark which is not always obvious at rest, but is conspicuous in flight.

Gaggle
Collective term for a number of Geese together on the ground (as opposed to 'skein' when the Geese are flying).
See Assembly

Gadwall

114

Galliformes

An order of mainly ground-feeding birds, often referred to as gallinaceous birds, the domestic fowl being a characteristic member. Sometimes called 'game birds', notably the Grouse and Pheasant families. The order comprises the following families:

Megapodes	Megapodiidae
Curassows	Cracidae
Grouse	Tetraonidae
Pheasants	Phasianidae
Guineafowl	Numididae
Turkeys	Meleagrididae
Hoatzin	Opisthocomidae

Gallinaceous

Resembling a domestic fowl (see above).

Gallinule

A name of several species of the genera Porphyrula and Porphyrio, having representatives in the New and Old Worlds, allied to the Rails and Crakes. Gallinule is also an alternative name for the Moorhen (*Gallinula chloropus*) in North America.

The N. American Purple Gallinule (*Porphyrula martinica*) has been recorded in Britain once, in 1958, on St Mary's, Isles of Scilly.

Game Bird

Sometimes used ornithologically to denote members of the Galliformes, but more appropriately applied only to certain species in that order, belonging mostly to the families Tetraonidae (Grouse) and Phasianidae (Pheasants). In certain parts of the world other families of the Galliformes are included, such as Meleagrididae (Turkeys) and Numididae (Guinea Fowl) particularly. The Bustards (Otididae) and certain 'waders' (Charadriidae), notably Snipe and Woodcock (Scolopacidae), are usually regarded as game birds although Ducks, Geese and Swans (Anatidae) are not. The term 'game' has a legal connotation in Britain and a game licence is required to shoot Partridge (*Perdix perdix*), Pheasant (*Phasianus colchicus*), Red Grouse (*Lagopus lagopus*), Ptarmigan (*Lagopus mutus*), and 'Black Game' or Black Grouse (*Lyrurus tetrix*). Woodcock (*Scolopax rusticola*) and Snipe (*Gallinago* spp) have a more limited status under the game laws. The need for special game laws to protect sporting rights originated from the fact that in English common law (not Scottish) wild animals in general

Hen Pheasant

were nobody's property until brought into possession by killing or capture. In the United States, game laws have had the object of protecting the birds rather than preserving enclosure rights.
Read: Fitzgerald, B. V., *British Game* (New Naturalist series), Collins, 1946.

Game Conservancy
An independent organisation financed by private subscription and formed in 1969 to undertake scientific research into the conservation of British game. Based at Fordingbridge, Hampshire, it publishes an annual report, bulletins, reports etc.

Gander
Male Goose.

Gannet
Name for some species of Sulidae (Pelecaniformes, sub-order Pelecani); commonly used in Britain for the single species encountered—the North Atlantic or Northern Gannet (*Sula bassana*). Another name for members of this family is 'Booby', generally applied to Gannets of tropical regions. The Gannet is a large white sea bird with narrow wings tipped with black. It is identifiable even at long range—especially when typical feeding behaviour is witnessed, the birds diving for fish from heights of 100ft (30m) or more. British nesting Gannets represent 20 per cent of the world's population of that species.
Read Nelson, B., *The Gannet*, Poyser, Berkhamsted, 1978
See Bass Rock; Booby; Grassholm

Garefowl
Alternative name for the extinct Great Auk (*Pinguinus impennis*).

Garganey (*Anas querquedula*)
A small surface-feeding Duck, slightly larger than Teal (*Anas crecca*). Summer visitor to Britain, breeding locally in very small numbers. The drake has a distinctive broad white band extending from the eye to the nape, and in flight pale blue forewing patches are visible.

Genus
Plural: genera. A taxonomic category, meaning a grouping of species. The definition given by Ernst Mayr, the famous American biologist, states that 'A genus is a systematic category including one species or a group of

species of presumably common phylogenetic origin which is separated from other similar units by a decided gap.' The category is a primary one in nomenclature, and it is obligatory that every species should be placed in a genus. If there is only one species, the genus is said to be 'monotypic; if there are two or more species, each is said to be 'congeneric', ie belonging to the same genus. The name of the genus constitutes the first word of the scientific name of each included species (or sub-species).
See Family

Gibraltar Point, Lincolnshire
Located 3 miles (5km) south of Skegness on the northern shore of the mouth of The Wash, this observatory originated back in 1948 when an agreement between the Lincolnshire Naturalists' Trust and Lindsey County Council to preserve the area as a nature reserve and use it for education and research paved the way for its establishment on a permanent basis. Excellent accommodation and laboratory space provide first-class opportunities to observe the migratory movements of birds and October particularly can produce such exciting species as Barred Warbler (*Sylvia nisoria*), and Red-breasted Flycatcher (*Ficedula parva*) and occasionally rarities like Pallas's Warbler (*Phylloscopus proregulus*) and Lesser Grey Shrike (*Lanius minor*).

Gizzard
The second part of a bird's stomach; it has strong muscular walls that break up food particles with grinding movements. Some birds swallow grit or small stones which collect in the gizzard to aid this action.
See Alimentary canal.

Glaucous
Literally, pale or translucent pale sea green, or with a pale bloom. The adult Glaucous Gull (*Larus hyperboreus*) is a pale grey-and-white bird with no black on the wing tips. Glaucous Gulls can vary markedly in size, some being as large as the Great Black-backed Gull (*Larus marinus*), others little larger than a Herring Gull (*Larus argentatus*). Young birds take three or four years to attain adult plumage, and in their first year they are a pale creamy-brown. An Arctic breeding species it is a regular winter visitor to Britain but a scarce one.

Gannet colony (opposite)

Glede (Gled or Glead)

Glaucous Gull

Glede (Gled or Glead)
Old name for Kite (*Milvus milvus*). Probably derived from its gliding flight.

Gloger's Rule
That in a given species, races in warm and humid areas are apt to be more heavily pigmented than those in cool, dry areas.

Goatsucker
An alternative general term, now mainly in American usage, for the Caprimulgidae (Nightjars). In Britain, formerly one of a number of local names for the Nightjar (*Caprimulgus europaeus*).

Godwit
Name for some long-legged, long-billed wading birds of the *Limosa* spp. In Britain these are the Black-tailed Godwit (*Limosa limosa*), which breeds in small numbers (around 50 pairs on the Ouse washes) and the Bar-tailed Godwit (*Limosa lapponica*), which

is a winter visitor with as many as 50,000 birds haunting suitable estuaries and other coastal areas.

Goldeneye (*Bucephala clangula*)
This diving Duck is mainly a winter visitor to Britain with large flocks to be found on estuaries around some coasts and smaller numbers at favoured inland waters. A small number breed in Scotland, encouraged by the provision of nesting boxes. The drake is a boldly patterned black-and-white bird with a large white spot near the base of the bill below and in front of the eye. It also has a

(above) Goldeneye (female at rear)

(below) Black-tailed Godwit

very obvious yellow eye—hence the name. However the Tufted Duck (*Aythya fuligula*) has a yellow eye, and this bird was also known locally at one time as the Goldeneye.

Goldcrest (*Regulus regulus*)
At only 3½in (90mm), it is Britain's smallest common bird. Present throughout the year, it likes coniferous woodlands, usually keeping to the higher branches with only its high-pitched 'zee-zee-zee' note to indicate its presence. At times it will feed low down, allowing a close approach, when the orange crest of the male or the lemon crest of the female are easily seen. However the 'crest' is usually merely a line of colour on the crown, and is never a true crest. In display the colourful crown feathers are spread out sideways.
See Firecrest

Goldfinch (*Carduelis carduelis*)
One of our most colourful finches, it is a seed eater particularly favouring thistles. Any patch of weeds will attract a 'charm' of these delightful birds. A resident, generally distributed throughout Britain and Ireland, with a total breeding population of around 30,000 birds.

Some local names give an indication of its coloration eg Gold Linnet, Redcap and Seven-coloured Linnet.

Goldcrest—restless and agile

The Goldfinch is at once identified by its red, white and black head, wings boldly marked with black and yellow, black-and-white tail and white rump

Gonad

Gonad
General term for the primary sex organs, testes (paired) in the male and ovary (single) in the female.

Gonys
The prominent ridge formed by the fusion of two halves of the lower jaw towards the tip, especially marked in the Gulls (*Larus* spp).

Gonys

Goosander (*Mergus merganser*)
Largest of the sawbilled diving Ducks. Basically a fresh-water bird, haunting rivers, lakes and lochs in the breeding season. Nesting mainly in Scotland and N England, with a population of around 2,000 pairs, it has also bred in Wales and N Ireland in recent years. Outside the breeding season it is found on large estuaries, lakes, rivers and reservoirs. Some migrants from Scandinavia swell the resident population to around 5,000 pairs. In North America this bird is called the Common Merganser.

Goose
Name of many species of Anatidae. Large semi-aquatic birds, their appearance is well known if only from domesticated birds or

Brent Geese

Goshawk (female)

from visits to wildfowl collections such as those maintained by the Wildfowl Trust.

Wild Geese in Britain are mainly winter visitors. These are generally referred to as 'Grey Geese' or 'Black Geese.' The Grey Geese include the Greylag (*Anser anser*)—ancestor of our domestic Goose and our only native breeding Goose—the White-fronted Goose (*Anser albifrons*) and the Pink-footed Goose (*Anser brachyrhynchus*), the three commonest species of this group. The Bean Goose (*Anser fabalis*) occurs in small numbers, while the Lesser White-fronted Goose (*Anser erythropus*) is only rarely noted. The Black Geese are represented by the Barnacle Goose (*Branta leucopsis*) and the Brent Goose (*Branta bernicla*), of which there are two forms—Light-bellied and Dark-bellied. The Canada Goose (*Branta canadensis*), introduced into Britain in the 18th century, is now a naturalised breeding species and is also included with the 'Black Geese', as is the very rare Red-breasted Goose (*Branta ruficollis*), a vagrant from Siberia.

Read Ogilvie, M. A., *Wild Geese*, Poyser, Berkhamsted, 1978

Gorget
A band of colour in some plumage patterns, on the throat or upper breast.

Goshawk (*Accipiter gentilis*)
A large broad-winged bird of prey, like a very big Sparrowhawk (*Accipiter nisus*); much favoured by falconers. The present limited British breeding population almost certainly stems from escaped and introduced birds. It is a much commoner species on the continent, where the larger areas of dense continuous woodland which it favours are to be found. There are also related birds of prey known as the Chanting Goshawks (*Melierax* spp), and the Gabar Goshawk (*Micronisus gabar*), which are African species.

Gould, John (1804-87)
A scientist and artist, he might be described as Britain's Audubon, as his output was certainly as great as that of the famous American artist; in fact no less than eighteen superb great folio works of paintings of birds and animals,

some in as many as seven volumes, are attributed to the Gould stable. Altogether he produced 2,999 different folio pictures, lithographed and coloured by hand. Some of the more popular works, such as *Birds of Great Britain*, were reproduced 500 times. However Gould did not create the bulk of his great plates on his own, having a team which included artists notable in their own right, such as Edward Lear, W. Hart, H. C. Richter and Joseph Wolf. As an artist Gould was inferior to some of those he employed, being more of an entrepreneur and promoter of his works; nevertheless it is his name that appears on these splendid examples of nineteenth-century 'bird art'.

Grassholm, Dyfed

Smallest of the famous Pembrokeshire islands, it lies 10 miles (16km) west of the mainland and covers some 22 acres (9Ha). An RSPB reserve, it has the second largest colony of Gannets in Britain (15,000-plus pairs). Additionally there are breeding Guillemots, Razorbills and Kittiwakes. Though landing can be difficult and infrequent it is one of the most accessible gannetries. Any visits must be made by arrangement with the RSPB Welsh Office in Newtown.

Great Auk (*Pinguinus impennis*)

The Great Auk was possibly never as abundant as the Passenger Pigeon, but it suffered a similar fate in that the hand of man contributed to its reduction in numbers and finally to its extinction, for by the year 1844 the Great Auk was no more. Largest of the Auks —about 30in (760mm) long—this flightless sea bird was able to swim underwater for considerable distances and looked very much like a giant Razorbill. Its usual breeding sites were the rocky islands of the North Atlantic Ocean. It was particularly common in the years prior to its extinction in the area of Newfoundland. However, finds of bones from other areas of Europe, notably Scandinavia, suggest a more extensive breeding range in earlier times, possibly including the Faeroes, St Kilda, the Outer Hebrides and the Orkney Islands. A book published in 1803 referred to the Great Auk as nearly extinct then and says "Examples are so rare in collections that a good specimen is now worth fifty guineas and even an egg will fetch from £20 to £30.' This trade in specimens of birds and eggs undoubtedly contributed to the passing of a species that was already heavily preyed upon by man.

See Garefowl; Passenger Pigeon

Read Eckert, A. *The Last Great Auk*, Collins, 1963.

Grebe

Name of all species of Podicipitidae (Podicipediformes); in the plural, general term for the family. Highly adapted for diving, they lead an almost exclusively aquatic life. Their lobed and partially webbed toes facilitate propulsion through the water and the legs are positioned at the very rear of the body. Grebes build floating nests and cover their eggs when leaving the nest. Their display includes weird head-shaking ceremonies and weed-exchanges. Another strange aspect of this group's behaviour is the feeding of feathers to the young.

In Britain, four species of Grebe breed. Perhaps the best-known is the Little Grebe (*Tachybaptus ruficollis*) or Dabchick, the smallest member of the family at 10in

Great Auk

A typical Grebe

Great Crested Grebe, a feature of many inland waters

(267mm). Even the tiniest pond will satisfy this bird's requirements. The Great Crested Grebe (*Podiceps cristatus*) is also well known, certainly in central and southern England, where the majority of the breeding population of 5,000 pairs is found. The Slavonian or Horned Grebe (*Podiceps auritus*) and Black-necked Grebe (*Podiceps nigricollis*) nest in small numbers locally in Scotland, but are more widely known as winter visitors to other parts of Britain. The Red-necked Grebe (*Podiceps grisegena*) is a somewhat scarcer winter visitor, with small numbers noted annually.

The Pied-billed Grebe (*Podilymbus podiceps*) is a North American species first recorded in Britain in 1963. There have been only half-a-dozen occurrences of this bird since that date.

Pied-billed Grebe

123

Slavonian Grebe

Greenfinch (*Carduelis chloris*)

A common member of the Finch family and very much a garden bird where peanuts are provided. In recent years the species has developed a fondness for this food and an ability to obtain it, clinging to nut-bags or other containers with the agility of Titmice. Total population of Britain and Ireland probably upwards of 2 million.

Greenshank (*Tringa nebularia*)

A medium-sized wading bird resident in small numbers (confined to NE Scotland and the Hebrides), but mainly known as a passage migrant in spring and autumn, when its musical triple 'tchu-tchu-tchu' call can be heard around lakes and reservoirs and on salt marshes and estuaries.

Read Thompson, D. and M., *Greenshanks*, Poyser, 1979

Greyhen

Name of the hen Black Grouse (*Lyrurus tetrix*).

Grey Geese

Those species of wild geese that are predominantly grey in colour are collectively referred to in this manner.

See Goose

Greylag

Usual shortened name of the Greylag Goose

(*Anser anser*). The largest and heaviest of the Geese, this species is the ancestor of the familiar farmyard bird. The term 'lag' is a contraction of 'laggard', for this is the species of Goose which stayed behind to breed when others migrated. Most breeding Greylags in Britain are feral, the truly wild population having been almost eliminated over the last 200 years. Probably only about a couple of hundred wild pairs now nest, in Scotland. About 600-800 pairs of feral birds are scattered throughout the UK with concentrations in County Down, Norfolk, Kent and the Lake District. In the winter the resident population is joined by 65,000 birds from Iceland.

Griffon

A Vulture (*Gyps fulvus*), this species is a vagrant to Britain. In Europe it breeds in parts of Spain, Sardinia, Sicily, Greece and Yugoslavia.

Grosbeak

The name of some species of Finch. There are two Grosbeaks which breed in Europe— the Scarlet Grosbeak (*Carpodacus erythrinus*), the smaller of the two, about the size of a sparrow, and the Pine Grosbeak (*Pinicola enucleator*). In both species the male is predominantly crimson, the female drab

Greylag Goose—an impressive sight when flying to and from the feeding grounds

Evening Grosbeak

brown in the case of the Scarlet Grosbeak and greenish in the Pine Grosbeak. Both species are vagrants to Britain. The Evening Grosbeak of North America belongs to a different genus.

Grouse

Name of many species of Tetraonidae, in the plural, general term for the family. There are 18 species, mainly ground-dwelling though some are partly arboreal in habit. The family is circumpolar and confined to the temperate zones of the northern hemisphere. In Britain the best-known is the Red Grouse (*Lagopus lagopus*), once considered the most British of birds, not occurring anywhere else in the world. However, recent thinking by taxonomists has placed the Red Grouse with the Willow Grouse. Whether exclusive or not, the Red Grouse still features large on the British

sporting calendar when the 'Glorious Twelfth' (12 August) signals the opening of the shooting season.

Characteristic of 'game birds', the Red Grouse is stout and short-winged, and when flushed it rises with whirring wings, usually calling loudly. Its rapid wing beats, followed by long glides on down-curved wings, are distinctive and when viewed from below the striking white underwing pattern contrasting with the dark body is diagnostic. The rufous-brown plumage looks very dark at a distance and only at close quarters can the white feathered legs and the red wattle over the eye be seen. The Ptarmigan (*Lagopus mutus*) is a

Red Grouse

125

Red Grouse—the adults feed mainly on young
heather shoots

Guillemots—bridled form on right

mountain-haunting Grouse, the male's plumage turning completely white in the winter to match his snow-covered habitat. The Black Grouse (*Lyrurus tetrix*) and the Capercaillie (*Tetrao urogallus*) are other British breeding game birds.
See Black Grouse; Capercaillie

Guano

The excrement of fish-eating sea birds, found especially on islands off the sea coasts of Peru, where such birds as the Peruvian Cormorant (*Phalacrocorax bougainvillii*), the Peruvian Booby (*Sula variegata*) and the Brown Pelican (*Pelecanus occidentalis thagus*) breed. Their accumulated droppings form valuable organic fertiliser which has been commercially exploited since the mid-19th century—and until comparatively recently with little thought for the producer, the bird. Nowadays the various bird islands are treated as sanctuaries and the annual production of guano is gathered like a crop. There are also other 'managed' guano islands in South Africa where the Cape Cormorant (*Phalacrocorax capensis*), the Cape Gannet (*Sula capensis*) and the Jackass Penguin (*Spheniscus demersus*) are the prime producers.

Guillemot (*Uria aalge*)

One of our commonest sea birds superficially resembling another member of the Auk family, the Razorbill (*Alca torda*), but having a slender pointed bill and thinner neck; and at close quarters its ostensibly black-and-white plumage is seen to be brown on the upper parts. There is also a 'bridled' form which has a white line round the eye and a white line running back from it over the sides of the head. This variety comprises about 2 per cent of the population in S and SW England, increasing northwards to about 25 per cent in the Shetlands. Total British and Irish population probably around 500,000 pairs, though the species has suffered considerably with other sea birds in recent years from oil spillages and other pollution of the sea and may well have declined since this figure was determined in 1969-70 by Operation Seafarer.
See Auk; Bridled; Razorbill

Guineafowl

The Guinea-fowl of our poultry yards is descended from the Helmeted Guineafowl (*Numida meleagris*) of Africa. There are seven other species of Guineafowl in the family Numididae and all these gallinaceous birds are restricted to that continent, Madagascar, the Comoro Islands and a small part of Arabia. In the wild state they are well known as sporting birds.

Gular

Pertaining to the throat

Gular pouch

Gull

Name of nearly all the species of the subfamily Larinae of the Laridae (Charadriiformes, sub-order Lari). In the plural, general term for the family.

Gulls are the most familiar of sea birds and popularly known as 'seagulls', though in truth they are more coastal than oceanic, with many species frequenting inland waters and marshes often far from the sea. The plumage is characteristically white with pale grey or darker colour on the back and wings. (In a few species the general appearance is dark, such as the Lava Gull (*Larus fulginosus*) of the Galapagos Islands.) Many have a dark hood or mask in the breeding season eg the Little Gull (*Larus minutus*) and Black-headed Gull (*Larus ridibundus*) and the webbed feet, legs and bill are bright red or yellow. The sexes are alike in plumage but immature birds are darker, often largely mottled brown. Full adult plumage is not attained for several years in the case of the larger Gulls. Mainly gregarious, they nest in large colonies. Being omnivorous they are able to exploit many sources of food.

In general the North Atlantic population of Gulls as a whole has increased dramatically in recent years, probably due mainly to their

Common Gull (top left)
Herring Gull (top right)
Great Black-backed Gull (above left)
Lesser Black-backed Gull (above right)
Black-headed Gull (right)
These Gulls breed round British coasts, as does
the Kittiwake (see next page)

(opposite) Herring Gulls (at Lerwick Harbour,
Shetland)

exploitation of the abundance of edible refuse provided by rubbish dumps and at fishing ports and harbours. Additionally the decreased interference by man, especially in the collection of eggs for food, has helped the increase of the 43 species of gull distributed throughout the world. The following breed in Britain:

Black-headed Gull (*Larus ridibundus*), present all the year and with the widest inland breeding distribution. Total British and Irish population between 150,000 and 300,000 pairs.

Common Gull (*Larus canus*), present throughout the year, and a common bird in Scotland, breeding widely northwards from the Solway. Total British and Irish population around 500,000 pairs.

Lesser Black-backed Gull (*Larus fuscus*): there are two distinct races of this bird. The British race (*Larus fuscus graellsii*) has a slate-grey back, the Scandinavian race (*Larus f. fuscus*), a passage migrant, has a blackish back.

Kittiwake on the Farne Islands, Northumberland

The British race are mainly summer visitors with the major proportion of the breeding population found in a relatively few areas. Walney Island (Lancashire) has one-third of the total population which was put at 47,000 pairs by the 1969-70 Operation Seafarer count but is certainly more than this now.

The Herring Gull (*Larus argentatus*) is present throughout the year, breeding round most of coastal Britain. It is estimated to be the second most numerous gull (and is still increasing). The British and Irish population was put at 300,000 pairs in 1970.

The Great Black-backed Gull (*Larus marinus*), largest and most voracious of the gulls, is present throughout the year. As a breeding bird it is found almost all along the west coast from the Shetlands to Cornwall. In Ireland it occurs predominantly around west and southern coasts. Total population was put at 22,000 birds in 1970.

The Kittiwake (*Rissa tridactyla*) breeds round most of Britain where suitable cliff nest sites occur. It is, however, mainly concentrated in the Orkneys and the Shetlands. Operation Seafarer found an estimated total of 470,000 pairs nesting in Britain and Ireland.

The Little Gull (*Larus minutus*) is mainly a passage migrant but has nested, so has the Mediterranean Gull (*Larus melanocephalus*), a much scarcer visitor. The Glaucous Gull (*Larus hyperboreus*) and Iceland Gull (*Larus glaucoides*) are regular winter visitors from the Arctic, and Sabine's Gull (*Larus sabini*) is less frequently noted.

Gyrfalcon (*Falco rusticolus*)

Largest of the falcons, it inhabits Arctic America and, in Europe, Iceland and Northern Norway. It is normally grey and white but one of its colour forms is almost pure white with a few black spots. A vagrant to Britain, it has been noted less than 50 times in the last 20 years.

Read Cerely, S., *The Gyr Falcon Adventure*, Collins, 1955

Gyrfalcon

Gnatcatcher

Substantive name of some species of the sub-family Polioptilinae of the Muscicapidae (Passiformes, sub-order Oscines). A group of tiny birds with long tails which they switch about continually. Usually found near marshes or swamps. There are 13 species (3 of which are called gnatwrens). The Blue-grey Gnatcatcher (*Polioptila caerulea*) is best known, being widely distributed in the United States of America.

Gobbling Ground

Name for the display area used by the Lesser Prairie Chicken (*Tympanuchus pallidicinctus*) of North America.

See Lek

Habitat

The environment in which a bird (or other organism) lives. Certain habitats, such as marshes, provide life support for many species of birds, while others support only a few species which have evolved to exist in such demanding places as deserts or mountain tops. Some birds change their habitat according to the season (and food supply), breeding in one habitat and wintering in another; eg many species of wading birds nest on the Arctic tundra but spend the winter on estuaries and mudflats around our coasts.

Birds cannot exist without a suitable environment and the destruction of any specialised habitat such as a marsh or forest means the loss of the birds which found life support within it. The preservation, and in many cases management, of habitats is therefore of the utmost importance in the conservation of birds and other wildlife.

The environment is composed of a multiplicity of components, each of which conforms to ecological principles that can be scientifically described, though complete standardisation of terminology may not be attainable; it is, however, possible to go some way towards this goal by using the definitions described in the *Handbook of the Birds of Europe, the Middle East and North Africa*, Volume I, *Habitat*, Glossary pp. 6-10.

Habitat preference

Birds will be found (in normal circumstances) in the habitat of their choice, ie the one that suits the means of existence they have evolved, where they can easily obtain food and find suitable nesting conditions. At certain times, eg on migration, habitat preference leads the bird to choose the setting that most nearly approximates to its usual habitat or provides sufficient life support. In such circumstances some species may be found in places that seem to be unusual settings for them when compared with their normal habitat.

Hack

Term used in falconry for an untrained bird. Also, 'hacking back' is the process of teaching a bird of prey taken from the wild before it is old enough to fend for itself to return to the wild and to catch its prey.

Hackle
The long slender feathers on the neck of a bird found especially on various game birds.

Halcyon
Name for the Kingfisher (*Alcedo otthis*), which in fable is the bird that raised its young on a nest floating on the sea, supposedly calming the waves to do so. Hence 'halcyon days' of calm and quiet.

Hallux
The first digit of the foot (ie the great toe). In most orders of birds this is the only toe to be directed backwards (ie the hind toe). It is very variable in size and totally absent in some species, eg the Kittiwake (*Rissa tridactylus*).

Hammerhead (*Scopus umbretta*)
Alternatively the Hamerkop, Hammer-headed Stork or Anvil-head; the name derives from the conspicuous long backward-pointing crest of this bird, the single species of the Scopidae (Ciconiiformes, sub-order Ciconiae) which is found throughout most of tropical Africa.

Hamulus
A hooked barbicel.
See Feather

Handbook
A volume or series of volumes which gives as complete a picture as possible of its defined subject matter, eg the birds of a certain area, or a particular facet of ornithology. *The Handbook of British Birds* comprises five volumes covering all British breeding birds and all accepted records at time of publication (1938-41). A comprehensive work, it deals in detail with 'Habitat', 'Field Characters' and 'General Habits', 'Display and Posturing', 'Breeding', 'Food and Distribution' (in Britain and abroad); it also includes a complete description of each bird in most of its plumages. Coloured plates by artists such as J. G. Keulemans, Gronvold, Lodge and others illustrate every species. Affectionately known as 'The Handbook', it has served ornithologists and birdwatchers for over 40 years and is still regarded by many as the finest complete work on British birds ever produced. Published by H. F. & G. Witherby Ltd, it was compiled by H. F. Witherby, F. C. R. Jourdain, Norman F. Ticehurst and Bernard W. Tucker. It has been reprinted seven times and is still in demand (despite the availability of more up-to-date productions),

with complete sets in virtually any condition commanding a high price. Though still an invaluable source of information it is now more sought as a 'collector's piece' as its rarity value increases, particularly that of the earlier editions.

Harem
A group of several females associated with one male and all laying eggs in one nest—a fairly uncommon type of polygamy among birds. A good example is provided by the Ostrich (*Struthio camelus*), the male bird usually having several females in his harem.
See Ostrich

Harlequin
More properly the Harlequin Duck (*Histrionicus histrionicus*). A bird of rough water though not a 'Torrent Duck'. There is a small breeding population of this holarctic species in Iceland. An accidental visitor to Britain, it has been recorded about 7 times.

Harrier
A type of bird of prey, the name for *Circus* spp. In the plural, general term for the sub-family Circinae of the Accipitridae (Falconiformes, sub-order Falcones). All harriers are slender, long-winged, long-tailed birds with

Female Hen Harrier

Montagu's Harrier

long legs and rather owlish faces. When hunting they fly low over the ground, systematically quartering in a manner characteristic of the group. They are birds of open country and feed mainly on small rodents and birds. In Britain the most frequently occurring is the Hen Harrier (*Circus cyaneus*), which in recent years has increased as a breeding bird, spreading from its stronghold in the Orkneys to other areas of Scotland and south into northern England and Wales. The present population is probably around 600 pairs. The Montagu's Harrier (*Circus pygargus*) is a scarce breeding bird and occasional passage migrant; and a few pairs of the reed-haunting Marsh Harrier (*Circus aeruginosus*) nest each year at a few localities in East Anglia.
Read Watson, D., *The Hen Harrier*, Poyser, 1977

Harris's Hawk

Harris, Edward (1799-1863)

American benefactor of Audubon, who named Harris's Hawk (*Parabutei univinctus*) after him. A black buzzard-type bird with a white rump and white band at the tip of its tail, it is found in the south-west of the USA and in parts of South America.

Hastings Rarities

During the first two decades of this century when the collecting of birds' eggs and bird specimens was still a passion among the well-to-do, considerable traffic in 'obtained' specimens of rare birds took place. Though undoubtedly carried on for commercial gain, this business, and the possession of a fine collection of locally 'taken' birds, carried considerable social prestige.

That rare and unusual birds do occur in various places now and then is of course well known and particularly in recent times the ever-increasing army of experienced bird-watchers greatly adds to the annual list of rarities observed in Britain. But not even today has any one area ever matched the remarkable total of unusual birds and extreme rarities that were 'obtained' in the Hastings district over a period from 1892 to 1930. The most strategically placed and constantly manned observatory has yet to equal, let alone surpass, the volume of 'Hastings rarities'. During the years 1903 to 1916, 49 species and vagrant races were added to the British list; of these, 32 originated from the Hastings area. Many more second, third, fourth etc, occurrences of 'obtained', 'shot' or 'taken' specimens found their way on to the market and into the record books. This plethora of rarities from such a relatively small area, and often in strange and vague circumstances, led some ornithologists to be suspicious of their origins, and investigations were made. That deception was taking place was fairly evident, and it was finally brought under control about 1930. However the manner and the details of the deception remain obscure even today. As a consequence of the investigation, which was finally wrapped up in 1962, a certain number of species which were on the British list on the strength of their occurrence in the Hastings area were deleted from it.

A detailed statistical investigation was also made of certain aspects of the many rare birds recorded in East Sussex and West Kent in the era 1894-1924, using the other areas in Kent and Sussex and a later era (1925-54) for comparison. If further evidence was needed, this again indicated the unlikeliness of so many rare birds ever ocurring in the Hastings area in the period of time in question. An entire issue of the magazine *British Birds* (Vol 55, No 8, August 1962) was devoted to this matter, and listed all the species of birds involved.

Hatching

The emergence of the developed chick from the egg after incubation. The term is applied to both egg and young, ie the eggs hatch, the young are hatched or hatch out.

Hawk

A diurnal bird of prey. The substantive name or part-name of many members of the Accipitridae (Falconiformes, sub-order Falcones). In American usage, the name applied to some species that in Britain are given a special name, eg Buzzard, Harrier, etc. The most obvious family characteristics are the decurved and pointed beak and the powerful gripping feet with strong talons. However size can vary considerably, from some minute Sparrowhawks to huge and powerful Eagles. In almost all birds of prey, however, the female of the species is larger than the male and often duller in colour.

In Britain the best-known 'Hawk' is the Sparrowhawk (*Accipiter nisus*), though the much more abundant Kestrel (*Falco tinnunculus*) is often mistakenly called 'Sparrowhawk'. Their mode of hunting is completely different, however, the Sparrowhawk never hovering in the characteristic manner of the Kestrel. The once very common and widespread Sparrowhawk is only now recovering from a population crash in the 1960s brought about by poisoning, originating from toxic seed-dressings: the birds accumulated lethal doses of organo-chlorine compounds ingested by the insectivorous and seed-eating birds on which they preyed, at the end of the 'food chain'. Sparrowhawks are now returning to areas from which they have long been absent. The total British and Irish population now stands at about 25,000 pairs.
See Falconiformes; Food Chain

Hawking

Synonymous with falconry. Also often used to describe the behaviour of a bird of prey of any kind flying in search or pursuit of prey.

Hawk Mountain

A particular spot on the Kittatinny Ridge near Drehersville, Pennsylvania, USA, where vast numbers of Hawks from all over New England and north of the St Lawrence in Canada converge during their autumn migration. Many birdwatchers gather at 'Hawk Mountain' each year to observe this annual spectacular.

Hawk Trust

A charitable trust concerned with the conservation of birds of prey, with breeding aviaries at Shrewsbury. The grounds are not open to the public.

Heath Fowl

Antique term (in British game laws) for Black Grouse (*Lyrurus tetrix*).

Heat Regulation

The process by which the correct body temperature is maintained; also called thermoregulation. Birds belong to the group of animals called 'homiothermal' (or warmblooded). The difference between these and 'poikilothermal' (cold-blooded) animals is that they are able to maintain a body temperature by internal physiological mechanisms although the temperature of the limbs is variable. Cold-blooded animals can regulate their body temperature only by suitable behaviour, eg basking in the sun. The body temperature of all species of birds is about 106°F when inactive, but this can exceed 110°F during periods of intense activity. Most birds rely on their feathers for conservation of heat, but in some birds such as Penguins (Spheniscidae), marine Ducks (Anatidae) and Petrels (Procellariiformes), subcutaneous fat is also important. Birds, unlike most mammals, do not have sweat glands and in order to cool themselves when necessary they dissipate heat by evaporation of body water through the respiratory passages by means of rapid panting. The rate can reach as much as 300 respirations per minute in domestic hens.

Hedge Sparrow

Alternative name and misnomer for Dunnock (*Prunella modularis*).

Heligoland Trap

So called as it was originally designed and built on the island of Heligoland when the

The Buzzard, one of our best-known 'Hawks'

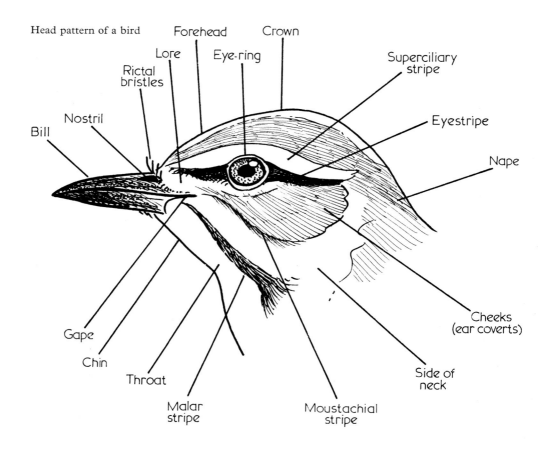

Head pattern of a bird

Rictal bristles

Forehead   Crown

Lore   Eye-ring   Superciliary stripe

Nostril   Eyestripe

Bill   Nape

Gape

Chin   Cheeks (ear coverts)

Throat   Side of neck

Malar stripe   Moustachial stripe

(below) Double Heligoland trap at Dyke on Fair Isle

observatory was first established there in 1909. This means of catching birds for ringing is basically a funnel of wire netting narrowing down to a catching box (see photograph). The trap is often sited in a gulley or other such natural feature which permits birds to be 'driven' towards the entrance of the trap. A plentiful growth of cover is especially advantageous and the provision of some open water inside the mouth of the trap also encourages birds to the area. A number of these permanent structures have been built and operated over a number of years at various observatories in Britain, though the advent of mist nets has possibly reduced the need for Heligoland traps, especially as they require constant repair and attention.
See Heligoland; Mist Net; Ringing; Traps

Hemipode

Member of the family Turnicidae, also called Button Quails. Small, Partridge-like birds, the 15 species of Hemipodes are found in Southern Europe, Asia, Africa and Australia. The Andulasian Hemipode (*Turnix sylvatica*) breeds locally in S and NE Spain and S Portugal.

Hen

A female bird; the female of the domestic fowl. A special term applies to females of some species, eg Pen (Swan), Greyhen (Black Grouse), Reeve (Ruff).

Hepatic

Liver-coloured, dark brownish-red, as the so-called hepatic phase of some adult Cuckoos (*Cuculus canorus*). This is an example of erythrism (reddishness), a not infrequently occuring colour abnormality in some species of birds.
See Erythrism

Hern, Hernshaw

Obsolete names in Britain for the Heron (*Ardea cinerea*), the latter variously spelt 'handsaw' by Shakespeare.

Heron

Name for most species of the Ardeinae, a subfamily of the Ardeidae (Ciconiiformes, suborder Ardeae). Herons are birds of moderate to large size, typically with long legs, long neck and long bill, adapted for wading. Most are found in the vicinity of water, usually rivers and lakes, swamps and marshes, but occasionally in sheltered bays of the sea. They eat mostly fish and other forms of aquatic life. Herons are mainly gregarious in the breeding season and most nest in colonies. A truly cosmopolitan group, Herons are represented in all continents. The majority

The female Black Grouse is commonly known as the Greyhen; the plumage is a strongly marked reddish brown, though less ruddy than that of the Red Grouse

of the world's 50 species are tropical or sub-tropical, and only two breed in Britain, the familiar Common or Grey Heron (*Ardea cinerea*) and the Bittern (*Botaurus stellaris*). The Grey Heron population fluctuates markedly as it suffers considerably in severe winters. Since counts were first made in 1928, the population has been recorded as being as low as 2,500 pairs, though the present number is probably around 7,000 pairs. Most Heronries are at traditional sites used year after year. In England and Ireland these are invariably in trees, but in Scotland they are often in low bushes or on cliff tops. The Bittern was once more widespread; it is now a scarce breeding species in Britain, mainly confined to a few areas of East Anglia.

Some rare Herons which occur in Britain on migration from southern Europe are the Night Heron (*Nycticorax nycticorax*) and Squacco Heron (*Ardeola ralloides*).
Read Elliott, H. F. I., and Hancock, J. *Herons, the World*, London Editions, 1978

Hesses' Rule
Birds which live in cooler parts of the range of the species lay more eggs per clutch than the races in the warmer part of the range.

Heteroic
Term used by Swynnerton (1918) to denote birds laying two or more distinct types of egg.

Hide
A construction designed to allow a number of people to observe birds (or other wildlife)

without disturbing them. These observation hides can be quite sophisticated—double-glazed and heated (as at the Wildfowl Trust's reserves on the Ouse Washes)—or the simplest of temporary concealments. One-man portable hides, usually of some strong material supported by poles, have long been used by bird and wildlife photographers. These are set up at a nest site or feeding place and removed when the photography has been completed. The process of erecting a suitable hide without disturbing the birds can be a lengthy one and requires particular care and restraint from the photographer.

Hill
A special term for the display ground (or lek) of the Ruff (*Philomachus pugnax*).
See Lek

Hirundines
Members of the Hirundinidae family, collective term for Swallows and Martins.

Hoatzin (*Opisthocomus hoazin*)
Sole member of the Opisthocomidae (Galliformes, sub-order Opisthocomi). A strange bird inhabiting the jungles of the Amazon

(opposite) Hide on the Ladywalk Wildfowl Nature Reserve (erected by the CEGB)

Typical hide

The Hobby will take over old nests, most often of the Carrion Crow

basin. Slenderly built, it somewhat resembles the Chachalacas (Cracidae). The head is remarkably small and bears a long, erect, bristly crest, which together with the long thin neck gives it the appearance of a Peacock when observed from the front. Though the wings are large in relation to the body, they are weak and are used more to steady the bird as it 'climbs' about amongst the branches than for flying. The young Hoatzin even has large claws on the first and second digits of its wings (recalling the wing structure of *Archaeopteryx*) to assist gripping and climb-ing; however these are lost on reaching maturity. The birds feed mainly on marshy plant foods and occasionally eat small fish and crabs.

Hobby (*Falco subbuteo*)
The most graceful and agile of British Falcons, it is capable of capturing Swallows and Martins on the wing, but it also feeds on large flying insects such as dragonflies. A summer visitor, it is a relatively scarce bird with probably only 100 pairs or so, breeding mainly in Southern England.
See Falconiformes

Holarctic
The palearctic and nearctic regions combined.
See Nearctic Region; Palearctic Region

Holme Bird Observatory
Established in September 1962, the observatory is attractively situated right on the coast with dunes and a shelter belt of fir trees, it enjoys views across freshwater marshes towards Holme-next-the-Sea which lies along the A149 just a couple of miles north of

Hobby chasing Swallow

Hunstanton, where the coast turns southwards into the Wash. Recognised by the British Trust for Ornithology in 1970, the observatory has a full-time warden and is manned daily from the middle of March until the middle of November. Ringing is strictly controlled, and unlike at most other observatories no visitors take part. The location of the observatory ensures the regular occurrence of interesting species and its tally of rarities (including, Pallas's Warbler, Collared Flycatcher, etc), is as impressive as that of nearby Blakeney Point or Cley. The reed-fringed area of water behind the dunes has two observation hides and 'Broadwater' as it is called frequently attracts aquatic species of note. Day permits are obtainable.
See Norfolk Ornithologists' Association

Homing Pigeon

A domestic Pigeon (*Columba livia* var) used for 'homing', particularly in the sport of Pigeon racing. Has been used to convey messages (hence 'Carrier Pigeon') since the days of the ancient Egyptians. Used quite widely during World War II, its role as a messenger is now probably defunct.

Homoiothermal

Warm-blooded.
See Heat Regulations; Poikilothermal

Honey Buzzard (*Pernis apivorus*)

Though similar in size to the Common Buzzard it is a slimmer-looking bird with slightly longer wings, longer tail and small head. Highly migratory, it frequently covers 6,000 to 7,000 miles when travelling to or from its winter quarters in Africa. It often migrates in large numbers, and many can be seen on the move at such places as Falsterbo in South Sweden or the Bosphorus and Gibraltar, particularly in the autumn. A scarce breeding bird in Britain, but a few pairs breed in Southern England each year. Its main diet consists of the larvae of wasps and bees.

Yellow-tufted Honeyeater (see next page)

Honeycreeper

Substantive name for some species of Thraupinae, a sub-family of the Emberizidae (Passeriformes, sub-order Oscines). Alternatively named 'Sugarbirds', particularly by aviculturists, most Honeycreepers suck nectar from flowers in the usual way by inserting the bill into the corolla opening, from a perched position. Some, however, pierce a hole in the side of the corolla tube, and have a bill adapted for the purpose: not surprisingly these are called Flower-piercers. The species are distributed throughout the West Indies, Central and South America.

Honeycreeper is also the substantive name for some species of Drepanididae (Passeriformes, sub-order Oscines), usually known as Hawaiian Honeycreepers. There is great diversity of form of bill and colour among this group of nectar-feeding birds, which are confined to the Hawaiian islands.

Honeyeater

Substantive name of many species of Meliphagidae (Passiformes, sub-order Oscines). A group of arboreal, mainly nectar-eating and fruit-eating birds of Australasia (with one representative in Africa).

Honeyguide

Substantive name of the species of Indicatoridae (Piciformes, sub-order Galbulae). Small dull-coloured forest birds of Africa and Asia, they earned their name from their habit of leading animals and men to bees' nests (though of the 14 species only 2 are definitely known to behave in this way). When the nest is opened up by the larger animal, the Honeyguide eats the wax. All Honeyguides are parasitic in their breeding habits.

Hood

1 An area of distinctive colour in some plumage patterns covering a large part of the head, as in the Black-headed Gull (*Larus ridibundus*) and Hooded Merganser (*Mergus cucullatus*)
2 In falconry, a small leather cap fitted over the head of a Hawk to keep it subdued.

Hoopoe (*Upupa epops*)

Sole species of the Old World family Upupidae (Coraciiformes, sub-order Coracii). A strikingly beautiful and unmistakable bird, it has a long curved bill, a black-tipped erectile crest (which is usually depressed) and pinkish-brown body plumage. The black-and-white

Hood

R.A.H.

Hoopoe—occasionally seen in Britain

bars on the wings form a distinctive pattern, especially when seen from the back or when the bird flies, its broad, rounded wings having a lazy, undulating 'open-and-shut' action. The name is derived from its low, far-carrying call, 'poo, poo, poo'. A bird of a warm, dry environment, it breeds in Europe eastwards across Asia and also in most parts of Africa. A summer visitor to Britain in small numbers, especially in spring, one or two pairs nesting in Southern England most years.

Hornbill

Name for all species of Bucerotidae (Coraciiformes, sub-order Bucerotes). In the plural, the general term for the whole family. Hornbills are so called because of their enormous bill, which gives them a top-heavy appearance but which in reality is usually an extremely light structure. The 45 species of Hornbill are distributed widely in the tropics of the Old World. During nesting the female is walled up in the hole of a tree with mud or dung, leaving just a slit through which she is fed by the male. Much still remains to be discovered about the life history of many of these birds.

Hovering

Many birds can hover by reducing their speed to that of the wind, and flying with an air speed above that of stalling but a ground speed of nil. When a bird hovers in still air, it has to take up an almost vertical body attitude and beat its wings backwards and forwards in a horizontal plane. This puts a great strain on the muscles, which tire quickly unless they are specially developed as in the case of the Humming Birds (Trochilidae). Other birds that hover when searching for food include the Kestrel (*Falco tinnunculus*), the Terns (Sterninae) and Kingfishers (Alcedinidae).

Huia

An extinct species of Wattlebird of the Callaeidae (Passiformes, sub-order Oscines), formerly inhabiting the forests of the southern part of North Island, New Zealand.

Humming Bird

Name of many species of Trochilidae (Apodiformes); in the plural, general term for the family. The name derives from the sound made by the rapid beating of the wings during flight. There are over 300 species of Humming Bird, all confined to the New World and particularly abundant in tropical parts of South and Central America. Most Humming Birds are brilliantly coloured, with long slender bills which are used to obtain nectar from flowers. They are unique in their flying abilities, being able to move backwards as well as forwards. The family includes the smallest of all birds—only 2½in (63mm) long. The most widespread North American species are the Ruby-throated Humming Bird (*Archilochus colubris*) and Rufous Humming Bird (*Selasphorus rufus*).

Hybrid

The result of interbreeding by two different species. Most hybrids show characters that are intermediate between the parental species. Under natural conditions hybridisation is rare but it quite frequently takes place among birds kept in captivity, more often within

Kestrel in hovering flight

certain groups than in others. Many species of Duck, for example, not only interbreed freely but have fertile offspring, so that multiple hybrids involving as many as 5 or 6 species sometimes occur.

Hybridisation, Zone of Secondary

An area in which two closely related forms make contact and freely interbreed, having earlier differentiated under conditions of geographical (or ecological) isolation. A classic case is that of the Carrion Crow (*Corvus corone*) and the Hooded Crow (*Corvus c. cornix*), two similar birds with a striking plumage difference. In their breeding areas they more or less divide the palearctic region between them, but come into contact across the Highlands of Scotland, along a line approximately that of the River Elbe, and along a line in central and eastern Asia. They are both the same species, but previously altered enough to become separate sub-species in isolation. Subsequently they have overlapped once more and freely interbreed.

A hybrid, Mallard x Pintail

143

Ibis

Name of most species of the sub-family Threskiornithidae (Ciconiiformes, sub-order Ciconiae). In the plural (Ibises), general term for the sub-family. Ibises are medium-sized to large wading-type birds with long, thin, decurved bills. Inhabiting mainly tropical and sub-tropical areas, they favour fresh water, where they feed on fish, crustaceans, worms, etc. There are no representatives of this sub-family breeding in Britain, though the Glossy Ibis (*Plegadis falcinellus*), which has bred in Spain, is very occasionally recorded and has in fact been noted annually (up to 4 in any one year) since 1972. The Glossy Ibis (*Plegadis f. falcinellus*) also occurs in North America, as does the White-faced Glossy-Ibis (*Plegadis mexicana*) and the White Ibis (*Guara alba*). The Wood Ibises belong to a different family.

The Sacred Ibis (*Threskiornis aethiopica*) is the symbol of the British Ornithologists' Union.

Icteridae

Family of the Passeriformes, sub-order Oscines. Sometimes called the American Orioles. There are 80 species in the New World where they are very widespread. Some of the more numerous of the North American representatives of this family are the Meadow-larks, Bobolinks, Redwinged Blackbirds and Grackles, and the Baltimore, Golden and Orchard Orioles.

Greylag Goose and naturally occurring cross between Greylag and Canada Goose. This cross is common in East Anglia, where feral flocks of both species are found, and nearly always takes the same form: basic Greylag shape with basic Canada plumage

Immature

A young bird which has reached the free-flying stage but has not yet attained maturity. In some species, adult plumage is not attained for several years, particularly in some of the larger Gulls (Laridae). Most birds are not mature (able to breed) until adult plumage is assumed, but some are exceptions to this, for example the Goshawk (*Accipiter gentilis*) and the Black Redstart (*Phoenicurus ochruros*).

Immigration

Migration into an area (the opposite of emigration). A similar distinction is implied by 'irruption' and 'eruption'.
See Irruption

Imprinting

Term applied to the learning pattern of young birds, especially related to the influences of their very early life. The name imprinting (*prägung* in German) was originally given to a type of learning found in the young of such birds as Geese and Ducks, which when raised in isolation from their parents reacted to their human keepers, following them about as they

The Sacred Ibis (opposite)

would their natural parents. It was also found that a similar reaction could be evoked by even inanimate objects. The German naturalist Oskar Heinroth first showed this some 50 years ago, though Konrad Lorenz is undoubtedly better known over the last 30 years for work on this aspect of bird behaviour. The imprinting shown by young Ducks and Geese cannot be demonstrated in nidicolous birds, but there is good evidence that in certain song birds something suggestive of imprinting takes place in the process of learning characteristic song. For instance, it has been found that Chaffinches (*Fringilla coelebs*) hand-reared in isolation produce a very poor version of typical Chaffinch song, lacking the usual phrasing and terminal flourish. Not only experiments but also observations in the wild have indicated that, without practising it at the time, young Chaffinches do learn their song from their parents, or other adults of the same species, in their formative days.

Read Lorenz, K., *King Solomon's Ring*, Methuen, 1961

Incubation

The process by which heat is applied to the egg after it has been laid in order to promote the development of the embryo. This is usually done by one or both of the parent birds, according to the species. In some cases however it may be done by other species, eg in Cuckoos (Cuculidae); whilst the Megapodes (Megapodiidae), lay their eggs in sand, the chicks hatching out in the warmth of the sun, or build a mound of rotting vegetation in which to lay their eggs, the necessary heat being created by fermentation. The length of time needed to incubate eggs varies considerably according to the species but is stable within the species. Most of the smaller Passerines require around two weeks with longer periods for larger birds. For example, the Royal Albatross (*Diomedea epomophora*) takes about 80 days, the Kiwis (Apterygiformes) take almost as long, with the Ostrich (Struthioniformes) and Cassowaries (Casuariiformes) needing 40-50 days. Penguins (Sphenisciformes) also take around 50 days and so do some birds of prey (Falconiformes).

Incubation is facilitated by the birds' bare brood patch. Most birds commence incubation proper after the full clutch has been laid, though some, notably the Owls (Strigi-

Red Grouse (female) on nest (opposite)

formes), start immediately the first egg is laid, so that the young hatch at intervals and are of different sizes during the first few weeks of life.
See Asynchronous hatching

Indigenous

Term applied to a species, meaning it is native to the area in question.

Injury-feigning

A common practice among ground-nesting birds: the parent bird imitates movements of an injured bird in order to lure predators from the nest site or from the young.
See Distraction Display

Insessores

A former ordinal name for the so-called 'perching birds', comprising the Passeriformes of today and various other groups.

Instinct

The innate capacity of a bird (or animal) to react in a particular way to environmental stimuli. A term less frequently applied by scientists, as more study reveals that a greater degree of learning is involved in a bird's regular life patterns than used to be supposed.

Instrumental Sounds

These are sounds produced by non-vocal means. Many birds make such sounds often as part of their display. The greeting ceremonies of Storks (Ciconiiae), when a great deal of bill clattering takes place, are well known but perhaps the best-known non-vocal sound is that made by Woodpeckers (Picidae), when the bird delivers a rapid succession of blows with its bill at a selected point on a tree. This 'drumming' has been most studied in the Great Spotted Woodpecker (*Dendrocopos major*). A number of species of birds make instrumental sounds with their wings, notably the Mute Swan (*Cygnus olor*), which alone among its kind produces a high-pitched throbbing note when in flight. Many species of Ducks (Anatidae) also create more or less musical whistling sounds with their wings when flying. Humming Birds (Trochilidae) also create sound with their wings (hence the name). Some Birds of Paradise (Paradisaeidae) produce rustling or rattling sounds with their wings and tails as part of their display rituals. The Nightjar (*Caprimulgus europaeus*) produces a series of wing claps when in gliding

flight, as many as 25 claps in succession. The Snipes (*Gallinago* spp) make a drumming or bleating sound during aerial evolutions over breeding territory. In the Common Snipe (*Gallinago gallinago*) this extraordinary noise is created by the vibration of the outer tail feathers, which are spread fanwise and detached from the remaining tail feathers as the bird descends in rapid angled flight, usually at some considerable height.
See Drumming

International Council for Bird Preservation (ICBP)

Founded by a group of ornithologists and conservationists who met in London in 1922, the ICBP was the first international conservation organisation to be set up. Its inspiration came from Dr Gilbert Pearson, then President of the National Association of Audubon Societies, USA, who had just completed a tour through Europe during which he found that bird protectionists knew little about (and took no interest in) what was happening in this field in other countries of Europe, America or any other part of the world. The main framework of the ICBP consists of National Sections, which form a recognised body of opinion and a tangible link between countries ready to help each other and to take concerted action where necessary. The British Section has always been one of the most active. It is directed by representatives of 20 national bodies, who constitute a central committee. Its achievements have been many. Among the most notable were efforts to protect migratory wildfowl throughout the whole of Europe, which brought about the introduction of wildfowl counts and the establishment of the Wildfowl Research Bureau, which has since developed into the International Waterfowl Research Bureau with workers all over the world. The British Section has also played a leading part in setting up the Advisory Committee for the Prevention of the Pollution of the Sea (chiefly by oil) and secured the first of a series of international conventions on the problem.

It has instigated research into the cleaning and rehabilitation of oiled sea birds. Also, in its fight to safeguard island birds—which are particularly vulnerable—ICBP acquired Cousin Island in the Seychelles and established the first international reserve in the Indian Ocean in 1968.

Details of the work of the ICBP and its British Section can be obtained from ICBP, c/o Natural History Museum, Cromwell Road, London SW7.

Symbol of the ICBP

International Ornithological Congress

Held every four years in a different country, it provides the world's leading ornithologists with a forum for scientific discussion and on occasions to decide on the future courses of action in international ornithological matters. There is an International Ornithological Committee of 100 members, meeting during the course of each congress, which decides on the running of the Congress, chooses the country in which the next Congress is to be held and elects a President for the succeeding Congress. There is also a small permanent Executive Committee which deals with matters arising between Congresses. The first Congress was held in Vienna in 1884. The XVIIth International Ornithological Congress was held in West Berlin in 1978; the XVIIIth Congress is scheduled for Moscow.

Invasion

Term, usually applied to the expansion of a species' range in a relatively short period, but frequently used as synonymous with irruption.
See Irruption

Iris

A thin opaque muscular membrane in front of the lens of the eye. The amount of contraction of the iris determines the size of the pupil, the opening in its centre. The colour of the iris can be quite a noticeable feature in some birds, particularly in Owls (Strigiformes) and some birds of prey (Falconiformes).

A brown pigmentation of the iris is very common in birds (resembling that found in many mammals); brilliant pigments, especially yellow, green and blue, are quite common, as are red or reddish eyes. Some examples of particular iris coloration are found among, for instance, Owls (Strigiformes), most of which have yellow irides; some waders (Charadrii), some Pigeons (Columbidae) and some Herons (Ardeidae), and many other groups also have yellow irides. Many groups include red-eyed birds, such as Rails (Rallidae), Pigeons (Columbidae), Grebes (Podicipedidae) and Herons (Ardeidae). A relatively infrequent colour found in birds' irides is green; an example is the Cormorant (*Phalacrocorax carbo*). The Blue-eyed Shag (*Phalacrocorax atriceps*) has blue irides, as does the Oilbird (*Steatornis caripensis*) and some other species. The Jackdaw (*Corvus monedula*) is a familiar species with an almost white iris. Iris coloration may change with age as in some Gulls (Laridae) and with the season. The colour of the iris must be distinguished from that of the orbital ring, the surrounding bare, sometimes hardened, skin round the eye of some species, or any circular pattern in the plumage in that position. The White-eyes (Zosteropidae) take their name from the white ring round the eye, not from iris colour.

Irish Wildbird Conservancy

A non-profit-making organisation run largely by volunteer workers. Its basic aim is to encourage a greater awareness and appreciation of Ireland's wildlife and to bring about improved legislation for its protection. The IWC holds conferences, arranges film shows and lectures, and also runs courses for young members at such places as the Cape Clear Bird Observatory. It undertakes various surveys and was responsible for the Irish records in *The Atlas of Breeding Birds in Britain and Ireland*. The IWS runs a number of sanctuaries, including Wexford Wildfowl Reserve (wintering place for half the world's Greenland White-fronted Geese), Little Skellig (second-largest breeding colony of Gannets in the world), Oilean Maistir (large Puffin colony) and Helwick Head (with many breeding seabirds). There are branches of the IWC in Cork, Dublin, Galway, North Munster, Waterford and Wexford and information on these and any aspect of their work can be obtained from the IWC, c/o Royal Academy, 19 Dawson Street, Dublin 2.

Irruption

Term applied to the irregular migratory movements characteristic of certain species of birds dependent on particular food requirements. When the preferred food is in short supply, birds invade other areas, 'erupting' from their usual range and subsequently irrupting into another area. Species notable for such irruptive behaviour are the Crossbill (*Loxia curvirostra*), the Nutcracker (*Nucifraga caryocatactes*) and the Waxwing (*Bombycilla garrulus*). Other species which irrupt from time to time include the Jay (*Garrulus glandarius*), Great Spotted Woodpecker (*Dendrocopos major*), Rough-Legged Buzzard (*Buteo lagopus*) and Bearded Tit (*Panurus biarmicus*).

Isabelline

A greyish-yellow colour, predominating on the plumage of the Isabelline Wheatear (*Oenanthe isabellina*), a vagrant to Britain from the Middle East and eastwards, and the Isabelline Shrike (*Lanius isabellinus*).

Isle of May, Fife

Situated at the mouth of the Firth of Forth, 5 miles (8km) south of the Fife coast and 10 miles (16km) north of the East Lothian coast, this small island, only 550m wide and 1.6km long, has been the site of an observatory since 1939, the second one to be set up in Britain. Although the observatory was established primarily for the study of migration (it has a considerable list of rarities to its credit including Thrush Nightingale, Olivaceous and Radde's Warblers), the large breeding seabird population has long attracted attention and its study forms an important part of the observatory's work today. There is no permanent warden and responsibility for manning the station and maintaining migration records rests with visiting observers. The island is a National Nature Reserve.

Isochronal Line

A line joining geographical localities at which the same event occurs at the same time, eg marking the arrival dates of migrant birds.
See next page.

Jacamar

Name of species of Galbulidae (Piciformes, sub-order Galbulae). The family comprises about 15 species of small to medium-sized insectivorous birds inhabiting the tropical wooded area of continental America.
See next page for example.

Jacana

Name of the species of Jacanidae (Charadrii-

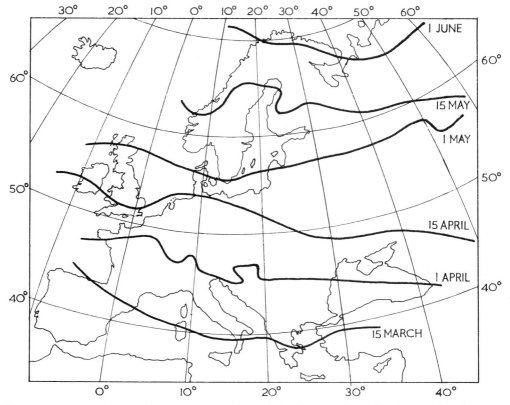

The advancing front of the Swallow's main northwards movement in spring, Sightings on the same date are shown by isochronal lines (heavy)

formes, sub-order Charadrii). The name is derived from the Brazilian word and should strictly be pronounced 'jaçaná'. A tropical and sub-tropical family of extraordinary long-legged birds with excessively elongated toes and straight claws; the claw of the hind toe is much longer than the toe and tapers to a fine point. They can move easily over floating vegetation, hence the alternative name 'Lily-trotter', especially of the African species.

Jack (**Snipe**) (*Lymnocryptes minima*)
The smallest Snipe, it is exceedingly difficult to observe on the ground but quickly distinguished from the Common Snipe (*Gallinago gallinago*) when flushed by its weaker but direct flight, shorter bill and lack of call note. A winter visitor to Britain, much less numerous than the Common Snipe.

Jackdaw (*Corvus monedula*)
Smallest of the Crows. Often found in the company of Rooks, where it can be quickly singled out, not only by its smaller size but

by its faster flight and quicker wing beats. At close quarters the grey nape and the pale eye are distinctive. A common resident, widely distributed throughout Britain and Ireland with probably about 500,000 pairs.

Jaeger
American name for Skua spp: Pomarine Skua or Pomarine Jaeger (*Stercorarius pomarinus*), Arctic Skua or Parasitic Jaeger (*Stercorarius parasiticus*), Long-tailed Skua or Jaeger (*Stercorarius longicaudus*). The Great Skua (*Catharacta skua*) is just known as Skua.

Jay (*Garrulus glandarius*)
Most colourful member of the Crow family, generally a shy and wary bird. An inveterate egg thief, its diet does, however, include fruit and insects. It has a fondness for acorns, and in the autumn can often be seen collecting

Jackdaw (above)

Jay—often shows just a flash of white rump and blue wing-patch as it disappears into a wood, calling harshly

these and burying them, supposedly for future use. Generally distributed throughout Britain, it is absent from some areas of Scotland and Ireland. Total population about 100,000 pairs.

Jizz

An expression of obscure origin used to convey the rather indefinable overall impression given by a bird in the field to an observer. The 'jizz' of a bird is not normally created by any particular feature of its plumage, nor any single behavioural characteristic, but by a combination of several things—it may be very difficult to single out the particular elements that contribute to it. Certain birds remain somewhat featureless and lack any special character, others have an instantly recognisable 'jizz', such as Robin, Dunnock and Skylark. The immediately identifiable species, such as Avocet and Kingfisher, do not really come into the same category—jizz tends to be more subtle, concerning shape, facial expression, stance, etc, as well as plumage marks, and eliciting such descriptive terms as 'restless', 'nervous', 'excitable', 'untidy', 'powerful', 'majestic', 'elegant', 'heavy' etc.

'Jizz' can, therefore, be appreciated even if the bird being watched is totally unfamiliar— but it is 'jizz' more than anything else which

enables someone to identify a familiar bird at a glance. For example, a Song Thrush can be separated from a Mistle Thrush without recourse to examination of the tail pattern or breast spotting; a Kittiwake can be identified by someone who knows the species even if he does not see bill or leg colour or precise wing-tip pattern—it is the 'jizz' that sings out loud and clear just what the bird is. Frequently, in the discovery of rare vagrants or birds new to the observer, it is the unfamiliar 'jizz' that catches the eye and stimulates the closer and more systematic examination of the field marks which results in a final conclusive identification.
See Field Marks

Juvenile
The young bird, at the stage of attaining its first full plumage of true feathers.
See Young

Kagu (*Rhynochetos jubatus*)
Sole member of the family Rhynochetidae (Gruiformes, sub-order Rhynocheti). An almost flightless bird about the size of a small Heron, with a short neck but longish legs and bill. Found only in New Caledonia, where

A pair of Kestrels

Kagu

though formerly common, it is now virtually restricted to remote mountain forests and is considered to be an endangered species.

Juvenile (left) and adult Herring Gulls. Noticeable differences include (adult features given in brackets): blackish bill (yellow with red spot), blackish eye (yellow), streaked brownish head and under parts (white), barred and mottled brown and black upper parts (unmarked pale grey), barred tail (white) and blackish wing tips (black with white spots). *See also* Plumage

Kestrel (*Falco tinnunculus*)
Britain's most numerous and widespread bird of prey, though outnumbered in some parts by other species eg in mid-Wales it is less abundant than the Buzzard (*Buteo buteo*) or Sparrowhawk (*Accipiter nisus*). It is notable for its characteristic hovering flight when hunting. In recent years it has become a familiar sight along motorway verges, attracted by the many small mammals on which it feeds. Total population of Britain and Ireland probably 100,000 pairs.

Killdeer
The Killdeer Plover (*Charadrius vociferus*) is one of North America's best-known birds and gets its name from its noisy call, 'kill-dee, kill-dee'. Similar in appearance to the Ringed Plover (*Charadrius hiaticula*), it is immediately distinguished by its two black breast bands.

Kingfisher—Europe's *Alcedo atthis*, the only Kingfisher which breeds in Britain

A vagrant to Britain, it has been recorded about 15 times in the last 20 years.

Kingfisher
Name of all species of Alcedinidae (Coraciiformes, sub-order Alcedines), except the few known as 'Kookaburras', in the plural general term applied for the whole family. There are 80 species of Kingfisher throughout the world ranging from the 4in (102mm) Pygmy Kingfisher (*Ispidina picta*) to the 18 inch (457mm) Giant Kingfisher (*Megaceryle maxima*), both of Africa. Kingfishers have short bodies, short necks and large heads, with long, sometimes massive, straight bills usually ending in a sharp point. The legs are very short and the toes are syndactyl, the third and fourth being united. Most are very colourful

with bright metallic greens, blues and purples predominating. Many Kingfishers feed on fish (and other aquatic creatures) for which they plunge headlong into the water, usually from a perch but often from hovering flight. Many Kingfishers, however, exist far from water, preying on large insects which are caught in a similar manner by a sudden swoop from a perch.

There are three sub-families: the Cerylinae, which includes the Belted Kingfisher (*Mega-ceryle alcyon*) of North America; the Alcedininae, which includes the European Kingfisher (*Alcedo atthis*), which breeds in Britain; and the Daceloninae, which comprises the 'Tree' Kingfishers (mainly arboreal and catching insects as Flycatchers do). The latter sub-family includes the well-known 'Kookaburra' or 'Laughing Jackass' (*Dacelo novaeguineae*) of Australia.

Kinglet
American name for *Regulus* spp (Goldcrests and Firecrests).

Kite
Name of the species belonging to the sub-family Milvinae, also of the sub-family Elaninae, members of the Accipitridae (Falconiformes, sub-order Falcones). True Kites are mainly found in the Old World, with the Black Kite (*Milvus migrans*) in its many races one of the most obvious birds of prey of warmer areas; it scavenges for food round the towns and villages of the East, often in hundreds, sometimes thousands. The Black Kite, however, is only a vagrant to Britain, with about 20 records over the last 20 years. On the other hand the Red Kite (*Milvus milvus*) is resident, but in small numbers and confined to Central Wales, where it is closely watched and protected by the RSPB and NCC. This is the species which centuries ago scavenged in the streets of London.

The *Elaninae*, the White-tailed Kites, are a nearly cosmopolitan sub-family of small or very small birds of prey of open country. They are found in America, the warmer parts of Europe, southern Asia, Africa and Australia. Grey-and-white Hawks, superficially like Falcons, they can hover like the Kestrel (*Falco tinnunuculus*). The Black-winged (or Black-shouldered) Kite (*Elanus caeruleus*) is an example which nests in Portugal, but is a vagrant to the rest of Europe.

Kittiwake
Name of two species of the Laridae; used on both sides of the Atlantic for *Rissa tridacytala*, the Kittiwake (which has black legs) and *Rissa brevirostris*—the Red-legged Kittiwake. The latter species is much less abundant and found only in the northern waters of the Pacific. The Black-legged Kittiwake is the familiar bird of our rockier shores, with large colonies found around the Scottish coasts and concentrations in the Orkneys and Shetlands.

The Red Kite, a magnificent bird on the wing; its gliding flight gave it one of its old names, Glead or Gled

Knot

Kittiwake

Kiwi

but the large ear aperture suggests a good sense of hearing. Mainly nocturnal, so very little study of them in the wild has been made so far.

Probably something like half a million pairs nest in Britain and Ireland.

Kiwi

The name of three species of the Apterygidae (Apterygiformes), a group of flightless birds all peculiar to New Zealand. Strange creatures with hair-like feathers, their eyesight is poor,

Knot (*Calidris canutus*)

One of our commonest shore birds; vast flocks of this bird are to be seen round our coasts during the winter months. It is particularly abundant on the Wash, Dee and Ribble estuaries. Total population between 300,000 and 400,000 birds.

Knot, at Hilbre, Cheshire

Kookaburra

Name of *Dacelo* spp. The best known of these Australian birds is the Laughing Kookaburra, or Laughing Jackass (*Dacelo novaeguineae*). The laughing effect is produced by three or more birds calling in unison. One starts and stimulates the others, the sound resembling that of a group of people laughing uncontrollably.

Kori

Alternative name for the Giant Bustard (*Ardeotis kori*).
See Bustard

Laggar (*Falco jugger*)

The Laggar Falcon or Lugger Falcon is an Indian species frequently used for falconry. Ashy brown above, white with brown markings below, its coloration distinguishes it from the Peregrine (*Falco peregrinus*). The Saker Falcon (*Falco cherrug*) can be distinguished by white spots on the central tail feathers.

Lammergeier

Alternative name for Bearded Vulture (*Gypaetus barbatus*). This impressive bird of prey has been driven from many of its original European haunts and is now far from numerous in Spain and Greece; a few pairs can still be found. It still breeds in the mountains of Syria, Lebanon, Jordan and Israel and eastwards to the Himalayas and Central Asia.

The adjective 'bearded' refers to the patch of black feathers running forward from the eye to the nostril, along the upper mandible and seemingly continuing on the lower mandible to end in a hanging tuft—the beard. In Spain the Lammergeier is called *quebrantahuesos*, which literally translated means bone-breaker, a name derived from its habit of carrying large bones and dropping them on rocks below to enable it to get at the marrow.

Lanceolate

The feathers of a bird's tail are said to be lanceolate when the two sides are evenly graduated to a point (lance-shaped). This shape is typical of a number of Warblers, particularly the Lanceolated Warbler (*Locustella lanceolata*). This bird is very much like the commoner Grasshopper Warbler (*Locustella naevia*) of the same genus, and is a rare vagrant to Europe from Asia. It has been recorded in Britain on several occasions, nearly always on Fair Isle (Shetland).

Landrail

An alternative name for the Corncrake (*Crex crex*), now rarely used.

Lanner Falcon (*Falco biarmicus*)

Much like a Peregrine (*Falco peregrinus*), the European race of Lanner (*Falco b. feldeggii*) is a slender, browner-looking bird. It breeds in Italy, Greece, Turkey and North Africa. Lanner Falcons have been used in falconry for centuries.

Lappet

A wattle, an unfeathered fold or flap of skin particularly near the gape. Lappets are often brightly coloured and found in such families as the Pheasants (Phasianidae), Turkeys (Meleagrididae), Plovers (Charadriidae), Jacanas (Jacanidae), Cotingas (Cotingidae), Honeyeaters (Meliphagidae), Starlings (Sturnidae) and Wattlebirds (Callaeidae). Their function is probably connected with display or recognition. They often show sexual dimorphism and their state may be subject to hormonal control.

Lapwing

The name for some *Vanellus* spp, eg the White-tailed Lapwing (*Vanellus leucurus*); some are called Plover, eg the White-crowned Plover (*Vanellus albiceps*). In Britain the Lapwing (*Vanellus vanellus*), with its green, black and white plumage and crest, is a familiar bird equally at home on pasture land, newly ploughed fields or moorland. Sometimes called the Green Plover, or the Peewit after its distinctive call, it breeds extensively throughout Britain and Ireland with an estimated population of around 200,000 pairs. Many more are present in the winter, following considerable immigration from northern Europe in the autumn.

Lark

Name of species of Alaudidae (Passeriformes, sub-order Oscines). In the plural, general term for the family. There are 76 species, found predominantly in the Old World. The Shorelark (*Eremophila alpestrus*) is the only representative in North America, where it is known as the Horned Lark. Larks are basically small to medium-sized birds of open country, generally quietly coloured but having very highly developed songs, a characteristic

Lapwing or Peewit: its nest is a scrape on open
ground

Woodlark (above) and Skylark (below)

Laying

Shorelark (or Horned Lark)

feature of the group. In Britain, the commonest and most widespread Lark is the Skylark (*Alauda arvensis*) with around 4,000,000 breeding pairs.

The Woodlark (*Lullula arborea*) is a much more locally occurring member of the lark family. The Shorelark, which in Europe breeds on the Arctic tundra, is mainly a winter visitor in small numbers, but has nested in Britain on one or two occasions. Some rare Larks which have been recorded in Britain include the Short-toed Lark (*Calandrella cinerea*), which breeds in Southern Europe, the Lesser Short-toed Lark (*Calandrella rufescens*), which breeds in Southern Spain, the Calandra Lark (*Melanocorypha calandra*) found in parts of Spain, France, Italy, Greece and Roumania, and the Crested Lark (*Galerida cristata*), which resembles the Skylark and breeds commonly on the continent of Europe. Vagrant Larks from Asia which have occurred include the White-winged Lark (*Melanocorypha leucoptera*) and the Bimaculated Lark (*Melanocorypha bimaculate*).

Laverock
Archaic name for the Skylark (*Alauda arvensis*).
See Lark

Laying
The act of depositing an egg. After the egg has been formed in the reproductive system it is then released from the body, passing from the uterus into the vagina, being pushed out by peristaltic action of the vaginal muscles. The expulsion of the egg may take 1 to 3 minutes, though in some parasitic birds such as Cuckoos (Cuculidae) it is only a matter of seconds. However, the Turkeys (*Meleagris gallopavo*) and Geese (*Anser* spp) are said to take 1 to 2 hours. A bird that cannot lay for some reason is called egg-bound. Egg laying starts when the female is sexually mature,

which in most wild birds is when they are about a year old. Larger birds take longer to mature, eg some Albatrosses (Diomedidae) may not start laying until their eighth year.

Egg laying is restricted to a particular season of the year, which is naturally related to all other reproductive activities and is generally timed so that the necessary food supply is available when the young hatch out. Some birds only lay at a particular time of day, eg many small Passerines usually lay around sunrise, Pigeons (Columbidae) in the afternoon, Pheasants (Phasianidae) in the evening. The interval between laying each egg is characteristic for a species. For most small Passerines this is 24 hours, as it is for many Ducks. For some larger birds the interval is 36 to 40 hours; for some, such as the Raven (*Corvus corax*), it is 3 days between eggs, while some of the Boobies (Sulidae) lay their eggs 5 days apart.
See Clutch; Egg

Leafbird
Substantive name of species in one genus of Irenidae (Passeriformes, sub-order Oscines). A small oriental group of fruit-eating forest birds that have bright whistling chattering calls. They are particularly numerous in Malaysia.

Learning
Adaptive changes in behaviour as the result of experience, in contrast with innate or instinctive behaviour. The word adaptive is used in order that the term 'learning' should not include changes in behaviour resulting from physiological effects due to fatigue etc, or structural effects due to injury. A basic example of learning is demonstrated by a bird being tamed and becoming used to human presence. Some birds can learn to do simple tricks, going through a sequence of actions culminating in a reward of food. In a sense this is only the result of a normal process of trial and error which it would undertake in the wild during its search for food, as when it learns a food source is available at a certain time in a certain place, eg at a garden bird table or nut dispenser.
See Imprinting

Leg
The term is usually applied to that part which is ordinarily visible, to include or exclude the foot. As an aid to identification, leg coloration can often play an important role.

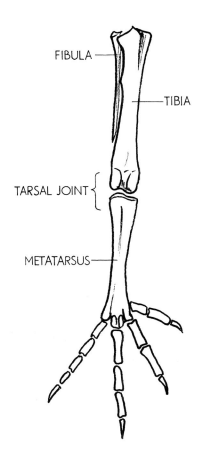

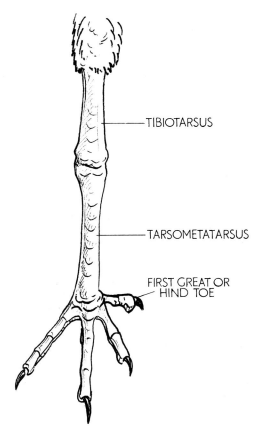

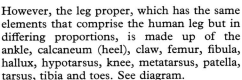

Bird's leg: (left) bone structure; (right) in the flesh

However, the leg proper, which has the same elements that comprise the human leg but in differing proportions, is made up of the ankle, calcaneum (heel), claw, femur, fibula, hallux, hypotarsus, knee, metatarsus, patella, tarsus, tibia and toes. See diagram.

The relative leg lengths of birds are extremely variable. Those that mainly walk or run have long legs, eg Flamingos (Phoenicopteridae), Storks (Ciconidae), Stilts (Recurvirostridae) etc, whereas most small birds that hop have relatively shorter legs. Birds that seldom walk have the shortest legs—such as Swifts (Apodidae) and Kingfishers (Alcedinidae). Birds which lead such highly aquatic lives as Grebes (Podicipitidae) have their legs set towards the rear of the body facilitating propulsion through the water but making walking almost impossible. The Petrels (Procellariidae), which spend all their time flying, only coming to land for nesting, also have weak limbs and are unable to walk in the usual manner.

Lek

Term originally used for an assembly of Blackcock (*Lyrurus tetrix*) but now extended to cover the ritualistic displays of groups of males of other species, notably Ruff (*Philomachus pugnax*). 'Lek' appears to come from the Swedish *leka*, to play, which can have a sexual connotation. The display arena where a lek takes place is generally referred to as a court, and these courts can be used year after year. Blackcock leks take place in early spring at dawn, when the birds strut about, posturing to one another, expanding and elevating the white feathers under the tail with the wings drooped, and making loud bubbling noises. Autumn 'leks' are also held in October though these are generally less intense.

The area where Ruffs display is called the hill, and may be no more than an imperceptible rise in an otherwise flat grassy area. The extensive and variously coloured head plumes that give the Ruff its name feature in the display ritual, but Ruff leks are exceptional in being entirely silent.

Leucism
Closely allied to albinism, it results from a varying degree of dilution of normal pigmentation rendering the bird's plumage (not the soft parts) paler in colour than is normal for the species.
See Albinism; Melanism

Life List
A list kept by some birdwatchers of all the birds they have seen. Each new bird is 'ticked off', hence another widely used term, 'tick list'. The term 'ticker' or 'tick hunter' is applied to the person deliberately and actively attempting to increase his list of birds seen. Some birdwatchers have separate life lists for the world, for Britain and even for other different countries or particular areas, though the usual division for British 'tickers', is between the world and Britain.

Lifer
Vernacular expression used by birdwatchers to describe a bird new to the observer. A birdwatcher seeing a bird new to him adds a 'lifer' to his life list.
See Life List

Lily Trotter
Name most often used for African species of Jacanidae.
See Jacana

Lime, Bird
A glutinous substance made from a type of bark. It is smeared on twigs in order to catch small birds (the practice is illegal in Britain). When the bird lands on a treated twig it cannot extricate itself. This abominable practice is still carried out in some parts of Europe. The term is also sometimes mis-applied to the white coating of bird excrement that collects on buildings, trees and rocks.

Limpkin (*Aramus guarauna*)
The only species of the family Aramidae (Gruiiformes, sub-order Grues). Much like a Rail with a long curved bill, it haunts wooded swamplands of the New World. Best known for its voice, a mixture of wailing, screaming and clucking notes most frequently heard at night: it is often called the 'Wailing' Bird or 'Crying' Bird.

Line Transect
A type of sampling used for woodland birds; sometimes called a belt transect. The observer walks as nearly as possible a straight line, and records the birds he sees and hears, but does not need to record his position or the position of the bird. Can be useful for assessing and comparing numbers of certain singing species but its accuracy is limited and dependent on a number of factors (not least regular and frequent sampling.)
Read Simms, E., *Woodland Birds*, (New Naturalist series), Collins 1971; Yapp, W. B., *Birds and Woods*, Oxford University Press, 1962

Linnaeus, Carolus (1707-78)
Swedish botanist and founder of modern scientific naming of life forms. The above is the Latinised version of his name, the original being Carl von Linné.
See Classification; Nomenclature

Linnet (*Acanthis cannabina*)
A common widespread breeding bird in Britain. The cock Linnet is an attractive species with its warm brown back, whitish, underparts, grey head and crimson forehead

Linnet (male) with young

crown and breast. It has a pleasant twittering song and was at one time a popular cage bird. Total breeding population in Britain and Ireland probably around 1 million pairs.
See Finch

Loafing

Certain types of birds spend much of their time standing about, either dozing or preening but presumably mainly digesting food. This aspect of bird behaviour is most noticeable in Gulls (*Larus* spp) and Ducks (Anatidae). Particular areas are regularly used for the purpose and these are called 'loafing' areas. 'Loafing' seems to form an essential part of these birds' daily routine.

Lobed or Lobate

Having toes separately fringed by lobes as distinct from webs: typically, Great Crested Grebe (*Podiceps cristatus*), Coot (*Fulica atra*), Phalaropes (*Phalaropus* spp).

Longspur

The North American name of *Calcarius* spp, including the Lapland Bunting (*Calcarius lapponicus*), a regular but locally occurring winter visitor to Britain in small numbers.

Long-tailed Duck (*Clangula hyemalis*)

A winter visitor to Britain which breeds in the holarctic; a basically marine species. It is unique in having three distinct plumage

Lobate foot

changes. In winter dress it is most handsome and it is then that the long tail streamers that give the bird its name are most obvious. In spring/summer (April-July) it is less distinct and in eclipse (August/October) it may be difficult to identify. In intermediate plumage phases it can often present a problem to the birdwatcher and at times might be mistaken for a female Common Scoter (*Melanitta nigra*) or Smew (*Mergus albellus*), or even Ruddy Duck (*Oxyura jamaicensis*). In North America it is known as 'Oldsquaw'.

Long-tailed Tit (*Aegithalos caudatus*)

A small black, white and pink bird with a long tail, a widely distributed resident in Britain where suitable habitat occurs. It

Long-tailed Tit: 3 inches of its total 5 inches are tail!

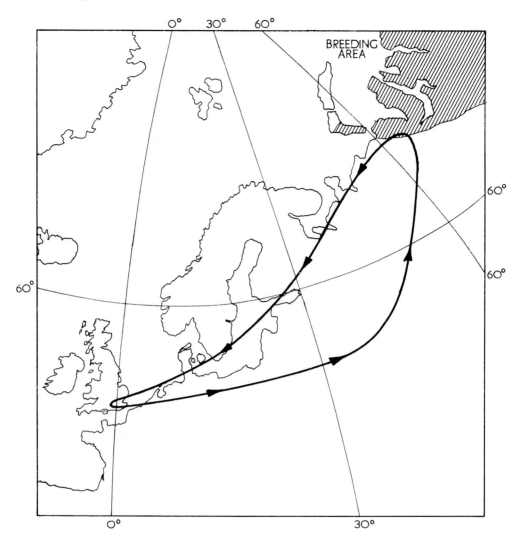

Loop migration. In this example, the European White-fronted Goose, which breeds in northern Russia, migrates to Britain by a fairly direct route in autumn, returning to the breeding grounds in spring by a different, more southerly, route

builds a remarkable domed nest of moss and cobwebs beautifully decorated with lichens and lined with many feathers. The total population of Britain and Ireland is probably around 150,000 pairs.
See Paridae; Tit

Loomery
A term applied to a breeding colony of Guillemots.

Locomotion
A bird's movement from place to place, other than by flight, often by swimming, or by walking, hopping or running. Most non-Passerines and some Passerines proceed on the ground by walking or running. Many of the small Plovers (Charadriidae) and Sand-pipers (Scolopacidae) can run at great speed— a well-known example is the Sanderling (*Calidris alba*). Other strong runners are to be found amongst the gamebirds (Galliiformes) and the Bustards (Otididae). However, it is

flightless birds (Ratites) that run as a means of moving from one place to another, particularly to escape their enemies—in such a highly developed way that at full speed an Ostrich (*Struthio camelus*) is said to be capable of a speed around 40mph (65kph).

Among the Passeriformes, most Crows (Corvidae) walk, as do Starlings (Sturnidae), Larks (Alaudidae) and Wagtails (Motacillidae), the last-named being among the smallest Passerine birds that walk and run. Some birds with short legs such as Ducks (Anatidae) and Pigeons (Columbidae) can do little more than waddle and take to the water or the air whenever a speedy escape is necessary. Birds like Divers (Gaviidae) and Grebes (Podicipitidae), with their legs positioned at the rear of their bodies, cannot maintain an upright position for long, and when moving on land, from water to nest, Divers push themselves forward on their breasts.

A further form of locomotion employed by some birds is climbing, with a number of species being specially adapted for this purpose, notably the Woodpeckers (Picidae), the Treecreepers (Certhidae) and the Nuthatches (Sittidae), walking more or less vertically up the trunks of trees (and in the case of the Nuthatch (*Sitta europaea*) downwards as well). The Wallcreeper (*Tichodroma muraria*) traverses rock faces in a like manner.

Longevity

In the wild, the lifespan of most birds is relatively short and, roughly, correlates with size, the largest birds living longest, the smallest perhaps not living longer than 12 months. Ringing has proved some individuals to be quite long-lived, eg Kestrel (*Falco tinnunculus*) 14 years, Curlew (*Numenius arquata*) 31 years, Swift (*Apus apus*) 21 years, Great Tit (*Parus major*) 7 years, Wren (*Troglodytes troglodytes*) 4 years 11 months. In captivity there are recorded instances of birds living to over 30 years of age and this includes 6 living to over 50 years.

Loon

North American name for the Gaviidae—the Divers.

Loop migration

Term used by Moreau (1961) to denote migration by different routes in spring and autumn between given breeding and winter quarters. For example, the Subalpine Warbler (*Sylvia cantillans*) is abundant in Egypt on spring passage but unknown there in autumn. Study suggests that this species travels much farther east in spring than in autumn. Also those Red-backed Shrikes (*Lanius collurio*) which breed in western Europe migrate first southwards in autumn, cross the Mediterranean and mostly strike the northern coast of Africa along a front of about 600 miles from Cyrenaica to Egypt. Returning in spring from eastern and southern Africa, the birds pass the Mediterranean zone much further to the east by Levant and Asia Minor. (For another example, see diagram opposite.)

Lore

The area between the base of the upper mandible and the eye on each side of the head. Plural 'lores'.
See Topography

Lorikeet

Name of small species of Lory (species of Parrot).
See Parrot

Lory

Name of species of Loriinae. In the plural, Lories, a general term for the sub-family.
See Parrot

Louse Flies

One of a number of different types of ectoparasite which are found on some birds. Louse flies (Hippoboscidae) are crab-like creatures which infest Swifts (Apodidae) and other predominantly aerial species.

LRP

The Little Ringed Plover (*Charadrius dubius*).

Lumper

A vernacular term used by birdwatchers to describe a taxonomist who is not inclined to classify small variations in a species across its range into subspecies, as opposed to a 'splitter' who considers morphological characteristics such as slight differences in measurements, shades of colour, etc, as sufficient to put a bird into a separate sub-species.
See Taxonomy

Lure

In falconry, a form of bait to bring the bird back to the falconer. A term also applied to an instrument for imitating bird calls, parti-

Rainbow Lorikeet

cularly as used by wildfowlers to bring birds within range.

Lyrebird
Name of two species of Menuridae (Passeriformes, sub-order Menurae). Restricted to eastern Australia, the birds are so named from the resemblance of their tails to a Greek lyre, although this is only shown momentarily when the bird is displaying.

Macaw
The name of some members of the Parrot family (Psittacidae). They are among the most spectacular and brightly coloured of all birds. In the wild they are to be found in the Americas from Mexico to Paraguay. Virtually all zoos and bird gardens have one or more of the most familiar species (often freeflying). The Blue-and-Yellow Macaw (*Ara ararauna*), often called the Blue-and-Gold Macaw, is one of the most usual. The Macaws are the largest of the Parrots, averaging 40in (1,016mm) in length.
See Parrot

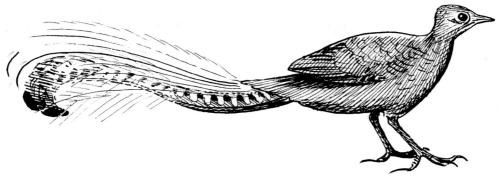

Lyrebird

Magpie (*Pica pica*)

This familiar member of the Crow family (Corvidae) is easily identified by its black and white plumage and long, graduated tail. Its large domed nest of twigs is a feature of many tall hedgerows and isolated trees over most of Britain and Ireland. The total population is probably well in excess of 250,000 pairs. In North America this species is called the Black-billed Magpie. The name Magpie is also used for certain *Gymnorhina* species in the family Craticidae (Passeriformes, sub-order Oscines)—Australian Butcherbirds or Bell Magpies.

Malagasy Region

The zoogeographical region formed by Madagascar and its off-lying islands, usually regarded as a sub-region of the Ethiopian region.

See Zoogeography

Malar

The area on the side of a bird's throat immediately below the base of the lower mandible

See Topography

Mallard (*Anas platyrhynchos*)

The best known of all our wildfowl, the drake Mallard or Wild Duck (term originally applied to the drake only, now obsolete) is a handsome and colourful bird, with bottle-

Magpies at carrion

165

Manakin

green head, yellow bill, white collar, grey back and flanks, distinctive curly black tail feathers and orange-red legs. As with all members of the Duck family, the female lacks the drake's bright plumage; her colouring is a mixture of browns, blacks and buffs. Widely distributed and nesting throughout the whole of Britain and Ireland, the breeding population could well be 150,000 pairs. In the winter visitors from Northern Europe may bring the total to half a million birds.

Manakin
Name of species of Pipridae (Passeriformes, sub-order Tyranni)—not to be confused with Mannikin (*Lonchura* spp). A neotropical group of nearly 60 species, Manakins are small stocky birds the size of Tits (Paridae).

Mandible
Term generally used for either jaw of a bird, and its horny covering. The adjective 'upper' or 'lower' is added as required.

Mannikin
Name for various *Lonchura* spp. In the plural, general term for the Amadini tribe of the family of Weaver Finches (*Estrildidae*). Commonly referred to as Waxbills, they are often kept as cage birds.

Man o' War Bird (Hawk)
Sailors' name for Frigatebirds (*Fregata* spp).

Marabou
Or Marabou Stork (*Leptoptilos crumeniferus*).

Mallard drake (the common 'Wild Duck')

An African species standing 4ft high with a wingspan of over 8ft. A carrion feeder, it gathers at animal corpses in the manner of Vultures and often in company with them. It has also evolved a similar wingform adapted for high soaring flight, when it looks a most impressive and powerful bird.

Marisma
Spanish word for marshy country, notably of the type found in the Guadalquivir delta. An internationally important bird habitat, 'Las Marismas', which comprises a vast area of reeds and mudflats with its attendant wildlife, were made widely known by the ornithological expeditions to the Coto Donaña of Field Marshal Viscount Alanbrooke, Sir Julian Huxley, Roger Tory Peterson, James Fisher, Guy Mountfort, Eric Hosking and others, particularly through the book *Portrait of a Wilderness* and the film of the expeditions, 'Wild Spain'.
Read Mountfort, G., *Portrait of a Wilderness*, David & Charles, 1968.

Marking
The commonest form of marking birds is by ringing them, but other methods are employed in the study of certain species of birds or bird populations, notably by the use of coloured dyes. Birds so marked are then readily distinguished in the field. This colour marking is generally confined to larger species such as Geese, Swans, Gulls, etc.

Marabou Storks with a solitary White-backed Griffon Vulture

Large birds can also be wing-tagged to enable identification in the field, and particularly this method has been employed on the British population of Red Kites (*Milvus milvus*). It should be stressed that no wild bird can be caught and marked without the permission of the Natural Environment Research Council, and invariably any particular study necessitating the marking of birds is made under the aegis of the British Trust for Ornithology.

See Ringing; Wing Tag

Martin

Substantive name of some species of Hirundinidae, notably in Britain the Sand Martin (*Riparia riparia*) and House Martin (*Delichon urbica*). The Sand Martin (smallest of the family) has mouse-brown upper parts and white underneath, and a brown band across the breast. Flight is more fluttering and erratic than the Swallow's, and its tail is also less forked, lacking the Swallow's long streamers. Like the Swallow it frequently

hawks for flying insects over lakes, reservoirs or rivers. The House Martin, with its white under parts, dark back and wings, is readily identified, as it swoops and flutters around buildings or over water, by its distinctive white rump. The Sand Martin tunnels into the banks of sand and gravel quarries or river banks to build its nest, while the House Martin constructs a distinctive inverted beehive type of nest made of small pellets of mud cemented together with its own saliva. The nests are usually fixed under the eaves of houses or other buildings and frequently under bridges. Both are summer migrants, the Sand Martin arriving in March and the House Martin in early April; both leave in September or October.

The Crag Martin (*Hirundo rupestris*) looks very much like the Sand Martin, but has white spots near the tip of the spread tail. It inhabits mountain gorges and rocky island cliffs in Spain and Southern Europe.

167

Martin Mere, Lancashire
Located 10 miles from Southport, this Wild-fowl Trust centre covers 360 acres (146Ha) of marshland on the site of what was once the largest mere in Lancashire. Visited by thousands of wild Geese, Ducks and waders, it offers wonderful opportunities for both the serious ornithologist and casual visitor. The collection contains over 1,500 wildfowl from all over the world and specialises in large flocks of Geese. There are spacious hides giving excellent views over the wild refuge, which contains an 18 acre lake. A Visitor Centre, of Norwegian log design, includes a large and well-equipped education centre, cinema, exhibition hall, gift and coffee shops and viewing concourse. Open daily (except 24 and 25 December).

Martlet
Archaic and heraldic name for a bird which may have been any of the Hirundines or perhaps the Swift (*Apus apus*).

Mate
Either member of a pair is mate to the other.

Mavis
Onetime widespread common name ·in Britain for the Song Thrush (*Turdus philomelos*).

Measurements
On birds, particular dimensions are commonly used as a general indication of size or

House Martin with its distinctive mud nest, and (below) Sand Martin at entrance to nest tunnel in vertical sandbank

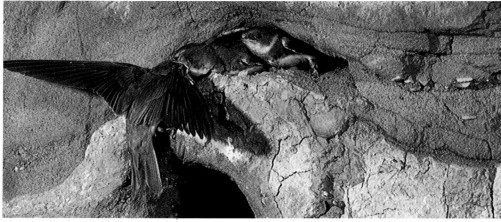

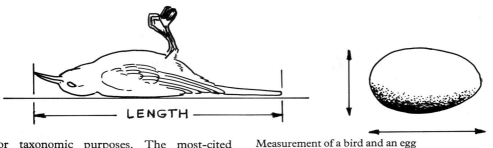

Measurement of a bird and an egg

for taxonomic purposes. The most-cited dimension is total length—this is measured in a straight line from the tip of the bill to the tip of the longest tail feather (taken from a freshly dead specimen laid on its back and without any undue stretching, with the bill in line with the body). Such measurements, invariably quoted in works of reference, can give a false impression of the size of the living bird, especially when bill, neck or tail are particularly long. However, they provide a rough idea of the comparative size of the species and the range of sizes within a group.

The wingspread or span is sometimes given. This is the distance between the wing tips (the ends of the longest primaries) when both wings are fully extended. For some of the larger, long-legged birds, standing height is a measurement which can help convey size.

More critical measurements of birds are made using dividers, either on living birds (usually made when caught for ringing) or on museum specimens. Such measurements have always been given in millimetres. Such precise measurements are usually confined to the wing, the tail, the bill and the tarsus. Eggs are measured with calipers: the usual dimensions cited are length and breadth.

Megapode

Substantive name of species of Megapodiidae (Galliformes, sub-order Galli). In the plural, general term for the family. Mainly confined to Australia, members of the family are characterised by the method of incubation employed for hatching their eggs. These are laid in mounds of rotting vegetation or in the ground, natural heat producing the required temperature for hatching. Birds in this group are commonly called 'mound birds', 'mound builders' and 'incubator' birds.

Megapodiidae

Family of the order Galliformes, sub-order Galli, comprising 12 species most of which are called Brush Turkey or Megapodes.

Melanism

Effectively the opposite of albinism, being a condition due to an excess of dark pigment in the plumage or eggs of a bird. Various degrees of melanism can occur, causing individual birds or eggs to appear darker than normal. The pigments usually involved are eumelanin (a blackish pigment) and phaeomelanin (a dusky or brown pigment).
See Albinism; Leucism

Merganser

Species of sea Duck, belonging to the group also known as the Sawbills, after their narrow bills with serrated edges. In Britain, the Red-breasted Merganser (*Mergus serrator*) and the Goosander (*Mergus merganser*) are the best known, both breeding in Scotland, Northern England, parts of Wales and Ireland. The Smew, another 'Sawbill' (*Mergus albellus*), is a locally occurring winter visitor in small numbers. The North American Hooded Merganser (*Mergus cucullatus*) is an accidental visitor to Britain and N Ireland.

Merlin (*Falco columbarius*)

A small Falcon of upland areas, preferring open moorland and fell country although it also frequents sea cliffs and coastal dunes. Present throughout the year, it nests widely in Scotland, N. England, Wales, SW England and Ireland, but nowhere is it common and the total population probably does not exceed 1,000 pairs. A speedy, agile flier, it preys on small birds which it seizes in short, twisting, turning chases. The male is slaty-blue above, the female a generally brown bird with a barred tail. In North America the Merlin is called the Pigeon Hawk.
Read Orton, D. A., *Merlins of the Welsh Marches*, David & Charles, Newton Abbot, 1980

Metabolism

A term derived from Greek, meaning change, and relating to the many chemical changes which take place in the cells and tissues of the body, but excluding those occurring in the digestive tract.

Mew Gull

Archaic or poetic name for a Gull, *Larus* spp. A local name for the Common Gull (*Larus canus*).

Red-breasted Merganser, mostly seen on salt water, and (below) the Goosander, more often on fresh water. On the water, the Goosander looks long and low; its bill is hooked at the tip

(opposite) Merlin (female)

170

Migration

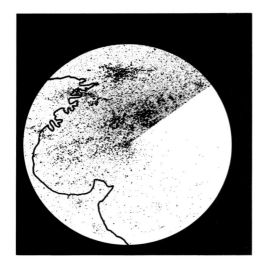

Migration seen on radar

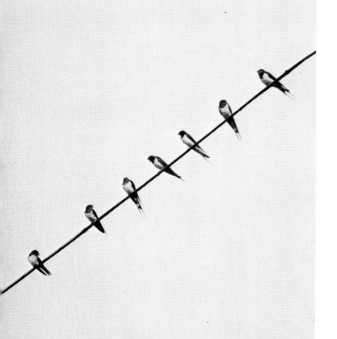

Swallows assembling on wire before migration

Migration

The regular movements of birds between alternate areas they inhabit at different times of year: generally, the movement to and from the areas where they breed and the areas where they spend their non-breeding period. The migration of birds is a phenomenon known to man from the earliest times. The movements of some birds when leaving or returning to their breeding areas, particularly the larger species, Geese, Cranes etc, are most noticeable and often quite dramatic events.

On the other hand the seasonal appearances and disappearances of most smaller species of birds are not easy to observe, and even until comparatively recent times were subject to many strange explanations, eg Swallows were thought to hibernate in mud at the bottom of ponds, Cuckoos to change into hawks, and birds were even believed to fly to the moon. Much of our knowledge of migration has only been obtained in the last 50 years or so. We know most of the places birds migrate to and from, and in many cases their routes, but the mystery of how it is accomplished remains largely unsolved. For a young Cuckoo to make the journey from England to Africa and return to the same neighbourhood in which it was raised is a staggering feat of navigation which cannot be totally explained, as is the case with many other migrants which carry out similar movements. Much of our information has been obtained through ringing birds but other main sources include:

Direct observation of 'visible migration', particularly at observatories.
Observation of birds at lighthouses and lightships, particularly at night when attracted by the light.
Moonwatching—birds can be observed crossing the face of the moon.
Tracking by radar.
Experiments on birds under controlled conditions, chiefly to study premigratory restlessness and orientation.

See Moonwatching; Orientation; Pre-migratory Restlessness

Read Dorst, J., *The Migration of Birds*, Heinemann, 1962; Mathews, G. V. T., *Bird Navigation*, University Press, Cambridge, 1968

Mimicry

This is the advantageous resemblance of one species to another. It is rare in birds, the few instances there are being mostly associated with breeding parasitism, eg some species of

Cuckoo (Cuculidae) show a striking similarity to some birds of prey, while the young of some Cuckoos resemble the young of the host species.

Mimicry, Vocal

It is well known that some birds incorporate the sounds of other species into their songs, and on occasion sounds of a non-avian type. Even plausible imitations of human speech can be produced by Parrots (Psittacidae) and Mynahs (*Acridotheres* spp) which have learned it while in captivity. In the wild, however, the most renowned mimics are the Starling (*Sturnus vulgaris*), the Marsh Warbler (*Acrocephalus palustris*), and the Mockingbird (*Mimus polyglottos*). The Starling is certainly the easiest to observe and listen to, and in two or three minutes of Starling song it is usually possible to pick out the calls of several other species without difficulty—what birdwatcher has not been fooled by a Starling as it gives a perfect rendition of a Curlew from a roof top? The Marsh Warbler, with its limited distribution in Britain—it is a Schedule 1 species—cannot be so readily heard, but those who are fortunate enough to know its song will appreciate its wonderful and varied repertoire, in which one can identify the notes of perhaps a dozen different species in a very short time. Though the Mockingbird is credited with great powers of mimicry,

evidence has been produced indicating that only 10 per cent of its song is actually mimicry. In Africa the best mimics are reputed to be the Robin Chats (*Cossypha* spp) and in Australia the Bowerbirds (Ptilonorhynchidae), the Lyrebirds (Menuridae) and the Scrub Birds (Atrichornithidae).

Mimidae

Family of the Passeriformes, sub-order Oscines. There are 31 species in this family, collectively called Mimine Thrushes. Distribution is limited to the New World, where some are variously known as Catbirds, Mockingbirds and Thrashers. The Mimine Thrushes are solitary in their habits and mostly sedentary. They are excellent singers and good mimics.
See Mimicry; Mockingbird

Minsmere

One of the RSPB's most notable reserves, situated on the Suffolk coast midway between Southwold and Aldeburgh. Covering 1,560 acres (631Ha), it comprises a wide variety of habitats, including freshwater reedbeds with open meres, duneland and seashore, mixed woodland and heaths. One of the strongholds for breeding Avocets in Britain is in part of the reserve known as the 'Scrape'—

Minsmere

a manmade area of shallow brackish water on which not only Avocets but up to 1,000 pairs of Terns breed (mainly Sandwich, but including some Common and Little Terns). Other reserve specialities include Marsh Harrier, Bearded Tit and Bittern. Though visiting is by permit only, there are public hides which can be reached from the beach providing excellent views across the Scrape.
Read Axell, H., and Hosking, E., *Minsmere: Portrait of a Bird Reserve*, Hutchinson, 1977

Mirror
Term used for the small white patches on the primaries of some gulls.

Mist Net
Used to catch birds for ringing, mist nets are so called because of their near-invisibility when in use. First introduced into Britain from Japan in 1956, they revolutionised ringing, enabling many more birds to be caught than by conventional traps. Easily transportable and made of a very fine material,

Minsmere—the Scrape

the nets are strung between poles at any suitable area as required, such as at breaks in hedgerows, or gaps in reedbeds. The birds then fly into the nets. After careful removal they are weighed, measured and ringed etc.
See Heligoland Trap; Ringing

Moa
Substantive name of the extinct order Dinornithiformes, large flightless birds probably standing 10ft (3m) high, inhabiting New Zealand. Extinction has come about only within the last few centuries and these birds were certainly known to the Maoris.

Mobbing
Term applied to the 'anti-predator' display made by most Passerines and some others when confronted by a predator. Most frequently applied to those occasions when small birds harass Owls or other species which appear to pose a threat to them. Also, within

174

Mist net with birds trapped for ringing

the vicinity of a nest with eggs or young, the parent birds will attempt to drive away a 'threatening' species, eg Lapwings will attack a Crow by diving at it. Many species mob human intruders too.

Mockingbird
Substantive name for some of the Mimidae (Passeriformes, sub-order Oscines). In the plural, general term for the family. A New World group, they bear resemblances to both the Thrushes (Turdinae) and larger Wrens (Troglodytidae).
See Mimicry, Vocal

Monotypic
A genus comprising only one species or a species which has no sub-species—contrasted with polytypic.

Montagu, George (1751-1815)
English ornithologist and author of an

Mist netting Sand Martins—the birds are being removed from the net and placed in catching bags before weighing and ringing

Montane

Ornithological Dictionary. The discoverer of Montagu's Harrier (*Circus pygargus*), which is named after him. Montagu's Harrier is a slightly smaller, slimmer bird than the Hen Harrier (*Circus cyaneus*), the male having a greyish instead of white rump and narrow black bars in the centre of the wings. The female Montagu's Harrier even more resembles the female Hen Harrier (which has a totally different plumage from the male), having dark brown upper parts, broadly streaked buffish underparts and a white rump and barred tail. When the observer is unable to be specific the bird is usually referred to as a 'Ringtail', which at one time was considered to be a distinct species. It was Dr John Heysham, a predecessor of Montagu, who in 1783 established beyond doubt that the 'Ringtail' was the female Hen Harrier by keeping young birds alive and noting their colour changes.
See Harrier

Montane

Appertaining to mountains; term applied to the avifauna of elevated areas where the bird life is strikingly different from that of adjacent lower areas.

Moonwatching

A means of studying bird migration by noting the slants and pathways of passing birds which appear as silhouettes when crossing the moon's face. The observer using a telescope visualises the moon as an upright clockface and records their directions (eg 3.30 to 8.30, or whatever it may be). This information, with other accrued data, has provided some very interesting facts, particularly from the United States of America where most moonwatching has been carried out.

Moor Fowl

An old name used in British game laws for the Red Grouse (*Lagopus lagopus*).

Moorhen (*Gallinula chloropus*)

Sometimes known as the Water Hen, this species is common in Britain, found wherever there is the smallest area of water; often no more than a wet ditch is sufficient for its needs. The long green legs, slaty-grey head and body, red frontal shield on the forehead, red bill with yellow tip and conspicuous

Montagu's Harrier

Moonwatching—seeing birds against the face of the moon, through a telescope

white undertail coverts divided by a black line down the centre identify it immediately. When nervous or excited the tail is flirted in a most characteristic manner. On the water it swims buoyantly, jerking its head, and though it does not obtain its food by diving, it will submerge rapidly when surprised to escape danger. Total breeding population of Britain and Ireland around 300,000 pairs.

Morillon

An obsolete name once used by wildfowlers for the immature Goldeneye (*Bucephala clangula*), once thought to be a different species.

Morph

A term introduced by J. S. Huxley to replace the less precise 'phase', denoting any one of the different forms of a species population subject to polymorphism.
See Polymorphism

Mother Carey's Chicken

Sailors' name for Storm Petrels of various species (Hydrobatidae). It originates from the term 'mater cara'.
See Petrel

Motmot

Substantive name of species of the Momotidae (Coraciiformes, sub-order Alcedines), birds of continental tropical America. They are allied to the Kingfishers (Alcedinidae) and the Todies (Todidae). One of their most noteworthy structural peculiarities is the serrated edges on their broad bills. There are eight recorded species of Motmots.

Moult

The periodic shedding and renewal of a bird's plumage. All birds moult at least once a year, many twice a year and some three times. The renewal of feathers is essential to the bird's wellbeing, not only in the maintenance of its health, facilitating such functions as temperature regulation and body protection, but also, for most birds, making flight possible. Additionally, any plumage

Moorhen (or Merehen)

Moult

Blue-throated Motmot

features which are necessary to the bird's successful courtship are important in the continuance of the species and may be present only during the breeding season—thus being affected by moult. The time of a bird's moult invariably correlates with its breeding cycle and with its migration, but though some species undergo a complete moult before migrating some do not moult until their migratory flights have been accomplished. Of particular note is the Shelduck (*Tadorna tadorna*), which undertakes a 'moult migration' at the end of the breeding season. The main body of birds from the British Isles fly to the sandbanks of Heligoland to spend their flightless period.

The cyclical occurrence of moult is determined by physiological factors in which the thyroid and hypothalamic-pituitary-gonadal systems are principally concerned, though physical influences also play a part. Of the latter, light appears to be the most important, but temperature is also a contributing factor.

Research has demonstrated the role of the thyroid gland in the regeneration of a bird's feathering, the failure of which results in the suppression of moult and feather growth. The thyroid acts selectively on different areas of the bird. The body feathering particularly reacts to thyroid secretion, whereas the head, neck, wings and tail are little affected. It is

believed, however, that the gonadal system is the main controlling factor.

During a bird's moult the primaries are usually shed in a definite order, most often being lost in succession from the innermost feathers outwards (generally referred to as descendant moult). Or the moult may begin with two feathers simultaneously, say the first and the seventh primaries, proceeding outwards from each. In other cases, however, the order appears to be irregular. The secondaries are commonly moulted from the outermost feathers inwards. (This, of course, occurs simultaneously on each wing.)

In contrast to all other Passerines, the Spotted Flycatcher (*Muscicapa striata*) moults its primaries from the outermost feathers inwards (ascendant moult), while the rectrices are moulted centripetally. The moult of the secondaries and the tail feathers in this species is also in reverse sequence to that of other Passerines. This reversal may have been originated by a single mutation.

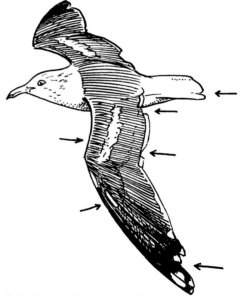

Adult Lesser Black-backed Gull in moult. A large conspicuous bird like this can be examined in the field for signs of moult. Here, the bird's two longest primaries on each wing are old and yet to be replaced; the next is new and three-quarters grown, and a white patch shows its missing covert; the rest are all freshly grown. Several secondaries are missing or still not fully grown and ragged white patches on the upper wing show where some of the coverts have been shed. Other feathers are missing from the tail. Dark winter feathers are appearing on the head

The simultaneous moult of all flight feathers (eclipse) occurs in the Anatidae, but the simultaneous moult of the remiges (wing feathers) is also found in Flamingos (Phoenicopteridae), Grebes (Podicipedidae), Divers (Gaviidae) and Darters (Anhingidae).

Certain families of birds have evolved certain moult sequences, for example in the Woodpeckers (Picidae) and Treecreepers (Certhiidae) the two central rectrices, so essential as support when climbing trees, are retained until the rest of the tail is fully replaced. In some Crows (Corvidae) areas of feathers are moulted simultaneously, while in some birds the procedure is prolonged, as in the Falconiformes; to see some of the larger birds of prey, eg Eagles, with primary feathers missing is not unusual. There are also instances in which the moult sequence differs according to the sex of the bird, such as the Black Grouse (*Lyrurus tetrix*), in which the cock moults twice a year, the hen only once. There may also be differences depending on age, as in some Shrikes (*Lanius* spp), which moult twice a year during the early years of their lives and thereafter only once a year. The timing of a moult is also affected by age, eg young Gulls moult earlier in the autumn than adults because they do not have the pressures of raising a family. Some species, eg some birds of prey, may moult earlier than usual if their attempt at breeding has failed for some reason.

Duration of the moult also varies according to the species. The Ostrich has a protracted moult, while in some Penguins it is rapid—in the Humboldt's Penguin it is over in 12 days.

Certain Passerine species, notably the Starling (*Sturnus vulgaris*), Linnet (*Acanthis cannabina*) and Brambling (*Fringilla montifringilla*), show more contrasting and colourful plumage when abrasion is coupled with their prenuptial moult—the pale edges of the growing feathers wear away to reveal bright colour beneath (abrasive or substractive moult). Possibly the actual colour of the remaining part of the feathers also becomes intensified, since the red of the male Linnet's breast becomes brilliantly scarlet as the breeding season advances.

Feathers accidentally lost are usually regenerated before the next normal moult.
See Abrasion; Eclipse

Moundbuilders
General term for some Megapodes, who lay their eggs in mounds of rotting vegetation to be incubated by the naturally generated heat.
See Megapodidae

Mousebird
Substantive name (alternatively 'Coly') of the species of Coliidae (sole family of the Coliiformes). In the plural, Mousebirds or Colies. Fruit-eating birds confined to the Abyssinian region; there are 6 recorded species.

Mousebird

Moustachial
A streak in some plumage patterns running from the base of the bill, giving the bird a 'moustached' or 'bearded' look, eg the Jay (*Garrulus glandarius*), Green Woodpecker (*Picus viridis*), Hobby (*Falco subbuteo*), Reed Bunting (*Emberiza schoeniclus*).
See Topography

Mouth Markings
A widespread characteristic of nestlings is a brightly coloured mouth, often with a number of contrasting spots on the tongue and soft palate. These are considered to be directive or target marks revealed when the nestling gapes in response to the arrival of the parent bird with food.

Murre
American name for Common Guillemot (*Uria aalge*), formerly used in Britain as a local name for this species.

Murrelet
Substantive name of a number of small Auks occurring in the North Pacific.

Bearded Tit

Muscicapidae

A family of the Passeriformes, sub-order Oscines, embracing a large number of mainly Old World, largely insectivorous, song birds. It comprises the following sub-families (of which several were previously accorded familial rank).

1 Turdinae: includes Thrushes, Robins and Chats
2 Timaliinae: includes the Babblers
3 Cinclosomatinae: Rail-babblers, Quail Thrushes, Logrunners
4 Paradoxornithinae: Parrotbills, Reedling
5 Polioptilinae: Gnatcatchers and Gnatwrens
6 Sylviinae: includes Old World Warblers and Kinglets
7 Malurinae: Australian 'Wrens'
8 Muscicapinae: includes Old World Flycatchers
9 Pachycephalinae: Shrike-thrushes and Whistlers

Mutation

A species of bird (or other animal) that has undergone some genetic change which when transmitted to its offspring gives rise to a heritable variation. This may not necessarily show in the bird's appearance, instead perhaps in its behaviour. Ernst Mayr suggested that the spread westwards of the Collared Dove (*Streptopelia decaocto*) was possibly due to a genetic mutation in the western peripheral population of this bird, as it is only this segment of the Collared Dove's total population that has spread so dramatically. Amongst the Wagtail group, inter-breeding occurs between distinctive sub-species and mutants occur. Birds which could not be separated from Sykes's Wagtail (*Motacilla flava beema*) have been noted in Britain, but it is believed these birds are mutants of independent origin and not from their true home in western Siberia.

See Wagtail

Muttonbird

Local name for various species of Petrel (Procellariidae). In New Zealand applied to the Sooty Shearwater (*Puffinus griseus*— a species which is a regular migrant to British waters—and in Australia applied to the Short-tailed Shearwater (*Puffinus tenuirostris*). In both these areas the young of both species were collected commercially for human consumption—hence the name.

Mynah

Substantive name of various Asian species of the genera *Acridotheres*, *Gracula* and *Sturnus*. The Indian Hill Mynah (*Gracula religiosa*), the largest of its kind, is one that is frequently kept in captivity and is perhaps the most famous for its talking abilities. One advantage Mynahs have in this respect is that birds which have learned to talk will do so in front of people, whereas Parrots often refuse to talk before an audience.

Naivasha, Lake

Considered to be one of the most beautiful of the African Rift Valley Lakes, and situated only 50 miles from Nairobi, this area is one of Kenya's top places for birds. With a shoreline of papyrus beds, secluded lagoons and vast areas of semi-submerged vegetation, it supports a wide variety of waders, Terns, Gulls and birds of prey as well as many other types.

Nakuru, Lake

This lake in Kenya is one of East Africa's top birding places, particularly noted for waterfowl, including Cape Wigeon, Maccoa Duck and Greater and Lesser Flamingo.

Name, Common

Or popular or vernacular name, of which some of our birds have many. These vary from region to region and even from county to county. They invariably reflect some aspect of the bird's appearance or behaviour, though some were corruptions of words from ancient languages not obviously explicable. Standardisation of birds' names brought about by usage through greater communication and the printed word has virtually removed such poetic and archaic names from the scene, but even in today's tidy world, one or two of the 'old names' continue to be used, certainly in anecdotal ornithological writings; eg Stormcock for Mistle Thrush, Tom Tit for Blue Tit, Sea Pie for Oystercatcher, etc.
Read Greenoak, F., *All the Birds of the Air— The Names, Lore and Literature of British Birds*, Deutsch, 1979; Kirkeswan, H., *A Dictionary of English and Folk Names of British Birds*, 1913, reprinted E.P. Publishing, Wakefield, 1977

Name, English

The usual name of a bird as opposed to its Latin or scientific name. English names are part of a living language and change with usage. Those current today are subject to change as much as any other terminology, though the tendency in recent years (certainly encouraged by ornithologists) has been to shorten cumbersome compound names, such as Gold-crested Wren to Goldcrest, or Leach's Fork-tailed Petrel to Leach's Petrel. The prefix 'Common' likewise is now omitted in many instances where it is really unnecessary, and the redundant second term in Fulmar Petrel, Eider Duck and others has been dropped. Also in recent years, some names have been changed in favour of a term more accurately reflecting the bird's classification, eg Buff-backed Heron is now Cattle Egret. Some of the names commemorating a bird's discoverer, or some other notable personage, have also been changed: for example, Eversman's Warbler became Arctic Warbler and Buffon's Skua became Long-tailed Skua.

Whether or not to use capital initial letters for the English names of species is a controversial point. Ordinary literary usage has preferred small letters and some ornithological publications follow this, but certainly for scientific purposes it is considered there are advantages in the use of capital letters: references to particular species are more easily picked out on a page, and also no ambiguities arise when names prefixed by such adjectives as Little or Great are used, eg Little Ringed Plover, Little Gull, Little Bustard, Great Bustard, etc.

Name, Scientific

See Nomenclature

Name, Substantive

Term used for the noun that is the chief element in the English name of a number of species distinguished from each other by qualifying adjectives, eg Plover: Little Ringed, Golden or whatever the adjective may be. For a few species a single word serves as the complete name, eg Avocet, Hoopoe, Siskin.

Natural Environment Research Council

Established by Royal Charter in 1965, its objects are to encourage, plan and execute research in those sciences—physical and biological—which relate to man's natural environment and its resources. Amongst the component establishments of the Council are the Nature Conservancy Council and the Institute of Hydrology. Address: Alhambra House, 29-33 Charing Cross Road, London WC2.

Naturalised Birds

The term applied to species that have been introduced deliberately (or have escaped from captivity), have successfully established themselves and are breeding regularly as wild birds in areas where they were not previously to be found. In Britain the longer-established introduced naturalised birds are the Pheasant (*Phasianus colchicus*) from Asia, the Red-

Canada Geese, in Britain introduced, naturalised birds

legged Partridge (*Alectoris rufa*) from Southern Europe, the Little Owl (*Athene noctua*) from Western Europe and the Canada Goose (*Branta canadensis*) from North America. In more recent times the Egyptian Goose (*Alopochen aegyptiaca*), the Wood Duck (*Aix sponsa*) from North America, the Mandarin Duck (*Aix galericulata*) from Asia, the Ruddy Duck (*Oxyjura jamaicensis*) from North America, the Golden Pheasant (*Chrysolophus pictus*), Lady Amherst's Pheasant (*Chrysolophus amherstiae*), have become established breeding birds and are considered as naturalised, being accepted on to the official British and Irish List.

Read Lever, C., *The Naturalised Animals of the British Isles*, Granada, 1979

Nature Conservancy Council

Established by Act of Parliament in 1973, the NCC is the official government body responsible for the conservation of flora and fauna and geological and physiographical features throughout Great Britain. It is financed by the Department of the Environment but is free to express independent views. The NCC establishes, maintains and manages National Nature Reserves throughout Great Britain.

Little Owl, a long-established naturalised bird in Britain

It advises the government on nature conservation policies and on how other policies may affect nature conservation. It provides advice and information for all whose activities affect the natural environment, and it commissions, supports and undertakes research. The NCC looks after 135 National Nature Reserves totalling nearly 300,000 acres (121,400Ha). Some are owned, some loaned, others established under a nature reserve agreement. In addition, over 3,000 sites of special scientific interest (SSSIs) have been notified to local planning authorities.

The NCC is also responsible for granting or approving certain licences in connection with Acts protecting birds, deer, seals and badgers. It produces numerous informative, advisory and promotional publications and details of these can be obtained from the Nature Conservancy Council Headquarters, 19 Belgrave Square, London SW1X 8PY. The Welsh headquarters is situated at Penrhos Road, Bangor, Caernarvonshire LL57 2LQ and the Scottish headquarters at 12 Hope Terrace, Edinburgh EH9 2AS. There are also various regional offices (see local directories).

Navigation
When used in relation to birds, their ability to orientate themselves in the absence of familiar landmarks.
See Migration; Orientation

Nearctic Region
The zoogeographical area comprising North America, from the Arctic Ocean in the north, the Bering Straits and the Pacific Ocean in the west, and the Atlantic Ocean in the east, southward to approximately the line of the northern edge of the tropical rain forests of Mexico.
See Zoogeography

Near-passerine
This refers to a small group of Orders which are close to the order Passeriformes in classification and which have same features more or less in common with the Passerines and more or less distinct from those non-Passerines such as Anseriformes and Chara-driiformes. Thus it is an unscientific term which groups together birds which might be grouped with the Passerines by a casual observer—including Apodiformes (Swifts and Hummingbirds), Coraciiformes (Kingfishers, Bee-eaters, Rollers, Hoopoes, etc) and Piciformes (Honeyguides, Woodpeckers, etc). The Passerines are distinguished by the form of the foot (four toes which are never webbed and with three directed forward, one back) and also often by their songs and calls, wing structure and the form of their spermatozoa and syrinx.

Ne-ne
Vernacular name for the Hawaiian Goose (*Branta sandvicensis*). Many of these geese

Ne-ne

have been reared in captivity at the Wildfowl Trust, Slimbridge, and returned to their native Hawaii, where they had become an endangered species.

Neotropical Region
The zoogeographical area comprising tropical America and the non-tropical parts of South America together with the West Indies and other adjacent islands. The region as a whole extends from the northern edge of the tropical rain forests of Mexico south to Cape Horn.
See Zoogeography

Neossoptile
Term applied to the natal down plumage, where present (from the Greek *neos*, young, and *ptilon*, feather), as contrasted with teleoptile, the final feathers.

Nest
The structure made by a bird in which the eggs are laid and incubated and in which the young may be raised to the fledgling stage. Many birds in fact make no nest in the accepted sense, laying their eggs directly on the ground (*see* Scrape) or in holes without nest material, whilst others lay their eggs in structures but do not incubate the eggs. A few species, particularly the Old World Cuckoos (*Cuculidae*), have no nests of their own, depositing their eggs in the nest of a host species. The Emperor Penguin (*Aptenodytes forsteri*) and King Penguin (*Aptenodytes patagonica*) incubate their single egg between the belly and feet, shuffling about with it held in that position until it hatches. Many nests are quite simple constructions, but among the Passerines (perching birds), in particular, some most complex nests are found. Birds of this group which nest in Britain and build sophisticated and what may be described as beautiful nests include the Long-tailed Tit (*Aegithalos caudatus*), the Goldcrest (*Regulus regulus*) and the Reed Warbler (*Acrocephalus scirpaceus*).

Other interesting structures are the nests of the Swallow (*Hirundo rustica*) and House Martin (*Delichon urbica*), the latter mainly built of wet mud mixed with the birds' saliva. The Song Thrush (*Turdus philomelos*) uses mud and pieces of rotten wood to reinforce the inside bowl of its nest, and the Nuthatch (*Sitta europaea*) is unique among

Long-tailed Tit's nest: for other nest types, see next page

Pheasant's nest and eggs (above)   Black Guillemot's nest and eggs (below)

Little Penguin on nest, with chicks (above)   Avocet at its nest (below)

British birds in tailoring a natural nesting hole to the right size by the use of mud.
Read Goodfellow, P., *Birds as Builders*, David & Charles, Newton Abbot, 1977
Campbell and Ferguson-Lees, *A Field Guide to Birds' Nests*, Constable, 1972

Nestbox

Charles Waterton, an early 19th-century Yorkshire squire, is believed to have been the first naturalist to put up boxes simply to encourage birds to nest—though nestboxes have their origins in the Middle Ages, when clay flasks were used in Holland and wooden cistulae (flasks) in Silesia. There were no conservation aims in mind at that time: the object was then to ensure that a ready source of food was available, the first broods of sparrows or starlings being taken for this purpose (a similar principle to the dovecote).

The idea of using nestboxes on any scale simply to attract birds to nest was applied in Germany in 1901 when 300 boxes were put up in woodland by a Baron von Berlepsch, with remarkable success—all 300 boxes were used, by 14 species of birds. The boxes used by von Berlepsch were the hollowed-out log type, the natural appearance probably being considered necessary, though it has been

White Stork

shown over the years that the rustic touch does not increase their attraction to birds—the external appearance seems of little consequence, the siting, proportions, and hole size being much more important. Traditionally wood is favoured for most nest boxes, though other materials such as plastic, cement and sawdust etc, have been used. The two major nestbox styles are the closed variety, with an entrance hole, designed mainly to attract Titmice, Pied Flycatcher etc and the open-fronted type suitable for Robins, Pied Wagtails, Spotted Flycatchers and Redstarts. These traditional designs have been adapted to attract various other species, with larger versions for Woodpeckers (the Upton box), Owls (the Owl chimney) and Kestrels, Stock Doves, Jackdaws and Ducks.

Artificial nests for House Martins have proved highly successful, and some conservation-minded architects even specify cavity bricks in their designs with the nesting requirements of the Swift in mind.

As well as nestboxes there are other means of encouraging certain birds to nest. Cartwheels or special platforms have been erected in Holland and elsewhere to encourage White

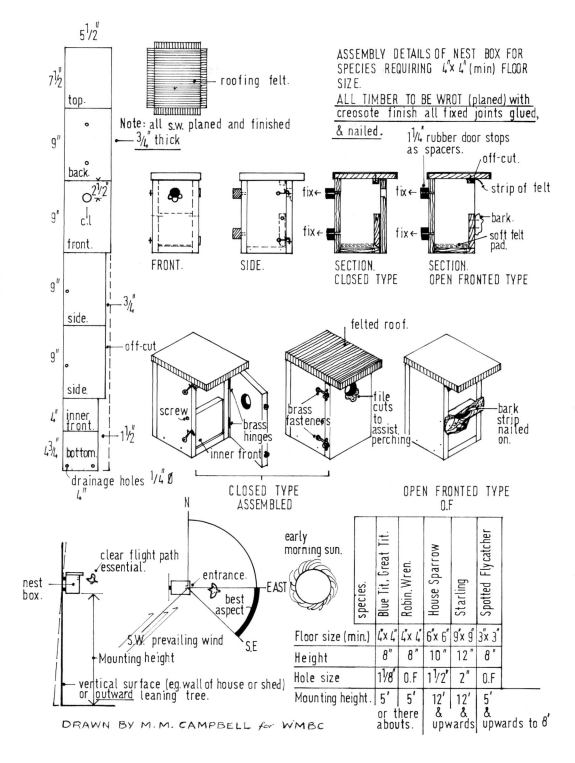

Storks, a practice going back several centuries, and this means has been used very successfully in N America to attract Ospreys. Duck baskets, also of Dutch origin, are widely used to encourage Mallard and other species.

The erection of a nestbox in a garden, if it is properly sited with suitable nearby feeding, will nearly always encourage a pair of Blue Tits or Great Tits to take up residence and the provision of many boxes in suburban gardens has surely helped to increase the population of these species. There have also been a number of schemes to box large areas of woodland, some by the Forestry Commission and many by County Naturalists' Trusts, all of which undoubtedly contribute to the breeding success of the species which can take advantage of them.
Read Flegg, J. J. M. and Glue, D. E., BTO Guide No 4, *Nest Boxes*

Nest Record Scheme

A long-running scheme organised by the British Trust for Ornithology. It grew out of the Hatching and Fledging Enquiry started by Sir Julian Huxley and James Fisher in 1939. It aim was to obtain fundamental information on the breeding biology of birds by collecting data on nests from observers all over Great Britain. Specially printed cards were produced for the scheme and 4,000 had been returned to the BTO by 1947. In the following 10 years the annual total rose to 15,000 cards. In recent years as many as 25,000 cards have been returned in a season. Information gathered relates to such aspects of breeding biology as the number of eggs laid and young reared, the length of the breeding season, how breeding success is affected by such factors as climate and human activity etc. Analysis of the accumulated data of around half a million cards is now made by computer and material is frequently published.
Read Gross, H. M., *The Nest Record Scheme*, BTO Guide No. 2.

Netting

Netting is the term formerly used for illicit capture of birds, but today it invariably refers to their capture for ringing purposes by the use of mist nets.
See Mist Net

A quantity of nest boxes have been provided on the Ladywalk Wildfowl Nature Reserve (opposite)

Neusiedl Lake

An area of great interest and much visited by birdwatchers, situated in eastern Austria less than 50 miles from Vienna. The lake straddles the Austrian-Hungarian border, though most of its 20-mile length lies on the Austrian side. A relatively shallow water, it has vast reed beds, some up to 3 miles wide, providing breeding areas suitable for Great White Egret and Little Egret, Spoonbill, Purple Heron, Bittern, Little Bittern, various Rails, Bearded and Penduline Tits. The surrounding region is also rich in bird life and the numerous saline lakes of the nearby Seewinter are notable for their wading birds and wildfowl. The Neusiedl ridge is good for Shrikes and various birds of prey and other interesting species.

New World Seed Eater

A member of the Fringillidae family. One of the largest bird families, it contains over 300 species and includes the Buntings, Finches and Sparrows.

New World Warbler

An alternative name for a complex family of songbirds that includes such groups as Tanagers (Thraupinae), Honeycreepers (Coerebinae), Cardinal Grosbeaks (Pyrrhuloxiinae) and Troupials (Icteridae), often called 'American Warblers' or 'Wood Warblers', the latter not to be confused with the Wood Warbler (*Phylloscopus sibilatrix*) of the western palearctic, which is one of the 'Leaf Warblers'.

Niche

The place in the total community that a species is enabled to occupy by virtue of its adaptations.

Nictitating membrane

A transparent skin-like membrane that can be drawn across a birds' eye without shutting off all light. Used as a cleansing medium and for protection (underwater), it is sometimes called the third eyelid. (Photograph page 192).

Nidicolous

Living in the nest—a term applied to birds whose young when hatched are helpless, with eyes closed, and which remain in the nest until more or less ready to fly, eg Passerines.

(above) Nidifugous birds—Curlew chicks   Nictitating membrane over eye of Tawny Owl

Nidifugous
Leaving the nest soon after hatching—a term applied to birds that have a covering of down and open eyes on hatching and can leave the nest area within a very short time, eg wading birds, game birds, etc.

Nighthawk
Substantive name of various New World species of Caprimulgidae (Nightjars). In the plural used for the sub-family Chordeilinae.

Nightingale
Substantive name of some *Luscinia* spp. In Britain used for *Luscinia megarhynchos*, a bird more widely known for its song than for its appearance. A summer visitor arriving mid-April and leaving in August, it breeds locally in England roughly south of a line from the Humber to the Severn. It does not breed in Ireland. It has declined considerably in recent years, total population now being probably under 10,000 pairs.

The Thrush-nightingale or Sprosser (*Luscinia luscinia*) is a darker, more olive-brown bird of the same size, having a brownish mottled breast. It breeds in Eastern Europe and eastwards into part of Asia. Similar in behaviour to the Nightingale, its song is equally musical and possibly more powerful. A vagrant to Britain, with under 40 records in the last 20 years.

Nightjar
Substantive name of the Old World species of Caprimulgidae (Caprimulgiformes, sub-order

Nightingale

Caprimulgi). In the plural, general term for the family. In North America the names Goatsuckers and Nighthawks are more often used, though some of the birds have special names derived from their calls, eg Whip-poor-will (*Caprimulgus vociferus*). There are about 70 known species of these nocturnal Hawk-like insectivorous birds, divided into two sub-families: the Chordeilinae—Nighthawks, and the Caprimulgae which include the European Nightjar (*Caprimulgus europaeus*), a summer visitor to Britain. A bird of the twi-light, it becomes active as darkness falls, when its vibrant churring or jarring song can be heard from May to July. When it rests, by day, its cryptic coloration, of grey-brown mottled, spotted, streaked and barred with dark brown, renders it almost invisible against a background of earth and plant debris. As a British breeding species it has declined considerably in recent years and is now mainly concentrated in Southern England. A few pairs nest in Ireland. Total population is probably less than 5,000 pairs. Vagrant Nightjars that visit Britain include the Red-necked Nightjar (*Caprimulgus ruficollis*) and Egyptian Nightjar (*Caprimulgus aegyptius*).

Nocturnal
Active at night. In the bird world, Owls (Strigiformes) are the most outstanding and best-known family of birds of this type. The Oilbirds (Steatornithidae) and Kiwis (Apterygidae) are also species that have adapted to

night-time activities. While Nightjars (Caprimulgidae) might be regarded as night birds, they are more crepuscular than nocturnal in their feeding habits. Some other species are only nocturnal when it comes to nesting activities, particularly the Petrels (*Procellariiformes*). Some wading birds (*Charadrii*) and some wildfowl (Anatidae) are partly nocturnal, frequently feeding at night, particularly during full moon periods.

Noddy
Substantive name (plural Noddies) of some species of Tern found throughout the tropical and sub-tropical oceans of the world. *Anous* species are the only dark brown Terns (except the immature Sooty Tern (*Sterna fuscata*) and the only Terns with a full rounded tail. Accidental in Europe.

Noddy Tern

194

Nightjar—only the male has the white on wings and tail

Nomenclature
The scientific naming of species, sub-species, genera, families and other categories in which species may be classified. Latin is used as the internationally accepted language for this purpose. So far as the animal kingdom is concerned (which includes birds) the practice of naming is governed by the International Code of Zoological Nomenclature. This system of rules and recommendations authorised by the International Congress of Zoology aims to promote stability and universality in the scientific naming of animals and to ensure that each name is unique and distinct.

The essence of the system is that every species is placed in a genus and bears the name of that genus plus its own specific name. Thus the House Sparrow is placed in the genus *Passer* (meaning Sparrow), and this is followed by the name *domesticus* indicating its association with man. Thus *Passer domesticus* (the generic name is always spelled with a capital letter). *See* Binominal System; Classification

Norfolk Ornithologists' Association
Primarily concerned with the study of bird migration in Norfolk, its main centre of

operations is the Holme Bird Observatory. Open daily, visiting permits are obtainable on the spot. The Association has an Information Centre at Salthouse and runs the Dodman Farm Reserve at Titchwell. An annual report is also published. For details of the NOA write to Aslack Way, Holme-next-the-Sea, Hunstanton, Norfolk
See Holme Bird Observatory

Nuchal
Pertaining to the nape.
See Topography

Numbers
Numbers of birds have always had a fascination to those who watch them and at present numbers are even more meaningful and important in the field of conservation. Scientifically based data are essential when arguing the importance or value of areas known to provide feeding or breeding places for birds. Over the last 30 years the British Trust for Ornithology has been pre-eminent in organising counts and censuses of various species and groups of birds. In particular the Common Bird Census monitors the changes in the populations of our commoner nesting birds, since 1961, while the Wildfowl Counts organised by the Wildfowl Trust have provided statistical evidence of the changing fortunes of our Ducks and Geese.

Of the world's sea birds, Wilson's Petrel (*Oceanites oceanicus*) is probably the most numerous, breeding in millions along the edge of Antarctica. Its migration annually takes it into the North Atlantic, but only a handful have ever been noted in British waters. There are other sea birds whose populations run into millions, such as the Sooty Tern (*Sterna fuscata*), also known as the Wideawake, with about 10 million breeding on one island of the Seychelles group alone. Britain's most numerous sea bird is probably the Guillemot (*Uria aalge*), which Operation Seafarer put at over half a million pairs in 1970.

About 8,600 different species of birds are known to exist in the world at present, and of this total some populations number a few thousand pairs, or in some cases only a few hundred or even less. However, there are many more populations that run into millions. The most abundant species in the world is reckoned to be the Red-billed Quelea (*Quelea quelea*), a small African Weaver Finch whose numbers are estimated to be as high as 10 billion. The only other land bird whose population is believed to have come anywhere near this figure is the now extinct Passenger Pigeon (*Ectopistes migratorius*) of North America, of which at one time there were estimated to be around 9 billion. After the Red-billed Quelea, the Starling (*Sturnus vulgaris*) is thought to be the most abundant bird, at around 2 billion.
See Population

Nun
Substantive name of some Mannikins, *Lonchura* spp. Popular cage birds.

Nuptial
Pertaining to the breeding season. A term applied especially to plumage and display.

Nutcracker (*Nucifraga caryocatactes*)
Similar in size to the Jackdaw, this member of the crow family (*Corvidae*) is a dark chocolate-brown in colour, boldly speckled with white, and with very conspicuous white under-tail coverts. A bird of the pine forests, it prefers more mountainous areas in the southern part of its range. The birds of Europe belong to the so-called Thick-billed sub-species *Nucifraga c. caryocatactes*, while those found further east into Asia belong to the Slender-billed sub-species *Nucifraga c. macrorhynchos*. The two forms are only safely identifiable in the hand, though the differences in bill shape are detectable to those who are familiar with both. The Nutcracker is subject to irruptive movements when its major food supply, the cone crop, fails, and then occurs in areas where it is not normally found. Large numbers of the Slender-billed form invaded Britain during 1968; over 300 sightings were made. Many also turned up in Holland, Germany and France and some were recorded as far south as Portugal. Clark's Nutcracker (*Nucifraga columbiana*) is a distinctive grey and black bird, the New World representative of the genus, being found exclusively in the western half of North America, from British Columbia to California. It is often very tame, particularly at camp sites, foraging amongst rubbish bins and sometimes even taking food from the hand.

Nuthatch
Substantive name of the more typical species of Sittidae (Passeriformes, sub-order Oscines), the name used in Britain for the common

195

Clark's Nutcracker

Nuthatch. Its presence is often detected by the loud tapping of its bill on a nut it has wedged in a crevice

European species (*Sitta europaea*). In the plural a general name for the family. All members of the family are climbing birds that seek their food in trees, or in a few cases on rocks. There are 21 species, most of which inhabit Asia and Europe. There are also four species in North America. Small birds ranging from 3¾in (840mm) to 7½in (1830mm) in length, Nuthatches are similar in form, with compact body, short tail and very strong claws. They do not use the tail for support as Woodpeckers (*Picidae*) do, but move up, down and sideways on trees, seemingly indifferent to gravity, using only their claws.

In Britain the slate-blue-grey upper parts and buff under parts, and the bold black streak through the eye of the Nuthatch (*Sitta europaea*), are familiar to birdwatchers who reside in England south of a line from the Mersey to the Wash, especially in woodland and parks where plenty of old timber abounds. In such places its loud boyish whistle, or its loud trilling call can be heard. The total population is probably around 20,000 pairs. Europe also has the Corsican Nuthatch (*Sitta whiteheadi*), confined to Corsica, the Rock Nuthatch (*Sitta neumayer*), found in Greece and the Balkans, and the Wallcreeper (*Tichodroma muraria*) which also belongs to this family and occurs in mountainous regions from Spain to the Balkans.
See Wallcreeper

Bird observatories in Britain and Ireland

Observatory

A centre for ornithological study, especially connected with migration and ringing. Observatories are located at some favourable place where migrant birds regularly occur, usually an island or headland. They may be manned throughout the year or only during part of the year, usually April to October or November. Self-supporting, they offer accommodation of varying standards for visiting birdwatchers who come to help with the ringing or other studies. The network of observatories round Britain is shown on the accompanying map.

The concept of observatories as trapping and ringing stations stemmed from the work of Heinrich Gatke on the North Sea island of Heligoland, where he spent much of his life (during the 19th century) collecting specimens and making daily surveys and counts of migrant birds. The 'daily census' of birds present, is today standard practice at all British bird observatories. The modern observatory at Heligoland, however, was not established until 1909, when the large-scale trapping and ringing of migrant birds was undertaken, using specially designed wirenetting traps, still universally known as 'Heligoland traps'.

The first British bird observatory was set up on Skokholm by R. M. Lockley in 1933, followed by another on the Isle of Man in 1934. It was not until after World War II that some of today's well-known observatories such as Spurn (1946), Fair Isle (1948) and Gibraltar Point (1949), were established; others, like Lundy (1946), Cley (1950) and Monks House (1951), are unfortunately no longer in operation.

The work at the various observatories has always been closely linked with the British Trust for Ornithology which from time to time has provided cash grants, especially to struggling young observatories. However, it is the Bird Observatories Council, formed in 1970, that in liaison with the BTO decides which projects the various observatories will undertake.

Some well-known European observatories are sited at Radolfzell in Western Germany, Ottenby and Falsterbo in Sweden, Revtangen in Norway, Blaavandshuk in Denmark and Texel, Holland.

197

Occiput

Read Durman, R. (ed), *Bird Observatories in Britain and Ireland*, Poyser, Berkhamsted, 1976

Occiput
The back of the head (*adj* occipital)
See Topography

Oceanic Birds
Usually taken to include any species capable of existing for long periods at sea, but generally applied to most of the order Procellariiformes which include such families as the Diomedeidae (Albatrosses), Procellariidae (Petrels and Shearwaters), Hydrobatidae (Storm Petrels) and Pelecanoididae (Diving Petrels).
See Pelagic

Ocella
Eye-like pattern on plumage, eg as in tail of Peacock (*Pavo* spp).

Oilbird (*Steatornis caripensis*)
Sole member of the neotropical family Steatornithidae (Caprimulgiformes, sub-order Steatornithes). Also known as Guacharo and in Trinidad, Diablotin. In appearance it is something between a large Nightjar (*Caprimulgidae* spp) and a Hawk (*Accipitridae* spp), though it has evolved behaviour unlike either of those two families or any other bird for that matter; it is the only nocturnal fruit-eating bird in the world. A gregarious species living in caves, oilbirds spend the day crouched on ledges. They fly out at night to feed on fruit, which is plucked on the wing by means of a strong hooked bill. In the pitch dark of their cavern homes they navigate by echo location, using a series of rapid clicking sounds. It also utters loud screaming and snarling calls. It breeds from Western Guyana through Venezuela and Columbia to Ecuador, Peru and Trinidad.
See Echo Location

Oil Gland
Situated above the root of the tail, it is also called the 'preen gland' or uropygial gland. The gland is found in the great majority of birds but is absent in the Ostrich (*Struthio camelus*), Emus, Cassowaries (*Casuariidae*), Bustards (*Otididae*) and some others. The function of the gland has been much debated, but for many birds it certainly supplies oil used for preening; the oil is applied via the bill to the feathers, maintaining their condition and waterproofing them. The gland tends to be very well developed in aquatic birds. It has been suggested that it may serve some purpose as a scent organ, but only in a few species does the secretion have any strong odour, and as birds in general are not credited with any acute sense of smell this seems unlikely.

Oil Pollution
Refers essentially to pollution of the sea by oil from ships—taking two basic forms, accidental spillage due to error, breakage or collision, and deliberate discharge of waste matter in contravention of the law. Probably the regular small discharges of oil and minor spillages cause the majority of bird deaths, although the occasional more spectacular incident (eg the wrecks of the *Torrey Canyon* and the *Amoco Cadiz*) create greater publicity and have immediate spectacular localised effects on birds. Further incidents, eg blow-outs of oil wells, have great disaster potential should they occur at the wrong place at the wrong time. The Shetlands, for instance, have extremely large and exceptionally vulnerable populations of seabirds which could be enormously reduced by a large, untimely spillage of oil from the variety of installations on and around the islands. Oil pollution affects very many species but certain groups, eg Auks, Divers, Gulls, Cormorants and Ducks, are especially subject to mortality when they encounter oil at sea.
Read Marine Oil Pollution and Birds, RSPB, 1980

Oldsquaw
North American name (spelt as one word) for the Long-tailed Duck (*Clangula hyemalis*).

Old World Flycatchers
Members of the family *Muscicapidae*, 134 species are distributed through Eurasia, Africa and Australia. These Flycatchers are small short-billed birds and vary greatly in coloration. Some are quite dull-looking, such as the Spotted Flycatcher (*Muscicapa striata*), a common summer visitor to Britain, while the Red-capped Robin Flycatcher (*Petroica goodenovii*), an Australian species, is a combination of black, white and red. Mainly birds of forest and woodland, a few live in more open habitats. Most feed on insects caught in the air; the bird makes a short flight from its perch to capture passing prey.

See Flycatcher; New World Flycatchers; Tyrant Flycatchers

Old World Warblers

Members of the family Sylviinae comprising 270-odd species of small, slender-billed, generally plain-looking birds. Most are forest-dwellers, but some inhabit marshes and some open scrubby country. Includes some of the most accomplished songsters of all birds.
See New World Warblers; Warbler

Oology

The scientific study of birds' eggs, with particular reference to external characteristics, such as shape, size, texture and coloration. Formerly a popular subject, particularly during the latter half of the 19th century. Much so-called oology was however merely the collecting of eggs, rather than their study. In recent times there has been great controversy over this practice and in effect no such study is now legal, as all birds' eggs and nests have been protected by law. Only with a special licence from the Natural Environmental Research Council can eggs be taken and this is usually done only to determine the cause of hatching failure in some particular species.

Operation Seafarer

A census taken in 1969-1970, when professional and amateur ornithologists throughout the British Isles combined to map and count all seabird colonies. Planned by the Executive Committee of the Seabird Group, and directed by them and a specially appointed census committee; the results provided invaluable information on the status of our seabirds.
Read Cramp, Bourne and Saunders, *The Seabirds of Britain and Ireland*, Collins, 1974.
See Seabird Group

Orbital

A distinctive area round the eye in some plumage patterns. Some groups, eg Gulls and birds of prey have a thin, fleshy orbital ring, often brightly coloured.

Order

A primary taxonomic category, being a subdivision of a class of a life form—in this instance the class Aves—birds. All ordinal names end in 'iformes' (formerly 'morphae'). The aim of an ordinal grouping is to express the phylogeneric relationships between families within the order. There is, however, great uncertainty at this level of division, and the content of orders has changed greatly in the light of new knowledge; today it is still subject to many differing views, with some authorities sceptical of the evidence of relationships and tending to support more separate orders, while others place more families together, thus reducing the number of orders (in the vernacular, the 'splitters and lumpers'). Many orders, of course, are not in serious dispute, and some comprise only a single family and merely express the fact that the order does not appear to have any near relationships.

A sub-order is a secondary taxonomic category; this is not a grouping of superfamilies and not all orders are divided into sub-orders, the category being used only when required. The names of sub-orders end in ordinary Latin plural forms ('i', 'ae'. 'es').

In listing orders it is customary to begin with those that are believed to be the most primitive and to proceed towards the more highly developed—Ostriches (Struthioniformes) to 'perching birds' (Passeriformes). At one time they were listed the other way round and occasionally this is done today. The world's birds are grouped into 27 orders:

Struthioniformes	Gruiformes
Rheiformes	Charadriiformes
Casuariiformes	Columbiformes
Apterygiformes	Psittaciformes
Tinamiformes	Cuculiformes
Sphenisciformes	Strigiformes
Gaviiformes	Caprimulgiformes
Podicipediformes	Apodiformes
Procellariiformes	Coliiformes
Pelecaniformes	Trogoniformes
Ciconiiformes	Coraciiformes
Anseriformes	Piciformes
Falconiformes	Passeriformes
Galliformes	

Oriental Region

Also known as the Indian region, it is one of the major zoogeographical divisions of the earth. Largely within the tropics, its northern boundary runs from the Hindu Kush mountains in the west along the entire length of the Himalayas and then east to include Yunnan and Szechnan. It continues south of the Yangtze Kiang basin to the East China Sea. From its western extremity the boundary runs south-west but excludes Afghanistan and Baluchistan, down the valley of the Indus to its mouth near Karachi in West Pakistan.

Orientation

Also includes Taiwan (Formosa) and Hainan, as well as the greater part of the Indonesian Archipelago, the Philippines, Borneo, Celebes and islands east to Timor.
See Zoogeography

Orientation

The ability of a migratory bird to determine its geographical position and thus move in a fixed direction to locate a required destination. Still one of the most complex puzzles of bird migration. Many theories have been advanced to explain this remarkable ability. Certainly the recognition of landmarks plays its part in determining a bird's travels over short distances, but over large featureless land masses (deserts), and particularly over miles of ocean, other factors as yet undetermined must come into it.
Read Dorst, J., *The Migration of Birds*, Heinemann, 1962
See Migration

Oriole

Substantive name of most species of Oriolidae (Passeriformes, sub-order Oscines). In the plural and in an Old World context, general term for the family. In North America the name is also used for some members of the Icteridae (Icterids).

In Britain the Golden Oriole (*Oriolus oriolus*) is an uncommon but regular summer visitor and some do nest here. Though the male is an unmistakable brilliant yellow with black wings and tail, it is a secretive bird and normally stays well hidden with only its fluty 'weela-weeo' call to betray its presence. The Northern Oriole (*Icterus galbula*) is a vagrant to Britain from North America.

Golden Oriole

Ornis

Greek word for bird (plural *ornithes*).

Ornithichnite

A geological term for a bird's footprint preserved in stone.

Ornitholite

A geological term for the fossilised remains of a bird.

Ornithology

The scientific study of birds as carried out by an ornithologist (one who studies birds); that branch of Zoology concerned with the class Aves. The term ornithology is sometimes misapplied to birdwatching, which is generally a recreational pursuit though birdwatchers and ornithologists often combine and numerous surveys and a great deal of census work could not be undertaken without the help of birdwatchers. For example the *Atlas of Breeding Birds of Britain and Ireland* could not have been produced without the aid of 10,000 birdwatchers over the five-year period needed for the project.
See Atlas

Ornithosis

Disease identical with or closely related to psittacosis. Caused by *Chlamydia psittaci*, an organism that can produce fatal pneumonia in humans. Initially Parrots and other psittacine birds were thought to be the only avian hosts.
Read Cooper, J. E. and Eley, J. T., *First Aid and Care of Wild Birds*, David & Charles, Newton Abbot, 1979.
See Disease

Ortolan

Alternatively Ortolan Bunting (*Emberiza hortulana*). This Yellowhammer-sized bird is a passage migrant in Britain, occuring in small numbers, mainly in autumn. At such times it is usually the immature birds that turn up and not the more readily identified adult males, which have pinkish-buff underparts and yellow throat, olive-green head and chest, olive moustachial stripe, yellow eye-ring and pink bill. Their presence is often only determined by their call notes, a soft 'tsee-up' and 'tsip', and a piping 'tseu'. The Ortolan breeds quite widely on the continent, preferring open hilly country, nesting on the ground in growing crops or weeds. Cretzschmar's Bunting (*Emberiza caesia*) is very similar, but breeds further east in Greece and west to Dalmatia. Elsewhere in Europe, it is a vagrant. The Ortolan Bunting is considered to be a

The Osprey

table delicacy and is taken for food in parts of Europe.

Oscines

A sub-order of Passeriformes; comprises some 40 families, generally termed song birds. *See* Passeriformes; Perching Birds

Osprey

Sole member of the family Pandionidae, this Eagle-like bird with its contrasting dark upper parts, white under parts, dusky breast-band and spectacular behaviour of plunge-diving for fish, is readily identifiable; to see one of these birds in action is one of the great thrills of birdwatching. It was eliminated as a breeding bird in Britain by the end of the nineteenth century due to persecution by gamekeepers and collectors. In the mid-1950s it began nesting again and 3 young were raised in 1959 at Loch Garten in Scotland, a success due to intensive protection of the nest by the RSPB, who have guarded the site ever since allowing controlled viewing. Ospreys now nest at several places in northern Scotland. Migrating birds occur at inland waters in spring and autumn throughout Britain.

Often called the Fish Hawk in North America.

When feathers were widely used in the millinery trade, the plumes of Egrets were often misnamed 'Osprey feathers'.
Read Brown, P., *The Scottish Ospreys*, Heinemann, 1979

Ostrich (*Struthio camelus*)

Sole species of the Struthionidae (Struthioniformes). In the plural Ostriches, a general term for the family and the order. Largest of living birds, standing nearly 8ft in height and weighing around 340lb (154kg), the appearance of this flightless bird must be familiar to everyone from illustration if not from television films, zoos and other means. Its strange appearance and behaviour have always focussed considerable attention upon it, with many myths and legends arising from its habits, particularly related to its appetite for unusual items (metallic objects etc). This is probably due to its habit of swallowing a great deal of grit to aid the digestion of its normal vegetable food, but why it should be credited with the burying of its head in the sand at the approach of danger is more difficult to appreciate. It may stem from the way in which incubating females will try to go unnoticed by an approaching predator by stretching out the head and neck along the ground. The normal method of escape is to run, the long powerful legs giving speeds of up to 40mph (25kmph) at full tilt. Ostriches have been farmed for their feathers (which are cut up to three times every couple of years) since the middle of the nineteenth century; even today it is still a profitable business.

Ostriches are polygamous, each male being accompanied by at least three hens. The hens all deposit their eggs in a common nest, a

Ostrich (female)

shallow scrape in sandy soil. Up to 30 eggs have been recorded in some nests. As a result of introductions of the Ostrich for domestication, a small feral population exists in one or two localities in South Australia.

Ousel

Substantive name of the Ring Ousel (*Turdus torquatus*), also spelt Ouzel. Sometimes called the Mountain Blackbird, the male resembles the Blackbird (*Turdus merula*) in many respects but can be quickly identified by a white crescent on the breast. Also the secondaries and coverts have greyish edges so that the closed wing appears pale grey, a feature also evident when it flies.

A summer migrant, arriving March or April and leaving September or October, the Ring Ousel is to be found in elevated areas of S W England, Wales, N England and Scotland, where suitable habitats occur. It has declined considerably in recent years, particularly in Ireland where few now nest. Total population of Britain and Ireland between 8,000 and 16,000 pairs.

Ouse Washes, Cambridgeshire

An extensive area of floodland lying between the course of the Old Bedford River and the New Bedford River (or 100 foot drain, as it is also known). Denver lies at the northern end and Earith at the southern extremity of this 20-mile stretch of outstanding ornithological interest. In the winter it is the home of many Bewick's Swans (up to 2,000) and large numbers of other wildfowl. In the summer there are breeding Shelducks, Black-tailed Godwits, Redshanks, Snipe and Ruffs. Most of the Washes are now protected and looked after by either the RSPB in conjunction with the Ely Naturalists Trust, or the Wildfowl Trust (Welney Reserve) the total protected area being over 2000 acres.
See Welney Reserve

Ovary

Female gonad, part of the reproductive system.

Ring Ousel or Mountain Blackbird

Ovenbird

Substantive name of typical species of Furnariidae (Passeriformes, sub-order Tyranni). A very diverse family, it comprises about 221 species, most of which are small brown birds found in the densely wooded regions of Central and South America. The family is named after the nesting habits of many of them: they build large oven-shaped nests of mud.

Overshooting

This is said to take place when a bird travels beyond its normal range or breeding area following migration from its winter quarters. For example some birds which are typical of Southern Europe are noted in Britain during the spring, having overshot their destination, possibly due to weather conditions.
See Accidental; Vagrant

Oviparity

Producing young by means of eggs (ova) which do not hatch until after they have been laid. Birds, some reptiles and amphibians and most insects are oviparous.

Owl

Substantive name of all species of the familes Strigidae and Tytonidae (Strigiformes). In the plural, general term for the order. These two families have a worldwide distribution and are in effect the nocturnal counterparts of diurnal birds of prey, though not all of them hunt exclusively by night.

In size Owls range from the tiny Pygmy Owls (*Glaucidium spp*) and Elf Owl (*Microthene whitneyi*)—no bigger than a House Sparrow (*Passer domesticus*)—to the giant-sized Eagle Owls (*Bubo spp*). The majority of the world's Owls have arboreal habits, though some live on grasslands, swamps and cactus deserts; all feed exclusively on animals, which may range from earthworms and large insects to crabs, fish, reptiles, birds and small to medium-sized mammals. Generally the prey is swallowed whole, indigestible matter such as fur, feathers, bones, etc, being regurgitated some hours later in the form of pellets. Most owls make no nest to speak of, using other birds' old nests, such as those of Crows (Corvidae) or holes in trees, buildings etc. The eggs are white and roundish, with clutch size varying from 1-14. Clutch size of some species depends on food availability—seasonal fluctuations of small rodents particularly affect such species as Snowy Owl (*Nyctea scandiaca*) and Short-eared Owl (*Asio flammeus*). Incubation starts with the laying of the first egg,

Owls—nocturnal birds of prey.
(left) the Little Owl, sometimes seen in daylight being mobbed by small birds; (below) Long-eared Owls, seldom seen by day unless found roosting. Opposite: (top) young Barn Owls; (below) the Short-eared Owl, which perches on posts, fences or trees in a more horizontal posture than that of other Owls

leading to great disparity in the size of the young; the smallest often fall victims to their advanced brothers and sisters in time of food scarcity. Unlike diurnal birds of prey, the young hatch with ears and eyes closed. They are covered with white down.

Generally credited with sharpness of vision, Owls have large forward-looking eyes, enabling them to see more effectively in poor light, but they cannot see in total darkness and prey is secured as much by hearing ability and by silent flight as by acute eyesight. The forward-looking eyes provide a very small angle of vision but this is compensated for by the Owl's ability to turn its head through a wide arc: in the Long-eared Owl this is reputed to be 270°.

In Britain, the Tawny Owl (*Strix aluco*) is probably the most common breeding Owl, with an estimated 100,000 pairs generally distributed, though it is not found in N W Scotland, the Hebrides, Orkneys, Shetlands or Ireland. The Barn Owl (*Tyto alba*) and Little Owl (*Athene noctua*) are possibly equally well known, but their numbers do not exceed 10,000 pairs for each species. The Long-eared Owl is much more locally distributed and though the total population is around 10,000 pairs, most of them are in Ireland, where they replace the Tawny as the commonest Owl. The Short-eared Owl is confined to moorland and coastal dunes as a breeding bird, so is less numerous and even in a good year (when the food supply is plentiful) probably no more than 1,000 pairs nest in total. It has nested on only two known occasions in Ireland. The rarest breeding Owl in Britain is the Snowy, which has nested in recent years in the Shetlands.

Vagrant owls from northern Europe include Tengmalm's Owl (*Aegolius funereus*), Pygmy Owl (*Glaucidium passerinum*), Hawk Owl (*Surnia ulula*) and from Southern Europe the Scops Owl (*Otus scops*).

Read Burton, J. A., *Owls of the World*, Eurobooks, 1972
Everett, M., *A Natural History of Owls*, Hamlyn, 1977
Soper, T. and Sparks, J., *Owls, their Natural and Unnatural History*, David & Charles, Newton Abbot, 1970

(left) Snowy Owl

Owlet Frogmouth
Substantive name of the species Aegothelidae (Caprimulgiformes, sub-order Caprimulgi). Alternatively Owlet Nightjar. The group is relatated to the Frogmouths (Podargidae) and consists of a single genus of small arboreal Nightjars almost restricted to the Papua-Australian area.

Oxpecker
Substantive name of 2 species constituting the sub-family Buphaginae of the Sturnidae: the Yellow-billed Oxpecker (*Buphagus africanus*) and Red-billed Oxpecker (*Buphagus erythrorhynchus*). Also called Tickbirds. Confined to Africa, they obtain all their food (ticks, etc) from the hides of larger African mammals, and from domestic stock.

Oxyurini
Tribe of the Anatidae, this group of extremely aquatic and largely nocturnal Ducks are known as Stifftails. In Europe the White-headed Duck (*Oxyura leucocephala*) is the naturally occurring representative of the genus, while the North American Ruddy Duck (*Oxyura jamaicensis*) is now established as a breeding bird in the West Midlands and parts of the South West and has been accepted on the British List.

Oystercatcher
Substantive name of all the species of Haematopodidae (Charadriiformes, sub-order Charadrii). General term for the family. There are 6 species found in both Old and New Worlds. Sometimes called Sea-pies, these largish waders are 16-21in (406-533mm) long, either black-and-white or wholly black. The bird we know in Britain, *Haematopus ostralegus*, is a common shore bird, immediately recognisable not only by its distinctive black-and-white plumage but by its long orange-red bill, blood-red eyes and pink legs. They are noisy, excitable birds, very gregarious, with spectacular piping displays. Though most breed near the coast, nests occur around inland lochs and along rivers, particularly in Scotland. Breeding population is around 30,000 pairs with many more in winter.

Paddy
Alternative name for Sheathbill (*Chionis* spp).

Painted Snipe
Substantive name for the two species of Rostratulidae (Charadriiformes, sub-order Charadrii). A sub-tropical and tropical group occurring in Africa, Asia, Australia and South America. The resemblance to Snipe (*Gallinago* spp) is superficial.

Pair
A male and a female bird of the same species believed to be mated together.

Pair Formation
The establishment of a special relationship between two birds of the opposite sex, normally brought about by an exchange of signals between potential mates over a period of time. These may be visual (through courtship display) or auditory, ie by song. Any relationship formed may be short-lived, as with several species which display at leks, eg Black Grouse (*Lyrurus tetrix*), the only interrelationship being copulation. With most Passerines, however, the relationship lasts for the breeding season, usually until the young are fully fledged. Some smaller birds seem to make even longer lasting pair bonds, as does the Bullfinch (*Pyrrhula pyrrhula*). In other species such as Swans and Geese the pair bond may last until one of the partners dies. Study

Oystercatcher, a noisy, familiar shore bird

at the Wildfowl Trust has shown that the divorce rate in Bewick's Swans (*Cygnus bewickii*) is non-existent, birds returning year after year with the same mate. Though monogamous relationships are the norm amongst birds, polygamy and polyandry do occur. Homosexual pairing is rare in the wild, though not uncommon in captive birds.
See Polyandry; Polygamy

Palaeontology
The study of fossilised animals and plants.

Palearctic Region
The zoogeographical region which comprises the whole of Europe, Africa north of the Sahara and Asia north to the Himalayas. It is this region that interests British birdwatchers particularly, as the British Isles lie within it.

'Palearctic', formerly the American spelling, now appears to have been generally accepted and 'Palaearctic' is disappearing. The simplified version is incorporated in the title of the *Handbook of the Birds of Europe, the Middle East and North Africa—The Birds of the Western Palearctic*, OUP, 1978, which no doubts sets the seal on its acceptance this side of the Atlantic!
See Zoogeography

Bewick's Swans

Palmate
Having three toes connected by webs.

Pamprodactyl
Having all four toes directed forwards (the first being movable) or capable of being moved into that position.

Panic
In connection with birds, a sudden wave of alarm that sometimes occurs in a colony of gulls or Terns, birds rising from their nests and flying seawards—if on the coast. Usually the 'dread', as it is also called, quickly passes and the birds very soon return to their nests. Often there is no apparent reason for such behaviour. 'Panic' is often noisy, whereas a 'true dread' is silent.

Parabolic Reflector
A dish-shaped device usually glassfibre, used by wildlife sound recordists to collect more sound energy from a particular direction. Also helps to exclude sound from other directions.
See Sound Recording

Parakeet
Substantive name for some of the smaller species of Parrots (Psittacidae).
See Parrot

Parasite
An organism that lives at the expense of another species, either in it (endoparasite) or on it (ectoparasite); both types of parasite can infest a host at the same time, invariably to its disadvantage, and though in birds often creating little more than discomfort, an infestation can be fatal.
See Disease; Ectoparasite; Endoparasite

Parasitic Birds
Several families of birds are known to include species that are parasitic in the sense that they lay their eggs in the nest of another species. Such behaviour is also variously called brood parasitism, breeding parasitism or social parasitism. The best-known example of this form of parasitism is of course found in the Cuckoos (Cuculidae), where the female

209

deposits her egg in the nest of a chosen host species, and on hatching the young Cuckoo heaves out the eggs or young of the foster-parent and is then raised by the host. In the Cuckoo family this behaviour is so highly developed that the egg colour and pattern has evolved to mimic those of the hosts.

Other birds which act in a similar manner, but not to such a highly developed degree as the Cuckoos, include the Black-headed Duck (*Heteronetta atricapilla*) of South America, which lays its eggs in other Duck's nests, some Weaver Finches (*Estrildidae* spp), some Icterids (*Icteridae*), particularly the Cowbird (*Molothrus ater*), and most of the Honeyguides (*Indicatoriadae*).

Pardalote
Substantive name, alternatively Diamond Bird of *Pardalotus* spp—Flowerpeckers, small birds mostly inhabiting the oriental and Australasian regions.

Parrot
Substantive name of many species of the

A Hedge Sparrow nestling lies dying on the rim of the nest, being followed by an unhatched egg—both ejected by a murderous 36-hours-old Cuckoo

Psittacidae—sole family of the Psittaciformes. There are in fact 328 recognised species, with names variously ending in Cockatoo, Lory, Lorikeet, Macaw, Parrot or Parrotlet. Found throughout the tropical and subtropical regions of the world, they vary in size from 4 to 40in (100 to 1,000mm) in length. All are highly colourful, many having long tails. The bills are characteristically short, strong and markedly hooked, having a bulging cere (sometimes feathered). Most are forest dwellers, often using the bill as an additional aid to movement through the branches. Usually gregarious, they are among the noisiest of birds, with harsh screaming calls. Food consists of fruit, berries and seeds, though the New Zealand Kaka (*Nestor meridionalis*) and Kea (*Nestor notabilis*) have acquired a taste for sheep meat in recent times. Hole nesters, they mostly use cavities in trees, though some burrow in the ground.

The Parrots for convenience are divided into the following sub-families:

New Zealand Kaka and Kea (Nestorinae)
New Zealand Owl Parrot (or Kakapo) (Strigopinae)
Lories and Lorikeets (Loriinae)
Pygmy Parrots (Micropsittinae)
Cockatoos (Kakatoeinae)
All other typical Parrots (Psittacinae)

Since the earliest times Parrots have been kept as cage and aviary birds and the order is well known from some of the more popular captive species, eg Macaws, Cockatoos, Budgerigars, etc. In present times a number of Parrots have become extinct, notably the Carolina Parakeet (*Conuropsis carolinensis*), the only Parrot to inhabit temperate North America: it was completely wiped out earlier this century.

Read Forshaw, J. M., *Parrots of the World*, David & Charles, Newton Abbot, 1978

Parrotbill

Substantive name of most of the species of the sub-family Paradoxornithidae of the Muscicapidae (Passeriformes, sub-order Oscines), considered by some authors a mere tribe of the Timaliinae (Babblers); others place it as a sub-family of the Paridae (Tits). The birds are small to medium size. Tit-like in appearance except for a peculiarly formed bill, very much compressed with strikingly convex outlines. Mostly confined to the oriental region, a few wide-ranging species overflow into the palearctic, and one aberrant species, the Bearded Tit or Reedling (*Panurus biarmicus*), extends as far west as Britain.

See Bearded Tit; Paradoxornithidae; Reedling

Partial Migrant

A term applied to species of which, in a given breeding area, some individuals are migratory and some are not. The Song Thrush (*Turdus philomelos*) and the Lapwing (*Vanellus vanellus*) are good examples in respect of their native British populations.

Partridge

Belonging to the Pheasant family (Phasianidae), Partridges are ground-living chicken-like birds, represented in Britain by the Grey Partridge (*Perdix perdix*) and Red-legged Partridge (*Alectoris rufa*). The Grey Partridge, a well-known game bird of the cultivated regions of Europe, is generally distributed throughout the British Isles, apart from NW Scotland, the Orkneys and Shetlands, and parts of central and coastal Wales. The present population is estimated at 50,000 pairs and though it has declined in recent years it is still a familiar bird of arable lands and pastures where its grating 'kirr-ic, kirr-ic' call can be heard.

The equally distinctive 'chucka-chucka-chucka' call of the Red-legged Partridge can be heard mainly in areas where dry, sandier soils are to be found, particularly East Anglia, where it is as common as the Grey Partridge if not more so. Sometimes called the French Partridge, it was introduced into Britain sometime during the eighteenth century and its present population is reckoned to be between 100,000 and 200,000 pairs.

Other European Partridges, which are not found in Britain, include the Rock Partridge (*Alectoris graeca*), Chukar (*Alectoris chucar*) and Barbary Partridge (*Alectoris barbara*), birds of dry, stony or semi-arid habitats.

See Chukar

Passage Migrant

A bird which merely passes through an area on its migrations, not remaining throughout either the summer or winter. Alternatively 'transient', though this is not in common usage today.

Passenger Pigeon

In the early part of the nineteenth century the numbers of the Passenger Pigeon or Wild Pigeon (*Ectopistes migratorius*) of North America were estimated in billions. A highly gregarious species, this bird migrated in vast flocks throughout its range, which before man's arrival on the scene included the deciduous forests of North America from the Great Plains of the west to the Atlantic Ocean in the east, northwards to Southern Canada and southwards to northern Mississippi. These migrations were not a regular occurrence and were less in some years. In a year when the birds were abundant, millions would be found together, so many that they darkened the sky. In 1871, a nesting area of Winconsin comprising 850 square miles was calculated to hold in the region of 136,000,000 birds! Even today it is hard to comprehend so many birds, and it was no doubt inconceivable at the time that within less than 50 years the species would be extinct.

The great naturalist writer and painter John James Audubon certainly did not think there was any danger to the Passenger Pigeon,

Grey Partridge (above); and below is the
Red-legged Partridge—easily distinguished from
the Grey by its heavily barred flanks, white face,
black-and-white gorget, red bill and red legs

despite the great slaughter which took place during the nineteenth century, to which he refers in Volume 1 of his ornithological biography.

That the denudation of its forest habitat would seriously reduce its numbers is without question, but possibly some Passenger Pigeons could have flourished even today in the remnants of the great deciduous forests that once supported so many of them had they not also been so heavily persecuted. The last wild specimen of the Passenger Pigeon was taken in 1899, though some were kept alive in captivity for a time after this date, the last individual, named 'Martha', dying in Cincinnati Zoological Gardens in 1914.

Passeres
Used as an ordinal name synonymous with Passeriformes—perching birds.

Passeriformes
The huge order of birds, alternatively Passeres, includes more than half of all the world's recognised species of birds. Generally described as perching and singing birds, its members are in the following sub-orders and families.
    Sub-order Eurylaimi
        Family Broadbills (Eurylaimidae)
    Sub-order Tyranni
    Super-family Furnarioidea
        Family
        Woodcreepers (Dendrocolaptidae)
        Ovenbirds (Furnariidae)
        Antbirds (Formicariidae)
        Gnat-eaters (Conopophagidae)
        Tapaculos (Rhinocryptidae)
    Super-family Tyrannoidea
        Family
        Pittas (Pittidae)
        Asitys (Philepittidae)
        New Zealand Wrens (Xenicidae)
        Flycatchers (Tyrannidae)
        Manakins (Pipridae)
        Cotingas (Cotingidae)
        Plantcutters (Phytotomidae)
    Sub-order Menurae
        Family
        Lyrebirds (Menuridae)
        Scrub Birds (Atrichornithidae)
    Sub-order Oscines—comprises 40 families

Passerine
Adjective pertaining to the order Passeriformes. Used to refer to all birds belonging to that order, all others being collectively known as non-Passerines.

Pastor
The substantive name of the Rosy Pastor or Rose-coloured Starling (*Sturnus roseus*).
Though similar in form and movement to the Starling (*Sturnus vulgaris*), it has an unmistakable rose-pink body with glossy black head, neck, wings and tail, and a distinctive crest. The juveniles are not so distinctive, being sandy-brown with dark wings and tail and lacking the crest. The Pastor breeds in SE Europe and is only a scarce and irregular visitor westwards to Britain. It is kept as a cage bird, and escapes frequently confuse the bird's true status as a migrant.

Peafowl
Probably the best known of this small group of long-legged game birds is the Blue Peafowl (*Pavo cristatus*)—or 'Peacock'. Originally from India, the species has been so widely dispersed by man that it has become woven into the stories and legends of many countries where it would never have occurred naturally. Noted for the splendour of its tail (which is not actually its true tail): the dazzling colours are caused by refractions and reflection from the surface layers of the feathers which look like so many eyes. Beautiful as it is, the far-reaching strident call is not one of its most endearing qualities in urban areas, especially as it is frequently uttered at night. Unlike the related Green Peafowl (*Pavo muticus*), it is a sociable bird and in captivity a number of individuals, even males, can be kept together without fighting.

The Congo Peafowl (*Afropavo congensis*) was not discovered until 1936, providing a great surprise to zoogeographers, for until then it was assumed that Peafowl were indigenous only to SE Asia. Though similar in some ways to the genus *Pavo*, it lacks the resplendent tail of the Blue or Green Peafowl.

The term Peacock is used for the male of the species and Peahen for the female.

Peakirk, Cambs
These Wildfowl Trust gardens are a charming combination of woodland and water, 5 miles (8km) from Peterborough. Situated on the site of an old osier bed through which passes the ancient Car Dyke, in Roman times one of the principal commercial waterways of East Anglia. The gardens are a favourite

Blue Peafowl cock with tail fanned

with photographers and contain more than 600 wildfowl of over 100 kinds, many of which are rare. Special attractions are the flock of Chilean Flamingos, the Black-necked and Coscoroba Swans and the Andean Geese, The Trumpeter Swans, descended from a group presented by HM The Queen, are also noteworthy and breed regularly in the grounds. Open daily (except 24 and 25 December).

Pecking Order
See Dominance

Pecten
A feature peculiar to the avian eye, attached to the optic nerve. It is smallest in nocturnal birds, larger in seed-eating birds, larger still in insectivores and largest of all in the diurnal predators such as Hawks and Eagles. Its function however is not fully understood.

Pectinate
Having a serrated comblike edge. The Herons

(*Ardeidae*), particularly, have this 'comb' on the claw of the third toe. It is used for cleaning plumage fouled by fish slime. When preening a Heron coats its feathers with a powdery material obtained from special glands. This substance reduces the stickiness of the fish mucilage which is then removed by the 'comb'.

Some species of Tetraonidae (Grouse) have this 'comb' on the sides of the toes.

Pectoral
Pertaining to the breast.

Pectoral Sandpiper (*Calidris melanotos*)
The commonest nearctic wader in Europe. Occurs regularly in Britain in small numbers, particularly in autumn. Slightly larger than a Dunlin (*Calidris alpina*), it has rich brown and black upper parts with pale stripes down its back like a Snipe (*Gallinago gallinago*). The throat and breast are finely streaked, giving the appearance of a pectoral band (hence the name), sharply demarcated from the white lower breast. The legs are greenish-yellow. The flight is fast and swerving.

The much rarer Siberian Pectoral Sand-piper (*Calidris acuminata*), or Sharptailed Sandpiper as it is now called, closely resembles the Pectoral Sandpiper but it does not have such a clean-cut breast-band and the legs are greenish-grey or black; the call is a Swallow-like 'tree-treep'.

Peewit
Alternative name for Lapwing (*Vanellus vanellus*).

Pelagic
Inhabiting the open waters of the sea. A term applied to such species as Albatrosses (Diomedeidae), Petrels and Shearwaters (Procellariidae), etc.
See Oceanic Birds; Petrels

Manx Shearwater, a bird of the open sea

Pelecaniformes

An order of fairly large-sized, mainly fish-eating, birds with webbed feet, having a cosmopolitan distribution and comprising the following sub-orders and families:

Sub-order Phaethontes
Family
Tropicbirds (Phaethontidae)
Sub-order Pelecani
Super-family Pelecanoidea
Family
Pelicans (Pelecanidae)
Super-family Suloidea
Family
Gannets (Sulidae)
Cormorants (Phalacrocoracidae)
Darters (Anhingidae)
Sub-order Fregatae
Family
Frigate Birds (Fregatidae)

Pelican

Substantive name of all species of Pelecanidae (Pelecaniformes, sub-order Pelecani). The Pelicans are among the largest of birds, 50 to 72in (127 to 183cm) long, and with their webbed feet are well adapted to an aquatic life. Their most characteristic feature is the very large bill with a distensible pouch capable of holding large quantities of fish, their principal food. Highly gregarious, they often fish in groups, either sweeping the shallows in line or dipping their heads under the water in unison. The majority of the 6-8 species of this mainly tropical family are white in colour, suffused with pink in the breeding season, and having black or dark primaries. Some have crests and in some the bill and gular pouch can be yellow, orange or red.

Also occurring in more temperate areas, the White Pelican (*Pelecanus onocrotalus*) breeds in Rumania, winters in Greece and is accidental west to Sweden, Germany and Spain. The Dalmatian Pelican (*Pelicanus crispus*) is very similar to the former species except in flight, when it shows dusky secondaries and black wing tips above and looks dirty-white on the under parts. Some breed in Greece, a vagrant elsewhere in Europe.

Pellet

The undigested portion of a bird's food that is regurgitated and ejected via the mouth.

Pelican (opposite)

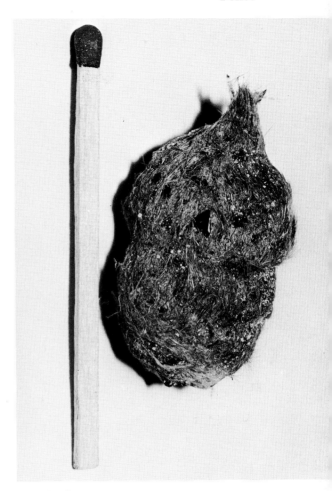

Kestrel pellet

Sometimes referred to as a casting. This habit is best known in birds of prey and Owls in particular, though many other types of birds eject pellets; more than 60 different species among British birds alone are known to do so, even seed- and insect-eating birds down to the size of the Goldcrest (*Regulus regulus*). The process can often be seen: after characteristic 'retching' movements, the pellet is brought up. An immediate search near the area should result in its discovery. The contents of a pellet can often provide valuable clues to the birds' diet; the dissection of Owl pellets particularly has shown in nearly all cases that they are not the villains they were thought to be. The analysis of pellets is best carried out by soaking the pellet in a dish of

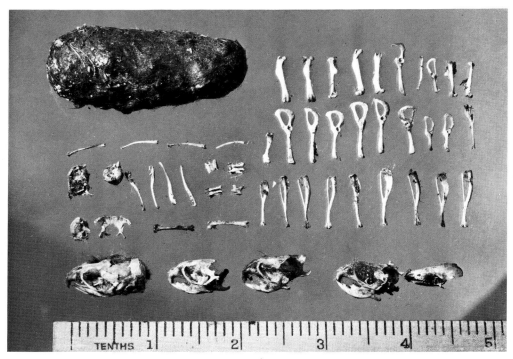

Barn Owl pellet (top left) and contents of another pellet, including five skulls

warm water and then separating the contents with a fine needle or forceps.

Read Glue, D., *Collecting and Analysing Bird Pellets*, (leaflet reprinted from the YOC magazine *Bird Life*).

Yalden, D. N., *The Identification of Remains in Owl Pellets*, Mammal Society, Harvest House, 62 London Road, Reading, Berkshire.

Pen

Special term for the male Swan.

Penduline Tit (*Remiz pendulinus*)

This small bird is distinguished from any other Tit by its striking greyish head and throat, and a broad black patch across the face. Inhabiting marshy localities, it builds an ovoid nest with a funnel-shaped entrance, suspended from the outer twigs of a bush or tree or in reeds. It breeds in SE Spain, S France, Italy and eastwards to Manchuria. It has been recorded in Britain only three times.

Penguin

Substantive name of all 16 species of Spheniscidae (sole family of the Sphenisciformes). In the plural, general term for the family and

Penduline Tit

order. Flightless sea birds of the southern hemisphere. Most are to be found along the coast of Antarctica, though one species, the Galapagos Penguin (*Spheniscus mendiculus*), is to be found at the equator. A familiar zoo bird, the most frequently kept species include the Adelie Penguin (*Pygoscelis adeliae*), Gentoo

Penguin (*Pygoscelis papua*), Emperor Penguin (*Aptenodytes forsteri*) and Macaroni Penguin (*Eudyptes chrysolophus*).
Read Sparks, J., and Soper, T., *Penguins*, David & Charles, Newton Abbot, 1970

Pepper Shrike
Substantive name of the two species of the sub-family Cyclarhinae of the Vireonidae (Passeriformes, sub-order Oscines). A neotropical group, they are heavily built birds, 6 to 7in (15 to 18cm) long, with large heads and powerful bills strongly hooked at the tip. Birds of open woodland, their food is mainly insects. Large prey is held down by one foot and pulled to pieces with the bill.

Perching Bird
Birds which are particularly adapted to gripping a branch or similar object with their feet. The Passeriformes are sometimes referred to as 'perching birds' because their toes are notably adapted to gripping. However many other birds are able to perch, even

Pair of King Penguins in a Gentoo rookery

though they lack the specialised foot structure found in this order.
See Passeriformes

Peregrine
The Peregrine Falcon (*Falco peregrinus*) typifies the larger Falcons (Falconiformes, sub-order Falcones), and could be described as the world's most successful flying bird. Cosmopolitan in distribution, with 17 races, its performance as a flier is scarcely equalled by any other bird and it is little wonder it has been the first choice for falconers in any country where this pursuit is followed. This bird stooping at its prey is one of the most spectacular sights in nature and no descriptions can convey its drama. Estimates of the speed achieved are put at 100mph (160kmph) or more. Aerodynamically it is probably capable of this, but it must rarely exceed 65-86mph (104-136kmph), which is quite sufficient to despatch its victims. In Britain, it is present throughout the year, being formerly

Peregrine

Two photographs of the Peregrine Falcon. In falconry, the female is the Falcon, the male the 'Tiercel'

more numerous than now. Many were shot during World War II in an attempt to protect Carrier Pigeons. In the mid-50s it declined due to the effects of organo-chlorine poisoning. However it is making a slow recovery thanks to greater protection, though it is still harassed by egg collectors and by removal of young from the nest. Most of the breeding population is in Scotland with some in N England, Wales and SW England. It nests sparsely in Ireland, population in Britain put at under 1000 pairs.

Read Treleaven, R. B., *Peregrine: the Private Life of the Peregrine Falcon*, Headland Publications, Penzance, 1977; Baker, J., *The Peregrine*, Collins, 1967; Ratcliffe, D., *The Peregrine Falcon*, Poyser, 1980

Petrel

Name or part-name of many species of the Procellariiformes (Tubinares). In the plural, a general term (sometimes 'Tubenoses') for the order. Comprises the four families Diomedeidae (Albatrosses), Procellariidae (typical Petrels and Shearwaters), Hydrobatidae (Storm Petrels) and Pelecanoididae (Diving Petrels). A distinct group of sea birds, having a deeply grooved, markedly hooked bill with prolonged tubular nostrils, the function of which is not fully understood: they may be concerned with either the excretion of excess salt by the nasal gland, or with a highly developed sense of smell (unusual in birds), something so marked in this order that it seems likely they locate their feeding area,

food, each other or breeding sites by smell. The birds themselves have a peculiar musky smell which may or may not be derived from oil secreted in the stomach. The four families total 90 species, of which the Procellariidae comprise over half, and these are distributed around the world's oceans.

All are totally marine, and their food usually consists of the larger zooplankton, fish, cephalopods and fish offal when available. Normally they only come ashore to breed, often on remote islands; having legs not developed for effective walking, they are vulnerable to predation and mostly return to their nesting sites after dark.

In Britain, the best-known of this order of birds are the Fulmar (*Fulmarus glacialis*), the Manx Shearwater (*Puffinus puffinus*), Storm Petrel (*Hydrobates pelagicus*) and Leach's Petrel (*Oceanodroma leucorhoa*). A number of other rarer Petrels have been recorded in Britain from time to time, such as Bulwer's Petrel (*Bulweria bulwerii*), Soft-plumaged Petrel (*Pterodroma mollis*) and Wilson's Petrel (*Oceanites oceanicus*).

Phalarope

Substantive name coined by the French naturalist Brisson in 1760 for the three species of Phalaropodidae (Charadriiformes, suborder Charadrii). In the plural, general term for the family. This group of small Sandpiper-

Storm Petrel—at sea by day and returns to nesting burrow at night

like birds have some characteristics quite unlike other waders; in particular they spend
much of their time on the water, where they
float as lightly as corks, frequently spinning (or
pirouetting), round and round on the surface
picking up small animal life from the water.
The stirring action is supposed to bring their
minute prey to the surface. Two of the three
species, the Red-necked Phalarope (*Phalaropus lobatus*) and Grey Phalarope (*Phalaropus
fulicarus*), are so adapted to an aquatic life
(the toes are partially lobed) that outside the
breeding season they are only to be found out
at sea and for most of the year they are in fact
totally oceanic, apparently quite capable of
dispensing with fresh water indefinitely. The
third member of the group, Wilson's Phalarope (*Phalaropus tricolor*), however, appears
to be essentially a freshwater inland bird,
feeding more on land than the other two. This
latter species breeds in North America,
wintering in the tropics and South America.
Its first recorded occurrence in Britain was
only in 1954, but since then one or two have
been noted in most years. The Red-necked
Phalarope breeds sparingly in Ireland, Outer

Red-necked Phalarope; it nests in a scrape in
grass or other vegetation

Hebrides, Orkney and Shetland, and is
usually to be found in small colonies in
suitable localities. During the breeding season
the male incubates the eggs and looks after
the young, a reversal of the normal sexual
relationship which is common to all three
species, the females also being the larger and
more brightly coloured.

Both the Red-necked and Grey Phalaropes
are circumpolar in breeding distribution,
occurring in North America, where the Grey
is known as the Red Phalarope (its breeding
plumage is predominantly a chestnut-red); the
Red-necked Phalarope is there called the
Northern Phalarope.

Phaneric
Opposite of cryptic, ie coloration or other
features making a bird or animal conspicuous.

Phase
Equivalent of morph.
See Morph

222

Pheasant

Substantive name of many species of Phasianidae (Galliformes, sub-order Galli). The males of those species called by that name are generally brightly coloured and elaborately marked birds and consequently frequently kept as ornamental fowl. Notably birds of Asia, many species have been introduced into Europe and other parts of the world where they do not normally occur. The Pheasant we know in Britain (*Phasianus colchicus*) was probably brought over by the Normans in the eleventh century with other introductions made in the eighteenth century. Now an established British bird, the Pheasant shows considerable variation due to the interbreeding of the two races *Phasianus c. colchicus* from the Caucasus (the earlier introduced species) and *Phasianus c. torquatus* from China, the more recently introduced species. This mixing produces some birds that are quite dark without white rings round their necks, while sometimes the so-called 'Ring-necked Pheasant' predominates. Artificial rearing in considerable numbers for shooting tends to give an unnatural distribution, though it survives quite well away from unmanaged areas and is found wherever suitable habitat occurs. The total British and Irish population may well be half a million pairs.

Three other species of Pheasant introduced into Britain are now breeding freely in the wild in some areas: the Golden Pheasant (*Chrysolophus pictus*), Lady Amherst's Pheasant (*Chrysolophus amherstiae*), and Reeve's Pheasant (*Syrmaticus reevesii*).

Read Delacour, J., *Pheasants of the World*, Spur, 1977

The Pheasant Trust

A public charity established in 1959 by a group of well-known ornithologists and aviculturists with the object of trying to save the world's rarest Pheasants and other game birds from extinction. At its headquarters at Great Witchingham, Norfolk, it maintains the largest collection of rare pheasants ever assembled in Britain. Of the 48 species of Pheasant in the world, 18 are considered to be in danger of extinction, and 8 of these are breeding regularly in the Trust's collection. Swinhoe's Pheasants (*Lophura swinhoei*) bred at the Trust have been released in their native Taiwan, and young Cheer Pheasants (*Catreus wallichi*) have also been raised and released into the wild of their native Simla. There are other birds and also mammals at the Great Witchingham Wildlife Park, which is located on the A1067, 12 miles out of Norwich.

Phenology

The study of visible appearances and seasonally occurring events—in the ornithological field, the first arrival dates and last departure dates of migrants, etc, and the relation of these with meteorological data.

Phoebe

Substantive name for some species of Tyrannidae (Passeriformes, sub-order Tyranni), North American Flycatchers.

Cock Pheasant

Photography

Since the earliest days of photography, birds have been popular subjects, the first pictures of them being taken around the middle of the last century. A hand-coloured photograph of a Long-eared Owl is credited with being the first published picture of a bird, and this was in 1868. The first 'real' bird photographers however were undoubtedly the brothers Kearton—Richard and Cherry. Observing that birds took no notice of animals, they got close enough to photograph nesting birds by using the skin of an ox, stretched life-like over a wooden frame in which they concealed themselves! This cumbersome and undoubtedly uncomfortable strategem was in effect the origin of the 'hide' that photographers use today.

As cameras and lenses improved, so the scope of bird photography increased, the invention of the dry plate greatly facilitating field photography. In the 1920s photographic naturalists like Arthur Brooke, Ralph Chislett, Arthur Gilpin, Walter Higham, Oliver Pike and Ian Thompson were producing 'masterpieces of bird photography' and a selection of the work of these and other photographers can be seen in a publication under that title. Of all bird photographers one name is pre-eminent, that of Eric Hosking, whose work extends over 50 years and who is surely the greatest living exponent of the art.

Bird photography is a popular pursuit for many with modern sophisticated equipment and high-powered telephoto lenses, which allow a freedom undreamt of years ago. However, even today 'hidework' is often the only means of obtaining the best natural shots, Though most photographers work with colour producing colour transparencies, there is still a place for black and white photography and many books and journals still use such material.

Anyone photographing birds must always have their welfare in mind and be fully conversant with the law relating to the disturbance of wild birds on or near the nest. A leaflet on *Bird Photography and the Law* can be obtained from RSPB, The Lodge, Sandy, Beds, SG19 2DL, and should be consulted.
Read Hosking, E., and Gooders, J., *Wildlife Photography—Field Guide*, Hutchinson, 1913; Hosking, E., *Eric Hosking's Birds: 50 Years of Photographing Wildlife*, Pelham, 1979; Hosking, E., *An Eye for a Bird*, Hutchinson, 1970

Photoperiodism

The regulation of cyclical changes in physiology and behaviour by light acting as an external stimulus, eg the lengthening days stimulating breeding, the shortening days encouraging migration.

Phylum

A taxonomic category in the classification of living things. Birds are placed in the sub-phylum Vertebrates of the phylum Chordata. The sequence classification runs: kingdom, sub-kingdom, phylum, sub-phylum, class, order, family, genus, species.

Piciformes

An order, alternatively Pici, comprising the following sub-orders and families:
Galbulae
    Super-family Galbuloidea
      Family
      Jacamars (Galbulidae)
      Puffbirds (Bucconidae)
    Super-family Capitonoidea
      Family
      Barbets (Capitonidae)
    Super-family Ramphastoidea
      Family
      Honey Guides (Indicatoridae)
      Toucans (Ramphastidae)
Pici
    Family
    Woodpeckers (Picidae)

Pigeon

Substantive name of species of Columbidae (Columbiformes, sub-order Columbae); in the plural, general term for the family. In normal usage 'Dove' refers to the smaller members of the family, Pigeon to the larger forms, though this is not always consistent; for instance the Stock Dove (*Columba oenas*) is more typically a Pigeon than a Dove. A cosmopolitan family, there are 280 species throughout the world which vary in size from that of the Diamond Dove (*Geopelia cuneata*), no bigger than a Skylark, to that of the Crowned Pigeons (*Goura* spp), which are nearly as large as hen Turkeys.

Most Pigeons are aboreal or partly so, while some are terrestrial and some cliff-haunting. Strong fliers, some are highly migratory and most are more or less gregarious, gathering in large flocks with a number breeding colonially. Food is almost entirely seeds, fruit, berries, or buds or other vegetable matter. Pigeons drink by immersing the bill and sucking, a habit shared with Sandgrouse and Button Quails,

Two of Britain's four 'Pigeons': Stock Dove (above) and Wood Pigeon (below)

while all other birds take a gulp and lift the head to swallow. The nest is a slightly-built but strong structure of interwoven twigs in which 1 or 2 unmarked white eggs are laid. The young, called squabs, are fed on re-gurgitated food known as Pigeon's milk.

In Britain the Wood Pigeon (*Columba palumbus*) is our commonest representative of the family, and with its fondness for vegetable crops, the 5 million resident pairs are considered to be quite a pest.

The Stock Dove (*Columba oenas*), on the other hand, is no serious threat to agriculture and it is rarely met with in any number. The total British and Irish population is in fact only put at around 100,000 pairs. The Stock Dove also has the distinction of being the only European Pigeon to nest in holes, which can be in a tree or building, outcrop of rock or even rabbit burrow.

Two other members of the Columbidae family which are found in Britain might cause some confusion, the Turtle Dove (*Streptopelia turtur*) and Collared Dove (*Streptopelia decaocto*). The former species is a summer visitor, arriving late April/early May, its presence often only detected by its incessant purring note, one of the typical sounds of summer in southern Britain, from Yorkshire and Lancashire southwards. The

Collared Dove (above) and Turtle Dove (below), Britain's other two 'Pigeons'

Collared Dove, however, is met throughout the British Isles, except in upland areas: yet before 1952 it was unknown in Britain. The spread of this bird across Europe from Asia Minor is one of the amazing success stories of the bird world, for in less than 50 years it has colonised most of Europe, and since 1955 when the first pair nested near Cromer, Norfolk, has become a familiar bird of suburbs and villages, also haunting granaries, docks and other places where grain is handled.

The Barbary Dove (*Streptopelia risoria*), a favourite cage bird, looks very similar to the Collared Dove but is smaller and creamier and does not have dark wing-tips; it sometimes escapes from captivity and has bred in the wild.

The Rufous Turtle Dove (*Streptopelia orientalis*) has found its way here from the Middle East on a few occasions and the Laughing Dove (*Streptopelia senegalensis*) may well do so one day.

See Pigeon's Milk

Read Murton, R. K., *The Wood Pigeon* (New Naturalist series), Collins, 1965

Crested Pigeon, an Australian species

Pigeon's Milk
A secretion produced in the adult crop of all Pigeons (Columbidae), on which the nestlings are fed during the first few days after hatching. It is rather similar in composition to mammalian milk, being very rich in proteins and fat.

Pinfeather
A growing feather still in its sheath, most frequently exhibited in young birds in the nest.

Pinion
A poetic word for a wing. Sometimes used in reference to part of the wing, usually the primary feathers, or sometimes to only a single feather.

Pinioning
The cutting of one wing at the carpal joint, removing the basis from which the primary feathers grow and thus rendering the bird

227

Pinkfoot

permanently flightless. This practice is carried on particularly where large birds are kept in the open for display or ornamentation.

Pinkfoot

Shortened name of the Pink-footed Goose (*Anser brachyrhynchus*), a colloquialism used by birdwatchers; plural Pinkfeet.

Pintail (*Anas acuta*)

A surface-feeding Duck. The drake has long slender tail feathers which give the bird its name. A few pairs nest in Britain, but it is best known as a winter visitor, with notable concentration in the Lancashire and Cheshire estuaries and in the Ouse Washes.

Pipit

A group of mainly ground-feeding and nesting birds, all fairly nondescript, having generally brownish plumage, pale under parts with dark streaks and white outer tail feathers. In some respects they are like Wagtails in behaviour, but have much shorter tails. In Britain the Meadow Pipit (*Anthus pratensis*) is by far the commonest, being a familiar moorland-nesting bird, but visiting more lowland and

Richard's Pipit

Pintail—four drakes and a duck

(above) Tree Pipit—of similar but sleeker appearance than the Meadow Pipit

(below) Meadow Pipit with young cuckoo in its nest

coastal areas in the winter. Its typical 'peep-peep-peep' call can be sufficient for the experienced birdwatcher to identify the species, and the best means of distinguishing it from the very similar but generally sleeker Tree Pipit (*Anthus trivialis*), which is a summer visitor preferring more wooded settings than the Meadow Pipit, though the two can often be found together. The Rock Pipit (*Anthus spinoletta*) is generally a much greyer-looking bird and slightly larger. It is a coastal-haunting species, occasionally noted inland. Some rarer Pipits which occur on passage include the Tawny Pipit (*Anthus campestris*), probably the most Wagtail-like of the Pipits, and Richard's Pipit (*Anthus novaeseelandiae*), one of the largest and longest-legged of this difficult group.

Piratic Birds
For one bird to rob another of its food is frequent practice amongst many species;

Great Skua

Starlings, for instance frequently rob Blackbirds (*Turdus merula*) or, often as not, each other. However, in a few species this robbery is a highly developed means of obtaining food; particularly amongst the Skuas (Stercorariidae), piracy appears to be the preferred way whenever possible. In general, once the hapless victim has been selected the Skua pursues it closely, following every twist and turn it makes, buffeting it with its wings, colliding with it, until finally (and sometimes the chase can be quite protracted) the food is disgorged and dropped. The Skua then retrieves the meal, often before it hits the water. The Arctic Skua (*Stercorarius parasiticus*) is a constant pirate of Terns, and on occasion harries other species. The Great Skua (*Stercorarius skua*) adopts the same techniques, even preying upon Gannets (*Sula bassana*) and pressing home attacks on water to the point of attempting to drown the victim by a paddling action of the feet.

Some Gulls indulge in such tactics periodi-cally though never with the same tenacity and rarely with any success; the Common Gull (*Larus canus*) is perhaps more frequently noted as adopting piracy.

Pitta
Substantive name of the 26 species of Pittadae (Passeriformes, sub-order Tyranni). Brightly coloured ground birds of tropical forests and jungles. Most superficially resemble plump short-tailed Thrushes.

Plains Wanderer
Alternatively Collared Hemipode (*Pedionomus torquatus*), sole member of the Pedionomidae (Gruiformes, sub-order Turnices).

Plantcutter
Substantive name of three species of Phytotomidae (Passeriformes, sub-order Tyranni).

Banded Pitta

Plover

The name of the majority of species of
Charadriidae (Charadriiformes, sub-order
Charadrii). Plovers are small to medium-
sized, compactly built birds, mostly having
short, straight, fairly stout bills of moderate
length. The wings are long, the tail short to
medium. A cosmopolitan family: a large
proportion of the 56 species are tropical
though a number are to be found in the higher
latitudes. For convenience they can be
divided into three main groups:

1 The Lapwings, which comprise mainly
species which have a crest, facial wattles and
wing spurs, characteristics not found in other
Plovers.

2 The Golden Plovers, which comprise four
species of *Pluvialis*.

3 The Sand Plovers, many of which have a
black breast-band. There are one or two
others, such as the Wrybill (*Anarhynchus*

Golden Plover (above)

Ringed Plover (below)

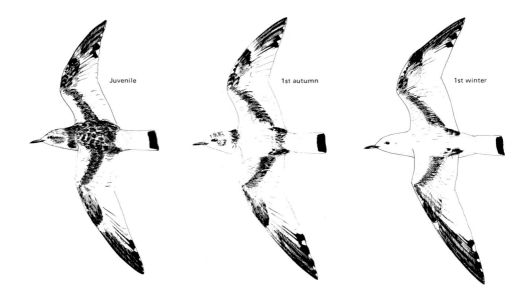

Juvenile   1st autumn   1st winter

frontalis) of New Zealand and the Dotterel (*Eudromias morinellus*), which do not fit into any of the three groupings.

In Britain the best-known Plover is the Lapwing or Green Plover (*Vanellus vanellus*), a dark greenish bird with a crest and distinctive 'Peewit' call which gives it one of its other names. A bird of agricultural and arable land, it also occurs on moorland. At times during autumn and winter it resorts to the tideline to feed, but on the shore it is generally the Ringed Plover (*Charadrius hiaticula*) which is the more familiar species. This rotund little shore bird with its prominent black collar, brown back and crown, orange-yellow legs and orange bill with black tip, can also be found nesting in suitable areas around our coasts.

Also frequenting the shoreline in winter is the larger Grey Plover (*Pluvialis squatarola*), its mournful 'tlee-oo-ee' echoing across the mudflats. At all times the distinctive black axillaries identify this bird in flight. The Golden Plover (*Pluvialis apricaria*) prefers open fields in which to feed, often associating with Lapwings. During the summer it breeds on upland moors when its beautiful golden-spangled upper parts deservedly suggest its name. Breeding at inland sand and gravel pits and sometimes on spoil tips and the margins of reservoirs, the Little Ringed Plover (*Charadrius dubius*), a slimmer, slightly smaller bird than the Ringed Plover with a

yellow ring round its eye, will be known to birdwatchers in the Midlands and SE England, where it was recorded as nesting for the first time in Britain in 1938. It is still slowly expanding its range and about 500 pairs now breed each year. However it is still not found in Wales, SW England or Ireland. The Kentish Plover (*Charadrius alexandrinus*) once nested in SE England, but is now only a scarce migrant.

Even rarer Plovers occur from time to time and in recent years such species as the Lesser Golden Plover (*Pluvialis dominica*) and the Killdeer Plover (*Charadrius vociferus*), both from North America, and Greater Sand Plover (*Charadrius leschenaultii*) and Sociable Plover (*Vanellus gregarius*) from Asia have been noted.

Plumage

A bird's covering of feathers—the outstanding character of the Class Aves, distinguishing it from all other animals. Besides protecting and insulating the body, feathers are an essential component of flight, combining high efficiency with minimal weight. A bird's plumage changes with age, through moults. Generally its first plumage (when it hatches) consists of natal down (termed neossoptile) which is shed in the nest as the bird grows. This gradually is replaced by the juvenile plumage, which consists of rather loose-structured feathers that the bird retains

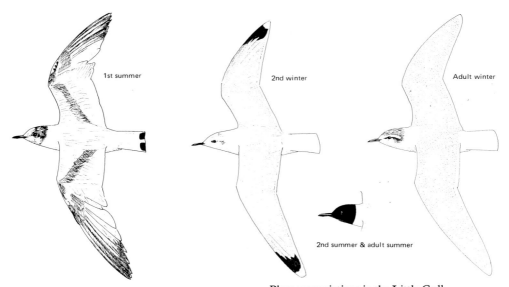

1st summer   2nd winter   Adult winter

2nd summer & adult summer

Plumage variations in the Little Gull

for a short while after leaving the nest; these are replaced by its first winter plumage. Then prior to the breeding season most Passerines assume their first nuptial or adult breeding plumage. After the breeding season the bird then moults again, assuming its winter plumage, the process continuing for as long as the bird lives.

There are some variations to this sequence with different species, but generally speaking birds have two different plumages, a breeding plumage and a winter plumage, often giving them a different appearance at different seasons. The plumage is very important to birds in determining recognition of other members of the same species, and often plays a major role in the breeding display. In some species, the colour of the plumage acts as camouflage, helping the bird to survive and avoid detection by predators or by its prey. *See* Contour Feather; Feather; Filoplume; Powder Down

Pochard (*Aythya ferina*)
A common diving Duck in Britain, found on most suitable stretches of water during the winter, when total population is probably over 50,000 birds. A rich chestnut head, black breast, grey sides and black stern immediately identify the drake and even in silhouette the dome-shaped head is distinctive. As a breeding bird it is scarce or local, about 500 pairs nesting here with a bias towards eastern England.

Poikilothermal
Cold-blooded—the opposite of homiothermal. *See* Heat Regulation

Pole Trap
An unselective, barbaric instrument, banned long ago, but still illegally used specifically to kill birds of prey. Such birds as Harriers, Falcons and Owls like to perch on top of an isolated post or pole—hence a spring trap set on such a vantage point is a simple way of killing them. Obviously any species is liable to be trapped and the birds hang upside down, usually with broken legs, until the trap is checked or until they starve to death, a process which may take several days. The pole trap is therefore both lethal and exceptionally cruel. Its use was the subject of a special RSPB campaign which revealed widespread utilisation of pole traps by gamekeepers, showing just how many gamekeepers and landowners were flouting the bird protection laws.

Polish Swan
An albinistic Mute Swan. The condition is particularly obvious in juvenile birds, as the pre-moult plumage of normal young birds is grey.

Polyandry
In birds, a sexual relationship between a female and two or more males. The term is

233

usually applied to the behaviour of species in which the female, after copulation and laying the eggs, takes no part in the incubation or raising of the young, instead moving to another male to establish a further sexual relationship. Polyandry is rare among birds and little study has been made of it. The Rheas (Rheidae) and some Tinamous (Tinamidae) are polyandrous.

Polygamy
The establishment of a pair bond between a male and more than one female, or between a female and more than one male. When referring only to the former state it is polygyny and if only the latter it is polyandry.

Polygyny
The establishment of a sexual relationship between one male and more than one female. A common occurrence among birds, particularly in the Pheasant and Grouse families. However the general term polygamy is probably the most appropriate in the case of birds that have established a ritualised pair bond.

Pochard—will sit for hours on stretches of fresh water, dozing or riding the waves

Polymorphism
The co-existence of two or more readily distinguishable 'morphs' or phases within a single inter-breeding population in numbers too great to be merely a recurrent mutation. The plumage phases differ markedly from each other independently of sex, age, season or geographical race. Familiar examples are found in the Arctic Skua (*Stercorarius parasiticus*) with dark and light morphs or phases, and the Ruff (*Philomachus pugnax*), the male bird assuming a variety of coloured breeding plumes. Some other birds which show colour morphs are the Screech Owl (*Otus asio*) and the Snow Goose (*Anser caerulescens*), both North American species.

Population
The total number of species for a given area: eg the population of British breeding Blackbirds is 7 million pairs. On a global basis, bird populations can vary from a very few in the case of some threatened species, such as the Whooping Crane with probably less than 50

individuals all told, to the probably 100 million world total of the Quelea. For some of the world's commoner species exact figures are difficult to obtain and only estimates can be made, but census work in recent years has been able to determine some bird populations, particularly of seabirds, more accurately.
See Numbers

Portland Bill, Dorset

Jutting out into the English Channel for some 6 miles (13km), the Bill provides an ideal site for an observatory. The Portland Observatory and Field Centre has been in operation there since 1955. Housed in the Old Lighthouse, it offers luxurious accommodation in comparison with most other observatories. Though the Bill is a tourist attraction with a large coach and car park, the observatory gardens and surrounding small stone-walled fields offer sanctuary for many passage migrants and many exciting 'rushes' regularly occur. Along with the more usual observatory species, the observatory has two 'firsts' for the British Isles to its credit—Calandra Lark and Desert Warbler. On occasions seawatching at the Bill can be profitable, and at times Sooty Shearwater, Great Skua, Grey Phalarope, Little Gull, etc, are noted, along with more usual sea birds.

Potoo

Name of the species of Nyctibiidae (Caprimulgiformes, sub-order Caprimulgi), alternatively Tree Nighthawks. Long-winged, long-tailed, cryptically coloured birds found in South America. They are related to the Nightjars and have a huge mouth which enables them to capture night-flying insects; they fly from a perch, in the manner of a Flycatcher.

Poult

A domestic chicken; sometimes applied to other species, usually certain game birds.

Poultry

A collective term for domesticated species used for food—not applicable to game.

Powder Down

Disintegrating feather material which breaks up into minute particles forming a dusty substance used by birds for cleaning their feathers. It is found only in the Herons (Ardeidae), Toucans (Ramphastidae), Parrots (Psittacidae) and Bowerbirds (Ptilonoryn-chidae). When present, powder down occurs in patches: the Herons have one on the upper breast and another behind each thigh.

Prairie chicken

American name applied to some Grouse—Tetraonidae (Galliformes, sub-order Galli).

Pratincole (*Glareola pratincola*)

In flight these birds look like a large Swallow (Hirundinidae) with long, pointed, dark wings and deeply forked tail with a white base; for this reason they are sometimes called Swallow-plovers, though they do in fact belong to the Glareolinae, a sub-family of Glareolidae (Charadriiformes, sub-order Charadrii). Widely distributed throughout the Old World, they are related to the Cursoriinae—the Coursers. Gregarious and often crepuscular, they capture insects in flight. In Africa they are called Locust Birds, from their habit of feeding on invading locust swarms. In Europe they breed in southern Spain, with pockets of birds found in S France, NE Italy and in Greece eastwards.

Pratincoles, or more fully Collared Pratincoles, turn up in Britain every year, though rarely more than 2 or 3. The rarer Black-winged Pratincole (*Glareola nordmanni*), which breeds in Rumania and eastwards, occurs even less frequently.

Precocial

Active immediately after hatching, as with quite a number of ground-nesting species, particularly game birds.

Predation

The act of one species (the predator) preying on another (the prey), to secure food.

Preening

The act of cleaning and arranging the plumage with the bill, often employing oil from the preen gland. A basic and most important function for birds, and they spend much time on it. Preening almost invariably follows bathing and also occurs after sunning, dusting and anting. When preening the bill is used to 'nibble' or 'draw' the feather through the mandibles, or it is used when closed to stroke the feathers.
See Feather; Oil Gland

Pre-migratory Restlessness

The inception of migration is preceded by a period during which birds show considerable

Pratincole (above)   Curlew preening (below)

restlessness. The well-known autumn flocking of the Swallow (*Hirundo rustica*) is a good example. It is deduced that the birds are preparing for departure and are awaiting the appropriate external stimulus. This restlessness has also been demonstrated by several species of migratory birds kept experimentally in caged conditions.
See Zugunruhe

Prey

A term generally applied to all living animal forms that are taken by a predator for food—as a Blackbird takes a worm, a Tern catches a fish, a Flycatcher an insect. However, in most birdwatchers' minds, 'prey' is taken by either Falconiformes (Eagles, Hawks, Falcons etc) or Strigiformes (Owls).

Primary

Or 'primary feather'. This may be any of the flight feathers from the carpal joint outwards. In most non-Passerine species there are ten, but Grebes (Podicipedidae), Storks (Ciconiidae) and Flamingos (Phoenicopteridae) have eleven. Most Passerine birds have only nine primaries or else the tenth, the outermost, is much reduced.

Prion

Substantive name of *Pachyptila* spp, a group of small Petrels also called Whale Birds. They inhabit the circumpolar seas of the southern oceans, breeding from the Antarctic main- land north to the Falkland Islands and islands around New Zealand.

Procellariiformes

An order comprising the Petrels or Tubenoses.
See Albatross; Petrel

Ptarmigan (*Lagopus mutus*)

A Grouse-like bird of the mountain tops. In Britain it is confined to the Scottish Highlands, with a total population of between 20,000 and 50,000 pairs. At all times the male has varying amounts of white in the plumage, while in the winter both sexes are completely white except for the black-tipped tail and, in the male, a black mark from the bill through the eye. It also has feathered feet which act like snowshoes.

Pterylae

Skin areas on which feathers grow.

Pterylosis

The distribution of the feathers on the skin— the arrangement of the pterylae.

Ptilopaedic

Clad in down when hatched.

Puffbird

Substantive name of some species of Bucconidae (Piciformes, sub-order Galbulae). Small

The Ptarmigan

to medium-sized birds with a puffy appearance, hence the name. They are closely related to the Jacamars (Galbulidae). Confined to continental tropical America. One of the largest and most widespread members of this family is the White-necked Puffbird (*Notharchus macrorhynchus*).

Puffin (*Fratercula arctica*)
Certainly the most popular of sea birds and probably the best-known member of the Auk

Puffins

family. Remarkable for its colourful Parrot-like beak and for nesting in an underground burrow it excavates itself or in one dug by rabbits. Colonies of this bird are concentrated in the Orkneys and Shetlands, and the western islands of Scotland, with other colonies scattered around the coasts of western Britain and Ireland. It has declined markedly in recent years and the present

population is probably no more than a half-million pairs, which at one time was less than the total number of birds on St Kilda alone.
Read Lockley, R. M., *Puffins*, Dent, 1953

Puffinosis
A disease occuring in the Manx Shearwater (*Puffinus puffinus*) and probably allied to psittacosis. It sometimes causes heavy losses amongst young birds.

Pullet
An immature female domestic fowl.

Pullus
A young bird until it is full grown and flying; also called a chick or nestling while remaining in nest. After the pullus stage the bird is described as a juvenile.

Quail (*Coturnix coturnix*)
A very small Partridge-like bird found throughout Europe, Asia and North and South America. It favours many types of open country, particularly tall grassland from where its distinctive call, likened to 'wet-my-lips' is the only indication of its presence. A highly migratory species, in some years it occurs in greater numbers than others. There are scattered instances of its breeding from most of Britain, though it is more frequently noted in southern England. Probably quite a common species in Britain in the eighteenth century it declined markedly in the nineteenth century. The Quail belongs to a distinct group of birds known as the Old World Quails, which differ from other members of the family found in North America—the American Quails.

Blue-breasted Quail

Quelea
A small Finch-like bird also called the Red-billed (or Black-faced or Sudan) Dioch (*Quelea quelea*). Probably one of the most numerous birds in the world, found throughout much of Africa where it does great damage to crops. Flocks of Quelea have been estimated in millions and extensive control measures, including the use of flame-throwers and explosives, are taken against it.
See Control

Quelea

Quetzal
Also called the Resplendent Trogon (*Pharomachrus mocinno*).
See Trogon

Quill
The calamus of a feather, a term used loosely for a flight or tail feather.
See Calamus; Feather; Rachis

Race
A sub-division within the geographical range of a species, usually determined by morphological characteristics, such as slight differences in measurement, shades of colour etc. The term is synonymous with 'sub-species' which is in fact the official term in the International Code of Zoological Nomenclature, though the expression 'race' is preferred by many ornithologists. Not all species are split into races or sub-species.
    The Yellow Wagtail (*Motacilla flava*) is a good example of one that is sub-divided. A summer visitor to Britain, the bird we know is yellow on the head (the male), while the central European Yellow Wagtail has a bluish crown and white eyestripe and chin, and is called the Blue-headed race (*Motacilla flava flava*). This race frequently occurs on spring migration in Britain (having overshot its normal range) and on occasions breeds with the Yellow Wagtail.
See Sub-species

Rachis
The distal portion of the shaft of a feather, bearing the vane.
See Feather

Radiation
In the evolutionary sense, divergence of forms of common ancestry with increasing dissimilarity as a result of differences in adaptation.

In the distributional sense, the geographical spread of a species or group of related species from the area where it originally evolved as a separate entity.

Radipole Lake, Dorset
Practically surrounded on all sides by the popular south coast resort of Weymouth, this artificially controlled backwater of the river Wey is an amazing area of lagoons and reedbeds, with an outstanding list of birds to its credit in what is now virtually a town park. Terns and waders are almost continually present in autumn whilst Little Gulls are probably more frequent here than anywhere else in England. There are Bearded Tits and Cetti's Warblers in the reedbeds and on passage anything might turn up. It is also, of course, the second-largest breeding colony of the Mute Swan in Britain (the largest is at nearby Abbotsbury). Only 5 minutes from the town centre and beach, Weymouth is the ideal place for the birdwatching father who does not feel he can deprive his family of a conventional holiday. (Portland Bill is also only a few miles away.) A large part of the Lake is an RSPB reserve.

Raft
Collective term for a number of birds together on the sea, mainly applied to Auks (Alcidae), eg a raft of Guillemots (*Uria aalge*). Also used particularly for a gathering of Manx Shearwaters (*Puffinus puffinus*); these birds collect together forming large rafts before their return to nesting burrows.

Rail
Name of many species of Rallidae (Gruiformes, sub-order Grues). There are over 130

A raft of Manx Shearwaters

species known throughout the world. Ground dwellers, many are aquatic, living in dense vegetation, their laterally compressed bodies allowing easier and quicker progress through reeds, grass etc, while long toes facilitate walking on floating vegetation. They are small to medium-sized birds, the bill varying from long and curved to short and conical. The diet is variable, mainly animal, but some prefer vegetable food. Though some are good flyers, covering long distances on migration, they are invariably loath to fly when disturbed, instead running for cover on their long legs.

In Britain the Water Rail (*Rallus aquaticus*) is our best-known Rail, if only from its squealing and grunting calls, which it utters from the depths of a marshy area. When seen it gives the appearance of a small dark Moorhen (*Gallinula chloropus*) with a long, red, curved bill. Total breeding population in Britain probably no more than 3,000 pairs, though the resident population is greatly increased by migrant birds in the autumn.
See Crake

Ramus
Barb of a feather.
See Feather; Plumage; Wing

Range
That portion of the world over which a particular species, genus, etc, extends: the geographical limits of a bird's breeding area or migrations.

Raphidae
Family of Columbiformes, sub-order Columbae, the best-known member being the extinct Dodo (*Raphus cucullatus*).
See Dodo; Extinct Birds

Raptor
A term used generally for birds of prey.

Rarities Committee
The British Birds Rarities Committee was founded in 1958 and since then has assessed all records of rare birds in Britain. The committee consists of ten voting members (often referred to as 'the Ten Rare Men'), with a non-voting honorary secretary. At least one member leaves the committee each year and is then replaced, after a postal election by the county and bird-observatory recorders. Over the years the chairmen have included such eminent field experts as P. A. D. Hollom, D. I. M. Wallace and P. J. Grant.

Between 600 and 1,000 records are circulated to the committee each year and are subsequently published in the annual 'Report on Rare Birds in Great Britain' in the monthly journal *British Birds*. A list of the species considered by the committee and copies of the special forms for submitting records may be obtained from the honorary secretary (now M. J. Rogers, 195 Vicarage Road, Sunbury-on-Thames, Middlesex TW16 7TP).

Ravens will feed on carrion, but evidence that they kill newborn lambs is rare

Ratite
A flightless running bird, lacking the 'keel' or breastbone of flying birds.

Raven (*Corvus corax*)
Largest and most powerful of the Corvidae in Britain, a bird of wild moorland and mountainous country and also some coastal areas. The stout bill and distinctive wedge-shaped tail should aid identification, while the deep 'pruk-pruk' of its flight call, and the throaty 'grock', are quite different from the similar but smaller Carrion Crow's 'karr' or its repetitive car-horn note. British and Irish population is about 5,000 pairs.

Razorbill (*Alca torda*)
This black-and-white sea bird is one of our most familiar Auks, breeding round certain rocky coastal parts of Britain. Probably 70 per cent of the world's population of this bird nest in Britain and Ireland. In 1970 this was estimated about 144,000 pairs. In America called the Razorbilled Auk.
See Alcidae; Auk; Guillemot; Puffin

Redbreast
Alternative name for Robin (*Erithacus rubecula*).

Red-headed Smew
Or Red-head. Colloquial name often applied to the Smew (*Mergus albellus*).

Redshank, known as 'warden of the marshes' as it is the first bird there to take wing at any alarm

Redpoll (*Acanthis flammea*)
Small streaked grey-brown Finch with a bright crimson forehead and black chin. In Britain it breeds widely in Scotland, N and E England and in Ireland, favouring birchwood, areas of alders and coniferous plantations. It has increased considerably in recent years. The present breeding population of Britain and Ireland is probably around 600,000 pairs. There are other races of the Redpoll which occur in Britain, namely the continental Mealy Redpoll (*Acanthis flammea flammea*), the Greenland or Greater Redpoll (*Acanthis flammea rostrata*) and occasionally the Arctic Redpoll (*Acanthis hornemanni*), a separate species with a 'hoar-frosted' look to the plumage on its head and nape. In N America it is known as the Hoary Redpoll.

Redshank (*Tringa totanus*)
A medium-sized wading bird, with vermilion-red legs that give the species its name. Present through the year, haunting estuaries and mudflats in the winter and breeding in salt marshes and waterside meadows and other damp places in the summer. A nervous, easily excited bird, it flies up at the slightest hint of danger, shrieking its triple 'tu-hu-hu' call. The Spotted Redshank (*Tringa erythropus*), a passage migrant (some winter), has dark red legs; in summer plumage it is sooty black speckled with white, while in winter it looks more like the commoner bird. Other Shanks include the Greenshank (*Tringa nebularia*) and much rarer Greater Yellowlegs (*Tringa melanoleuca*) and Lesser Yellowlegs (*Tringa flavipes*). Formerly called Greater Yellowshank and Lesser Yellowshank respectively, they are both rare visitors from N America.

Redstart (*Phoenicurus phoenicurus*)
A summer visitor to Britain, this colourful bird favours old deciduous woodland, parkland, heaths and commons, where it nests in holes in trees, buildings or walls. It quite readily accepts nestboxes. Locally distributed in suitable areas, scarcer in E and S England, sparse in N E England and absent from the Hebrides, Orkneys and Shetlands. There are only sporadic nesting records from Ireland. The total population is between 50,000 and 100,000 pairs.

Redstart is also the substantive name for some species of American Warblers (*Setophaga* and *Myioborus* spp).

BTO Register of Ornithological Sites—the Site Register form (opposite)

British Trust for Ornithology

Register of Ornithological Sites

Please read accompanying instructions

and then complete as much of this

form as possible

FOLD

Observer/Address[1]	Site Name[2]
R.E. YOUNGMAN 53 SEYMOUR PARK RD, MARLOW, BUCKS	WEST WYCOMBE HILL

Hectares[3]	Altitude limits/Aspect[4]	Grid Reference[5]
2 5	300-500 feet / HILL TOP	S U 8 2 7 9 5 0

Years/Seasons surveyed[6]
(tick boxes)

	1968-72			1973			1974			1975			1976		
	P✓	S✓	W✓	P✓	S✓	W✓	P	S	W	P	S	W	P	S	W

Site Status[7] (tick *all* relevant boxes)

National NR	
RSPB Reserve	
County Trust R	
Forest NR	
Wildfowl Refuge	
Other Reserve	
SSSI	
Other Stat Area	
Common Land	
Forestry Comm	
Min of Defence	
Crown Estate	
National Trust	✓
Private Owner	
Miscellaneous	

Sketch Map[8] (show scale, north, and site boundaries clearly)

WOOD
BLEDLOW RIDGE
FOOTPATH
500 ft CONTOUR
N
SCALE: APPROX 2½" = 1 mile
xxxx = SITE BOUNDARIES
A40
OXFORD
LONDON
B4010

Habitats[9]
(use classification code and place roughly in order of decreasing area)

A	B
1	1
6	0
6	3
0	5
0	4
6	8

Site Description[10]

A mainly open grassland and arable farmed hilltop at the southern tip of a long narrow Chiltern hill ridge. The hill is dominated by an iron age fort and the church which stands within it. There is a small wood mainly of yew, and isolated lime, beech and ash trees.

Main Ornithological Interest[11]

Typical chalk downland / scrubland bird communities.

Breeding Cirl Buntings.

An excellent vantage point.

General Comments[12]

There is public access at all times to the hill which is very popular. Attractions include the church, hillfort, a mausoleum, caves and a cafe. The grassland areas support a rich variety of chalk downland plants including orchids, Clustered Bellflower and Felwort.

OFFICE USE ONLY

Example of the front of the new Site Register form completed for a site

Reedling
Shortened alternative name for Bearded Reedling or Bearded Tit (*Panurus biarmicus*).

Reeling
Term usually applied to the rapid and uniform high-pitched trill of the Grasshopper Warbler (*Locustella naevia*). This song has a peculiarly mechanical effect not unlike the running of an angler's reel (hence the term), but more sustained and often lasting as long as 2 minutes. Inaudible to some people, it has considerable carrying power in favourable conditions, sometimes being heard at a quarter-mile's distance or more. When delivering the song the bird turns its head from side to side which gives a ventriloquial effect.

The Savi's Warbler (*Locustella luscinioides*) also has a somewhat similar song, but lower-pitched, fuller and often of much shorter duration.
See Warbler

Reeve
The female Ruff (*Philomachus pugnax*).

Reflex
An innate, relatively simple and stereotyped response involving the central nervous system and occuring very shortly after the stimuli which evoke it. It specifically involves only a part of the organism, though the whole may be affected, and is usually a response to localised sensory stimuli (Thorpe 1951).

Refuge (Wildfowl or Wildlife)
Synonymous with reserve or sanctuary, the term is more favoured in the USA, though now possibly used globally more than it used to be.
See Reserve; Sanctuary

Register of Ornithological Sites
A survey to document sites of ornithological value on a nationwide scale. Work has been going on since 1973. Organised by the BTO and financed by the Nature Conservancy Council, it has been described as a 'modern Domesday Book'. As a follow-up to the *Atlas of Breeding Birds* it will serve as a yardstick to measure the state of bird habitats and be of tremendous value to conservationists and planners working on long-term environmental planning. Contact the BTO, Beech Grove, Tring, Herts, for details.

Relict
Term used for small populations of birds that were once larger populations or formed part of a more continuous distribution of the species in question.

Relict Form
A race or species that has become geographically isolated in a small part of its former range.

Remex
A main flight feather. Remiges (plural) are the primary and secondary feathers in the wing.
See Feather; Plumage; Wing

Remicle
A small feather occurring on the wing of some species, considered to be a vestigial primary feather.
See Feather; Plumage; Wing

Resident
A bird that remains in its breeding area throughout the year. A summer resident is only present during the breeding season and a winter resident is present only in the non-breeding period.

Retina
Part of the eye—the inner membrane which receives images.
See Iris

Retrix
A main tail feather. The retrices (plural) are the tail feathers, in effect the whole tail.

Reverse Migration
The movement of migratory birds in the direction opposite to the one they started out on—brought about by adverse weather encountered during a stage of migration, or possibly when the migratory urge wanes after they have set forth.

Rhea
A large running Ratite, member of the Rheidae (Rheiformes), a group of Ostrich-like birds restricted to South America.

Rheiformes
An order of Ratite birds, comprising only one family, Rheidae—the Rheas.
See Ratite; Rhea

Rictal
Pertaining to the gape, often applied to the bristles that some birds have in that area.

Rhea, a running bird (above)

A Goldcrest after ringing

Ring Dove

Alternative name for Woodpigeon (*Columba palumbus*), but also applied to a domesticated variety of one of the sub-species of Collared Dove (*Streptopelia decaocto*).

Ringer

One who rings wild birds.
See Mist net; Ringing; Trapping

Ringing

Fitting a ring, bearing a unique serial number and an address, to the leg of a bird, so that in future it will be possible to recognise that bird as an individual. Initially the main reason for ringing birds was to find out where they go and how long they live. More recently ringing has allowed other aspects of the bird's life cycle to be studied, such as mortality rates, weight variations and moult. With increasing pressures on our remaining wild areas, ringing has been able to provide facts about the importance of certain sites to birds. To cite but one example, ringing of waders at estuaries has shown how, although the total number of birds present may be static, an

estuary supports different populations of birds at different seasons, and that one individual bird may be dependent on several estuaries in the course of a year.

Although marking wild birds in one way or another can be traced back to years before Christ, the first ringing of a bird *as an individual* was by Danish ornithologist H. C. Mortensen who, in 1899, ringed 164 Starlings with numbered and addressed rings. In Britain, ringing started in 1909 with two independent schemes. That started by A. Landsborough Thomson at Aberdeen University came to an end during World War I, but the other scheme, started by Harry Forbes Witherby in connection with *British Birds*, continued. In 1937 the Witherby scheme was transferred to the British Trust for Ornithology to become the ringing scheme we know today. Most current rings bear the address 'British Museum, London SW7' and this was the headquarters of the scheme until 1963, when it was transferred to the then new BTO headquarters at Beech Grove, Tring.

The ringer is trying to discover what an ordinary, healthy wild bird does, so even leaving humanitarian feelings aside, it is essential that the capture of the bird and the ring it wears do not affect it adversely. To this end the British Trust for Ornithology issues ringing permits, and all ringers must undergo an extensive period of training before being allowed to operate on their own. The Protection of Birds Act governs ringing in Britain and all ringers must have a licence issued by the Nature Conservancy Council. Even trainee ringers and helpers who handle birds must have obtained a restricted licence.
See Cannon netting; Heligoland Trap; Mist Net; Rocket netting
Read Mead, C. *Bird Ringing*, BTO Guide No 16

Ring-necked Duck (*Aythya collaris*)
A North American species of diving Duck, superficially resembling a black-backed

Ring-necked Duck

Scaup (*Aythya marila*). The ring of dull chestnut colouring round the neck which gives the bird its name is only visible at extremely close range and the two white rings which cross the bill in the drake are much more readily seen. It has been recorded about 75 times in the last two decades and has become more frequently noted in recent years. That it can make a successful return flight across the North Atlantic has been demonstrated by a bird ringed at Slimbridge, Gloucestershire, being subsequently shot in south-east Greenland.

Ring-necked Parakeet (*Psittacula krameri*)
Also called the Rose-ringed or Green Parakeet. The species is found north of the equator from Senegal and Nigeria to Sudan and Uganda, through Mauritius and the Seychelles eastwards to Burma, India, Sri Lanka, Malaysia and south-western China. A colourful and attractive member of the Parrot (Psittacidae) family, it has long been kept as a cage bird. Over the years many have escaped (and in some instances have been deliberately released when found to be difficult birds to handle), and they are now breeding freely in the wild in some southern parts of Britain, particularly in the SE where they are believed to be quite well established. They readily feed from bird tables and as fruit eaters they are also rapidly earning a bad reputation for their attacks on apples, pears and plums.

Ring-necked Pheasant
See Pheasant

Ritualisation
A term used to denote the development of stereotype patterns of behaviour into more highly complex activities, eg basic activities such as preening, feeding etc have become ritualised, forming part of the bird's display.

Road Runner (*Geococcyx californianus*)
An American species of Cuckoo that runs on the ground. It inhabits dry, open, stony desert areas.

Robin (*Erithacus rubecula*)
Of all British birds, the Robin is our best loved. It has appeared on our postage stamps, is annually featured on millions of Christmas cards and was voted our National Bird. A regular garden visitor, it can become tame enough to take food from the hand and quite often stays to nest. From August to mid-winter it is strongly territorial and aggressively

Robin

American Robin

drives off its own kind as well as other species, from whichever area it chooses as its own. It normally feeds out in the open, hunting small insects and spiders, also eating some seeds, fruit and berries. On the Continent it is a bird of deep woodland, where it is shy and retiring, the complete reverse of its extrovert behaviour this side of the Channel. The sexes are indistinguishable.

The Robin was not associated with Christmas festivities until the coming of the Christmas card in 1860. The fact that postmen in the mid-nineteenth century wore red tunics and were nicknamed 'Robin' did not escape Victorian commercial artists: 'Robin the postman' was soon changed to 'Robin the bird' on card designs, and has been with us ever since.

The name Robin has been misapplied to birds in many parts of the English-speaking world, as in North America, where the American Robin (*Turdus migratorius*), a Thrush, was so called by the colonists because it had a red breast, eg the Magpie Robin and Bush Robin of Australia, the Scrub Robin and Robin Chat of Africa.

Read Lack, D., *The Life of the Robin*, Witherby, 1941 (4th ed 1965)

Rocket Netting
This works on the same principle as cannon netting, except that the net is actually propelled by rockets attached to it. This technique for catching birds has now largely been superseded by the less cumbersome cannon net, although the Wildfowl Trust still possesses rocket-netting equipment for ringing Geese.

Roding
Display flight of the Woodcock (*Scolopax rusticola*). From March through to July, each dawn and dusk, the male traverses a variable circuit round its breeding territory, flying quite fast, but with slow Owl-like wing action, a little above the tree-tops, frequently calling with a low croaking sound. It also utters a thin 'tsiwick' note but this is given in non-roding flight as well.

See Woodcock

Roller
Name of the species of the sub-family Coraciinae of the Coraciidae (Coraciiformes, sub-order Coracii). Typical Rollers are an Old World group of mostly brightly coloured, stoutly built birds of around 9½-13in (230-

Abyssinian Roller

330mm) in length. Rollers get their name from their habit of somersaulting and rolling in the air during display flights. Mainly insect eaters, most Rollers are found in Africa, though there is a European Roller (*Coracias garrulus*), which breeds in southern and eastern Europe, being an uncommon migrant to Britain.

Rook (*Corvus frugilegus*)
A familiar member of the Crow family, it is a resident generally distributed throughout Britain and Ireland. A highly social and gregarious species, Rooks not only nest in colonies or rookeries, building large bulky nests of twigs in the tops of tall trees, but also feed together, foraging in fields in large flocks. In recent years the species has declined dramatically in some areas. In order to check the extent of this bird's decrease it was the subject of a BTO survey in 1975.

Rookery
A colony of nesting birds, particularly of Rooks (*Corvus frugilegus*) but also applied to the colonies of other birds, including Cormorant and Penguin.

The Rook (left) and the rookery (below) are thought of as an intrinsic part of the farmland scene. But for how much longer ?

Pied Wagtail roost

Roost

A bird's resting or sleeping place, but in general birdwatchers' parlance usually referring to an area or place where large numbers of birds gather to rest or sleep—eg Starling roost, Gull roost. In the case of the Starling (*Sturnus vulgaris*), a building or buildings in a city centre, or bushes or trees in the country, might be the site of a regularly used roost where thousands gather for the night. With Gulls (*Larus* spp), a roost inland is frequently at a large reservoir, and during the late afternoon and evening many birds can be observed flying in from the surrounding areas where they have been feeding during the day. Other species which roost communally in large numbers include Ducks, Geese, waders (often in the day, when their feeding areas are then covered by the tide), Rooks, Jackdaws, Wagtails and some Thrushes.

The general requirement for a suitable roost depends upon the species, but basically it needs to be secure from predators. During the breeding season birds will roost near the nest (male), the female probably sleeping on the nest. In winter there is greater need for protection from the elements and many species seek holes or cavities in trees or buildings. Some birds will use nestboxes, particularly Tits and Wrens.

See Loafing
Read Dobinson, H. M., *Bird Count: A Practical Guide to Bird Surveys*, Penguin, 1976

Ross, Sir James Clark (1800-62)

British explorer of the Arctic and Antarctic. Ross's Gull (*Larus rosea*) is named after him. This bird was first sighted in 1823 when two specimens were collected by the then Lt Ross, who in company with Polar explorer W. E. Parry was attempting to find the North West Passage. The adult Ross's Gull is a beautiful bird with the head, under parts, rump and tail white suffused with a soft rosy pink. A rare visitor to Britain, recorded only a handful of times.

Royal Society for the Protection of Birds (RSPB)

The RSPB is a registered charity and Europe's largest voluntary wildlife conservation body. With a professional staff of over 300 and the backing of well over 300,000 members, plus another 100,000 in the junior branch, the Young Ornithologists Club (YOC), the society has the will and the means to oppose activities threatening the welfare of birds. It is

Ross's Gull

concerned with *wild* birds and their place in nature, not captive and feral birds.

Members come from all walks of life and all age groups—the majority probably simply taking pleasure in seeing the wild birds of the garden and countryside, wanting to know more about them and caring enough about their future survival to support an organisation geared to taking informed action on their behalf. Expert ornithologists are inevitably in the minority. The RSPB began in 1889 and gained its Royal Charter fifteen years later, its purpose being the better conservation and protection of wild birds. In its early days the society was active in bringing about legislation to protect birds, in fighting pollution, protecting endangered species and in creating reserves, but until the 1960s this was all on a relatively small scale. Then the membership began to grow—from being under 10,000 in 1960 it has risen to over 300,000 and the rise continues.

The headquarters are in Sandy, Bedfordshire, with regional offices established in nine other areas. Over 70 reserves covering more than 85,000 acres are owned or leased, most of them wardened and open to visitors. Several educational and visitor centres are also maintained, as the work of the RSPB involves not only conserving birds and their habitats but also informing and educating the public.

Other activities include investigation of alleged offences under bird-protection laws and special protection schemes, scientific research, monitoring of pollution, and conservation planning and consultation with local and national government, international liaison especially within the European Economic Community, the production of material for schools and teachers, running teachers' courses and publication of a full-colour magazine *Birds* (and *Bird Life* for the YOC) as well as many leaflets, reports, booklets and posters. A major aspect of RSPB work is the production of films which are shown at 300 performances annually (excluding those using hired RSPB films) and the running of a network of over 150 member groups and 100 local representatives.

For details of the RSPB write to The Lodge, Sandy, Bedfordshire SG19 2DL.
See Conservation; Minsmere; Reserve; YOC

Ruff (*Philomachus pugnax*)
A member of the Scolopacidae (Charadriiformes, sub-order Charadrii), the Ruff is perhaps unique among this group of birds, which are generally referred to as Snipe and Sandpipers. In general appearance it shows a more erect stance than some of the smaller Sandpipers and also there is considerable size difference between the male, which is about 11½in (279mm) long and the female or Reeve which is about 9½in (229mm) long. In full breeding plumage the male is unlike any other Sandpiper, having a large erectile ruff and eartufts which vary considerably in colour between individuals—an instance of polymorphism. This ornamentation is used in the species' ritual display or tournaments which take place at special places or 'hills'. These are called leks.

Most Ruff breed in Northern Europe and into Asia. They formerly bred in many places in England but declined in the eighteenth and nineteenth centuries largely due to drainage and consequent loss of suitable nesting habitat, its extinction as a breeding bird being hastened by egg collectors. In the early 1960s nesting was suspected in the Ouse Washes and in 1963 this was proved for the first time in 41 years. Since then a number of pairs have bred in that area, much of which is now protected by the RSPB, the Wildfowl Trust and the local County Trust.
See Lek

Sabine, Sir Edward (1788-1883)
English general and physician. Sabine's Gull (*Larus sabini*) is named after him.

RSPB

Formerly considered to be quite a rare visitor to British waters, this Arctic Gull is now recorded annually, mostly in the autumn. In summer plumage the head has a slate-grey hood bordered by a narrow black collar, which turns to a mottled, dusky white in winter. When it picks food in buoyant flight from the surface of the water, it might be confused with the Little Gull (*Larus minutus*) or immature Kittiwake (*Rissa tridactyla*) but the flight pattern of black outer primaries and the triangular area of broad white behind them contrasting with grey wing coverts should identify it without problem. The tail is much more strongly forked and the lack of any dark wing bar on the coverts should rule out the other two species.

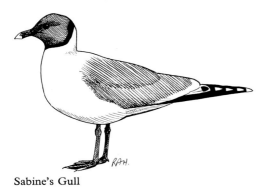

Sabine's Gull

The Ruff's erect stance and sedate ways of feeding help to distinguish it from other waders such as the Redshank

Saddlebill
Sometimes used alone as the name of the Saddle-billed Stork (*Ephippiorhynchus senegalensis*). A very large black-and-white Stork with a distinctive black-and-yellow bill, widely found in small numbers throughout the Ethiopian region.

Saker (*Falco cherrug*)
A bold, ferocious Falcon, distinguished from the Peregrine (*Falco peregrinus*) by its earth-brown (not slate-blue) upper parts and wings which have buffish emarginations, its whitish crown and nape streaked with dark brown, and narrow indistinct moustachial streak; also the white under parts are streaked with brown and not barred. Breeding on the plains of central Europe and Asia, it is highly migratory and in autumn birds fly south to the plains of west Pakistan and north-west India. Some birds do wander eastwards and the species has been noted in Europe on occasions. As it is a favourite falconer's bird, a Saker Falcon sighted in Britain might be an escapee.

Salt Gland
Part of the excretory gland. The salt gland helps to eliminate excess salt from the system and is highly developed in sea birds.

Sanctuary
See Bird Sanctuary; Reserve

Sanderling (*Calidris alba*)
A small plump active little shore bird, in winter the whitest of the small waders, with almost totally white plumage, short black bill and legs. A familiar species around our coasts, preferring sandy shores and flats. A passage migrant and winter visitor; the maximum number present in Britain during the autumn is probably around 30,000 birds. A few stay during the summer, when the upper parts, head and breast are chestnut, speckled blackish, contrasting with a pure white belly.

Sandgrouse
Name for species of Pteroclididae (Columbiformes, sub-order Pterocletes). In the plural (unchanged), the general term for the family. About the size of small Pigeons, to which group they have some affinity, Sandgrouse are ground-living birds, with long wings and long tails, but short legs that only allow them to waddle. Their general plumage coloration

Sanderling: it takes its prey from the tide-edge, racing after the retreating waves and dodging oncoming breakers

is like that of the mainly dry, arid areas in which they live, a sandy-brown with much spotting and barring. The drinking habits of Sandgrouse are unique. Some species (mainly those that live in deserts) drink first thing in the morning, and some drink in the evening. Sandgrouse have their favourite watering places and will travel up to 40 miles to reach them, often collecting in their thousands. They drink like Pigeons, leaving the bill in the water continuously without raising the head to swallow; as many as 44 gulps have been counted.

Of the 16 species of Sandgrouse, most are found in Africa and Asia, though the Pintailed Sandgrouse (*Pterocles alchata*) breeds in the south of France, Spain and Portugal, and the Black-bellied Sandgrouse (*Pterocles orientalis*) is resident in Spain and Portugal. A few other species are occasionally noted in Europe, particularly Pallas's Sandgrouse (*Syrrhaptes paradoxus*), which is prone to

periodic irruptive movements westwards, sometimes in large numbers, after which some have nested, as they did in Britain after the last big invasion in 1908.

Sandpiper

The substantive name for many members of the Scolopacidae (Charadriiformes, sub-order Charadrii). Sandpipers are wading birds, ranging in size from small, 5in (127mm), to moderately large, 24in (610mm), which in many cases includes a long bill. The legs are often long and in some species so is the neck. The plumage is generally mottled brown and grey on the upper parts, with pale under parts sometimes streaked or spotted. The sexes are generally alike but there is often a seasonal change affecting both. Winter dress tends to be paler than the breeding plumage. Most Sandpipers are birds of open country in the vicinity of water, many species breeding in desolate regions of the Arctic and sub-Arctic. Many have elaborate courtship displays. The nest is usually on the ground, sometimes concealed in vegetation and in other cases quite in the open. A few

The Common Sandpiper, wading

species use the old nests of tree-nesting birds and frequently perch in trees. The eggs, usually 4, are well camouflaged. The downy young are precocial and are ready to follow their parents a short time after hatching.

The family Scolopacidae, which comprises about 70 species, is mostly found in the northern hemisphere, in marked contrast to the Charadriidae family in which a great majority of the species are tropical. However, Sandpipers are highly migratory and are widely spread over the world as non-breeding birds.

Generally the Scolopacidae are divided into four sub-families:

1 Curlews and Tringine Sandpipers (Red-shank and Greenshank, Common Sand-piper etc)
2 Woodcock and Snipe
3 Godwits, Dowitchers, Calidrine Sand-pipers (Knot, Dunlin, Stints, etc).
4 Turnstones

In Britain the best-known bird whose substantive name is Sandpiper is the Common

Sandpiper (*Tringa hypoleucos*). One of the small Tringine Sandpipers, it can be quickly identified by the constant up-and-down movement of its tail end as it perches on a rock or boulder in a stream or by a lake. Equally characteristic is the flight, usually a foot above water, a regular peculiar flickering wing-beat and momentary glide on down-curved wings, an action unique to this bird. A summer visitor, the Common Sandpiper breeds widely in Wales, N England and Scotland. It also nests in Ireland, mainly in the eastern half. The total breeding population is around 50,000 pairs.

The Green Sandpiper (*Tringa ochropus*) superficially resembles the Common Sandpiper but in flight shows a white rump and black underwing. It also has a distinctive 'Klu-weeta-weeta' call. Frequently noted on passage, particularly in the autumn; a few stay through the winter and it has nested on occasions.

The third in the trio of the more commonly met 'Sandpipers' is the Wood Sandpiper (*Tringa glareola*). Though it has a white rump, the grey under-wing and 'chiff-chiff' call

Solitary Sandpiper

helps to distinguish this bird from the other two species. A few pairs nest in Scotland, though it is mainly known as a passage migrant, particularly in autumn.

Some rarer Sandpipers which have occurred in Britain include the Solitary Sandpiper (*Tringa solitaria*) and Spotted Sandpiper (*Tringa macularia*).

Sandwich Bay, Kent
The most easterly of the British observatories, situated on the Kentish coast midway between the Stour estuary and the town of Deal to the south. Founded in 1952 as a ringing station it became an official observatory in 1959. The observatory headquarters and trapping area are situated on the Sandwich Bay estate 2½ miles (4km) from the town of Sandwich and are manned throughout the year. Some notable occurrences at the observatory have been Red-flanked Bluetails, Olivaceous Warbler, Thrush Nightingale, Black-headed Bunting, Royal Tern, Sociable Plover and Terek Sandpiper. Though all birdwatchers are

welcome, priority is given to qualified ringing-permit holders wishing to visit, especially during peak migration periods.

Sapsucker
Substantive name of a number of American Woodpeckers (Picidae). One of these, the Yellow-bellied Sapsucker (*Sphyrapicus varius*) is a vagrant to Britain. The first record of it was on the Isles of Scilly in September 1975.

Sawbill
General term for the Mergansers (*Mergus* spp), derived from the tooth-like serrations on the bill.

Scapulars
The feathers above the shoulder. Most noticeable on some Ducks.

Scaup (*Aythya marila*)
A highly marine species rarely to be found on inland waters, occurring in large numbers on certain estuaries in winter, particularly in the Firth of Forth. A diving Duck feeding on molluscs, it superficially resembles the Tufted Duck (*Aythya fuligula*) but has a grey back and lacks the latter bird's distinctive crest. The females are somewhat harder to distinguish, though in the Scaup the area of white round the bill is much more extensive. In Britain peak numbers of this species are found from December to February, when probably around 20,000 are present, representing about one-eighth of NW Europe's total population.

Schedule I
This refers to the First Schedule of the Protection of Birds Acts; the species it lists are usually referred to as 'Schedule I Birds'. They are the species to which special protection is afforded (they must not be disturbed at or near a nest with eggs or unflown young) and special penalties are applied to people proved to have disturbed them. Birdwatchers would do well to know about this schedule, as apart from the obvious species (eg Avocet, Red Kite, Osprey, Snowy Owl), many birds which are regularly watched by large numbers of people in the breeding season cannot legally be disturbed at the nest without a licence—eg Chough, Divers, Kingfisher, Barn Owl, Little Ringed Plover, Sparrowhawk, Little Tern, Marsh Warbler and Woodlark. Scores of well-intentioned birdwatchers actually break the law every year by visiting the nests or breeding sites of such species and disturbance can be considerable. With birdwatching now so popular and the knowledge of the whereabouts of rare birds now so widespread, it should be remembered, especially, that a brief visit—apparently harmless—may just be one of several during a particular day or weekend. The cumulative effect may become intolerable for the birds concerned.
See Bird Protection Acts

The Common Scoter, usually seen in large straggling flocks

Scoter

Substantive name of *Melanitta* spp, the best-known being the Common Scoter (*Melanitta nigra*). This is a sea-going species preferring shallow inshore waters. It can be seen in varying numbers anywhere round the coasts of Britain at almost any time of the year. It first bred in Scotland in 1855 and Ireland in 1905. About 50 pairs now breed annually in Scotland and about 150 pairs in Ireland. The drake is totally black except for a spot of orange on the bill. The female is brownish with a light cheek-patch. The similar Velvet Scoter (*Melanitta fusca*) can easily be distinguished by the white wing patches, though these are often only visible when the bird flaps its wings or when flying. A winter visitor, the Velvet Scoter is less numerous than the Common Scoter, with probably no more than 5,000 birds in winter located at favoured areas.

Scottish Ornithologists' Club (SOC)

Founded in 1936. Membership is a must for Scottish birdwatchers. It publishes an internationally known quarterly journal, *Scottish Birds*, holds an annual weekend conference and organises weekend field meetings to the Solway and other areas. It has the best ornithological library in Scotland, available for reference during office hours and at other times by arrangement. It also runs a bird bookshop, where practically any bird book can be obtained. The SOC has local branches in Aberdeen, Ayr, Dumfries, Dundee, Edinburgh, Glasgow, Inverness, St Andrews and Stirling, with groups in New Galloway, Thurso and Wigtown. Each has its own programme of lectures and field meetings. The emblem of the SOC is the Crested Tit, which features on the club tie, badge etc. For details write to The Scottish Ornithologists' Club, The Scottish Centre for Ornithology and Bird Protection, 21 Regent Terrace, Edinburgh EH7 5BT.

Scrape

Some birds construct little or no nest, merely scraping a shallow depression in which to lay their eggs. Many wading birds, particularly the Plovers (Charadriidae), do this.

An area of the RSPB reserve at Minsmere, especially constructed for wading birds, is generally called and widely known as 'the Scrape'.

Screamer

Substantive name of 3 species of the Anhimidae (Anseriformes, sub-order Anhimae). Distantly related to the Flamingos and wildfowl, they are Goose-sized, but larger-legged, with much longer and spreading toes, webbed only slightly at the base. They have a curved, sharp-pointed spur on the forward edge of both wings, providing a formidable weapon. The Crested Screamer (*Chauna torquata*) is perhaps the best known. Its common name, 'Chaja', is taken from its double-noted, trumpeting call, which can be heard more than a mile away. The Screamers are confined to South America.

Crested Screamer

Scrub Bird

Substantive name of 2 species of Atrichornithidae (Passeriformes, sub-order Menurae). Primitive ground-loving song birds, found only in Australia. The first species, the Western Scrub Bird (*Atrichornis clamosus*) was only discovered in 1842, and in view of its loud voice was given the English name Noisy Bush Bird, later changed to Noisy Scrub Bird. Up to 1889 only 20 specimens were known and after that date none were seen or heard until 1961 in SW Australia. Others were later located in that area and the first authenticated nest was found in 1963. The Rufous Scrub Bird (*Atrichornis rufescens*) is much more numerous but occurs in Eastern Australia. The nests of both species are bulky, globular structures with a side entrance. The interior is lined with a kind of papier-mache, made by the bird chewing up plant fibres; when dry this looks like grey cardboard.

Scrub-bird

Scrub Fowl
Name sometimes applied to some Megapodes.

Scrub Warblers
This group, mostly of the genus *Sylvia*, consists of birds with more distinct markings than the Tree Warblers, some having a capped appearance. Mainly haunting thickets, bushes and scrubby areas, four of the 'Scrub Warblers' breed in Britain. The Dartford Warbler (*Sylvia undata*) is a very dark-looking bird with slate-grey head shading to dark brown upper parts, under parts purplish-brown, the chin and throat spotted with white. As a breeding bird it is confined to the gorsy commons and heaths of southern England between Devon and Sussex, where about 500 pairs are to be found. Vulnerable to severe weather, this number can be much reduced after a long, cold winter.

The Whitethroat (*Sylvia communis*) is a summer visitor, favouring open country with bushes and tangled vegetation, untrimmed hedges and the edges of woodland, from where it will proclaim its presence with its scratchy little song, often delivered in display flight. Once much commoner, a population crash in 1969 reduced the breeding population by 75 per cent. About 500,000 pairs are now to be found throughout Britain and Ireland, still well below the 1968 peak.

The Lesser Whitethroat (*Sylvia curruca*) is more secretive than the former species and often its 'rattling' song, rather like that of the Yellowhammer (*Emberiza citrinella*), is the only indication of its presence. Also a summer visitor, between 25,000 and 50,000 pairs are to be found throughout Britain. It is entirely absent from Ireland.

The Blackcap (*Sylvia atricapilla*) is possibly the finest songster among the Scrub Warblers, its rich warbling and melodic phrasing putting it on a par with the Nightin-gale (*Luscinia megarhynchos*) in some people's opinion. The male is easily identified by his black cap, but this is rich chestnut-brown in the female. A summer visitor, arriving early April, it favours copses, spinneys and woodland, with dense undergrowth. The total population is around 200,000, being well distributed in England and Wales, becoming locally scarce northwards to Scotland and scarce in Ireland. Some stay through the winter, often visiting bird tables.

Among the rarer 'Scrub Warblers' to visit Britain, the Barred Warbler (*Sylvia nisoria*), nesting in Eastern Europe, is perhaps the most frequently noted. Every autumn a number occur at coastal sites, mainly immature birds lacking the barred appearance of the adult. But their heavy-looking appearance, stout bills and stout blue-grey legs help to identify them. The Orphean Warbler (*Sylvia hortensis*), Sardinian Warbler (*Sylvia melanocephala*) and Sub-alpine Warbler (*Sylvia cantillans*) are others of this group which have occurred in Britain from time to time.
See Acrocephalus Warbler; New World Warblers; Swamp Warblers; Tree Warblers.

Dartford Warbler

Whitethroat

Scutellate
Covered with scales—as the leg and foot of a bird, on which the scales are usually large and overlapping.

Seabird Group
Formed in 1966 to promote and improve the co-ordination of sea-bird studies, its major achievement was the organisation of Operation Seafarer in 1969-70. This was the first time a national census of breeding seabirds had been carried out anywhere in the world. Following a somewhat dormant period, plans are in hand to decide the best way to repeat Operation Seafarer, and a photographic coverage of UK cliff colonies is being organised. Other major seabird studies will be centred on: census techniques; birds at sea; oil victims.

To enquire about membership of the Seabird Group write to T. R. Birkhead, Zoology Dept, The University, Sheffield.
See Operation Seafarer

Sea Gull
A common term in ordinary speech for any species of Gull, whether it is pelagic or not. A non-ornithological expression.

Sea Swallow
A popular name for Terns (*Sterna* spp), derived from the superficial resemblance of these birds' forked tails and long streamers to those of the Swallow (*Hirundo rustica*).

Secondary
Or secondary feather. Any one of the flight feathers on the forearm (ulna), as contrasted with the 'primaries' borne on the manus. They are sometimes called cubitals.
See Ulna; Wing

Secretary Bird (*Sagittarius serpentarius*)
Sole species of the Sagittariidae (Falconiformes, sub-order Sagittarii). Found only in Africa. A very long-legged bird, it stands over 3ft (1m) tall. The bill and face are Hawk-like, while a remarkable crest of elongated feathers protrudes from behind the eye looking like the 'quill' pen behind the ear of a clerk or secretary, hence the name. It feeds on a wide variety of animal prey and wages incessant war on snakes, beating them to death with its powerful feet.

Sedentary
A sedentary species is one that is non-migratory, staying in or near the area where it was raised.

Seed Snipe
Species of Thinocoridae (Charadriiformes, sub-order Charadrii). A group of plump, ground-feeding birds, about Partridge size. They feed almost entirely on seeds, and have

Secretary Bird (opposite)

the zig-zag flight of a Snipe (*Gallinago gallinago*) but are not related. All 4 species of Seed Snipe are found only in South America.

Senses

In birds, the sense of vision is usually very acute (there are exceptions, notably the Kiwis), and hearing is also normally well developed. However, the sense of smell appears limited (except perhaps in some of the Procellariidae). The sense of taste is probably quite poor, whereas the sense of touch is acute, eg the Snipe (*Gallinago gallinago*) locates its food with the highly sensitive tip of its bill.

Serin (*Serinus serinus*)

A tiny, streaked, yellowish Finch with a stubby bill and bright yellow rump. This bird is a common species in continental Europe, occurring in parks, gardens and vineyards. It displays its presence, singing from treetops or telegraph wires or in flight, with a rapid sibilant jingle of notes interspersed with Canary-like trills. Its visits to Britain are becoming much more frequent, particularly in southern England, where successful breeding

has taken place on a number of occasions in recent years.

Sexual dimorphism

Differences in appearance between male and female members of a species of the same age and of the same season, eg in the Bullfinch (*Pyrrhula pyrrhula*).

Shag

The name is interchangeable with Cormorant (*Phalacrocorax* spp), but in Britain is applied only to *Phalacrocorax aristotelis*—though this species is sometimes called the 'Green Cormorant'.

Shank

Popular term for the whole or some part of the leg.

Such species as the Redshank (*Tringa totanus*), Greenshank (*Tringa nebularia*) and some others are frequently termed 'Shanks' as a group.

The Shag is smaller than the Cormorant, and its plumage is dark greenish-looking; in the breeding season it has a short crest

Shearwater

Substantive name of certain species of Procellariidae, oceanic birds, only visiting land for breeding. Shearwaters literally shear the water in flight, banking and gliding on long, narrow, stiff wings. They have slender bills and are longer-bodied than the smaller Petrels, coloured generally dark above and white underneath. In Britain the Manx Shearwater (*Puffinis puffinus*) is the best-known of this group, with large colonies breeding from the Shetlands down the W coast south to the Isles of Scilly. Some of the larger concentrations are to be found on Skokholm (35,000 pairs), Skomer (95,000 pairs) and Rhum (100,000 pairs). The total British and Irish population could well be over 300,000 pairs. Manx Shearwaters can be seen particularly during their autumn movements south, as they fly just offshore, sometimes in almost continuous procession along the horizon. At such times birdwatchers are looking out for more unusual species of Shearwater such as Cory's Shearwater (*Puffinus diomedea*) or Greater Shearwater (*Puffinus gravis*). Perhaps the most frequently met of the rarer Shearwaters, however, is the Sooty Shearwater (*Puffinus griseus*), which looks black at a distance and does not give the 'white—then black' appearance of the 'Manx' as it banks and glides over the water. Sometimes Sooty Shearwaters occur in quite large numbers.

Sheathbill

A family of the Charadriiformes, sub-order Charadrii. There are 2 species, small white shore birds superficially resembling Pigeons. Called Sheathbills from the rough horny sheath which covers the base of the short stout bill, and also known as Paddies, they are the only birds with webbed feet found on the shores of the Antarctic continent.

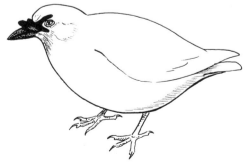

Black-billed Sheathbill (Paddy)

Shelduck (*Tadorna tadorna*)

Sometimes written Sheld Duck or Sheldrake. This Goose-like bird looks very black and white at a distance, hence the name 'Shield Duck', which means pied Duck, having no connection with a shield. However, at close quarters it will be seen that the bird has boldly contrasting plumage, with a greenish-black head and neck and a broad chestnut band around the forepart of the white body. There is also a dark stripe down the centre of the underparts and black bands on the

Shelduck

261

Shoebill

upperparts. The bill is red and the legs pink. Found round most of coastal Britain and Ireland, particularly on mudflats and sand dunes, it has increased considerably as a breeding bird in recent years and has even begun to colonise inland areas, notably the Ouse Washes. Many Shelduck undertake a special moult migration in the autumn, thousands gathering on the mudflats off Heligoland.

The Ruddy Shelduck (*Tadorna ferruginea*) is a vagrant to Europe from Asia and has been recorded in Britain on a number of occasions.

Shoebill (*Balaeniceps rex*)
The Shoe-billed Stork or Whale-headed Stork is a bird of African swamplands. The sole member of the Balaenicipitidae family, it is usually placed in the order Ciconiiformes, sometimes in the sub-order Ardeae and sometimes in the sub-order Ciconae; some authorities place it in a sub-order of its own.

Shorebird
In North America a term generally applied to those families of the Charadriiformes called 'waders' by British birdwatchers.

Shoebill

Shorelark (*Eremophila alpestris*)
The Horned Lark in American usage.
See Lark

Shoveler (*Anas clypeata*)
A handsome surface-feeding or dabbling Duck. It has a very large spatulate bill with which it sieves the watery ooze for food. The drake has a dark green head, white breast and chestnut-brown flanks. In flight it shows large blue shoulder patches. The female lacks the drake's bright colours but is easily identified by the distinctive bill. Shovelers

Shoveler

breed locally in small numbers with probably no more than 1,000 pairs in Britain and Ireland. There are also some winter visitors from the Continent.

Shrike

Substantive name of most species of Laniidae (Passeriformes, sub-order Oscines), a widespread but mainly Old World family. Shrikes are bold, aggressive birds, feeding on large insects, small reptiles, birds and small mammals. Many species will impale their prey on thorns or barbed wire, or hang it from a branch, forming so-called 'larders', for which reason they are sometimes known as 'Butcher-birds'. There are 70 recorded species of true Shrikes, most of which are found in Africa. In Britain the Red-backed Shrike (*Lanius collurio*) is a summer visitor, breeding locally in East Anglia and SE England in small numbers, the population having declined markedly in recent years. A handsome bird, the male has a chestnut back,

Red-backed Shrike (female)

a pale blue crown and wings and a broad black mark across the face. The under parts are pinkish-white. The black-and-white tail is often swung from side to side.

By September most Red-backed Shrikes

Woodchat Shrike

263

have left, but then the Great Grey Shrike (*Lanius excubitor*), which breeds in Spain and Europe, arrives. A larger bird, its general colouring is white and grey, with black face markings. It is commoner in some years than others, but always a solitary species. Some rarer Shrikes that occasionally turn up during migration include the Woodchat Shrike (*Lanius senator*) and the Lesser Grey Shrike (*Lanius minor*).

Within the Shrike family there are four sub-families, the true Shrikes as above, the Bush Shrikes, the Helmet Shrikes of Africa, and a single near relative occuring in Borneo —known as a Bristle-head (*Pityriasis gymnocephala*).

Sibling species

Two or more closely related species that are morphologically very similar but are reproductively isolated (ie able to inhabit the same area without interbreeding); sometimes called 'cryptic species'. For example, the Marsh Tit (*Parus palustris*) and Willow Tit (*Parus montanus*).

Singing

Bird song is generally understood to be a series of notes, usually of more than one type, uttered in succession and so related as to form a recognisable pattern. However the so-called song of some species, such as many waders, may be nothing more than a succession of call-notes. It is among the Passeriformes, in the sub-order Oscines (which literally means song birds), that the most highly developed forms of singing are found, the Warblers and the Thrushes particularly being recognised as songsters.

As bird language, song is essentially a means by which the male bird defines the area of his territory and attracts a mate. But there are often different forms of song related to the component parts of these forms of behaviour—to the actual courtship, nest-site selection, nest building, etc.

Different species of birds have evolved particular ways of delivering their song. Many sing from a perch, often in quite an exposed situation; others sing hidden from view in deep vegetation. Others have particular song flights, flying round in a circle, or singing in upwards flight like the Skylark (*Alauda arvensis*), while some ascend for only a short distance and then 'parachute' down to the ground or a perch singing all the time—as the Tree Pipit (*Anthus trivialis*).

Identifying a bird by its song is not always easy, but to know a bird's song and the manner in which it is delivered can be most useful. Sometimes it might be the way in which the bird's presence is first detected, and with some similar-looking species, such as Reed Warbler (*Acrocephalus scirpaceus*) and Marsh Warbler (*Acrocephalus palustris*), may be the only way to distinguish between the two.

The amount of singing a bird does usually correlates to its breeding activities; it is generally at its maximum level in the spring but as the nesting period varies between the species, so does the song period. Some species begin their song period quite early in the year, eg the Song Thrush (*Turdus philomelos*) is often singing quite strongly in February, the Blackbird tending to start a little later, usually March. Some species continue to sing when most others have ceased: typical of the summer months is the Yellowhammer (*Emberiza citrinella*), whose monotonous wheeze is one of the few songs still heard in July. Some sing intermittently all through the year, such as the Wren (*Troglodytes troglodytes*) and Dunnock (*Prunella modularis*). When describing various types of bird song the following definitions should be useful:

Chatter Loud harsh notes, unmusical and often merely a rapid repetition of one note.

Slur When two or more notes of different pitch are connected by a gradual change instead of an abrupt one.

Trill A rapid repetition of one note with a more or less tremulous or quavering effect.

Twitter Notes not so connected as a trill, generally unmusical—though some such utterances might be described as a warbling twitter where they are of better tonal quality!

Warble A sequence of notes of different pitch but connected so that the effect is liquid and flowing, more or less musical, and pleasing to the human ear. In some cases it may be monotonous, in others very diversified.

See Dawn Chorus

Read Armstrong, E. A. *Discovering Bird Song* Shire Publications, 1975

Siskin (*Carduelis spinus*)

An active little Finch. The male is predominantly yellow-green with a black crown and chin and a yellow rump. In flight, two yellow bars on the wing and yellow patches either side of the tail are noticeable. The female has no black cap or chin and is greyer looking and streakier underneath. In Britain

Sedge Warbler singing

the species is more widely known as a winter visitor and can be found wherever there are alder trees or birch, where they feed on the seeds, hanging upside-down in Tit-like manner.

Quite a number breed in N Scotland, and parts of Ireland, while conifer plantations elsewhere in Britain have encouraged them to nest in many scattered localities. Since about 1963 numbers of Siskins have visited suburban gardens in England, feeding on nuts put out for Tits.

Size Dimorphism
In many species male and female are of different size. The male is usually slightly larger, and sometimes this difference is marked, as in the Capercaillie (*Tetrao urogallus*), for example. However, in birds of prey (Falconiformes) the females are always much larger and often hunt different prey.

Skein
A flock of wild Geese when in flight.
See Assembly

Skimmer
Skimmer or Scissor Bird is the substantive name of the species of Rynchopidae (Charadriiformes, sub-order Lari). Allied to the Gulls and Terns, the Skimmer is unmistakable when feeding. It flies low above the water,

265

skimming the surface, with its much longer lower mandible ploughing through the water until some small fish or other aquatic life is encountered. This is then picked up with a quick backward movement of the head, or in the case of plankton literally scooped up by this unique bill. There are three species of Skimmer: the Black Skimmer (*Rhynchops nigra*) of the Americas, the African Skimmer (*Rhynchops flavirostris*), which is found over much of that continent, and the Indian Skimmer (*Rhynchops albicollis*) breeding in India and Indo-China.

Skokholm
The island of Skokholm lies about 4 miles (6.4km) north west of St Ann's Head off the extreme south-west tip of Dyfed (formerly Pembrokeshire). To the north is the large neighbouring island of Skomer, and the islet

Great Skua (left) and (below) Arctic Skua and chick—dark phase bird

of Grassholm lies 6 miles (10km) to the west. This 50 acre (20 Ha) island, with its mainly rocky shoreline, has been a bird observatory since R. M. Lockley established it in 1933. The island was leased to the West Wales Field Society in 1948 and the observatory was administered by the Field Studies Council until 1969. Since then the island has been run by the West Wales Naturalists' Trust, in conjunction with the Edward Grey Institute. The observatory undertakes migration studies and ringing, and has four Heligoland traps. Longterm studies of sea birds, particularly the Manx Shearwater, have been undertaken. The observatory is open from March to October and up to 14 visitors can be accommodated each week throughout the season.

Skomer

Lying 1 mile off the Welsh coast, it is the largest and most accessible—and considered by many to be the best—of the four Dyfed (Pembrokeshire) islands. Declared a National Nature Reserve in 1959 it is administered by the West Wales Naturalists' Trust. The 750-odd acres are the summer home of many sea birds—Manx Shearwaters and Puffins, Razorbills, Guillemots, Kittiwakes, Fulmars, nesting on the towering 200ft (60m) cliffs. The island is open daily during the summer.

Skua

Substantive name of all members of the Stercorariidae (Charadriiformes, sub-order Lari). They are Gull-like birds but generally having dark plumage. There are 4 species widely known for their habit of chasing other seabirds in order to make them disgorge or drop their food. All 4 species occur in Britain, two of which breed. The Great Skua (*Stercorarius skua*) or Bonxie is larger and stockier than a Herring Gull (*Larus argentatus*), having uniformly dark plumage with white patches in the wings which are very conspicuous in flight. It preys upon the larger Terns and Gulls and will even chase Gannets (*Sula bassana*) and force them to disgorge. The Great Skua breeds in small numbers in the Orkneys and Shetlands and also on the Scottish mainland.

The Arctic Skua (*Stercorarius parasiticus*) is the Skua most frequently met, and in autumn particularly it is common to see several together as they attack and harry the Terns along the coast. There are two forms (morphs) of this species, a light form which has a dark cap, white face and underparts, and a dark form which is uniform blackish-brown all over, while some are intermediate between the two. This species also breeds in the Orkneys and Shetlands and in the Hebrides and on the Scottish mainland, though the total population is only around 1,000 pairs. The Pomarine Skua (*Stercorarius pomarinus*) which breeds in the Russian tundra, is much rarer in British waters, but some are noted around our coasts, particularly in the autumn when the blunt, twisted tail of the adult helps to identify the species. There are also light and dark forms of this bird.

Perhaps the rarest of the four Skuas is the Long-tailed Skua (*Stercorarius longicaudus*), which is also the smallest. It has a long wafty tail and distinctive dark cap contrasting with a broad white collar. This bird also feeds in the Arctic tundra, occurring in Britain only on passage.

In America these birds are known as Jaegers.
See Piratic Birds

Smew (*Mergus albellus*)

A small, short-billed 'Sawbill'. The drake looks all white with a black eye patch; the duck is quite different, having a chestnut cap and white cheeks and throat. An Arctic-breeding species, and a winter visitor to Europe. Small numbers are noted in Britain some of the London reservoirs being particularly favoured, with perhaps 20 or 30 to be seen on occasions. However the total winter population in the British Isles is probably no more than 150.
See Red-head; Sawbill

Smoke Bathing

Some birds on occasions seem deliberately to sit near a source of smoke and carry out comfort or drying movements. Typically such species as Starlings (*Sturnus vulgaris*) and Jackdaws (*Corvus monedula*) will do this on chimney-pots. Little study has been made of this behaviour but it is believed the smoke or the fumes might have some effect on body parasites.

Snake Bird

Alternative name for species of Anhingidae, the Anhingas or Darters. Also a common name in Britain for the Wryneck (*Jynx torquilla*), derived from its writhing snake-like head actions and snake-like hissing when disturbed in its nest hole.

Snipe

A member of the family Scolopacidae (Charadriiformes, sub-order Charadrii), the Snipe (along with the Woodcock) is placed in the sub-family Scolopacinae, birds having long straight bills with flexible tips that can be opened below ground and grasp any prey they locate. In Britain 3 species occur, one of which breeds—*Gallinago gallinago*, the Common Snipe. A secretive bird of marshy places, its rich brown and black plumage, strongly striped with golden-yellow on the back, with a dark stripe through the eye and on the crown, help to conceal its whereabouts as it hides among the reeds and grasses. It is more often

Snipe and eggs—cryptic coloration

seen in flight as it suddenly bursts from cover with a harsh call, zig-zagging away low over the ground, before gaining height: it is for this reason regarded highly as a 'sportsman's bird'. It nests extensively in Britain and Ireland where suitable habitat occurs, the total British and Irish population being around 100,000 pairs, a number greatly increased by winter immigrants.

The much smaller Jack Snipe (*Lymnocryptes minimus*) does not breed, but may be located from September to March in haunts similar to those of the Common Snipe, though rarely in any number. When flushed it does not zig-zag and very soon settles again.

The Great Snipe (*Gallinago media*) also has a more direct flight, rising silently, and is frequently to be found in much drier situations, stubble fields, heaths etc. Much rarer than the Jack Snipe—only one or two are noted in any year.

Snow Finch (*Montifringilla nivalis*)

A mountain species of Sparrow, found above 6,000ft (2,000m) in the summer. It descends to lower altitudes in winter. A warm chocolate-brown above and creamy-white below, it nests in rock crevices, walls, etc. In Europe it is confined to the Pyrenees, the Alps and mountains of Yugoslavia and Greece; it is a vagrant elsewhere.

Soaring

A mode of flight whereby the bird glides on rising air currents without actively flapping its wings. This energy-saving method of flying is typical of large birds of prey, like Vultures, Eagles and Buzzards. Gulls also frequently spiral in a similar manner.

Society for the Promotion of Nature Reserves (SPNR)

A voluntary organisation founded in 1912 and incorporated by a Royal Charter in 1916. Its principal objects are to collect and collate information about areas of land interesting for their flora and fauna, to prepare schemes showing which areas should be acquired as nature reserves, to acquire and manage land in nature reserves and to promote interest in nature conservation as widely as possible.

Snipe are numerous at favoured feeding-grounds, where wisps of 12 or more may be seen flying around (opposite)

Soft Parts

The Society acts as the national association of the many county naturalists' trusts. It publishes a twice-yearly magazine for its members, *Conservation Review.*

Soft Parts

A term somewhat absurdly applied to those part of a bird not normally covered by feathers, usually including the bill, legs and feet, parts which are in fact fairly hard.
See Topography

Solan Goose

Former alternative name for the Gannet (*Sula bassana*).

Songbirds

Birds credited with exceptional singing ability, usually those of the sub-order Oscines (Passeriformes).

Song Post

A perch from which a bird normally sings within its territory. Two or more song posts are often used and these might be a tree, bush, garden shed, roof, T.V. aerial, or any prominent elevated position.

Sonogram

Made up from an abbreviation of 'sound spectrogram'. Sometimes called an audio-spectrogram, a sonogram is a visual representation of a sound pattern. Basically it is a graph showing the distribution of sound energy, in three parameters: a) frequency (pitch) on the vertical scale b) time (duration) in the horizontal scale c) amplitude (loudness) in the depth of shading, from pale grey to black. Sonograms may be a little difficult to interpret for some but they standardise the presentation of a bewildering and often misleading range of written descriptions of bird utterances. They are used throughout the *Handbook of the Birds of Europe, The Middle East and North Africa.*

Sound Recording

The first known recording of bird song in the wild is credited to Cherry Kearton (one of the Kearton brothers of bird photography fame) as early as 1900, when he put a few notes of the songs of a Nightingale and Song Thrush onto a wax cylinder. In 1910 HMV issued a single-sided 80 rpm disc of a captive Nightingale singing, and in 1927 a 10in 78rpm disc of dawn song and of a Nightingale was produced. By the late 1920s recordings of birds were being made in America at Cornell University, and in 1929 Ludwich Koch published some recordings of birdsong he had obtained in Africa. It was particularly the work of Ludwich Koch, who came to Britain as a refugee from Germany in 1936, that brought the attention of the public to bird song on records and in 1936 and 1937 commercial recordings by him under the titles 'The Song of Wild Birds' and 'More Songs of Wild Birds' were issued. From then until the late 1950s he was widely known as a recordist of birdsong and other wildlife sounds through his broadcasts for the BBC, and was regarded as unique in the field (as indeed he was) for many years. As with photography it was the development of equipment that brought sound recording within the reach of the public, today's portable tape recorders bearing little resemblance to the cumbersome disc-cutting machines (which with their ancillary items probably weighed half a ton) used by Ludwich Koch in the early days of recording before World War II. Magnetic wire recording, and then the advent of magnetic tape machines, revolutionised the techniques of recording in general; their application to bird song and other wildlife sounds has become a major recreational pursuit in its own right, while many birdwatchers use a tape recorder and parabolic reflector, in addition to binoculars and telescope, to secure evidence, or to help identification of an unknown bird at a later date.

Playing back birdsong or calls, in order to lure certain species into view, or to encourage their vocal performance, when practiced to excess is not considered to be in the interest of the bird and there have been cases of some birds driven 'frantic' in their attempts to protect their territory against 'taped' invaders.
See British Library of Wildlife Sound; Parabolic Reflector; Wildlife Sound Recording Society
Read Margoschis, R., *Recording Natural History Sounds*, Prints & Press Services, Barnet 1977; Simms, E., *Wildlife Sounds and their Recording*, Elek, 1979

Sound Recordings

Today there are innumerable records and tapes commercially available to the bird-watcher of many species of birds from many parts of the world—a far cry from the days of Ludwich Koch's 'The Songs of Wild Birds' and 'More Songs of Wild Birds', issued in 1936 and 1937. Modern recordings can be of immense value in helping the bird-watcher to learn to identify songs and calls of birds, as well as providing great pleasure. The 'Witherby Sound Guide' from the recordings of Myles North and Eric Simms, first issued in 1958, has long been a classic of its type and provides 300 characteristic sounds of nearly 200 species in systematic order. There are, of course, others but the list is too great to include here.

See Bird Sound Recording; British Library of Wildlife Sound; The Wildlife Sound Recording Society

Read British Birds Magazine, Vol 72, No 5, May 1979; 'Recommended Bird-recordings', Ron Kettle

Sparrow

Substantive name of minor species of Passerinae (Ploceidae). In the plural, the general name for the sub-family. The Passerinae were formerly considered to be Finches (Fringillidae) but are now placed in the Ploceidae—the Weavers: small birds 4-7in (101-178mm), all have mainly brown and grey coloured plumage (except for white in the Snow Finch), being mainly ground-feeding seed-eaters. They nest in a variety of situations, but most frequently in holes in rocks or buildings, although sometimes in trees. In Britain (and in most other parts of the world where it has been introduced) the House Sparrow (*Passer domesticus*) or English Sparrow is one of our most familiar birds, seemingly totally dependent on man, living from his husbandry and wasteful activities. Though so widely distributed in Britain and Ireland, it is not in fact our most abundant bird, the total breeding population being around 5 million pairs. The Tree Sparrow (*Passer montanus*) is even less numerous, with a total British and Irish population of about 250,000 pairs. A neater, warmer-brown-coloured bird, its rich chestnut cap and dark ear coverts distinguish it from its common relative without difficulty.

Other European Sparrows include the Spanish Sparrow (*Passer hispaniolensis*), Rock

House Sparrow (male birds)

271

Species

Sparrow (*Petronia petronia*) and Snow Finch (*Montifringilla nivalis*).
See Snow Finch
Read Summers-Smith, J. D., *The House Sparrow*, (New Naturalist series), Collins, 1963

Species

A 'kind' of bird (or other organism), or more precisely, as expressed by Ernst Mayr, 'Species are groups of actually or potentially breeding populations which are reproductively isolated from other such groups, ie a distinct species that does not interbreed with any other distinct species.' A species may be a single population or a virtually homogeneous group of populations, termed monotypic. Or it may be a series of populations showing considerable geographical variation over a wide and perhaps discontinuous range, termed polytypic. In the latter case there may be geographical 'races' sufficiently distinct to be allotted sub-species status, or there may be a more or less geographical gradation of characters termed a cline. There might also be sympatric (having the same area of distribution) and interbreeding 'phases' or 'morphs' showing greater differences than the usual level of individual variation within a population: this is termed polymorphism. *See* Cline; Morph; Phase; Polymorphism; Sub-species

Specific

Referring to a species, eg a specific name.

Spoonbill

Speculum

A patch of distinctive colour on the wings, usually the secondaries, in some plumage patterns, especially the 'metallic' patch seen in dabbling Ducks.

Spoonbill

Substantive name of the species of Plataleinae, a sub-family of the Threskiornithidae (Ciconiiformes, sub-order Ciconae). The most distinctive feature of these birds is the long bill which is flattened and broad at the end, giving it a spoon-like appearance. Six species of Spoonbill occur in tropical and sub-tropical regions of the world. All except one are white, and they are similar in appearance and behaviour, wading on their long legs in shallow water, sieving the ooze for food often with a distinctive 'sweeping' side-to-side motion.

In Europe, the Spoonbill (*Platalea leucorodia*) breeds in Holland, Southern Spain, SE Europe, much of Asia and Northern Africa. It is a regular visitor to Britain, birds no doubt coming from Holland, often during the summer months. Individuals or small groups frequent parts of eastern England. It once nested in the Fenlands and there are high hopes that it will do so again.

Sprosser

A German name for the Thrush-Nightingale (*Luscinia luscinia*) and often used in preference to the latter fabricated one. Very like

Wood Pigeon squabs

the Nightingale (*Luscinia megarhynchos*), it has a darker more olive-brown appearance, and at close quarters its brownish mottled breast is apparent. Its song is equally musical with typical 'chook-chook-chook' commencing notes but distinguished from the Nightingale's by the absence of rising crescendo phrases.

Breeding in eastern Europe into Asia, it is a vagrant to the rest of Europe and Britain, with only one or two recorded in any year.

Spurn

A 3 mile (5.6km) long peninsula, little more than 105ft (35m) wide in places, forming the furthest extremity of the northern shore of the mouth of the Humber, in south east Yorkshire. In 1945 a bird observatory was set up here, the first to be established in mainland Britain. In 1960 the Yorkshire Naturalists' Trust purchased the peninsula, which became a nature reserve with a full time warden, administered by the Trust; hostel accommodation is available providing opportunities to study migration throughout the year. It has an impressive list of rarities to its credit, while every season regularly produces such birds as Great Grey Shrike, Barred Warbler and Yellow-browed Warbler.

Squab

An unfledged nestling Pigeon.

Squacco

Squacco (*Ardeola ralloides*)
Or Squacco Heron. A bird of Southern Europe, breeding southwest into Asia and in Africa. An infrequent visitor to Britain, only recorded about a dozen times in the last 20 years.
See Heron

Squeaking
Making high-pitched squeaking noises by rubbing a cork on a bottle, or by other means: such sounds encourage small birds, whose own notes are in a similar frequency range, to investigate the source of the sound and thus reveal themselves, when in thick vegetation.

Starling
Substantive range of many species of Sturnidae (Passeriformes, sub-order Oscines). Primarily tropical birds, there are 110 different species with many found in Africa, India and the East Indies. Several species also breed in Europe. Medium or rather large, ranging from 7-17in (129-432mm), they are chunky-looking birds with strong legs and bill. Many are more or less black, but often with iridescent plumage. Some of the more beautiful members of the family occur in Africa, notably the Superb Starling (*Spreo superbus*) and the Emerald Starling (*Lamprotornis iris*). There are two other Starlings to be seen in Europe—the Rose-coloured Starling (*Sturnus roseus*) of SE Europe and the Spotless Starling (*Sturnus unicolour*), which breeds in Spain, Portugal, Corsica, Sardinia and Italy—it has not been recorded in Britain.
See Pastor

Sterna
Used in reference to Terns, *Sterna* spp. Birdwatchers' slang for the group of similar 'Sea Terns' that consists of the Common Tern (*Sterna hirundo*), Arctic Tern (*Sterna paradisaea*), Little Tern (*Sterna albifrons*), Sand-

Superb Starling, from Kenya

wich Tern (*Stèrna sandvicensis*) and Roseate Tern (*Sterna dougallii*).
See Commic Tern; Tern

Stifftail

Stifftail Ducks belong to the tribe of the Oxyurini, a group of aquatic and largely nocturnal freshwater Ducks, most of which have stiff retrices (tails) which no doubt facilitate underwater control. Of the 6 species in the genus, the White-headed Duck (*Oxyura leucocephala*) is the only naturally occurring Stifftail in Europe, breeding in Southern Spain, Sardinia, Southern Italy and one or two other isolated spots in SE Europe. It is a vagrant northwards to Holland, France and Germany. The North American Ruddy Duck (*Oxyura jamaicensis*) is an introduced species in Britain; having escaped from captivity it is now breeding freely in the wild.

Stilt (*Himantopus himantopus*)

A member of the Recurvirostridae (Charadriiformes, sub-order Charadrii)— the same family as the Avocet. The Stilt is found throughout most of the world, there being 5 geographical races (which are accorded species rank by some). It occurs in Europe, breeding in Spain and isolated parts of France and Germany and in Greece eastwards. Unmistakable, with its 10in (254mm) long pink legs and black upper parts contrasting with white under parts, a bird of marshes, lagoons and floodwaters, where it wades deeply, probing and picking with its long, needle-like bill. Its occurrence in Britain is not regular but there have been 60 records

Black-winged Stilt

in the last 20 years. There is one isolated incident of the bird nesting in Britain: two pairs bred at a Nottingham sewage farm in 1954. Also breeding widely in Africa; other races occur in N and S America, Australia and New Zealand.

Stint

Name for some of the small Sandpipers, wading birds mainly of the genus *Calidris*. The two species most likely to be seen in Britain are the Little Stint (*Calidris minuta*), a tiny wader only 5¼in (133mm) long, distinguished from the Dunlin (*Calidris alpina*) by a straight short black bill, black legs and smaller, neater appearance. The rarer Temminck's Stint (*Calidris temminckii*) is a much greyer-looking bird, its legs usually greenish, sometimes brownish, but not black. Its behaviour is also different, towering like a Snipe when flushed and calling with a short trill. The Temminck's Stint has bred in Britain on one or two occasions. The Least Stint (*Calidris minutilla*)—which is even smaller than the Little Stint—is a vagrant to Britain from North America. American birdwatchers refer to all small 'shore birds' (waders) such as Stints as 'Peeps'.
See Peep

Temminck's Stint

Stonechat (*Saxicola torquata*)

Similar to the Whinchat (*Saxicola rubetra*), this species is a plumper more upright bird, perching on the tops of bushes, constantly flicking its tail and flicking its wings—frequently calling, the harsh 'wee-tack tack' sounding like two pebbles being struck together—hence the name. In summer the male's head is black with white patches on the sides of the neck, and it has a white wing patch and whitish area on the rump. The

275

Stonechat (male)

Stone Curlew—panting in hot weather

under parts are orange-chestnut and the tail is dark. The female is a drabber version of the male and lacks the white rump and neck patch. As a resident in Britain it has declined markedly in recent years and is now a sparse breeding bird inland, being mainly confined to western coastal regions. Quite widespread in Ireland. Total population around 50,000 pairs.

Stone Curlew (*Burhinus odicnemus*)
A member of the family Burhinidae (Charadriiformes, sub-order Charadrii). In Britain it is a bird of dry, stony, open ground, chalk downland, sandy heaths and shingles, but increasingly found in cultivated fields and woodland fire breaks in the areas where it occurs. A few may winter, but it is mainly a summer visitor, when it is found mostly in the Brecklands of East Anglia and on the downlands of Wiltshire. Probably no more than 500 pairs are present in any one year. Particularly active at dusk, it can be heard calling, with its plaintive wailing note, well into the night during the breeding season. A large Plover-like bird, its streaked sandy-brown plumage makes it difficult to see on the stony sandy soil it favours, but the pale yellow legs and large yellow eyes give it an unmistakable appearance.
See Thick-knee

Stoop
Term used to describe a bird-of-prey's rapid, steep dive on to its flying quarry. Particularly applied to the dive of the Peregrine Falcon (*Falco peregrinus*), the species probably most renowned for this act.

Peregrine stooping at Redshank

277

Stork

Substantive name of most members of the Ciconiidae (Ciconiiformes, sub-order Ciconiae). Large to very large birds, 30-60in (760-1520mm) in length, some with a standing height of 4ft (1.2m) and having very long legs and long bills, some straight, some curved or decurved. They are strong fliers, many performing long migrations. Mostly gregarious, they often occur in large numbers, particularly on migration. The majority nest in trees, but sometimes on cliff ledges and in the case of the White Stork (*Ciconia ciconia*) on buildings or specially-erected platforms. This is the species best-known in Europe, breeding in Holland and eastwards into Germany and Russia and southwards to Asia Minor. It also breeds in the Iberian Peninsula and North Western Africa. In Britain it has never been more than a vagrant and as the continental population decreases its visits to Britain are likely to diminish. About a dozen records occur most years with over 170 sightings in the last 20 years.

The Black Stork (*Ciconia nigra*) is even less frequently noted in Britain with just over a dozen records in the last 20 years. Mainly breeding in the forests of eastern Europe, with some found in SW Spain, it may become more frequently noted in view of its apparent recent extension northwards and westwards of the breeding range in Europe, first breeding in France in 1976.

Storm Petrel

Substantive name of species of the Hydrobatidae (Procellariiformes)—Petrels.
See Mother Cary's Chicken; Petrel

Strutting Ground

A special term in North America for the social display ground of the Sage Grouse (*Centrocercus urophasianus*).

Subsong

Not full song, but sometimes comprising fragments of the full or primary song, often including imitations of other species. Usually uttered from an inconspicuous place, and often the beak may be closed. Normally a quiet extended warbling, the subsong can be heard during the bird's full song period, though usually at other times.

Painted Stork (opposite)

The sub-species of Black-eared Wheatear; white-throated form (left) and black-throated form

Sub-species

A population distinguishable from the members of other populations within the species to which they belong. The term 'race' or 'geographical race' is used synonymously, and is perhaps more indicative of the concept. Ernst Mayer described a sub-species as 'geographically defined aggregates of local populations which differ taxonomically from other subdivisions of a species.' For example, the Pied Wagtail (*Motacilla alba yarrellii*), the bird which occurs in Britain, is a sub-species of the White Wagtail (*Motacilla alba alba*), which is found on the continent of Europe. (In the scientific classification, sub-species are given a third name to identify the race.) In this example, the White Wagtail is the nominate race, ie it was described and given a Latin name before the Pied Wagtail which breeds in Britain and shows slight colour differences. The two races can interbreed and sometimes do when migrating White Wagtails passing through Britain pair with resident Pied Wagtails and stay to nest.
See Cline; Race; Species

Sugarbird

Substantive name of 2 species of *Promerops*, a genus of the Meliphagidae (Passeriformes, sub-order Oscines). Occurring in Africa, the genus is remarkable for its wide geographical separation from this mainly Australian family of Honeyeaters. The male Cape Sugarbird (*Promerops cafer*) has an extremely long, slender tail which can attain a length of 12in (305mm).

Cape Sugarbird

Summer Visitor

A species which visits an area during the summer months for the purposes of breeding (though some individuals may not actually do so), then returning to a different area for the winter, eg Swallow (*Hirundo rustica*), Cuckoo (*Cuculus canorus*).

Sunbird

Substantive name of most species of Nectariniidae (Passeriformes, sub-order Oscines), a family of 116 species of brightly coloured little birds with long, slender, decurved bills with which they feed on nectar, hovering in front of flowers like Hummingbirds. Most species are found in Africa, with others in India, Ceylon, Burma, Malaya, the East Indies and Australia. A sumptuous monograph of the family was produced by Shelley in 1876-80.

Sunbittern (*Eurypyga helias*)

Sole member of the family Eurypygidae (Gruiformes, sub-order Eurupygae). About 18in (457mm) in length, it is a graceful stout-bodied bird, long-necked, long-legged, with most intricately barred, spotted and mottled plumage. As part of its nuptial display it spreads its wings to reveal a large, round shield of deep orange-chestnut colour set in the midst of an area of pale orange-buff in the centre of each wing, likened to a sun darkly glowing in a sunset-tinted sky. A shy, solitary species it forages along watercourses, keeping

to the shady parts of the forests of Central and South America.

Superciliary

A marking above the eye in some species of birds, usually a stripe.

The superciliary—on Radde's Warbler

Swallow

Substantive name of most species of Hirundinidae (Passeriformes, sub-order Oscines). Another substantive name, Martin, is also used within the family, but the distinction has little significance and on different sides of the Atlantic both are used to describe the same species. In Britain, *Riparia riparia* is known as the Sand Martin, in N America as the Bank Swallow.

Throughout the world there are 78 different species, all smallish birds from 3¾in (95mm) to 9in (229mm) in length, with short necks, slender bodies and long pointed wings, often with a forked tail and the tails of some have elongated outer feathers. The legs are short and the feet weak but have strong claws. The bill is short but the gape is made to facilitate the capture of flying insects.

In Britain the Swallow (*Hirundo rustica*) is one of our most familiar birds and its coming is eagerly awaited each spring. Found over almost the whole of Britain and Ireland (but absent from parts of Scotland), the total population is probably half a million pairs. The House Martin (*Delichon urbica*) is the only 'European Swallow' with a white rump and is equally familiar, nesting under bridges and the eaves of houses, constructing its unique inverted beehive nest of mud. Also widely distributed, though more local, and probably as many House Martins as Swallows visit Britain each year.

The Sand Martin excavates a long tunnel in the banks of rivers, in cliffs and in sand and gravel quarries, and is rarely far from water or its nesting areas; consequently it is not quite so well known as the other two. However, it has the distinction of being one of the

Swallow—long wings and forked tail with long streamers

Swallow collecting nest materials

Grasshopper Warbler

earliest of our summer migrants to arrive, often turning up in early March. About 250,000 pairs nest each year. Gregarious birds in the early spring, all 3 species can be seen together hunting for flies over lakes, rivers and reservoirs; in the autumn, Swallows and Sand Martins gather in large numbers, roosting in reedbeds.

A rare visitor to Britain, the Red-rumped Swallow (*Hirundo daurica*) breeds in Spain and Greece, Africa and Eurasia. It has been noted just over 50 times in the last 20 years. The Crag Martin (*Hirundo rupestris*) might be confused with the Sand Martin at a distance, but it does not occur in Britain, inhabiting mountain gorges and rocky inland and coastal areas of Southern Europe.

Swallow Tanager (*Tersina viridis*)
Sole member of the family Tersininae, this small brilliant turquoise-blue Passerine of Central and South America is both a fruit and insect eater. It bears some resemblance to the Tanagers (Thraupinae) but is longer-winged and shorter-legged, amongst other things. Outside the breeding season it forms flocks that, unlike those of most other tropical birds, never associate with other species.

Swamp Warblers
Inhabiting mainly marshy or damp areas, the birds in this grouping also include Warblers which can be further categorised as streaked or unstreaked (with or without markings on the back). Of the unstreaked 'Swamp

Warblers', the Reed Warbler (*Acrocephalus scirpaceus*) is the best known. Brown above and buffish-white below, this reed-haunting species is a summer visitor to Britain, nesting locally where suitable habitat exists. Noted for its neatly constructed nest woven round several reed stems, it is often a host to the Cuckoo (*Cuculus canorus*).

The not-so-well-known Marsh Warbler (*Acrocephalus palustris*) is a similar-looking bird but has a completely different song, remarkable for its diversity and amazing mimicry. It builds in a different setting, constructing a 'basket handle' slung nest. A scarce summer visitor in Britain, it is confined mainly to the Severn and Avon valleys as a breeding bird. Savi's Warbler (*Locustella luscinioides*) and Cetti's Warbler (*Cettia cetti*) are species common on the Continent which in recent years have begun to colonise Britain and in some areas have become quite well established as breeding birds. The Great Reed Warbler (*Acrocephalus arundinaceus*) is a rare visitor to Britain. It looks like a Reed Warbler but is much larger, 7½in (190mm) long and has a much bolder, harsh, chattering song.

Among the streaked Swamp Warblers, the Sedge Warbler (*Acrocephalus schoenobaenus*) is the commonest in Britain, easily distinguished by its prominent creamy stripe over the eye, with a boldly streaked back and

Mute Swan

crown. Though found in reeds and other waterside vegetation it is frequently found in much drier situations and is consequently much more widely distributed than the Reed Warbler. A summer visitor, arriving in April, leaving in August-September.

The Grasshopper Warbler (*Locustella naevia*) is a secretive skulking bird and would often go undetected but for its peculiar mechanical song, a rapid high-pitched trill (or reeling), often lasting for up to 2 minutes. It favours areas of thick low cover which can be either damp and marshy or dry and heathy. Also a summer visitor, it arrives in late April, leaving August-September.

The Moustached Warbler (*Acrocephalus melanopogon*) and Aquatic Warbler (*Acrocephalus paludicola*) are rare passage migrants.

Swan
Substantive name of some of the Anatidae (Anseriformes), notably *Cygnus* spp, of the tribe Anserini. There are 6 species in the world, all very large, long-necked birds; those found in the northern hemisphere are wholly white (except for some colour on the bill in all but the Trumpeter Swan (*Cygnus buccinator*)) and those of the southern hemi-

sphere are wholly black or black and white, with red on the bill.

In Britain the Mute Swan (*Cygnus olor*) must be one of our best-known birds, virtually domesticated. A family of Swans is a feature of practically every river, stream and canal, lake, reservoir or pond of any size. The total population is probably around 15,000 birds. The largest concentration of this species occurs on the Stour Estuary in East Anglia, where as many as 1,000 gather for the summer months. Another flock almost as large is on the Fleet behind Chesil Beach in Dorset, a site which includes the long-established breeding colony at Abbotsbury. The Mute Swan has long been studied, and was the subject of the BTO's earliest census.

The two 'wild' swans which visit Britain in the winter are more wary and less approachable. The Bewick's Swan (*Cygnus bewickii*), from Arctic Russia, arrives around October and stays until mid-March. Of the total winter population of around 2,000, over half are to be found on the Ouse Washes. The Whooper Swan (*Cygnus cygnus*) in Britain comprises two separate populations totalling

around 3,500 birds. Most of these are from Iceland, and winter mainly in Scotland and Ireland. Those from the Scandinavian-Russian breeding stock are to be found in East Anglia and in other scattered localities, usually in small flocks of less than 100 on estuaries, lakes and reservoirs.

The North American species comprise the Trumpeter Swan, once almost extinct (there were only about 60 in 1935), and the Whistling Swan (*Cygnus columbianus*), which is very similar in appearance but a much commoner species. Other species are the Black Swan (*Cygnus atratus*) of Australia and the Black-

Black Swan

necked Swan (*Cygnus melanocoryphus*) of South America. The Coscoroba Swan (*Coscoroba coscoroba*), though similar to the Swans, is not of the same genus.

Read Scott, Peter, *The Swans*, Michael Joseph, 1972; Wilmore, S. B., *Swans of the World*, David & Charles, Newton Abbot, 1974

Swan Goose (*Anser cygnoides*)
Restricted to Asia in its wild state, but it has been domesticated for 2,000 or 3,000 years and in this form is known as the Chinese

Goose or African Goose and found in many parts of the world.

Swan Upping

The Mute Swan (*Cygnus olor*) was highly prized, and considered to be a royal bird and the property of the crown for many centuries. The monarchs had the right to grant to favoured subjects the privilege of keeping them, provided they were pinioned and so could not fly. There was considerable prestige attached to such a dispensation. As the Swans were kept on open waters and not enclosed they could be stolen. Therefore it became customary (from as far back as the eleventh century) to mark birds by a series of nicks or cuts on the webs of the feet or legs, or more frequently to mark the orange-coloured upper mandible where it could more easily be seen. Over the centuries elaborate patterns evolved which determined ownership of the Swans, as cattle brands do in America today. The practice of marking Swans lasted well into the eighteenth century, with the annual practice of rounding-up young birds called 'Swan upping'. Swan keeping has virtually died out but a traditional Swan-upping cermony is still carried out on the Thames each year where birds are marked for the Queen by the Worshipful Companies of Vintners and Dyers.

Swift

Substantive name for species of Apodidae and Hemiprocnidae (Apodiformes, sub-order Apodi). Swifts are the most aerial of all birds, feeding entirely in the air and regularly spending the night on the wing. They also collect windborne materials in flight for their nests and copulate in the air, unique among birds. There are some 71 species of Swift (Apodidae), spread throughout Europe, Africa and America; most are tropical. Some breed in northern parts of Europe, Asia and America all migrating to the tropics for the winter. The sub-family Chaeturinae includes 20 small species of Cave-swifts of SE Asia and the Pacific Islands. They live in caves, finding their way by echo-location.

All Swifts are dull-coloured birds, and typical is the Common Swift (*Apus apus*), which is a summer visitor to Britain. There is some superficial resemblance to the swallow family, but the narrow scythe-like wings and short tail without the long streamers should prevent confusion. In Britain the Swift is one of the latest migrants to arrive and is not

Swift

to be seen much before the end of April. By August most have gone. Generally distributed throughout Britain and Ireland, the total population is around 100,000 pairs.

The Alpine Swift (*Apus melba*), which is much larger and paler, breeds in southern Europe, but about half a dozen are recorded in Britain every year. The smaller Pallid Swift (*Apus pallidus*) also breeds in southern Europe but is not so numerous; it has been seen twice in Britain. The Hemiprocnidae or Crested Swifts (3 species) are confined to SE Asia and the Western Pacific from India to the Solomon Islands.

Read Lack, D., *Swifts in a Tower*, Methuen, 1956

Swiftlet
Sometimes used as the substantive name for species of the Apodidae.

Sylvia Warblers
Typical warblers of the genus *Sylvia*, which includes such species as Blackcap (*Sylvia atricapilla*), Garden Warbler (*Sylvia borin*) and Whitethroat (*Sylvia communis*). These birds and others in this group often occur together on migration in 'movements', 'falls' or 'rushes' at observatories and are referred to by birdwatchers in this way.

Sympatric
Term used for related species found in the same geographical area—contrasted with allopatric.

Syndactyl
Having two toes joined for part of their length, as in the Kingfisher (*Alcedo atthis*).

Syrinx
Vocal organ unique to birds. Situated at the lower end of the trachea, where this divides into the bronchi, it forms part of the bird's respiratory system, and the place where the bird's voice or song is produced. The size and shape of the syrinx varies from species to species.

Tail
The feathers protruding more or less backwards from the rump of a bird. The feathers which comprise the tail are called retrices; the complete tail is the retrix. In some species the tail may be quite a feature of their appearance, in some it may be much reduced or even absent. Most birds have 12 tail feathers, but the number may vary from 6 to 32. The shape of the tail can vary considerably; it may be short and stumpy, of moderate or substantial length or greatly elongated.

The Kiwis (Apterygidae), Cassowaries (Casuariidae), Emu (Dromaiidae) and Rheas (Rheidae) are practically tailless, having no special tail feathers—or no feathers recognisably different from any other plumage of the hinder parts.

The Ostrich (*Struthio camelus*) is an exception among ratite birds in having something of a tail. In Grebes (Podicipitidae) the tail is rudimentary and in many other aquatic birds it is very short.

At the other extreme, very long tails are found in Pheasants (Phasianidae) and in certain Parrots (Psittacidae). Some Passerine families also sport long tails, eg Tyrant Flycatchers (*Muscivora* spp) and the Paradise Flycatcher (*Terpsiphone paradisa*). The end of the tail, depending on the length of the paired retrices, may be square, rounded, forked or wedge-shaped, and in the identification of certain species of birds this shape can be important. The movement of the tail can also be a characteristic feature of a species or family, as in the case of the Common Sandpiper (*Tringa hypoleucos*) or the Wagtails (*Motacilla* spp). The tail may often be cocked and lowered, as by the Stifftailed Ducks (Oxyurini), eg the North American Ruddy Duck (*Oxyura jamaicensis*); or as in the Blackbird (*Tardus merula*) cocked momentarily when alighting. Shrikes (*Lanius* spp) wag their tails from side to side and frequently fan and close them.

Usually, if the tail is of any considerable proportion, whether it is particularly ornamental or not, it features in courtship or any display postures carried out by the species.

Talon
A claw (toe) especially of a bird of prey; mainly used in the plural.

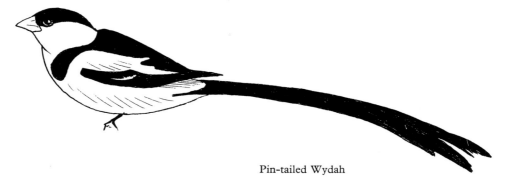

Pin-tailed Wydah

Summer Tanager

Tanager

Substantive name of species of Thraupinae (Passeriformes, sub-order Oscines). A family of 233 recorded species, some of which have the substantive names *Euphonia* Chlorophonia, Dacnis, Honeycreeper, or Flowerpiercer; one is called Conebill and one Orangequit. Small to medium-sized, brightly coloured birds, found mainly in the tropics of the western hemisphere. The name Tanager comes from 'Tangara', a South American Indian name. Tanagers have a highly modified bill and tongue for drawing nectar from flowers.

In North America the Western Tanager (*Piranga Ludoviciana*), Summer Tanager (*Piranga rubra*) and Scarlet Tanager (*Piranga olivacea*) are well known songbirds of the south-western States. The Summer Tanager winters in Central and South America, and is a visitor to the eastern States. A single bird of this species was trapped on Bardsey in September 1957.

Tapaculo

Substantive name of some species of Rhinocryptidae (Passeriformes, sub-order Tyranni). Ground-dwelling birds of Central and South America. There are 30 species ranging from the size of a Wren to that of a Thrush.

Tarsus

Or, fully, tarso-metatarsus. The bone of that part of a bird's leg formed by the fusion of tarsal and metatarsal elements.

Taste

The taste buds (or sensory receptors) which determine the degree of this sense in birds are small in number compared to mammals. Whereas a rabbit has 17,000 taste buds, a domestic Pigeon on average has only 37. This suggests that a bird's sense of taste is rudi-mentary, and it seems to play little part in a bird's selection of its food.

Tattler

Or, fully, Wandering Tattler (*Heteroscelus incanus*). A medium-sized North American wading bird favouring rocky shores. The Grey-tailed Tattler or Grey-rumped Sandpiper (*Heteroscelus brevipes*) breeds in Eastern Siberia through eastern Asia to Australia.

Grey-tailed Tattler

Taxidermy

The art of stuffing and mounting dead animals and birds, once widely practised; in the late nineteenth century many homes possessed a glass case of specimens, purely as ornamentation. Bird Protection Acts and a greater appreciation of the living bird has led to its decline and outside museums little taxidermy is now carried on. In any case it is now illegal to obtain specimens of many species for mounting.

Taxon

The general term (plural taxa) for any category used in classification, or any particular example of such category. The fundamental taxon is the species, which represents a real biological entity and can be defined generally in objective terms. All other taxa are either sub-divisions of a species or groupings of a species.

The primary groupings and sub-divisions (taxa) are now

Class
Phyllum
Order
Family
Genus
Species
Sub-species

See separate entries for these

Teal—when disturbed it will take off almost vertically from the water, hence the wildfowlers' term 'a spring of teal'

Taxonomy

The science of classification—orderly arrangement of life forms, also referred to as 'systematics'.

The taxonomist is a scientist who studies taxonomy and who works within several disciplines, notably anatomy, but also considers biochemical, physiological and behavioural aspects of the life-form being studied.

Teal

Europe's smallest Duck, the Teal (*Anas crecca*) is present in Britain throughout the year, breeding in Scotland, northern England, East Anglia, SE England and occasionally elsewhere. It is widely but thinly distributed as a nesting species in Ireland. The total breeding population is around 5,000 pairs. Many more however visit Britain in winter, with probably as many as 75,000 birds present. The similar Green-winged Teal (*Anas crecca carolinensis*), which breeds in north America, is occasionally recorded in Britain. Its main distinguishing feature is a vertical white band down the sides of the breast instead of the white horizontal band along the scapulars of the commoner species.

The Blue-winged Teal (*Anas discors*) is another rare visitor from N America, which as well has having a blue forewing can be easily identified (the drake, that is) by a white crescentic patch between the bill and the eye on the dark head.

Telescope

The invention of the telescope in the early seventeenth century is credited to a Dutch spectacle-maker, Hans Lippershey. In 1608 he was selling a small telescope in the Netherlands. Very soon other spectacle-makers throughout Europe were producing them. Over the years developments and improvements were made by Galileo, Johannes Kepler and others, but the performance of early telescopes was restricted by the poor-quality lenses, which gave blurred images and produced chromatic aberrations. Not until the nineteenth century were lenses able to provide really good results. No doubt ornithologists in the seventeenth and eighteenth centuries used telescopes on occasions, though at that time most study was made on specimens rather than on the living bird.

The widespread use of telescopes by bird watchers is a fairly recent practice and was probably not widespread until after World War II, when the well-equipped birdwatcher sported not only a pair of ex-WD fieldglasses but also a leather-bound, brass, multi-draw-tube telescope. Some skill was needed to gain the best results, for when fully extended it could be a yard long (an advantage in some ways, as from a reclining position it could be rested on the knees). Even though some models had a $2\frac{1}{2}$in (63mm) or 3in (76mm) diameter object lens, performance at high

The author using telescope and stand

magnification was poor, except in the brightest of conditions. Very few of this type of telescope are now in use and most birdwatchers choose the shorter, lighter, prismatic type which usually has only one draw tube and is focussed by turning a small knob or the eye piece, rather than pushing a tube in and out. Most of the modern telescopes have a 60mm object lens and usually provide a magnification range of 20 x to 60 x. As with binoculars, the market is dominated by the Germans and Japanese. Though the modern telescope with its optics is vastly superior to the old drawtube types, for the best performance it is still essential it is held steady, and a tripod is therefore needed. There are good lightweight tripods available and telescopes are usually fitted with the standard photographic mount for this purpose. A telescope is essential for sea watching, or estuary work. The proper and sensible use of a telescope can provide even greater pleasure from birdwatching—don't let it be something slung round the shoulders and just so much more weight to carry.

See Binoculars; Chromatic Aberration

Tern

Substantive name of most species of the subfamily Sterninae of the Laridae (Charadriiformes, sub-order Lari). In the plural, general term for the family. In some respects Terns are like Gulls, but they are generally smaller, with long wings and forked tails, giving rise to the popular name 'Sea Swallow'. Plumage is mainly white with grey backs and wings and dark crowns (in the breeding season). The feet are webbed and in some species feet and legs are bright red, in others yellow or dark. The bill is tapered and pointed, except in the Gull-billed Tern (*Gelochelidon nilotica*), and can be red, red-and-black, black-and-yellow or black, according to the species and the season. Markedly gregarious, they often breed together in large colonies, called terneries. Most nest on the ground, often on sand or shingle. Food is mainly fish and other marine animals, characteristically taken by plunging into the water though not usually completely sub-

Sandwich Tern, the largest Tern breeding in Britain; and (below) the Common Tern, closely resembling the Arctic Tern (top, opposite)

merging. However some species, which are referred to as 'Marsh Terns', pick food from the surface of the water or catch insects in flight, and build floating nests in marshy situations; these are mainly birds of inland rather than coastal settings. There are 5 species of 'Sea Tern' or 'Sea Swallow', also sometimes referred to by the generic name 'Sterna' Terns, which breed in Britain: the Sandwich Tern (*Sterna sandvicensis*) is the largest; it has dark legs and a black bill with yellow tip. The Common Tern (*Sterna hirundo*) and Arctic Tern (*Sterna paradisaea*) are very similar and at times difficult to distinguish from each other. The Little Tern (*Sterna albifrons*), the smallest of our Terns, has a characteristic hovering flight before it plunges into the water for food. The Roseate Tern (*Sterna dougallii*), with its long tail streamers, is the most graceful of this group and the rarest breeding Sterna Tern, with less than 1,000 pairs nesting at a few colonies round Britain.

The most frequently noted 'Marsh Tern' in Britain is the Black Tern (*Chlidonias nigra*) which in summer has dark plumage except for white under-tail coverts. It is mainly a bird of passage, noted in both spring and autumn, though it has nested on occasions. Other Marsh Terns are the White-winged

Black Tern (*Chlidonias leucopterus*) and Whiskered Tern (*Chlidonias hybrida*), and every year a number of these birds which breed in SE Europe and eastwards are noted in Britain.

The Gull-billed Tern and Caspian Tern (*Sterna caspia*) are also recorded from time to time.

Terns have a worldwide distribution but the largest numbers are to be found in the Pacific Ocean, where for example one colony of Sooty Terns (*Sterna fuscata*)—also known as the Wideawake Tern because of its perpetual

(top) Arctic Tern, our most numerous nesting Tern; and (below) Little Tern, rarely seen in large numbers

screaming 'ker-wacky-wack'—in the Seychelles was reckoned to have over one million pairs. The Noddies are also Terns of tropical waters and perhaps the most delightful of the 5 species of Noddy Terns is the Small White Noddy or Fairy Tern, which has totally white plumage and large dark eyes. This bird lays its single egg on the branch of a tree; the chick when it hatches is able to hang on, even head-downwards, by its claws.

The Inca Tern (*Larosterna inca*) is the only species of the genus, a beautiful, slate-coloured bird with crimson bill and legs, yellow gape-wattles and a whisker-like ornamental plume near each eye. A bird of the west coast of South America, it nests in burrows, an unusual habit among Terns.

Territory

In the simplest terms, a 'defended area'. Many animals, both vertebrate and invertebrate, not only birds, defend a territory for themselves. It was Elliot Howard who first really studied this aspect in the behaviour of birds and drew attention to its widespread occurrence and importance, back in 1920. The variety of territories held or defended is enormous, and the areas may be large or small. The owners may be individual males or females, pairs, families or large groups. Territories might only be defended in the breeding season, or during part of it, or even the whole year round. In the case of most small perching birds, the breeding territory may be about an acre or just over, whereas a Golden Eagle (*Aquila chrysaetos*) may patrol an area of 30 square miles. In this way the population of a species becomes dispersed throughout the suitable habitat during the breeding season, which has the effect of spacing out nesting pairs, giving them a greater chance of breeding success. The defence of a bird's territory is equally important in colonial-nesting species and the spacing out of individuals also takes place, for example, even within the crowded confines of a Gannet (*Sula bassana*) colony, each nest being constructed just outside the pecking distance of the next bird as it sits on its nest.

Some species maintain feeding territories as well as nesting territories. The Oystercatcher (*Haematopus ostralegus*) shows an example of this dual territorial behaviour. Some birds whose food is not confined to a particular area, eg aerial species such as Swifts and Swallows, which feed on flying insects, do not demonstrate any territorial rights whilst feeding and even in the breeding season feed socially, away from their nest sites.
Read Howard, E., *Territory in Bird Life*, Murray, 1920.

Tetrad

A 2 x 2 kilometre square (a set of 4 square kilometres) used to plot bird distribution in a more detailed way than the 10 kilometre square grid of the breeding-bird survey used in the *Atlas of Breeding Birds in Britain and Ireland*.
See Atlas

Texel

Largest of the Frisian Islands which extend northwards from the line of the Dutch coast, Texel has long been regarded as one of Europe's major bird centres. Large areas of the dunes and polders which form virtually all the western coast of the island are protected as a bird reserve by the State Forestry Departments and the Netherlands Society for the Promotion of Nature Reserves. Many species breed, including Avocet, Common Tern, Shelduck, Redshank and Ruff, while many more occur on passage—over 300 species have been recorded on the island. Fast becoming a British birders' 'weekend' place.

Thick-knee

Substantive name commonly used for some species of Burhinidae (Charadriiformes, sub-order Charadrii). Other names used are Stone Curlew, Stone Plover, Dikkop (Afrikaans), Wilaroo (Australian) and Goggle-eye. A widely distributed family within the Old World, and 2 species occur in the neotropical region.

Plover-like birds, they also bear a superficial resemblance to Bustards (Otididae), though of course are much smaller. The large, proud head and the large eyes are characteristic of the family, which is generally found in dry, stony habitats, the sandy, dark-streaked plumage blending with the surroundings. Shy birds, they tend to rest a great deal in the day, becoming active at dusk and noisy at night, particularly during the breeding season.
See Stone Curlew

Thrasher

A substantive name of some species of Mimidae (Passeriformes, sub-order Oscines). They are mainly ground-feeding desert birds.

Throstle

A common name for the Thrush, cf German Drossel.

Robin in territorial display, presenting his red breast to a rival robin (opposite)

Thrush

Substantive name of some species of the sub-family Turdinae of the Muscicapidae (Passeriformes, sub-order Oscines). In general Thrushes are medium-sized, slender-billed birds, most of which are good songsters. There are approximately 300 species found throughout the world, inhabiting various types of terrain, from arid deserts to dense equatorial forests; many species occur in farmland and gardens, in close association with man. Amongst the latter are birds which are referred to as the 'true' Thrushes, those centred round the genus *Turdus*, which includes the familiar Blackbird (*Turdus merula*) and Song Thrush (*Turdus philomelos*). This genus is more widely distributed than any other of the sub-family and has about 63 species, many of them migratory, eg the the American Robin (*Turdus migratorius*). Some of them breed up to the tree line in Canada and winter in the southern States of the USA. This species has been recorded in Britain about a dozen times over the last 20 years. Other vagrant thrushes from N America which have been noted in Britain include the Olive-backed Thrush or Swainson's Thrush (*Catharus ustulatus*) and Hermit Thrush (*Catharus guttatus*).

Of course there are also our own 'Winter Thrushes', the Fieldfare (*Turdus pilaris*) and Redwing (*Turdus iliacus*), most of which come from Scandinavia, while the Ring Ousel (*Turdus torquatus*) is a summer visitor from Africa. Rare Thrushes from Eastern Europe and Siberia occasionally reach these shores and in recent years the Eye-browed Thrush (*Turdus obscurus*) and Black-throated Thrush (*Turdus ruficollis*) have both been observed. Within this sub-family Turdinae are also species that are generally smaller and have weaker songs than the 'true' Thrushes; these are generally referred to as 'Chat-like Thrushes' or just 'Chats', and include the Redstarts (*Phoenicurus* spp) and Stonechats (*Saxicola* spp), also Robins and Nightingales.

Read Simms, E., *British Thrushes* (New Naturalist series), Collins, 1978

Tibiotarsus

A bone of the leg, in birds formed by the fusion of the tibia and the proximal tarsals; often just called 'tibia'.

Tick-bird

This name is often applied to 2 species of African birds which feed on ticks taken from the backs of animals.

See Oxpecker

Tick-hunter

A generally derisive term for a 'birdwatcher' (or birder) whose main preoccupation is to see as many new birds as he can as often as he can, or to see as many species as he can in a given time, usually over a 12 month period, January to December, ticking them off on his list as they are seen. Also called tallyhunter, pot hunter, ticker and more usually 'twitcher'.

See Lifer; Life List; Twitcher

Tiercel

A special term for a male Falcon, from the French 'tierce' (to divide into three) referring to the size of the bird; it is about one-third smaller than the female, which is generally called the Falcon.

Tippet

The elongated facial feathers of typical Grebes (*Podiceps* spp), as distinct from other types of head-ornamentation in this group, eg the facial disc (the well-defined area of short feathers on the face), and auricular fan (the elongated feathers on the side of the head behind the eye). The Great Crested Grebe (*Podiceps cristatus*) has both tippets and facial discs. The Black-necked Grebe (*Podiceps nigricollis*) has an auricular fan of golden plumes in its summer plumage.

The term tippet was earlier applied to a woman's cape made of Grebe feathers ('Grebe fur').

Tit

Substantive name, abbreviated from Tit-mouse, of most species of Paridae (Passeriformes, sub-order Oscines). In the plural, general term for the family. Small active woodland birds, feeding mainly on insects and other invertebrates, the family is widely distributed throughout the world but excluding South America, Madagascar and Australia. There are three distinct sub-families: the typical Tits (Parinae), the Long-tailed Tits (Aegithalinae) and the Penduline Tits (Remizinae).

The Parinae comprises 43 species and in Britain includes such well-known garden visitors as Great Tit (*Parus major*) and Blue Tit (*Parus caeruleus*). Not quite so widely known, though commonly found in woodland and agricultural country, are the Coal Tit (*Parus ater*), which shows a preference for coniferous woodland, the Marsh Tit (*Parus palustris*) and Willow Tit (*Parus montanus*). Marsh and Willow Tits are similar-looking birds, to distinguish between them being a test of skill even for experienced birdwatchers. In North America the Black-capped Chickadee (*Parus atricapillus*) is one of the commonest representatives of the sub-family, and was at one time considered to be conspecific with the Willow Tit. All are hole-nesting birds, the Great and Blue Tits readily accepting nestboxes. The Coal Tit will sometimes nest in a hole in the ground, while the Willow Tit excavates its nesting hole in rotting treestumps.

The Aegithalinae comprises 6 species, 4 of which are found in the Himalayas and China, 1 in Java and the best-known, the Long-tailed Tit (*Aegithalos caudatus*), having a wide distribution in Europe and Asia. Not such a frequent garden visitor in Britain, this delightful pink, white and black bird is mostly tail, which gives it a top-heavy appearance when in flight. Most frequently met in the winter months, when roving bands of these birds draw attention to their presence with their constant contact calls: a low, abrupt 'tupp', a trilling 'tsirrup' and a penetrating 'zee-zee-zee'. The Long-tailed Tit is of course

Blue Tit (or Tom Tit) at nestbox; (below) Coal Tit, smallest of the Tit family and even more restless and active than the others

Great Tit

noted for its remarkable domed nest of moss, cobwebs and hair, beautifully decorated with grey lichens and lined with many feathers. It is susceptible to long periods of severe weather. The present population of Britain and Ireland is probably around 150,000 pairs.

The sub-family Remizinae comprises 6 African species, 1 North American species and 1 found in the Palearctic from Europe to China. This species, the Penduline Tit (*Remiz pendulinus*), breeds in SW Spain, Southern France, Italy, and other parts of Eastern Europe. It builds an ovoid nest with a funnel-shaped entrance, which is suspended from the outer twigs of bushes or trees or in reeds. It mainly prefers marshy areas, but is also to be found in drier conditions. There is one recent record of this species observed in Britain.

The Bearded Tit (*Panurus biarmicus*) is a member of the Paradoxornithinae.
See Bearded Reedling
Read Barnes, J. A. C., *Titmice of the British Isles*, David & Charles, 1975; Perrins, C., *British Tits*, Collins, 1979

Titlark
A common name for Meadow Pipit (*Anthus pratensis*) and some other similar small birds.

Titmouse
Name for a member of the Paridae, but usually abbreviated to Tit. Now more often used as a group term (Titmice).

Tody
Substantive name of the 5 species of Todidae (Coraciiformes, sub-order Alcedines). In the plural, Todies. Small forest bird, found only in the West Indies.

Broad-billed Tody

(opposite) Great Tit again—its 'teacher-teacher-teacher' song is familiar in the garden from January to mid-June

Tongue

Tongue

In birds the tongue is highly variable in size, form and function and is particularly adapted, depending on the bird's food. In a few species the tongue is used instead of the bill to collect food, notably the Green Woodpecker (*Picus viridis*), which possesses an exceptionally long tongue covered with a sticky secretion to help in catching ants and other insects. The Wryneck (*Jynx torquilla*), another ant-eater, also has a long tongue—which is nearly two-thirds the length of its body. Sunbirds (Nectariniidae) and Humming Birds (Trochilidae) have long, tube-like tongues, used for forcing out nectar and insects. Mainly, the tongue is used as an eating organ, and is not protruded. Flamingos (Phoenicopteridae) have tongues which fill the whole cavity of the lower mandible and are moved rapidly backwards and forwards to sift food from soft mud. Seed-eating birds tend to have thick, fleshy tongues which help to discard unwanted husks. In those species which swallow their food whole, the tongue is unnecessary and is therefore rudimentary.

In singing birds, the tongue can be seen to move when the bird is singing, though it plays no actual part in song production.

Topography

The detailed description of a bird's superficial features by the use of the appropriate terms for the different parts or areas of the body as a whole. Most are self-explanatory, the few needing clarification being dealt with in this book under their separate headings. The boundaries of the various areas of a bird cannot be precisely defined (except in the case of particular groups of feathers, eg secondary feathers), and these are indicated on the diagram shown here. Many beginners find such diagrams complicated and off-putting, but in fact only a handful of new terms need be learned and the benefits of understanding the basic anatomy and parts of a bird can be great. In describing a bird for one's own use or in order to inform someone else of its appearance, it is vastly better to use proper descriptive terms (eg greater coverts, rump) than to give ambiguous information.
See Field Notes

Torpidity

A state of inactivity and lowered body temperature enabling a bird to conserve energy during a perod when food might be short. This is particularly known in Swifts (Apodidae), which become torpid when cold, wet weather reduces their food supply. It has also been observed in Humming Birds (Trochilidae) and some Nightjars (Caprimulgidae). There is at least one known case of a bird, Nuttall's Poor Will (*Phalaenoptilus nuttallii*), being found hibernating in a rock crevice (in California, USA).

Toucan

Substantive name of species of Ramphastidae (Piciformes, sub-order Galbulae). The name comes from 'tucano' in the language of the Tupi Indians of Brazil, where many Toucans are found. Confined to the tropical parts of the American continents, they are noted for their enormous bills, which in some species exceed the body length of the bird and almost equal it in bulk. It is, however, quite light, consisting of a network of bony fibres ramifying through the space within the horny shell, which is invariably highly coloured.

There are about 38 species, which range in size from about 12in (305mm), such as the Emerald Toucanet (*Aulacorhynchus praisinus*), to about 24in (610mm) in length—the Toco Toucan (*Ramphastos toco*). Toucans are frequently kept in zoos.

Towhee

The substantive name of a number of large American Sparrows of the genus *Pipilo*. One of the most widely distributed and well known is the Rufous-sided Towhee (*Pipilo erythrophthalmus*, which has wandered to Britain on a couple of occasions.

Tragopan

Substantive name of some large colourful Pheasants which inhabit the wet forests of Assam, Burma, Tonkin and China. They are exceptional in this family in building large bulky nests in trees.

Transient

See Passage Migrant

Trapping

The legal trapping of birds is carried out for the purpose of scientific study. The captured bird is weighed, measured, examined for its state of moult and breeding condition, and for parasites, and finally ringed; or if the bird has been previously ringed, the ring number and its origin are recorded. Trapping today is usually done by mist net or Heligoland trap, occasionally by rocket netting or cannon netting.

See British Trust for Ornithology; Cannon Netting; Heligoland Trap; Mist Net; Rocket Netting.

Treecreeper
Substantive name of the species of Certhiidae (Passeriformes, sub-order Oscines). Treecreepers are small brownish birds, streaked above and white below. They have slender decurved bills, strong claws and stiff tails. As the name implies they have the habit of climbing trees, creeping up the vertical surface or along the undersides of branches, using their stiff tails for support in the manner of the Woodpeckers (Picidae). Found in both deciduous and coniferous woodland they also favour well-timbered parkland. The family, comprising 5 species, is confined to the northern hemisphere in both Old and New Worlds. In Britain the Treecreeper (*Certhia familiaris*) is generally distributed where suitable habitat occurs, with an estimated population of between 180,000 and 300,000 pairs. There is considerable geographical variation within this species and a dozen or more races are recognised in a series of clines, but over much of continental Europe to the south of Britain and Scandinavia it overlaps with the very similar Short-toed Treecreeper (*Certhia brachydactyla*), which has brownish flanks (not white) and a different call. In North America *Certhia familiaris* is called the Brown Creeper.

Tree Warblers
Among the Tree Warblers only the Garden Warbler (*Sylvia borin*) breeds in Britain, arriving in early April and leaving in September. A brownish bird with pale under parts, it has no real distinguishing features, the continuous, rapidly-uttered warbling song providing the best means of putting a name to it. The song of a Blackcap (*Sylvia atricapilla*) is similar but usually of much shorter duration and of richer quality.

The Icterine Warbler (*Hippolais icterina*) and Melodious Warbler (*Hippolais polyglotta*) are difficult to distinguish in the field and can often only be identified as 'Hippolais' Warblers when they occur as passage migrants, mainly in the autumn. The Olivaceous Warbler (*Hippolais pallida*) is one of the rarer Hippolais Warblers to visit Britain and has been noted on less than ten occasions in the last 20 years.

Treecreeper—in winter sometimes seen with roaming flocks of Titmice and Goldcrests

Tribe
Along with the classification of sub-family and super-family, 'tribe' is a secondary category of nomenclature, which is sometimes used within a family, where the genera are sufficiently diverse and can be further grouped. The assessment of degrees of difference is subjective, and what one author may regard as a number of separate families, another may treat as sub-families or even as tribes of a single family. Some authorities regard the tribal category as being superfluous. But in the case of a large family of birds, it may help

299

where there is relatively little diversity. Thus the Anatidae may be considered divisible into no more than three sub-families but can be further divided into ten tribes. In the case of a tribe the Latin name ends in 'ini'.

Trinominal System
See Binominal System; Nomenclature

Trochilidae
Family of Apodiformes, sub-order Trochili—the Humming Birds.

Trogon
Substantive name of most species of Trogonidae (sole family of the Trogoniformes). They are tree-haunting species of the Neotropical, Ethiopian and Oriental regions, and rank among some of the world's most beautiful birds.

Tropicbird
Substantive name of the species Phaethontidae (Pelecaniformes, sub-order Phaethontes), birds of tropical and sub-tropical water. There are only 3 species of the sole genus, *Phaethon*. The long central tail feathers, which can exceed the body length, give them an unmistakable appearance in flight, and the white plumage with a black bar across the eye, some black in the flight feathers, and a stout, slightly curved vivid red or yellow bill, are

Red-billed Tropicbird

distinctive. Tropicbirds feed by plunging into the water for fish or squid. They are sometimes called the 'Bosunbirds', possibly because of their shrill, trilling call resembling the call of a boatswain's pipe.

Troupial (*Icterus icterus*)
A species of the Icteridae (Passeriformes, sub-order Oscines)—the American Orioles. Sometimes used in the plural, in place of Oriole, as a group name for the family.

Trumpeter
Substantive name of 3 species of Psophiidae (Gruiformes, sub-order Grues). They are birds of the South American rain forests, with loud trumpeting calls. About the size of a domestic fowl, they have a somewhat hump-backed appearance.

Tubenose
A general term for birds with tube-like nostrils—members of the order Procellariiformes, the Albatrosses and Petrels.
See Fulmar

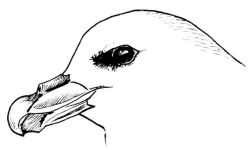

A tubenose—a Fulmar

Turaco
Substantive name (sometimes spelt Touraco) of most species of Musophagidae (Cuculiformes, sub-order Musophagi). A purely African group, there are 22 recorded species, tree-haunting, fruit-eating birds. Also included in the family are the Go-away Birds and Plantain-eaters.

Turkey
Substantive name of two species of Meleagrididae (Galliformes, sub-order Galli), large, gallinaceous, terrestrial birds, which in the wild state are confined to North America. The Common Turkey (*Meleagris gallopavo*) is undoubtedly the most important domesticated creature to have come from the New World. The first Europeans to reach Mexico found the Aztecs were raising Turkeys for consumption and it was not long before birds were imported to Europe, where they were quickly distributed throughout several countries. The name Turkey derives from

'Turkie Fowl', for in the sixteenth and seventeenth centuries anything brought in from the area known as the 'Near East' was called 'Turkish'.

The association of the Turkey and American Thanksgiving Day is as well known as its connection with Christmas festivities! Domesticated Turkeys resemble their wild ancestors but selective breeding has increased their weight and rendered them flightless. The wild Turkey can still fly, and apart from two species of Bustard is the largest of all game birds.

Turnstone (*Arenaria interpres*)
A distinctive shorebird with characteristic feeding behaviour of turning over small stones, seaweed and other tideline debris in search of sandhoppers and other creatures. The Turnstone (or Ruddy Turnstone) is present throughout most of the year in Britain, distributed on suitable coasts, particularly in autumn. Many winter and non-breeding birds are frequently observed in the summer. Breeding on the northern Tundra of the holarctic, it has been suspected of nesting in Britain on more than one occasion.

The Black Turnstone (*Arenaria melanocephala*), which is found in North and Central America, resembles the Turnstone in size, shape and behaviour, but lacks the former bird's rich, bold summer plumage of chestnut-brown and black.

Twitcher
A general slang term for a birdwatcher whose sole object is to see rare birds and who travels extensively to achieve this aim—literally twitching from one place to the next. (Twitching to the European continent from Britain is becoming quite a usual expedition.) An extensive grapevine exists with a number of key-links (by telephone) which can advise of the appearance of a rarity almost as soon as it is seen. When a rare bird appears somewhere, though normally one or two birdwatchers would occasion no problem, the sudden influx of 'twitchers' (a hundred or more in a day is not unknown) can and does create strained relations between landowners and 'twitchers', for sometimes damage is done and the bird is disturbed. The presence of a rare bird seems to do something to some usually rational individuals, who can be a nuisance in their desire to get a better view, to see it fly, etc.
See Tick Hunter

Twite (*Acanthis flavirostris*)
A small Linnet-type bird, but lacking the commoner bird's summer crimson forehead and breast. The male has a pink rump and yellow bill, the female a yellow bill but no pink on the rump. The call, a nasal 'chweer', is also quite different from that of *Acanthis cannabina*, the Linnet. Sometimes called the Mountain Linnet, in Britain the Twite nests locally in the Pennines and NW Scotland, the Hebrides, Orkneys and Shetlands. In winter it occurs on salt marshes, stubble fields and waste ground, usually near the coast when it is often seen in association with Linnets.

Tyrant Flycatcher
Substantive name for many of the Tyrannidae family. There are over 360 species of Tyrant

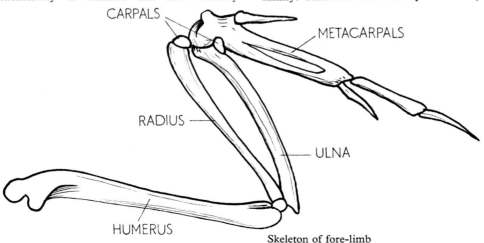

Skeleton of fore-limb

Tystie

Flycatchers, all confined to the Americas, inhabiting forests and semi-open country. Small to medium-sized Passerines, they live on insects caught in the air.

Some of the commoner and more widespread representatives of this large family are the Eastern Kingbird (*Tyrannus tyrannus*) and Western Kingbird (*Tyrannus verticalis*) Great Crested Flycatcher (*Myiarchus crinitus*), Traill's Flycatcher (*Empidonax traillii*), Hammond's Flycatcher (*Empidonax hammondii*) and Eastern Phoebe (*Sayornis phoebe*).

Tystie
A name sometimes used for the Black Guillemot (*Cepphus grylle*).

Ulna
A bone of the forelimb.
See Topography; Wing

Umbrella-bird (*Cephalopterus ornatus*)
A member of the Cotingidae (Passeriformes, sub-order Tyranni). A bird with a black, umbrella-like crest and a feather wattle as long as the bird itself hanging from its throat.
See Cotinga

Under Parts
The lower surfaces of a bird, from the chin to the top of the tail.
See Topography

Undulating Flight
A mode of flight characteristic of some species, notably the Woodpeckers (Picidae).
See Woodpeckers

Upper Parts
The upper surfaces of a bird from the forehead to the top of the tail.
See Topography

Uropygial Gland
See Oil Gland

Uropygium
The rump.

Vagrant
A term used for a bird which has wandered outside its normal migration range.
See Accidental

Vane
The part of a feather consisting of the barbs extending from each side of the rachis. Alternatively vexillum.
See Feather

Vanga
Substantive name of most species of Vangidae (Passeriformes, sub-order Oscines). In the plural, alternatively 'Vanga Shrikes', the general term for the family. Vanga was the original native name for the Hook-billed Vanga (*Vanga curvirostris*) but the name is now applied to all 12 species in the group. Vangas vary from 5in (127mm) to 12in (305mm), being mostly boldly patterned in black and white or blue with black, browns and greys. The bill is variable but usually heavy, often with a pronounced hook at the tip. Some bear a superficial resemblance to the true Shrikes (Laniidae). All Vangas are restricted to Madagascar.

Vascular System
Consisting essentially of three components: the arterial system, conveying the blood at high pressure from the heart to all parts of the body; the venous system, in continuity with the arterial system through a capillary network within the organs and tissues of the body, returning the blood to the heart; and the lymphatic system. Lymph glands are developed in only a few families of birds.

Vector
An animal that is a carrier of parasites or infections to another species, sometimes only as an intermediate host accomplishing only part of the life cycle; ie a biological vector as contrasted with a mechanical one.

Veery (*Catharus fuscescens*)
One of a group of North American Thrushes, it is a small secretive woodland species, not unlike the Hermit Thrush (*Catharus guttatus*) but having a distinctive song, a series of notes on a descending scale, 'vee-ur, vee-ur, veer veer', from which it gets its name.

Solitary Vireo

Griffon Vulture

Vireo

Substantive name of most species of the sub-family Vireoninae of the Vireonidae (Passeriformes, sub-order Oscines). Small plain-looking birds, between 4in (102mm) and 7in (178mm), thought by some to be related to the American Wood Warblers (Parulidae) and by others to the Shrikes (Laniidae). There are 39 species in the family, which includes some known as Pepper Shrikes and some as Greenlets. Woodland birds, haunting thickets and secondary growth, of North, Central and South America. They are mainly insect feeders but some fruit is taken. They are not generally considered to be accomplished singers. Among the more widespread representatives of this family in North America is the Solitary Vireo or Blue Head Vireo (*Vireo solitarius*), Red-eyed Vireo (*Vireo olivaceus*) and Warbling Vireo (*Vireo gilvus*). The Red-eyed Vireo has been recorded in Britain.

Visitor

A bird present in an area only at certain times of the year: summer visitors and winter visitors.

See Accidental; Passage Migrant; Vagrant

Volant

Means in the act of flying or capable of flight, also a heraldic term for a bird flying or with wings outstretched.

Vulture

Substantive name for most of 14 species of birds of prey which belong to the family Accipitridae (Falconiformes, sub-order Falcones). In the plural, generally referred to as 'Old World Vultures'. They are large birds some having up to a 9ft (3m) wing span. Unlike most other birds of prey there is little size variation between the sexes, and in some the male may even be larger than the female. The plumage in most species is brown or black, except on the Egyptian Vulture (*Neophron percnopterus*) which is dingy white, Palm-nut Vulture (*Gypohierax angolensis*) which is white with a black back and the Lammergeier or Bearded Vulture (*Gypaetus barbatus*), which is greyish-black on the upper parts and yellowish-orange underneath with an orange breast. Apart from the Lammergeier and Palm-nut Vulture they are all characterised by having part of the neck and head bare, most having a distinct ruff of

feathers at the base of the neck. The bill is hooked and powerful but the feet are weak and not adapted for clutching. The long broad wings enable them to soar for lengthy periods as they hunt for prey, which is any form of carrion (except for the Palm-nut Vulture, which feeds principally on the fruit pericarp of the oil palm). Old World Vultures inhabit the warmer parts of Europe, the whole of Africa and parts of Southern Asia. The Egyptian Vulture, Black Vulture (*Aegypius monachus*) and Griffon Vulture (*Gyps fulvus*) can be found in mountainous regions of Spain, Southern France, Sardinia, Italy and Greece, while the Lammergeier is becoming scarcer in its Spanish and Grecian haunts. *See* Lammergeier

Wader

A general term commonly used for species belonging to the sub-order Charadrii of the Charadriiformes, ie birds which wade in search of food. Mainly applied to Snipe, the Oystercatcher, Plovers, Sandpipers, the Avocet, Phalaropes and the Stone Curlew. In North America the term 'shorebird' is more often used for these species, the Herons, Bitterns, Storks and Spoonbills (Ciconiiformes) being referred to as 'waders'.

Wagtail

Substantive name of some members of the family Motacillidae (Passeriformes, sub-order Oscines). Small to medium-sized birds, mainly terrestrial in habit, running on the ground and characteristically wagging their tails with an up-and-down motion. Throughout the world there are 54 species of the Motacillidae which includes some with the substantive names Pipit and Longclaw. There are 10 Wagtails found in the genus *Motacilla* and 3 of these breed in Britain. The Pied Wagtail (*Motacilla alba*) is the commonest, a distinctive black-and-white bird found virtually anywhere, quite frequently in towns and cities, feeding in parks or on flat roof-tops, making frequent fluttering leaps to chase small gnats and flies. Usually it is to be seen singly, but it does often roost in quite large numbers, on factory roofs or in greenhouses or other buildings during the winter. A resident, generally and widely distributed throughout Britain and Ireland; the total population is probably around 500,000 pairs.

The White Wagtail (*Motacilla a. alba*)

(left) Egyptian Vulture

Yellow Wagtail

replaces the Pied Wagtail on the Continent. It has a pale grey back and rump. A number occur in Britain on migration, particularly in spring. The Yellow Wagtail (*Motacilla flava*) is a summer resident in Britain, arriving in early April when the cock birds are a bright lemon-yellow on the face and upper parts, the back green. The female is duller looking. As a breeding bird its numbers have declined in recent years, and it is now mainly found from the Midlands northwards, becoming scarcer towards the Scottish border. A few nest in Wales, SW and S England. It formerly nested in Ireland but now there are only isolated occurrences. Total population around 25,000 pairs. There are quite a number of geographical races of Yellow Wagtails (or Flava Wagtails as they are sometimes called). The most likely identifiable race to be seen in Britain is the Blue-headed Wagtail (*Motacilla f. flava*). The male has a blue head and white eye-stripe and chin. Blue-headed Wagtails and Yellow Wagtails sometimes interbreed. Other races of Flava Wagtails occurring in Europe include Spanish Wagtail (*M.f. iberiae*), breeding in Spain and Portugal, Ashy-headed Wagtail (*M.f. cinereocapilla*), breeding in Italy,

(above) Pied Wagtail (female)   (below) Grey Wagtail, in winter

Corsica, Sardinia, Sicily and Albania, Grey-headed Wagtail (*M.f. thunbergi*), breeding in Sweden, Norway and Finland, and Black-headed Wagtail (*M.f. feldegg*), breeding in the Balkans.

The Wagtails are a complex group; some taxonomists classify the various forms as distinct species, but intergradation occurs where the ranges overlap and mutants resembling other races breed with birds of normal appearance, particularly in the case of the Flava Wagtails; in the field one must often call them all 'Yellow Wagtails'. There is however the Citrine or Yellow-headed Wagtail (*Motacilla citreola*), the male having canary-yellow head, neck and under parts (the female is duller), which has occurred in Britain once or twice; it is a vagrant from Siberia.

The Grey Wagtail (*Motacilla cinerea*) is present throughout the year, being quite common and widespread in Scotland, Wales and Ireland. It breeds sparingly in Eastern and Central England and is absent or scarce from other areas which do not have the fast-flowing rocky upland streams it prefers to nest by. Considered by some to be our most graceful Wagtail; its longer tail with conspicuous white outer tail feathers certainly gives it a more elegant appearance than either Pied or Yellow. In summer the male has a distinctive black patch on the throat, a white stripe above and below the eye, bright yellow under parts and a slate-grey back. The female lacks the dark throat patch and is less yellow underneath. In winter it often frequents city centres, feeding from the pools of water which collect on flat roof-tops.

Read Smith, S., *The Yellow Wagtail* (New Naturalist series), Collins

Wallcreeper (*Tichodroma muraria*)

A close relative of the Nuthatch (*Sitta europaea*), this small but distinctive bird, 6½in (165mm) long, has brilliant crimson on its blackish rounded wings, showing large white spots on the edges of these and its tail when it takes flight in fluttering butterfly fashion. A bird of rocky mountainous areas, it probes the cracks and crevices for insects with its curved bill. Nesting in cracks in rocky ravines and occasionally in buildings, it is rarely found below 6,000ft (2,000m). In Europe it is largely confined to the Pyrenees, Alps, Apennines and Carpathian mountains. It is quite common in Switzerland, Austria and Yugoslavia. A vagrant to Britain, it has been recorded on only a few occasions.

Walney, Lancashire

Walney Island lies to the south-west of the Lake District and forms the most westerly point of Morecambe Bay. Approximately 10 miles (16km) long, it varies between 350m and 1500m in width. It is connected to the mainland by a road bridge crossing a tidal channel about 500m wide. The observatory is situated at the south end of the island. It was formed in 1965 and currently operates four Heligoland traps. Walney has long been known for its colonies of breeding Terns and Gulls and more recently Eiders. In recent years the colony of Herring Gulls and Lesser Black-backed Gulls has continued to increase at the expense of the Terns, and in 1970 Operation Seafarer put the Lesser Black-backed Gull total at 47,000 pairs, which was one-third of the total British and Irish population. There is cottage accommodation.

Warbler

Substantive name for most species of the sub-family Sylviinae of the Muscicapidae (Passeriformes, sub-order Oscines). Commonly known as Old World Warblers, as opposed to New World Warblers or Wood Warblers (Parulidae). Warblers are generally small or very small, from 3½in (89mm) long, plainly coloured, usually greenish, brownish or greyish (some tropical species are more brightly coloured), with thin pointed bills—being mostly insectivorous and tree-haunting, though some inhabit low scrub, reeds and grassy areas. Many species of Warbler resemble each other closely and identification can be exceedingly difficult by observation alone, in some instances impossible. In such cases small structural differences, such as wing formulae, have to be determined and this can only be done if the bird is caught.

The Sylviinae comprise about 340 species, of which about 40 breed in Europe. For convenience they can be divided into four groups generally reflecting the habitat where they are found: Swamp Warblers, Tree Warblers, Scrub Warblers, Leaf Warblers.
See under these headings

Waterfowl

A general vague term, usually applied to freshwater birds, especially Swans and Ducks (Anatidae), particularly when kept for ornamental purposes, being maintained artificially and under some degree of captivity.

Waterhen

An alternative name in Britain (now rarely

used) for the Moorhen (*Gallinula chloropus*).

Waterthrush
Substantive name for two of three species of the genus *Seiurus* which belong to the family Parulidae (Passeriformes, sub-order Oscines) —American or Wood Warblers. Being the most terrestrial of this predominantly arboreal family, they share with the Ovenbird (*Seiurus aurocapillus*) the habit of walking rather than hopping when on the ground. The Waterthrushes also have a tail-bobbing motion like that of a Wagtail (*Motacilla* spp) or a Common Sandpiper (*Tringa hypoleucos*). The Northern Waterthrush (*Seiurus noveboracensis*) has been recorded twice in Britain. Its congener the Louisiana Waterthrush (*Seiurus motocilla*) has not been noted this side of the Atlantic.

Wattle
A fleshy appendage on the head or throat of some birds.
See Lappet

Wattlebird
General term for the Callaeidae (Passeriformes, sub-order Oscines). Medium-sized arboreal birds restricted to the forests of New Zealand, their most conspicuous common characteristic is paired fleshy wattles at the gape.

Waxbill
A substantive name for various members of the family Estrildidae—so called as many have sealing-wax-like red beaks. There are over 100 species of these small brightly coloured Finch-like birds which are found in Africa, Asia and Australia, often called Weaver Finches along with the Grass Finches and

Common Waxbill

Mannikins. Many species of Waxbill are kept as cage birds and particularly the Cordon Bleu (*Uraeginthus angolensis*), Bluish Waxbill (*Estrilda caerulescens*), Zebra Finch (*Poephila guttata*) and Java Sparrow (*Padda oryzivora*).

Waxwing
Substantive name of three species of the subfamily Bombycillinae of the Bombycillidae (Passeriformes, sub-order Oscines). In Britain the Waxwing (*Bombycilla garrulus*), in American usage Bohemian Waxwing, is a winter visitor from Northern and Eastern Europe, occurring annually in varying numbers. A pinkish-brown Starling-sized bird with a prominent crest, it gets its name from the red sealing-wax-like tips of the secondary flight feathers. An irruptive species in some years—large numbers occur in areas where they are not normally known. In North America the Cedar Waxwing (*B. cedrorum*) also occurs; though similar it is considerably smaller. There is also the Japanese Waxwing (*B. japonica*) which is native to Eastern Siberia.
See Irruption

Weaver
Substantive name of many species of Plocei-

The wattle—on Pheasant and Ptarmigan

dae (Passeriformes, sub-order Oscines). The family comprises 150 species of this Old World, largely African, group. Mainly Sparrow-type birds, the family includes such well-known species as House Sparrow (*Passer domesticus*) and Red-billed Quelea (*Quelea quelea*).

Weaver Finch

A fabricated name for the Estrildidae (Passeriformes, sub-order Oscines).
See Waxbill

Web

A fleshy membrane between two toes, or the vane of a feather.
See Feather; Foot; Vane

Welney, Norfolk

The Wildfowl Trust Welney Refuge comprises over 800 acres (320Ha) of the famous Ouse Washes which constitute one of the most important areas for wildfowl in Europe. Over 1,000 Bewick's Swans spend the winter here together with tens of thousands of Wigeon, Mallard, Teal, Shoveler and other Ducks. In spring and summer Black Tern, Ruff and Black-tailed Godwit are among the many birds which have bred in the Washes. The refuge has a number of hides and a spacious observatory which give excellent views of birds. The wild flowers are a special feature in the summer, whilst on winter evenings the Swans can be observed by floodlight. Open daily (except 24 and 25 December).

Three types of visit can be made to the Welney Refuge: unescorted visits (daily); warden-escorted visits (Sat/Sun only: 10 am and 1.45 pm); evening visits (1 Nov-1 Mar; parties of 20 or over only).

Wexford Wildfowl Reserve

Established in 1969 by the Department of Lands in Association with the Irish Wildbird Conservancy and with assistance from the World Wildlife Fund, the reserve is part of the Sloblands on the northern shore of Wexford harbour in the south-east corner of Ireland. Of considerable national importance, it holds the largest winter concentration of Greenland White-fronted Geese, with 6,000-7,000 birds present, comprising about 50 per cent of the world's total population (a further 20 per cent winter in other parts of Ireland). Other Geese which occur in the winter include Brent Geese (about 600),

small numbers of Bean Geese and Canada Geese and the occasional Pink-footed Goose. Large numbers of Ducks are also present, with 2,000-plus Wigeon an average maximum in December. The reserve area (in two parts) covers 400 acres and has a car park, picnic area, observation tower, lecture hall, laboratory and library.
Read The Wexford Wildfowl Reserve, Forest and Wildlife Service, The Department of Lands, Dublin 2.

Whaup

A local popular name (in Scotland) for the Curlew (*Numenius arquata*).
See Curlew

Wheatear

Substantive name for various *Oenanthe* spp. The best-known of this genus in Britain is the Wheatear (*Oenanthe oenanthe*). One of the earliest of summer migrants to return (often in early March), the male, with his pearl-grey upper parts, buffish under parts, broad white stripe over the eye, black ear coverts and wings, is a most handsome bird. However it is the distinctive white rump which usually catches the eye as the bird flies (in swift, jerky style) to land on a stone wall or fence. They are birds of open country, and nest in holes or cavities, under rocks, or in stone walls or rabbit burrows. The population of Britain and Ireland is probably around 80,000 pairs.

The Greenland Wheatear (*Oenanthe o. leucorrhoa*) is a more brightly coloured subspecies, occurring on migration, when it can be identified—particularly in spring, not normally arriving before May. Some rarer Wheatears which occur from time to time in Britain include the Black-eared Wheatear (*Oenanthe hispanica*), which breeds in Southern Europe, and the Black Wheatear (*Oenanthe leucura*), which breeds in Spain.

Whiffling

Behaviour of Geese, mainly; when coming in to land, birds will sideslip and change course rapidly in an erratic manner.

Whimbrel (*Numenius phaeopus*)

A species of Curlew, it is slightly smaller than *Numenius arquata* and has a boldly striped crown. A summer resident and passage migrant, it breeds in the Shetlands, the Orkneys and the Outer Hebrides. A few nest on the Scottish mainland, but all told the

population is only about 200 pairs. In other parts of Britain it is known mainly as a passage migrant, particularly in the autumn, when flocks of Whimbrels are noted moving south, from July through to October. It is then that the distinctive rapid tittering call of even emphasis can be heard; this has given rise to its common name of Titterel or Seven Whistler.

Whinchat (*Saxicola rubetra*)
A summer resident in Britain, arriving late April. It nests only locally in S and E England, but is to be found more widely in the upland areas of Wales, N and W England. The bulk of the Irish population is concentrated in the central lowlands. Total population of between 20,000 and 40,000 pairs. It might be confused with the Stonechat (*Saxicola torquata*) when seen at a distance perched on top of a bank or wall, but the striking head-patterns of browns and black, with a bold white eye-stripe, are distinctive at close range. Also in flight there are broad white wing

(left) Wheatear (male)

Whimbrel

marks which are very evident, and the sides to the tail are noticeably white.
See Chat

Whip-poor-will (*Caprimulgus vociferus*)
A North American species of Nightjar.

White-eye
Substantive name of many species of Zosteropidae (Passeriformes, sub-order Oscines). Other names are Silver-eye, Spectacle Bird and Zosterops. White-eyes are found in Africa and Australasia. In most species there is a ring of shining white feathers round the eye, though the birds are misnamed as the iris is dark in most species.
See Iris

White-eyed Pochard
Alternative name for the Ferruginous Duck (*Aythya nyroca*), a rare visitor to Britain from Eastern Europe. Slightly smaller and more neatly built than the Tufted Duck (*Aythya fuligula*), both sexes have a rich dark mahogany head, neck and breast, white belly and wing

bar. At a distance this Duck might be confused with a female Tufted, but is usually distinguishable by the white under-tail coverts. The male has white eyes, hence the name.

Whitefront
Colloquial short name for White-fronted Goose (*Anser albifrons*).

Whitethroat
Substantive name of *Sylvia communis* and *S. curruca*.
See Scrub Warblers; Warblers

Whooper
Name sometimes used alone for Whooper Swan (*Cygnus cygnus*).
See Swan

Whydah
Substantive name, alternatively Widow or Widow Bird, for some members of the genus *Vidua*. Currently placed with the Ploceidae, the 9 species of Whydahs are brood-parasitic, using the nest of Estrilidine Finches, in which the young of both are raised side by side.

Wigeon: flocks may be seen grazing as well as taking food from the water

Wideawake
Alternative name for Sooty Tern (*Sterna fuscata*).
See Tern

Wigeon (*Anas penelope*)
A surface-feeding or dabbling Duck. Some breed, though this is mainly a winter visitor to Britain. The male is distinguished by a chestnut head with yellow forehead, grey body and pinkish breast. As a breeding bird it first colonised Britain in the nineteenth century, nesting in Sutherland. Most breeding records still come from Scotland, though there are scattered occurrences in Northern England and East Anglia. Probably in all around 500 pairs nest annually. It does not breed in Ireland. Winter population around 200,000.

Wildfowl
General terms for those species sought after by a wildfowler, usually comprising species of the Anatidae (Ducks and Geese), though also frequently extended to include Waders (Charadrii). In North America, 'Waterfowl' is more commonly used in this sense.
See Waterfowl; Wildfowling

Wildfowl Counts

Since 1948 the Wildfowl Trust has organised regular monthly counts, during the winter months, of wildfowl present at major haunts throughout Britain. These counts have subsequently been widened to include most of Europe, and over the years it has been possible accurately to monitor the Duck population in this way.

See International Council for Bird Preservation

Wildfowlers' Association of Great Britain and Ireland (WAGBI)

Founded in 1908, it aims to preserve responsible and legitimate wildfowling and rough shooting and to promote practical conservation throughout Great Britain and Northern Ireland. It works closely with the Nature Conservancy Council and Wildfowl Trust, and has been concerned with the introduction of reared Ducks and Geese into the wild—mostly Mallard and also Greylag Geese.

At the Wildfowl Trust, Slimbridge, Gloucestershire

Wildfowling

The practice or sport of taking wildfowl, which in the past involved many forms of capture, often the use of nets. Now generally confined to the shooting of wild Geese, Ducks and some Waders. In Europe, wildfowl are principally shot (by 'wildfowlers') when flighting. By contrast, in North America nearly all wildfowl are shot when coming into artificial decoys, where the 'sport' is known as Duck-hunting and the participant is the 'Duck-hunter'.

See Duck Decoy; Wildfowlers' Association of Great Britain and Ireland.

Wildfowl Trust

A registered charity founded by Sir Peter Scott in 1946. Its headquarters are at Slimbridge in Gloucestershire. Centred around

313

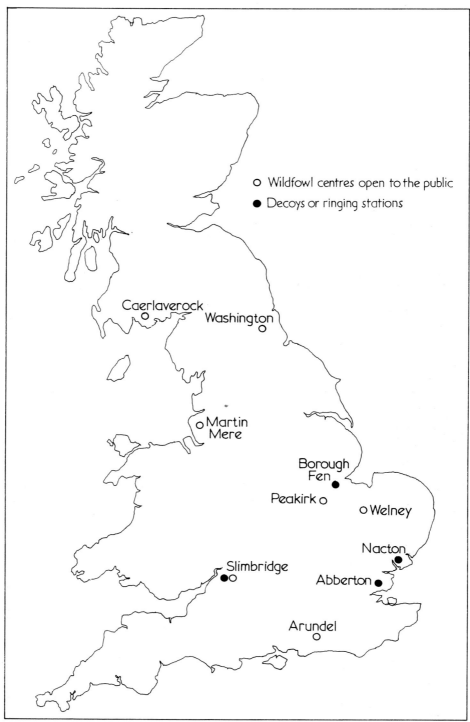

Wildfowl centres open to the public
Decoys or ringing stations

Caerlaverock
Washington
Martin Mere
Borough Fen
Peakirk
Welney
Nacton
Slimbridge
Abberton
Arundel

The wildfowl centres

the 'New Grounds', adjacent to the Severn Estuary, traditional wintering area for visiting White-fronted Geese, it has become the world's leading organisation concerned with research into wildfowl and their conservation. The Research Department at Slimbridge houses the International Waterfowl Research Bureau, works on studies of populations, behaviour, migration, nutrition and disease, and the balance between wildfowl conservation and agriculture. The Trust's wildfowl collection is world-famous and contains many rare and endangered species. One special feature of the Trust's work is research into the rearing of wildfowl species threatened with extinction, and a number of successes have been achieved, notably with the Hawaiian Goose and the White-winged Wood Duck. As

well as Slimbridge, there are six other centres in various parts of the country—at Arundel in Sussex, Caerlaverock in Dumfries, Martin Mere in Lancashire, Peakirk in Northants, Washington in Tyne and Wear and Welney in Cambridgeshire.

For full details write to the Wildfowl Trust, Slimbridge, Gloucestershire GLT 7BT.

Wildlife Sound Recording Society, The
Formed in 1968, its aim is to advise and assist in matters of technique and equipment for recording wildlife sounds. Members are invited to submit examples of their work and demonstrations of recording techniques for inclusion in a tape-recorder programme which is circulated four times a year. The society also publishes a journal twice a year. Full membership is available to those residing in the British Isles. For details contact the British Library of Wildlife Sounds, London.

Wing
The forelimb of a bird specially modified for flight, or in the case of Penguins (Spheniscidae) for swimming—when it is called a flipper.

A Pintail being x-rayed at the Wildfowl Trust

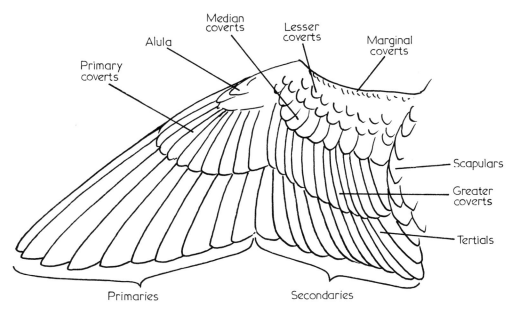

The wings of flying birds vary enormously in shape and size according to the bird's evolved state and its mode of life. Thus birds such as Buzzards, Eagles and Vultures which need to soar to great heights have broad, rounded wings, while Humming Birds' wings are pointed and narrow. The length of wing is also of great variability, measuring 4½ft (137cm) in the case of the Wandering Albatross (*Diomedea exulans*) to a few inches in the case of many small Passerines.

Wings are also used by some diving and swimming birds to propel them under water. All birds use their wings for balancing, particularly when perched on a moving object or in strong wind. During courtship

Upper wing

and breeding periods the wings are frequently used not only in display but also as weapons. Spur-wing Plovers (*Vanellus spinosus*) fight while in flight, striking their opponent with the wing which carries a spur capable of inflicting serious, even fatal, injury. The Spur-winged Goose (*Plectropterus gambensis*) is also believed to use its spurs as an aggressive weapon.

Wing Formula

The relationship between the length of various primary feathers. In certain groups of birds it is a valuable aid to in-the-hand identification of closely allied species that are difficult to differentiate in some plumages. It is especially useful in dealing with Old World Warblers (Sylviinae), also Tyrant Flycatchers of the New World (Tyrannidae) and the Vireos (Vireoninae).

Wing Tag

In order to track particular birds in the field, certain species have been marked with a wing tag. Made of light durable material and fixed to the wing or the carpal joint, it usually carries a code letter and number. This applies to large birds, particularly some birds of prey; Kites (*Milvus* spp) in particular have been so marked in order to study their dispersal. As for all ringing or marking of wild birds, a

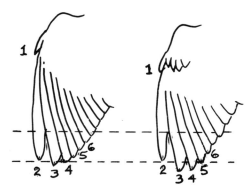

Wing formula showing comparative lengths of primary feathers on Reed Warbler and Blyth's Reed Warbler

permit from the National Environmental Council is necessary to carry out this activity. *See* Ringing

Winnowing Flight
When wings are rapidly fanned in forward flight through a very shallow arc, eg the winnowing flight of a Hobby (*Falco subbuteo*).

Winter visitor
A bird which spends the winter in a different area from the one in which it breeds. In Britain exemplified by such birds as Great Grey Shrike (*Lanius excubitor*), Jack Snipe (*Lymnocryptes minimus*) and several species of wildfowl, eg Bewick's Swan (*Cygnus bewickii*), Brent Goose (*Branta bernicla*).

Woodchat
Alternative name for the Woodchat-shrike (*Lanius senator*). Breeding in West, Central and Southern Europe, SW Asia and North Africa, about a dozen or so are recorded each year in Britain. The male has a rich chestnut crown and nape, broad black face markings, black wings and mantle, conspicuous white shoulder patches, and a noticeable white rump in flight. However birds noted in Britain are frequently immatures, looking very like young Red-backed Shrikes but more thickly barred with a trace of a wing patch.

Woodcock (*Scolopax rusticola*)
A solitary woodland species, it is most likely to be seen during the course of its roding display flights. On the ground it feeds as a Snipe (*Gallinago gallinago*), probing deeply, its long straight bill feeling for worms with its highly sensitive tip. When flushed from woodland cover it rises silently, and with its bill held characteristically downwards dodges through the trees with twisting evasive flight. Much larger and stouter than a Snipe, its upper parts are beautifully marked with rich brown, buffs and black, the under parts finely barred with dark brown. When the bird is sitting on eggs this cryptic colouring renders it virtually invisible against a background of dead leaves and litter. Present throughout

Woodcock

Woodcreeper

the year in Britain and Ireland, it is widely distributed as a breeding bird, with a population of about 50,000 pairs. There is considerable immigration from the continent in the late autumn. The Woodcock is highly regarded as a sporting bird, and much of our knowledge of its status in Britain before the Second World War is based on records kept of birds shot. A survey of the species was carried out in 1934-35 and a report by W. B. Alexander was later produced.

Woodcreeper
Substantive name of most species of Dendrocolaptidae (Passeriformes, sub-order Tyranni) —about 50 species, found in the woodlands of Central and South America. They are medium-sized, mainly dull brown, Passerines which search for insects on tree trunks in Woodpecker fashion.

Wood Hoopoe
Substantive name of species of Phoeniculidae (Coraciiformes, sub-order Coracii). Also called Tree Hoopoes. A small group of 8 species restricted to Africa, bearing no general resemblance to the true Hoopoes (Upupidae), though treated by some authors as being a

sub-family of them. Insect-eaters, they are typically birds of savannah and thorn country.

Woodlark (*Lullula arborea*)
A locally scarce resident in Britain. The species was formerly much more widespread but is now confined to a few localities in Wales, East Anglia, SW and S England, with a total population of less than 500 pairs. Highly regarded as a songster, it utters a sequence of short phrases comprising a few rich mellow notes interspersed with a liquid trilling 'lu-lu-lu-lu' which is usually delivered from a constant height as the bird circles over a wide area. It also frequently sings from a tree or from the ground and often at night. It can be heard regularly from the beginning of March to mid-June. It is very similar in appearance to the Skylark but has a whitish eyestripe meeting across the nape and a dark mark near the bend of the wing which the commoner bird lacks.

Woodpecker
Substantive name of most species of Picidae

Lesser Spotted Woodpecker (opposite)
Great Spotted Woodpecker (below)

Green Woodpecker

(Piciformes, sub-order Pici). The name is derived from their tree-haunting behaviour and feeding habits. A few of the 206 recorded species in this family have special names such as Flicker and Sapsucker (mainly found in N America), and some of the smaller Woodpeckers (mostly found in S America) are known as Piculets.

Most species are small to medium-sized, 3¼in (83mm)—13¼in (337mm), but a few are large, up to 22½in (571mm). General coloration may be black, white, yellow, red, brown or green, usually a combination of several with one or two predominating; the sexes are almost identical, with usually some red or yellow on the head of the males to distinguish them. Many are barred, spotted or streaked. Some are crested. The stiff wedge-shaped tail (rarely rounded) of the true Woodpeckers, sub-family Picinae, serves to support the bird when climbing. The straight chisel-like bill aided by powerful neck muscles is used for drilling into bark for insect food and for excavating nest holes in the wood itself. The nests are unlined and the eggs are white. The legs are short, the feet strong, having large

curved claws. Almost all Woodpeckers have a loud harsh voice, and some have 'laughing' or 'ringing' cries. Many species produce instrumental sounds by 'drumming'.

In Britain there are two species of 'Spotted' Woodpeckers. The Great Spotted Woodpecker (*Dendrocopos major*) is resident and well distributed in Britain and Ireland, with a total population of between 30,000 and 40,000 pairs; the Lesser Spotted Woodpecker (*Dendrocopos minor*) is scarce or locally common in parts of Southern England, virtually unknown north of Lancashire and totally absent from Ireland, the total population probably not exceeding 10,000 pairs. In Britain the Green Woodpecker (*Picus viridis*) is widely met with, though it is absent from parts of N Scotland and unknown in Ireland. This conspicuous, handsome greenish-yellow bird is as likely to be seen on the ground as in a tree, for it feeds extensively on ants. Its loud 'laughing' call or 'yaffle' is also frequently heard, proclaiming the bird's presence if it is not to be seen.

In Europe there are a number of other Woodpeckers, including the largest European species, the Black Woodpecker (*Dryocopus martius*), which is as big as a Rook (*Corvus frugilegus*). Breeding as near as Holland, this bird has yet to be recorded in Britain. The Middle Spotted Woodpecker (*Dendrocopos medius*), the White-backed Woodpecker (*Dendrocopos leucotos*), Grey-headed Woodpecker (*Picus canus*), Syrian Woodpecker (*Dendrocopos syriacus*) and Three-toed Woodpecker (*Picoides tridactylus*), are other species that can be encountered. The sub-family Jyaginae includes two species, the Red-breasted Wryneck (*Jynx ruficollis*) of tropical Africa and the Wryneck (*Jynx torquilla*), a summer visitor to Britain in small numbers. The sub-family Picumninae comprises the tiny Piculets found in tropical South America and South East Asia, on the island of Haiti, and in W and Central Africa. They do not have such powerful bills as the Picinae, and search for their insect food and excavate their nest holes only in rotten wood.

See Drumming; Instrumental Sounds; Wryneck

Read Sielmann H., *My Year With the Woodpeckers*, Barrie & Rockcliff, 1958

Wood Swallow

Substantive name—alternative is Swallow

Wood Swallow

Shrike—of the Artamidae species (Passeriformes, sub-order Oscines). An Australasian group of 10 species, they are inappropriately named, being neither Swallows (Hirundinidae) nor Shrikes (Laniidae). Strongly built birds, they feed on insects in the manner of Flycatchers.

Wood Warbler

In Britain the name for *Phylloscopus sibilatrix* in the sub-family Sylviinae of the Muscicapidae (Passeriformes, sub-order Oscines). A summer visitor and one of the Leaf Warblers. In North America an alternative general term for the American Warblers or Parulidae.

Wreck

Term for those occasional disasters affecting sea birds, when they are swept ashore or inland by persistent gales. The species most frequently affected are the Storm Petrel (*Hydrobates pelagicus*), Leach's Petrel (*Oceanodroma leucorhoa*) and Little Auk (*Plautus alle*).

Wren

Substantive name of the species Troglodytidae (Passeriformes, sub-order Oscines). There are 59 species of these small to medium-sized birds, found only throughout the New World, with the exception of *Troglodytes troglodytes*, the familiar Wren we know in Britain, which has established itself in much of temperate Eurasia and N Africa. Active, mainly insect-eating, birds with slender curved bills, strong feet and relatively short rounded wings, they tend to frequent dense, fairly low vegetation, where they proclaim their presence by loud song, a highly developed feature of this family. It includes some of the world's finest singers, such as the Quadrille Wren or Song Wren (*Cyphorhinus aradus*) of South America, where the greatest concentration of Wren species is to be found.

In Britain the peak population of the Wren is in the region of 10 million pairs, though the species suffers high mortality in long periods of freezing weather. Wrens are well known for their multiple nest building (cock nests), an innate behaviour which apparently evolved in the tropics primarily as a procedure enabling the species to find shelter from predators. For those species (including *Troglodytes troglodytes*, known as the Winter Wren in N America) found in the temperate zones it has become an adaptation facilitating polygamy and no doubt also a survival factor during bad weather.

The name Wren is also applied to many species of the sub-family Malurinae of the Muscicapidae (Passeriformes, sub-order Oscines), the Australian Wrens or Australian Warblers, and also to three out of four species of Xenicidae (Passeriformes, sub-order Tyranni), a distinctive group peculiar to New Zealand—the New Zealand Wrens, being a general term for the family, which is also called Acanthisittidae. A well-known bird of this family is the Rifleman (*Acanthisitta chloris*).

See Cock Nest
Read Armstrong, E. A., *The Wren* (New Naturalist series), Collins, 1955

Wryneck (*Jynx torquilla*)

In Britain, this summer visitor and passage migrant has declined markedly this century. From being a common breeding species found over most of Central and SE England and other parts of Britain, it now only occasionally nests here, in its once traditional Kent and Surrey stronghold. However since 1969 Wrynecks have been recorded breeding in parts of Scotland, and the British breeding population is now concentrated north of the border. Hopefully this colonisation, presumably by Scandinavian birds, will continue and the bird will become established here as it was 150 years ago.

Wren—only 3½in (95mm) long

The cryptic coloration of the Wryneck, with its closely patterned greys, browns and buffs, somewhat resembles that of the Nightjar (*Caprimulgus europaeus*), but its behaviour is more like that of a Passerine, though it is related to the Woodpeckers. It frequently feeds on the ground, searching for ants and their pupae, and on autumn passage sometimes occurs in gardens, attracted by the food obtainable there. It has a shrill 'pee-pee, pee-pee' call not unlike that of a bird of prey.

See Cuckoo's Mate; Woodpecker

Xanthochroism

The occurrence of excessive yellow pigmentation.

Yaffle

A common name for the Green Woodpecker (*Picus viridis*) derived from its 'laughing', yaffle-like call.

See Woodpecker

Year List

Some birdwatchers annually list the total number of species they see each year, aiming to improve on the previous year's total. For the average birdwatcher a year's total of species seen in Britain could be a little over

200, depending on how much travelling he undertakes to achieve this goal. There are people whose ambition is to see as many different species as possible and who give the whole of their spare time to achieving this end: a total of 250 or more in a year for Britain alone is accomplished frequently.
See Tick Hunter; Twitcher

Yellowhammer (*Emberiza citrinella*)
Also, but less frequently, called the Yellow Bunting. This familiar bird is a widely distributed resident species in Britain, but found only locally along parts of the Pennines and in the Scottish Highlands, being scarce in the Hebrides and Orkneys and absent from the Shetlands. The male has a bright lemon-yellow head and under parts and has the distinction of being one of the few species singing all through the summer months; its monotonous rattling wheeze is heard regularly from the early part of the year through till August. Total British and Irish population probably around 1 million pairs.

Young
A vague term applicable to a bird from the time of hatching (when it ceases to be an embryo) until the attainment of sexual maturity. Technically, a young bird, until it is full-grown and flying, is a 'pullus'. The ability to fly is the usual criterion (except of course in flightless species). Whilst still in the nest it is usually termed a 'nestling', or for active species a chick. After the pullus stage, a bird is described as a juvenile while wearing its first plumage of true feathers.

Certain terms describe the condition of pulli in different kinds of species. The young of some species are 'precocial', ie capable of locomotion more or less immediately after hatching. Others are altricial, ie incapable of locomotion. The young may be 'ptilopaedic', covered with down (usually dense) when hatched, or they may be 'psilopaedic', naked or with only sparse amounts of down (and usually blind) when hatched. Young that leave the nest immediately or soon after hatching are termed 'nidifugous'; those that remain in the nest are termed 'nidicolous'. Nidifugous young are necessarily both pre-

King Penguin which has appropriated the Gentoo Penguin's chicks!

cocial and ptilopaedic, but nidicolous young are not always psilopaedic or even wholly altricial. There are a number of special colloquial terms for the young of certain species: Swan (cygnet), Duck (duckling), Falcon and Eagle (eyass), Goose (gosling), Owl (owlet).
See Altricial; Nidicolous; Nidifugous; Pullus

Young Ornithologists' Club (YOC)
The Young Ornithologists' Club is run by the Royal Society for the Protection of Birds. It caters specifically for young people up to the

Young birdwatchers

age of 15, running courses and competitions. It has local groups and organises surveys: the annual 'phone-in' of arriving summer migrants is one such national event. The 100,000 members receive a copy of its own colour magazine *Bird Life* every two months. Details of the YOC are obtainable from RSPB, The Lodge, Sandy, Beds SG19 2DL.
See Bird Life Magazine

Zoogeography
The study of the geographical distribution of animals. In connection with this study the world has been divided into a number of faunal regions or zones. These faunal zones are:

1 The Australasian region (Australia, New Guinea and New Zealand, with neighbouring islands).

2 The Ethiopian region (Africa south to the Sahara, sometimes including Madagascar,

A party of young birdwatchers at a Sand Martin
colony

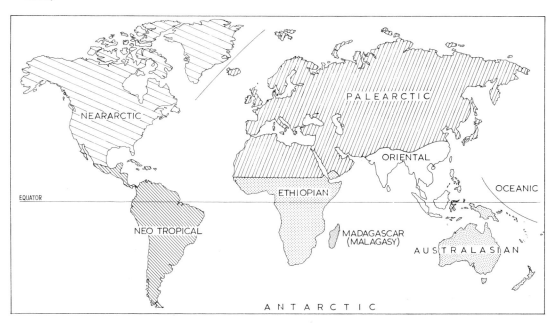

The world's faunal regions

Zoology

though this is now considered a separate region—Malagasy—in its own right).

3 The Nearctic region (North America south to Central Mexico).

4 The Neotropical region (South America and most of Central America and the Caribbean).

5 The Oriental Region (Southern Asia and its islands, Borneo, Celebes etc).

6 The Palearctic Region (Europe, Northern Asia and Northern Africa).

7 The Oceanic Islands are often considered as a separate faunal region.

8 The Antarctic. This is also considered as a separate faunal region.

The Nearctic and Palearctic are often called the Holarctic.

Zoology

The scientific study of animals, and one of the main divisions of biology. Zoology may be sub-divided according to the particular classes of animals under study. Study of birds (Class Aves) is one branch of it, known as ornithology.

Zosterops

Generic name often used as a common name for the White-eye.

Zugunruhe

German term, sometimes used in English writings, for pre-migratory restlessness.

Zygodactyl

Having two toes directed forward and two back.

See Woodpecker

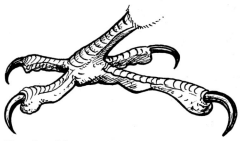

Zygodactyl foot

Acknowledgements

In compiling *The Birdwatcher's A-Z* I have consulted many sources and particularly the following:
Cramp & Simmons, *The Handbook of Birds of Europe, the Middle East and North Africa*, Vol I, Oxford University Press, 1977
Gooders, John, *Birds of the World*, Vols I to IX, IPC (partwork)
Peterson, R., *A Field Guide to Birds*, Houghton Mifflin, Boston
Peterson, R., *A Field Guide to Western Birds*, Houghton Mifflin, Boston
Peterson, R., Mountfort, G., and Hollom, P. A. D., *A Field Guide to the Birds of Britain and Europe*, Collins
Sharrock, J. T. R., *The Atlas of Breeding Birds in Britain and Ireland*, BTO, 1976
Thompson, A. Landsborough, *A New Dictionary of Birds*, Nelson, 1964
Witherby, *et al*, *Handbook of British Birds*, Vols I–V, Witherby, 1938-41
Wood, Gerald L., *The Guinness Book of Animal Facts and Feats*, Guinness Superlatives, 1976
British Birds magazine, Macmillan

A great number of other publications which were consulted are recommended as further reading, under relevant headings in the book.
I would also like to thank the following organisations for their help in various forms and in some cases for illustrative material which they supplied, duly acknowledged where appropriate: the British Trust for Ornithology, the British Ornithologists' Union, the Irish Wildbird Conservancy, the Nature Conservancy Council, the Royal Society for the Protection of Birds, the Scottish Ornithologists' Club and the Wildfowl Trust.
My special thanks to Rob Hume, who not only provided nearly all the line drawings, but also contributed a number of entries, such as those for the RSPB, Bird Protection Laws, Pole Traps, 'Jizz' and others. His opinion on other entries has been much valued and I am also grateful to him for checking proofs. I also thank my brother Clive, who provided diagrams for binocular vision, moonwatching, the size of eggs and radar migration, at a moment's notice; Philip Ireland, Ringing Secretary of the West Midland Bird Club, for the entries on Ringing, Rocket Netting and Cannon Netting; Bruce Campbell for some good advice during the formative period of this book; Lawrence Holloway, R. T. Mills and M. C. Wilkes; and also N. Baksa of Opticron Limited for assistance in compiling the item on telescopes.

The Illustrations

Photographs supplied by Aquila Photographics. Photographers are as follows:

Black and White
F. V. Blackburn: Lesser Spotted Woodpecker, Dartford Warbler, Red-backed Shrike, Robin displaying; S. C. Brown: Fulmar in flight, Bewick's Swans, Snipe, Common Gull, Great Crested Grebe, Great Spotted Woodpecker, Marabou Storks, Woodcock, Long-tailed Tit; CEGB: Hide in Ladywalk Wildfowl Reserve, nestboxes at Ladywalk; A. W. Cundall: Hen Capercaillie; G. F. Date: Little Owl, Stonechat; J. A. Dick: Spoonbill; Dennis Green: Buzzard (2), Grey Partridge eggs, flock of Dunlin, Merlin (2), trained Goshawk, Mute Swan's nest, flock of Knot, female Goshawk, Guillemots, Pheasant's nest, Black Guillemot's nest, young Barn Owls, Great Skua; H. A. Hems: Wheatear, Greylag-Canada Goose Cross; E. A. Janes: Brambling, Wood Pigeon drinking, Jackdaw, dead Hedge Sparrow and Cuckoo in nest, Common Sandpiper, Wood Pigeon squabs, Pied Wagtail; Tom Leach: African Crowned Crane, Wader flock on Dee, Secretary Bird; T. D. Longrigg: Sacred Ibis; R. T. Mills: Adult Gannet, birdwatchers, Greater Flamingos, Cape Clear observatory, Cormorants tree-nesting, Corncrake, making field notes, Coot, Brent Geese, mist net, mist netting Sand Martins, Curlew preening, Goldcrest after ringing, Solitary Sandpiper, Sedge Warbler, wisp of snipe, Mute Swan, Egyptian Vulture, Pied Wagtail roost, rookery; W. S. Paton: Razorbill, Mallard drake, Ostrich dust bathing, Kittiwakes on Farne Islands, female Red Grouse on nest, Swallows on wire, Ostrich, Peregrine, Superb Starling, Herring Gulls at Lerwick Harbour, House Martins; A. J. Richards: Cley-next-the-Sea, Salthouse Broad; J. L. Roberts: Blackcock at lek, Blackcap brooding young, Sandwich Tern colony, White Stork nest site, Pratincole, Curlew chicks, Carrion Crow; RSPB: Bempton Cliffs Reserve (Michael Richards), Minsmere (Michael Richards), the Scrape at Minsmere (Anthony Clay), young birdwatchers (2) (Michael Richards), RSPB warden at Ouse Washes; J. Russell: Puffins, Rook, Swallow collecting nest material; D. A. Smith: Peregrine calling, Clark's Nutcracker, Manx Shearwater, Red-necked Phalarope, raft of Manx Shearwaters, Griffon Vulture; Eric Soothill: Whimbrel; A. F. Taylor: Montagu's Harrier, nictitating membrane, Barn Owl pellet; E. K. Thompson: Gannets on Bass Rock, Common Tern, Arctic Tern, Ringed Plover's distraction display, Oystercatcher eggs, Eider's nest, Greater Flamingo, Gannet colony, Herring Gull, Greater black-backed Gull, Lesser black-backed Gull, Black-headed Gull, Heligoland trap, Avocet at nest, Snowy Owl, Arctic Skua, Great Tit; Winfried Walter: Kestrel pellet; P. D. Weaving: Green Woodpecker; Gary Weber: Emu, Yellow-tufted Honeyeater, Pelican, Crested Pigeon, Great Bower Bird, Little Penguin on nest; G. D. Wilson: Gentoo Penguins, pair of King Penguins, King Penguin with Gentoo chicks; Wildfowl Trust: Barnacle Geese at Caerlaverock (E. E. Jackson), Slimbridge duck decoy, catching net, decoy dog (B. A. Crosby), at the Wildfowl Trust (K. Portman), Pintail being x-rayed (K. Portman); M. C. Wilkes: Sparrowhawk bathing

(2), Yellow Wagtails' threat display, House Sparrow drinking, Fieldfare, hen Pheasant, Pintail drakes and duck, House Sparrows, Alan Richards with telescope, Grey Wagtail

Colour
T. Andrewartha: Ptarmigan; F. V. Blackburn: Corn Bunting, Coot, Crossbill, Goldcrest, Hobby, Kestrels, Woodlark, Nightjar, Long-eared Owl, Turtle Dove, Grasshopper Warbler; J. B. Blossom: Brent Geese, Red-breasted Merganser, Goosander, Common Scoter; A. J. Bond: Collared Dove, Sanderling; S. C. Brown: Tree Pipit, Red-legged Partridge, Reed Warbler; G. F. Date: Barn Owl, Pied Flycatcher; R. H. Fisher: Lapwing; R. Gill: Sooty Albatross; Dennis Green: Bullfinch, Whinchat, Stonechat, Curlew, Dotterel, Merlin, Jay; H. A. Hems: Wheatear, Canada Geese; R. A. Hume: Ruff; N. Jagannathan: Painted Stork; E. A. Janes: House Martin, Wood Pigeon, Arctic Tern, Little Tern; E. T. Jones: Snow Bunting; G. R. Jones: Blue-footed Booby, Magnificent Frigatebird; R. Kennedy: Snipe; H. Kinloch: Sedge Warbler, Puffin, Starling, Spotted Flycatcher, Red Grouse, Linnet, Long-tailed Tit, Ring Ousel, Meadow Pipit, Slavonian Grebe, Whitethroat, Shag, Yellow Wagtail, Wren; A. T. Moffett: Magpie, Nuthatch, Hawfinch, Ravens, Coal Tit; E. Morgan: Grey Partridge; W. S. Paton: Greylag Goose, Hen Harrier, Eider, Short-eared Owl, Oystercatcher, Peregrine, Ringed Plover, Pochard, Swallow; D. Platt: Guillemot, Golden Eagle; D. K. Richards: White-fronted Bee-eater; RSPB/Michael Richards: Osprey, Bearded Tit; J. L. Roberts: Black Guillemot, Avocet, Blackcap, Chaffinch, Redstart, Dipper, Fulmar, Skylark, Little Owl, Golden Plover, Sandwich Tern, Common Tern, Blue Tit; R. Siegal: Black Redstart, Red Kite; D. A. Smith: Bittern, Greyhen, Storm Petrel; E. Soothill: Woodcock, Dunnock, Black-tailed Godwit, Mallard, Redshank, Shelduck, Shoveler, Teal, Treecreeper, Wigeon; G. W. Ward: Razorbill; P. D. V. Weaving: Goldfinch; G. Weber: Rainbow Lorikeet, Black Swan; M. C. Wilkes: Reed Bunting, Greenfinch, Kingfisher, Sand Martin, Moorhen, Pheasant, Stock Dove, Rooks, Nightingale, Robin, Swift, Great Tit, Great Spotted Woodpecker; E. K. Thompson: Red-throated Diver, Black-throated Diver, Blue Peafowl